Frank McAlpine

Treasures From the Prose World

With Portraits and Biographical Sketches

Frank McAlpine

Treasures From the Prose World
With Portraits and Biographical Sketches

ISBN/EAN: 9783744694254

Printed in Europe, USA, Canada, Australia, Japan

Cover: Foto ©Thomas Meinert / pixelio.de

More available books at **www.hansebooks.com**

TREASURES

FROM THE

PROSE WORLD.

WITH

BIOGRAPHICAL SKETCHES,

BY

PROF. FRANK McALPINE.

ILLUSTRATED.

Sold by Subscription Only.

CHICAGO AND PHILADELPHIA:
ELLIOTT & BEEZLEY.
1886.

MANUFACTURED BY
ELLIOTT & BEEZLEY'S PUBLISHING HOUSE,
CHICAGO AND PHILADELPHIA.

INTRODUCTION.

MILTON has said: "A good book is the precious life-blood of a master-spirit, embalmed and treasured up on purpose to a life beyond life." For our readers, we have tried to gather such selections only as are worthy to be "embalmed and treasured up."

If we have succeeded in avoiding anything like a *text-book* upon literature, we have carried out the plan of our work. If we have succeeded in gathering up selections that are worthy of being called *treasures*, we have accomplished the object that we had in view. Then if our book finds a warm place in the heart of the reading public, our most earnest desire will be fully gratified.

Literature may be viewed as a mighty river taking its rise in the dim past and running parallel with the crystal stream of time. In tracing this river from its source to where it flows into the great ocean of the present, we enter the province of a text-book upon literature. We should view the tributaries from the different tongues of the world,—their nature and the influence they have had upon the progress and usefulness of the main channel. We should note this magnificent river pausing in classic Greece "to purify itself and gain strength of wave for due occasion," and at Rome,—Rome that sat on her seven hills and from her throne of glory ruled the world—to receive the tributary that added vigorous grandeur to its flow. We should examine its tributaries from tongues that spoke on the banks of the Nile, and in India and China, and on the sacred plains of Judea ; from the thoughtful fields of Germany, central Europe and fashionable France, till finally it was swelled to almost boundless proportions and influence by that greatest of all tributaries, —the one from the English tongue.

But we have viewed the literary world as a bountiful harvest from which to gather abundant stores of mental food. After having taken a careful survey of the entire field, sickle in hand, we have gone to the most fertile spots and gathered sheaves of the tallest, ripest and most perfect grain. As the judicious husbandman saves the best seed in anticipation of an improved and abundant harvest, so these sheaves of tall, ripe grain—this " precious life-blood " of the " master-spirits " —we have garnered up in TREASURES FROM THE PROSE WORLD.

FRANK MCALPINE.

CONTENTS.

ADVICE TO A WOULD-BE CRIMINAL	Victor Hugo	65
ADMIRATION OF GENIUS	Lord Lytton	72
AT THE OPEN WINDOW	B. F. Taylor	75
AND SUCH A CHANGE	B. F. Taylor	76
AUTUMN AT CONCORD, MASS.	Hawthorne	175
AUTOCRAT OF THE BREAKFAST TABLE	Holmes	218
ANGLO-SAXON INFLUENCES OF HOME	Geo. P. Marsh	331
ARIEL AMONG THE SHOALS, THE	Cooper	345
ABORGINES OF AMERICA	Bancroft	362
BEAUTY	Emerson	154
BUDS AND BIRD VOICES	Hawthorne	170
BLIND PREACHER	William Wirt	195
BALD-HEADED MAN, THE	Little Rock Gazette	355
CHILD'S DREAM OF A STAR, A	Dickens	27
CANDID MAN, THE	Lord Lytton	128
CHANGES OF MATTER	Yeomans	151
CHARACTER OF WASHINGTON	Jefferson	156
CHRISTIANITY	Charles Phillips	206
CHILDREN AND THEIR EDUCATION	Horace Mann	290
CHESTERFIELD'S LETTERS TO HIS SON	Chesterfield	392
DEATH OF LITTLE JO	Dickens	30
DOG-DAYS	Gail Hamilton	399
ELEONORA	Edgar A. Poe	208
ENGLISH LANGUAGE	Wm. Mathews	215
EVENING WALK IN VIRGINIA	J. K. Paulding	357

CONTENTS.

Escape of Harry Birch and Captain Wharton	Cooper	884
Fall of the Leaf, The	Ruskin	106
Grave, The	Irving	48
Glass of Cold Water, A	J. B. Gough	68
Good Man's Day, A	Bishop Hall	228
Goodrich Jones, Jr., To	J. G. Holland	234
Gentle Hand	T. S. Arthur	841
How Tom Sawyer Whitewashed His Fence	Mark Twain	36
Happiness	Colton	55
Heart Beneath a Stone, A	Victor Hugo	62
Home	T. S. Arthur	110
Happiness in Solitude	J. J. Rosseau	140
How Curious it is	H. P. Shillaber	148
Happiness of Temper	Goldsmith	816
Head-Stone, The	Wilson	880
Indian Summer	B. F. Taylor	17
In the Garret	Knickerbocker	828
Joan of Arc	Thomas DeQuincy	144
Jerusalem	Benj. Disraeli	222
Last Days of Pompeii	Lord Lytton	123
Love of Life and Age	Goldsmith	138
Little Eva	Harriet B. Stowe	267
Lily's Ride	Judge Tourgee	281
Little Woman, The	Dickens	810
Letters	Mitchell	818
Mother's Vacant Chair	Talmage	34
Music of Child Laughter, The		56
Musing by the Fire	B. F. Taylor	78
Marriage	Jeremy Taylor	192
My Mother's Bible		244
Mocking Bird	Alexander Wilson	246
Maxims of George Washington	Washington	306
Napoleon Buonaparte	Victor Hugo	60
Our Revolutionary Fathers	Webster	50

CONTENTS. 7

OLD-FASHIONED MOTHER, THE	B. F. Taylor	79
OMENS	Sir Humphrey Davy	101
OLD CHURCHYARD, THE	MacDonald	109
OLD AGE	Emerson	155
ON REVENGE	Samuel Johnson	186
OLD AGE	Theo. Parker	188
ORDER IN NATURE	Yeomans	199
OF BEAUTY	Lord Bacon	280
OUR OLD GRANDMOTHER	Anonymous	318
OUR BURDEN	Addison	323
OUTCASTS OF POKER FLAT, THE	Bret Harte	388
POETRY AND MYSTERY OF THE SEA	Dr. Greenwood	19
PARADISE ON EARTH, A	Victor Hugo	59
PERSONALITY AND USES OF A LAUGH	Anonymous	100
PRECIPICES OF THE ALPS	Ruskin	106
PARENTS	T. S. Arthur	113
PURITANS, THE	T. B. Macaulay	149
POOR RICHARD	Dr. Franklin	158
PUTTING UP STOVES	Anonymous	166
PLEA FOR THE ERRING, A	Wm. Mathews	177
PROGRESS OF SIN, THE	Jeremy Taylor	190
PENN'S ADVICE TO HIS CHILDREN	Wm. Penn	203
PICTURES OF SWISS SCENERY AND OF THE CITY OF VENICE	B. Disraeli	227
PLEDGE WITH WINE	Anonymous	270
PROSPERITY AND ADVERSITY	Lord Bacon	288
PICTURES	H. P. Shillaber	305
RURAL LIFE IN ENGLAND	Irving	44
RURAL LIFE IN SWEDEN	H. W. Longfellow	90
REBECCA'S DESCRIPTION OF THE SIEGE	Scott	252
SCHOOLMASTER, THE	Verplanck	69
SCENE AT THE NATURAL BRIDGE	Burritt	96
SKY, THE	Ruskin	107
SPIDER AND THE BEE, THE	Jonathan Swift	117
SPRING	Hawthorne	174

CONTENTS.

SHAKESPERE'S STYLE	Wm. Mathews	182
SKYLARK, THE	Jeremy Taylor	194
SILENT FORCES	Tyndall	232
STUDIES	Lord Bacon	279
TRAMP, TRAMP, TRAMP	J. G. Holland	241
TWO RACES OF MEN, THE	Charles Lamb	273
THOUGHTS ON VARIOUS SUBJECTS	Jonathan Swift	334
UNCLE TOM READS HIS TESTAMENT	H. B. Stowe	268
VOICES OF THE DEAD	E. H. Chapin	376
WORK	Thomas Carlyle	81
WELCOME TO LAFAYETTE	Edward Everett	203
WORKS OF CREATION, THE	Addison	260
WONDERS OF AN ATOM	Hunt	245

INDEX OF AUTHORS.

ADDISON, JOSEPH.
 OUR BURDENS, - - - - 328
 THE WORKS OF CREATION, - - - 260

ARTHUR, T. S.
 HOME, - - - - - - 110
 PARENTS, - - - - - - 118
 GENTLE HAND, - - - - - 841

BACON, LORD.
 STUDIES, - - - - - - 279
 BEAUTY, - - - - - - 280
 PROSPERITY AND ADVERSITY, - - - - 288

BANCROFT, GEORGE.
 THE ABORIGINES OF AMERICA, - - - 862

BURRITT, ELIHU.
 SCENE AT THE NATURAL BRIDGE, - - - 96

CARLISLE, THOMAS.
 WORK, - - - - - 81

CHAPIN, E. H.
 VOICES OF THE DEAD, - - - - - 376

CHESTERFIELD, LORD.
 LETTERS TO HIS SON, - - - - - 892

INDEX OF AUTHORS.

COOPER, J. FENIMORE.
    ARIEL AMONG THE SHOALS, - - - - 345
    ESCAPE OF HARVEY BIRCH AND CAPTAIN WHARTON, - 384

COLTON, WALTER.
    HAPPINESS, - - - - - - 55

DAVY, SIR HUMPHREY.
    OMENS, - - - - - - 101

DE QUINCY, THOMAS.
    JOAN OF ARC, - - - - - 144

DICKENS, CHAS.
    DEATH OF LITTLE JO, - - - - 30
    CHILD'S DREAM OF A STAR, - - - - 27
    THE LITTLE WOMAN, - - - - - 310

DISRAELI, BENJ.
    JERUSALEM, - - - - - 222
    PICTURES OF SWISS SCENERY AND THE CITY OF VENICE, 227

EMERSON, RALPH W.
    BEAUTY, - - - - - - 154
    OLD AGE, - - - - - - 155

EVERETT, EDWARD.
    WELCOME TO LAFAYETTE, - - - - 202

FRANKLIN, BENJAMIN.
    POOR RICHARD, - - - - - 158

GOUGH, J. B.
    A GLASS OF COLD WATER, - - - - 68

GOLDSMITH, OLIVER.
    LOVE OF LIFE AND AGE, - - - - 138
    HAPPINESS OF TEMPER, - - - - 316

GREENWOOD, DR.
    POETRY AND MYSTERY OF THE SEA, - - 19

INDEX OF AUTHORS.

HALL, BISHOP.
   A GOOD MAN'S DAY, - 228.

HAWTHORNE, NATHANIEL.
   AUTUMN AT CONCORD, MASS., - 175
   BUDS AND BIRD VOICES, - 170
   SPRING, - 174

HARTE, BRET.
   THE OUTCASTS OF POKER FLAT, - 338

HAMILTON, GAIL,
   DOG-DAYS, - 397

HOLMES, O. W.
   AUTOCRAT OF THE BREAKFAST TABLE, - 218

HOLLAND, J. G.
   TO GOODRICH JONES, JR., - 234
   TRAMP, TRAMP, TRAMP, - 241

HUGO, VICTOR.
   ADVICE TO A WOULD-BE CRIMINAL, - 65
   NAPOLEON BUONAPARTE, - 60
   A HEART BENEATH A STONE, - 62
   A PARADISE ON EARTH, - 59

HUNT, LEIGH.
   WONDERS OF AN ATOM, - 245

IRVING, WASHINGTON.
   THE GRAVE, - 43
   RURAL LIFE IN ENGLAND, - 44
   IN THE GARRET, - 328

JEFFERSON, THOMAS.
   CHARACTER OF WASHINGTON, - 156

JOHNSON, DR. SAMUEL.
   ON REVENGE, - 186

INDEX OF AUTHORS.

LAMB, CHARLES.
    THE TWO RACES OF MEN, - · · · - 273
LONGFELLOW, H. W.
    RURAL LIFE IN SWEDEN, - · · · · 90
LYTTON, LORD BULWER.
    LAST DAYS OF POMPEII, · · · 123
    THE CANDID MAN, · · · - 128
    ADMIRATION OF GENIUS, · · · 72
MANN, HORACE.
    CHILDREN AND THEIR EDUCATION, - · · - 290
MATHEWS, WM.
    ENGLISH LANGUAGE, - · · · 215
    A PLEA FOR THE ERRING, - · · · · 177
    SHAKESPERE'S STYLE, - · · - 182
MACAULAY, T. B.
    THE PURITANS, - · · · · 149
MACDONALD, GEO.
    THE OLD CHURCHYARD, · · - 109
MARSH, GEO. P.
    ANGLO-SAXON INFLUENCES OF HOME, · · 331
MITCHELL, DONALD G.
    LETTERS, - · · · · - 313
PARKER, THEODORE.
    OLD AGE, · · · · - 188
PAULDING, JAS. K.
    AN EVENING WALK IN VIRGINIA, - · · 357
PENN, WM.
    PENN'S ADVICE TO HIS CHILDREN, - 203
PHILLIPS, CHARLES.
    CHRISTIANITY, - · · · - 206

INDEX OF AUTHORS. 13

POE, EDGAR A.
 ELEONORA, - - - - - 208

RUSKIN, JOHN.
 THE FALL OF THE LEAF, - - - 106
 THE SKY, - - - - - - 107
 THE PRECIPICES, - - - - - 106

ROSSEAU, J. J.
 HAPPINESS IN SOLITUDE, - - - - 140

SHILLABER, H. P.
 PICTURES, - - - - - - 305
 HOW CURIOUS IT IS, - - - - - 148

STOWE, HARRIET BEECHER.
 LITTLE EVA, - - - - - - 267
 UNCLE TOM READS HIS TESTAMENT, - - - 268

SCOTT, SIR WALTER.
 REBECCA'S DESCRIPTION OF THE SIEGE, - - - 252

SWIFT, JONATHAN.
 THOUGHTS ON VARIOUS SUBJECTS, - - - - 334
 THE SPIDER AND BEE, - - - - - 117

TAYLOR, B. F.
 AT THE OPEN WINDOW, - - - - 75
 INDIAN SUMMER, - - - - - 17
 THE OLD-FASHIONED MOTHER, - - - - 79
 MUSING BY THE FIRE, - - - - - 78
 AND SUCH A CHANGE, - - - - - 76

TWAIN, MARK.
 HOW TOM SAWYER WHITEWASHED HIS FENCE, - - 36

TOURGEE, A. W.
 LILY'S RIDE, - - - - - - 281

INDEX OF AUTHORS.

TAYLOR, JEREMY.
 MARRIAGE, - - - - - - 192
 PROGRESS OF SIN, - - - - - - 190
 THE SKYLARK, - - - - 194

TALMAGE, T. DE WITT.
 MOTHER'S VACANT CHAIR, - - - - - 34

TYNDALL, JOHN.
 SILENT FORCES, - - - - - 232

VERPLAUCK,
 THE SCHOOLMASTER, - - - - - 69

WIRT, WILLIAM.
 THE BLIND PREACHER, - - - 195

WEBSTER, DANIEL.
 OUR REVOLUTIONARY FATHERS, - - - - 50

WASHINGTON, GEORGE.
 MAXIMS, - - - - - - 306

WILSON, ALEXANDER.
 THE MOCKING BIRD, - - - - 246
 THE HEAD-STONE, - - - 380

YEOMAN, PROF.
 ORDER IN NATURE, - - - - 199
 CHANGES OF MATTER, - - - - 151

BIOGRAPHICAL SKETCHES.

CHARLES DICKENS,	24
WASHINGTON IRVING,	40
VICTOR HUGO,	57
BENJAMIN FRANKLIN TAYLOR,	78
HENRY WADSWORTH LONGFELLOW,	88
JOHN RUSKIN,	105
LORD LYTTON,	121
OLIVER GOLDSMITH,	136
RALPH WALDO EMERSON,	152
NATHANIEL HAWTHORNE,	168
DR. SAMUEL JOHNSON,	184
EDWARD EVERETT,	200
OLIVER WENDELL HOLMES,	216
JOSIAH GILBERT HOLLAND,	233
WALTER SCOTT,	249
HARRIET BEECHER STOWE,	265
HORACE MANN,	289
DONALD G. MITCHELL,	312
BRET HARTE,	336
GEORGE BANCROFT,	360

From the hour of the invention of printing, books, and not kings, were to rule in the world. Weapons forged in the mind, keen-edged, and brighter than a sunbeam, were to supplant the sword and the battle-axe. Books! light-houses built on the sea of time! Books! by whose sorcery the whole pageantry of the world's history moves in solemn procession before the eyes. From their pages great souls look down in all their grandeur, undimmed by the faults and follies of earthly existence, consecrated by time.

        Edwin P. Whipple.

TREASURES

FROM

THE PROSE WORLD

Indian Summer.

The Year has paused to remember, and beautiful her memories are. She recalls the Spring; how soft the air! And the Summer; how deep and warm the sky! And the harvest; how pillar'd and golden the clouds! And the rainbows and the sunsets; how gorgeous are the woods!

Indian Summer is nature's "sober, second thought," and to me, the sweetest of the thinking. A veil of golden gauze trails through the air; the woods *en déshabillé*, are gay with the hectic flushes of the Fall; and the bright sun, relenting, comes meekly back again, as if he would not go to Capricorn. He has a kindly look; he no longer dazzles one's eyes out, but has a sunset softness in his face, and fairly blushes at the trick he meditated. Round, red Sun! rich ruby in the jewelry of God! it sets as big as the woods; and ten acres of forest, in the distance, are relieved upon the great disc—a rare device upon a glorious medallion. The sweet south wind has come again, and breathes softly through the woods, till they rustle like a banner of crimson and gold; and waltzes gaily with the dead leaves that strew the ground, and whirls them quite away sometimes, in its frolic, over the fields and the fences, and into the brook, in whose little eddies they loiter on the way, and never get "down to the sea" at all.

Who wonders that, with this mirage of departed Summer in sight, the peach trees sometimes lose their reckoning, fancy Winter, pale fly-leaf in the book of Time, has somehow slipped out, and put forth their rosy blossoms only to be carried away, to-day or to-morrow, by the blasts of November.

And with the sun and the wind, here are the birds once more. A blue bird warbles near the house, as it used to do; the sparrows are chirping in the bushes, and the wood-robins flicker like flakes of fire through the trees. Now and then a crimson or yellow leaf winnows its way slowly down through the smoky light, and "the sound of dropping nuts is heard" in the still woods. The brook that a little while ago stole along in the shadow, rippling softly round the boughs that trailed idly in its waters, now twinkles all the way, on its journey down to the lake. It is Saturday night of Nature and the Year—

> "Their breathing moment on the bridge where Time
> Of light and darkness, forms an arch sublime."

There is nothing more to be done; everything is packed up; the wardrobe of Spring and Summer is all folded in those little russet and rude cases, and laid away here and there, some in the earth, and some in the water, and lost, as we say, but after all, no more lost than is the little infant, when, laid upon a pillow it is rocked and swung, this way and that, in the arms of a careful mother. So the dying, smiling Year is all ready to go.

> "Aye, thou art welcome, heaven's delicious breath,
>   When woods begin to wear the crimson leaf,
>   And suns grow meek, and the meek suns grow brief,
> And the year smiles as it draws near its death.
> Winds of the sunny south! oh, still delay,
>   In the gay woods and in the golden air,
>   Like to a good old age, released from care
> Journeying in long serenity, away."

TREASURES FROM THE PROSE WORLD. 19

"With such a bright, late quiet, would that I
Might wear out life like thee, 'mid bowers and brooks:
And dearer yet, the sunshine of kind looks,
And music of kind voices ever nigh.
And when my last sand twinkles in the glass,
Pass silently from men as thou dost pass."

Poetry and Mystery of the Sea.

[Our Treasures would not be complete without the following beautifully sublime selection from the pen of Dr. Greenwood. Kind reader, if you love poetry and beautiful word pictures, you can never weary in reading the following:]

"The sea is His, and He made it," cries the Psalmist of Israel, in one of those bursts of enthusiasm in which he so often expresses the whole of a vast subject by a few simple words. Whose else, indeed, could it be, and by whom else could it have been made? Who else can heave its tides and appoint its bounds? Who else can urge its mighty waves to madness with the breath and wings of the tempest, and then speak to it again in a master's accents and bid it be still? Who else could have peopled it with its countless inhabitants, and caused it to bring forth its various productions, and filled it from its deepest bed to its expanded surface, filled it from its center to its remotest shores, filled it to the brim with beauty, and mystery, and power? Majestic ocean! Glorious sea! No created being rules thee or made thee.

What is there more sublime than the trackless, desert, all-surrounding, unfathomable sea? What is there more peacefully sublime than the calm, gentle-heaving, silent sea? What is there more terribly sublime than the angry, dashing, foaming sea? Power—resistless, overwhelming power—is its attribute and its expression, whether in the careless, conscious grandeur of its deep rest, or the wild tumult of its excited wrath. It is awful when its crested waves rise up to make a compact with the black clouds and the howling winds, and the thunder and the thunderbolt, and they sweep on, in the joy of their dread alliance, to do the Almighty's bidding. And it is awful, too, when it stretches its broad level out to meet in quiet union the bended sky, and show in the line of meeting the vast rotundity of the world. There is majesty in its wide expanse, separating and enclosing the great continents of the earth, occupying two-thirds of the whole surface of the globe, penetrating the land with its bays and secondary seas, and receiving the constantly pouring tribute of every river of every shore. There is majesty in its fulness, never diminishing, and never increasing. There is majesty in its integrity, for its whole vast substance is uniform in its local unity, for there is but one ocean, and the inhabitants of any one maritime spot may visit the inhabitants of any other in the wide world. Its depth is sublime; who can sound it? Its strength is sublime; what fabric of man can resist it? Its voice is sublime, whether in the prolonged song of its ripple or the stern music of its roar—whether it utters its hollow and melancholy tones within a labyrinth of wave-worn caves, or thunders at the base of some huge promontory, or beats against a toiling vessel's sides, lulling the voyager to rest with the strains of its wild monotony, or dies away with the calm and fading twilight, in gentle murmurs on some sheltered shore.

The sea possesses beauty in richness of its own; it borrows it from earth, and air, and heaven. The clouds lend it the various dyes of their wardrobe, and throw down upon it the broad masses of their shadows as they go sailing and sweeping by. The rainbow laves in it its many-colored feet. The sun loves to visit it, and the moon, and the glittering brotherhood of planets and stars, for they delight themselves in its beauty. The sunbeams return from it in showers of diamonds and glances of fire; the moonbeams find in it a pathway of silver, where they dance to and fro with the breezes and the waves, through the livelong night. It has a light, too, of its own,—a soft and sparkling light, rivaling the stars; and often does the ship which cuts its surface leave streaming behind a milky way of dim and uncertain luster, like that which is shining dimly above. It harmonizes in its forms and sounds both with the night and the day. It cheerfully reflects the light, and it unites solemnly with the darkness. It imparts sweetness to the music of men, and grandeur to the thunder of heaven. What landscape is so beautiful as one upon the borders of the sea? The spirit of its loveliness is from the waters where it dwells and rests, singing its spells and scattering its charms on all the coasts. What rocks and cliffs are so glorious as those which are washed by the chafing sea? What groves and fields and dwellings are so enchanting as those which stand by the reflecting sea?

If we could see the great ocean as it can be seen by no mortal eye, beholding at one view what we are now obliged to visit in detail and spot by spot,—if we could, from a flight far higher than tho eagle's, view the immense surface of the deep all spread out beneath us like a universal chart—what an infinite variety such a scene would display! Here a storm would be raging, the thunder bursting, the waters boiling, and rain and foam and fire all mingling together; and here, next to this scene of magnificent confusion, we should see the bright blue waves glittering in the sun and clapping their hands for very gladness. Here we should see a cluster of green islands set like jewels in the bosom of the sea; and there we should see broad shoals and gray rocks, fretting the billows and threatening the mariner. Here we discern a ship propelled by the steady wind of the tropics, and inhaling the almost visible odors which diffuse themselves around the Spice Islands of the east; there we should behold a vessel piercing the cold barrier of the north, struggling among hills and fields of ice, and contending with Winter in his own everlasting dominion. Nor are the ships of man the only travelers we shall perceive upon this mighty map of the ocean. Flocks of sea-birds are passing and re-passing, diving for their food or for pastime, migrating from shore to shore with unwearied wing and undeviating instinct, or wheeling and swarming around the rocks which they make alive and vocal by their numbers and their clanging cries.

We shall behold new wonders and riches when we investigate the sea-shore. We shall find both beauty for the eye and food for the body, in the varieties of shell-fish which adhere in myriads to the rocks or form their close, dark burrows in the sands. In some parts of the world we shall see those houses of stone which the little coral insect rears up with patient industry from the bottom of the waters, till they grow into formidable rocks, and broad forests, whose branches never wave and whose leaves never fall. In other parts we shall see those pale, glistening pearls which adorn the crowns of princes and are woven in the hair of beauty, extorted by the relentless grasp of man from the hidden stores of ocean. And spread round every coast there are beds of flowers and thickets of plants, which the dew does not nourish, and which man has not sown, nor cultivated, nor reaped, but which seem to belong to the floods alone and the denizens of the floods, until they are thrown up by the surges, and we discover that even the dead spoils of the fields of ocean may fertilize and enrich the fields of earth. They have a life, and a nourishment, and an economy of their own; and we know little of them except that they are there in their briny nurseries, reared up into luxuriance by what would kill, like a mortal poison, the vegetation of the land.

There is mystery in the sea. There is mystery in its depths. It is unfathomed and perhaps unfathomable. Who can tell, who shall know, how near its pits run down to the central core of the world? Who can tell what wells, what fountains are there to which the fountains of the earth are but drops? Who shall say whence the ocean derives those inexhaustible supplies of salt which so impregnate its waters that all the rivers of the earth, pouring into it from the time of the creation, have not been able to freshen them? What undescribed monsters, what unimaginable shapes, may be roving in the profoundest places of the sea, never seeking— and perhaps, from their nature, never able to seek—the upper waters and expose themselves to the gaze of man! What glittering riches, what heaps of gold, what stores of gems there must be scattered in lavish profusion in the ocean's lowest bed! What spoils from all climates, what works of art from all lands, have been engulfed by the insatiable and reckless waves! Who shall go down to examine and reclaim this uncounted and idle wealth? Who bears the keys of the deep?

And oh! yet more affecting to the heart, and mysterious to the mind, what companies of human beings are locked up in that wide, weltering, unsearchable grave of the sea! Where are the bodies of those lost ones over whom the melancholy waves alone have been chanting requiem? What shrouds were wrapped round the limbs of beauty, and of manhood, and of placid infancy, when they were laid on the dark floor of that secret tomb? Where are the bones, the relics of the brave and the timid, the good and the bad, the parent, the child, the wife, the husband, the brother, the sister, the lover, which have been tossed and scattered and buried by the washing, wasting, wandering sea? The journeying winds may sigh as year after year they pass over their beds. The solitary rain cloud may weep in darkness over the mingled remains which lie strewed in that unwonted cemetery. But who shall tell the bereaved to what spot their affections may cling? And where shall human tears be shed throughout that solemn sepulchre? It is mystery all. When shall it be resolved? Who shall find it out? Who but He to whom the wildest waves listen reverently, and to whom all nature bows; He who shall one day speak and be heard in ocean's profoundest caves; to whom the deep, even the lowest deep, shall give up its dead, when the sun shall sicken, and the earth and the isles shall languish, and the heavens be rolled together like a scroll, and there shall be *no more Sea.*

CHARLES DICKENS.

CHARLES DICKENS was born at Landport, a suburb of Portsmouth, England, February 7, 1812, and he died at his home, known as Gadshill House, near Rochester, Kent, June 9, 1870. His father, John Dickens, was a clerk in the navy pay-office.

Young Dickens received part of his education at Chatham, whither his parents had moved in 1816. His principal studies, however, were "Robinson Crusoe," "Don Quixote," "Gill Blas," and other novels. In 1822 his father became bankrupt and was sent to prison for debt. Charles' family then removed to London, where the boy was put to work in a blacking factory. His father, now relieved by a small legacy, became a reporter for the "Morning Chronicle." After attending school for two years, the boy was placed in an attorney's office. Subsequently, he learned short-hand and became Parliamentary reporter for "The True Sun." Four years later, he was joined to the staff of the "Morning Chronicle."

At the age of nine, Dickens commenced his literary work by writing a tragedy, entitled *Misnar, the Sultan of India*. In 1834, appeared his first published sketch, *Mrs. Joseph Porter Over the Way*. A series of sketches followed in the "Old Monthly Magazine," over the signature of "Boz." For want of pay these sketches were discontinued, and afterward resumed in the "Chronicle" where they attracted much public attention.

CHARLES DICKENS.

In 1836 these sketches were published in two volumes. The tide of Dickens' popularity had now fully set in, and sketches and books flowed from his pen like the steady movement of a mighty river. The *Posthumous Papers of the Pickwick Club*, upon the introduction of "Sam Weller," in the fifth number, grew in popularity, and upon completion of the "Papers," the author was famous.

Oliver Twist, two anonymous volumes entitled *Young Gentlemen* and *Young Couples, Memoirs of Joseph Gramaldi, Nicholas Nickleby, Old Curiosity Shop,* and *Barnaby Rudge,* quickly followed.

In January, 1842, in company with his wife, Dickens sailed for the United States, and on the 22d, landed at Boston. He was received with great enthusiasm. Upon his return home he published *American Notes*. He was severely censured for his exaggerations in speaking of American customs. In 1844 appeared *Martin Chuzzlewit*. Then followed a year's travel in Italy, after which he became editor of the London "Daily News." In the "News" appeared his *Pictures from Italy*. His editorship was discontinued at the end of four months. *Dombey and Son* appeared in 1848, and *David Copperfield*, in 1850. In 1850 he established "Household Words;" this being discontinued, in 1859 he started "All the Year Round." At this time he wrote a popular *Child's History of England*. Omitting his other works we will only record the productions of *A Tale of Two Cities*, published in 1860; *Great Expectations*, 1861; *Our Mutual Friend*, in 1865.

Visiting the United States again in 1867, he gave public readings from his works, in the Eastern and Middle States.

Dickens was an almost perfect actor, and his laborious study had prepared him to make his readings in this country the most successful part of his life work.

In a financial, as well as in a literary sense, his life work was eminently successful. *The Child's Dream of a Star*, which we have selected for this book, has been issued in a beautiful, illustrated edition. His writings are so well known that we will make no further record of them here.

Dickens' social history is brief. He was the second of eight children. In 1836, he married Catherine, the eldest daughter of George Hogarth, an editorial writer for the "Chronicle." They had seven children, but in 1858 arranged a formal separation, the reasons for which have never been made public. He once refused a baronetcy. He willed that no public announcement be made of his burial; that his name be inscribed on his tomb in plain English letters, without any title. He wished no monument, but said: "I rest my claims to the remembrance of my country upon my published works." A grateful world will remember him. Leaving *The Mystery of Edwin Drood* unfinished, he died at the time given in the beginning of this sketch, from a stroke of apoplexy, and was buried privately in the poet's corner of Westminster Abbey.

The Child's Dream of a Star.

There was once a child, and he strolled about a good deal, and thought of a number of things. He had a sister, who was a child, too, and his constant companion. These two used to wonder all day long. They wondered at the beauty of the flowers; they wondered at the height and blueness of the sky; they wondered at the depth of the bright water; they wondered at the goodness and the power of God who made the lovely world.

They used to say to one another, sometimes, "Supposing all the children upon the earth were to die, would the flowers, and the water, and the sky be sorry?" They believed they would be sorry: "For," said they, "the buds are the children of the flowers; and the little playful streams that gambol down the hillsides are the children of the waters; and the smallest bright specks playing at hide-and-seek in the sky all night, must surely be the children of the stars; and they would all be grieved to see their playmates, the children of men, no more." There was one clear, shining star that used to come out in the sky before the rest, near the church-spire, above the graves. It was larger and more beautiful, they thought, than all the others, and every night they watched for it, standing hand in hand at the window. Whoever saw it first, cried out, "I see the star!" And often they cried out both together, knowing so well when it would rise, and where. So they grew to be such friends with it, that before lying down in their beds, they always looked out once again, to bid it good-night; and when they were turning round to sleep, they used to say, "God bless the star!"

But while she was still very young, O, very, very young, the sister drooped, and came to be so weak that she could no longer stand in the window at night; and then the child looked sadly out by himself, and when he saw the star, turned round and said to the patient, pale face on the bed, "I see the star!" and then a smile would come upon the face, and a little weak voice used to say, "God bless my brother and the star!" And so the time came, all too soon! when the child looked out alone, and when there was no face on the bed; and when there was a little grave among the graves, not there before; and when the star made long rays down toward him, as he saw it through his tears.

Now, these rays were so bright, and they seemed to make such a shining way from earth to heaven, that when the child went to his solitary bed, he dreamed about the star; and dreamed that, lying where he was, he saw a train of people taken up that sparkling road by angels.

And the star, opening, showed him a great world of light, where many more such angels waited to receive them.

All these angels who were waiting turned their beaming eyes upon the people who were carried up into the star; and some came out from the long rows in which they stood, and fell upon the people's necks, and kissed them tenderly, and went away with them down avenues of light, and were so happy in their company, that lying in his bed he wept for joy.

But there were many angels who did not go with them, and among them was one he knew. The patient face that once had lain upon the bed was glorified and radiant, but his heart found out his sister among all the host.

His sister's angel lingered near the entrance of the star, and said to the leader among those who had brought the people thither,

"Is my brother come?"

And he said, "No."

She was turning hopefully away, when the child stretched out his arms, and cried,

"O sister, I am here! Take me!" And then she turned her beaming eyes upon him and it was night; and the star was shining into the room, making long rays down toward him as he saw it through his tears.

From that hour forth the child looked out upon the star as on the home he was to go to, when his time should come; and he thought that he did not belong to the earth alone, but to the star, too, because of his sister's angel gone before.

There was a baby born to be a brother to the child; and while he was so little that he never yet had spoken a word, he stretched his tiny form out on his bed and died.

Again the child dreamed of the opened star, and of the company of angels, and the train of people, and the rows of angels with their beaming eyes all turned upon those people's faces.

Said his sister's angel to the leader,

"Is my brother come?"

And he said, "Not that one, but another."

As the child beheld his brother's angel in her arms, he cried,

"O, sister! I am here! Take me!" And she turned and smiled upon him, and the star was shining.

He grew to be a young man and was busy at his books when an old servant came to him and said,

"Thy mother is no more. I bring her blessing on her darling son!"

Again at night he saw the star, and all that former company.

Said his sister's angel to the leader,

"Is my brother come?"

And he said,

"Thy mother!"

A mighty cry of joy went forth through all the stars, because the mother was reunited to her two children. And he stretched out his arms and cried, "O mother, sister, brother, I am here! Take me!" And they answered him, "Not yet." And the star was shining.

He grew to be a man whose hair was turning gray, and he was sitting in his chair by the fireside, heavy with grief, and with his face bedewed with tears, when the star opened once again.

Said his sister's angel to the leader,

"Is my brother come?"

And he said, "Nay, but his maiden daughter."

And the man who had been the child saw his daughter, newly lost to him, a celestial creature among those three, and he said,

"My daughter's head is on my sister's bosom, and her arm is round my mother's neck, and at her feet is the baby of old time, and I can bear the parting from her, God be praised!"

And the star was shining.

And thus the child came to be an old man, and his once smooth face was wrinkled, and his steps were slow and feeble, and his back was bent. And one night, as he lay upon his bed, his children standing round, he cried, as he had cried so long ago,

"I see the star!"

They whispered one another, "He is dying."

And he said, "I am. My age is falling from me like a garment, and I move toward the star as a child. And O, my Father, now I thank thee that it has so often opened, to receive those dear ones who await me!"

And the star was shining; and it shines upon his grave.

Death of Little Jo.

Jo is very glad to see his old friend; and says, when they are left alone, that he takes it uncommon kind as Mr. Sangsby should come so far out of his way on accounts of sich as him. Mr. Sangsby, touched by the spectacle before him, immediately lays upon the table half-a-crown; that magic balsam of his for all kinds of wounds.

"And how do you find yourself, my poor lad?" inquired the stationer, with his cough of sympathy.

"I'm in luck, Mr. Sangsby, I am," returns Jo, "and don't want for nothink. I'm more cumfbler nor you can't think, Mr. Sangsby.

I'm wery sorry that I done it, but I didn't go fur to do it. sir."

The stationer softly lays down another half-crown, and asks him what it is that he is so sorry for having done.

"Mr. Sangsby," says Jo, "I went and giv a illness to the lady as wos and yit as warn't the t'other lady, and none of 'em never says nothing to me for having done it, on accounts of their being ser good and my having been s' unfortnet. The lady come herself and see me yes'day, and she ses, 'Ah, Jo!' she ses. 'We thought we'd lost you, Jo!' she ses. And she sits down a smilin' so quiet, and don't pass a word nor yit a look upon me for having done it, she don't, and I turns agin the wall, I does, Mr. Sangsby. And Mr. Jarnders, I see him a forced to turn away his own self. And Mr. Woodcot, he come fur to give me somethink for to ease me, wot he's allus a doin' on day and night, and wen he comes a bendin' over me and a speakin' up so bold, I see his tears a fallin', Mr. Sangsby."

The softened stationer deposits another half-crown on the table. Nothing less than a repetition of that infallible remedy will relieve his feelings.

"Wot I was thinkin' on, Mr. Sangsby," proceeds Jo, "wos as you wos able to write very large, p'r'aps?"

"Yes, Jo, please God," returns the stationer.

"Uncommon, precious large, p'r'aps?" says Jo, with eagerness.

"Yes, my poor boy."

Jo laughs with pleasure. "Wot I wos thinkin' on, then, Mr. Sangsby, wos, that wen I wos moved on as fur as ever I could go, and couldn't be moved no furder, whether you might be so good, p'r'aps, as to write out, wery large, so that any one could see it anywheres, as that I was wery truly hearty sorry that I done it, and that I never went fur to do it; and that though I didn't know nothink at all, I know'd as Mr. Woodcot once cried over it, and was allus grieved over it, and that I hoped as' he'd be able to forgive me in his mind. If the writin' could be made to say it wery large, he might."

"It shall say it, Jo; very large."

Jo laughs again. "Thankee, Mr. Sangsby. It's wery kind of you, sir, and it makes me more cumfbler nor I wos afore."

The meek little stationer, with a broken and unfinished cough, slips down his fourth half-crown—he has never been so close to a case requiring so many,—and is fain to depart. And Jo and he upon this little earth shall meet no more. No more.

(*Another Scene.—Enter Mr. Woodcourt.*)

"Well, Jo, what is the matter? Don't be frightened."

"I thought," says Jo, who has started, and is looking round, "I thought I was in Tom-All-Alone's agin. An't there nobody here but you, Mr. Woodcot?"

"Nobody."

"And I an't took back to Tom-All-Alone's, am I, sir?"

"No."

Jo closes his eyes, muttering, "I am wery thankful."

After watching him closely a little while, Allan puts his mouth very near his ear, and says to him in a low, distinct voice: "Jo, did you ever know a prayer?"

"Never know'd nothink, sir."

"Not so much as one short prayer?"

"No, sir. Nothink at all. Mr. Chadbands he wos a prayin' wunst at Mr. Sangsby's, and I heerd him, but he sounded as if he wos a speakin' to hisself, and not to me. He prayed a lot, but I couldn't make out nothink on it. Different times there wos other gen'l'men come down to Tom-All-Alone's a prayin', but they all mostly sed as the t'other wuns prayed wrong, and all mostly sounded to be talkin' to theirselves, or a passin' blame on the t'others, and not a talkin' to us. We never know'd nothink. I never know'd what it wos all about."

It takes him a long time to say this; and few but an experienced and attentive listener could hear, or, hearing, understand him. After a short relapse into sleep or stupor, he makes of a sudden, a strong effort to get out of bed.

"Stay, Jo, stay! What now?"

"It's time for me to go to that there berryin'-ground, sir," he returns, with a wild look.

"Lie down, and tell me. What burying ground, Jo?"

"Where they laid him as wos wery good to me; wery good to me, indeed, he wos. It's time for me to go down to that there berryin'-ground, sir and ask to be put along with him. I want to go there and be berried. He used fur to say to me, 'I am as poor as you to-day, Jo,' he ses. I wants to tell him that I am as poor as him now, and have come there to be laid along with him."

"By-and-by, Jo; by-and-by."

"Ah! P'r'aps they wouldn't do it if I was to go myself. But will you promise to have me took there, sir, and laid along with him?"

"I will, indeed."

"Thankee, sir! Thankee, sir! They'll have to get the key of the gate afore they can take me in, for it's allus locked. And there's a step there, as I used fur to clean with my broom. It's turned wery dark, sir. Is there any light acomin'?"

"It is coming fast, Jo."

Fast. The cart is shaken all to pieces, and the rugged road is very near its end.

"Jo, my poor fellow!"

"I hear you, sir, in the dark, but I'm a gropin'—a gropin'—let me catch hold of your hand."

"Jo, can you say what I say?"

"I'll say anythink as you say, sir, for I knows it's good."

"Our Father."

"'Our Father!' Yes, that's wery good, sir."

"Which art in heaven."

"'Art in heaven!' Is the light a comin', sir?"

"It is close at hand. 'Hallowed by thy name.'"

"Hallowe⎯l⎯be⎯thy⎯name!"
The light has come upon the benighted way. Dead. Dead, your majesty. Dead, my lords and gentlemen. Dead, right reverends and wrong reverends of every order. Dead, men and women born with heavenly compassion in your hearts. And dying thus around us every day.

Mother's Vacant Chair.

I go a little farther on in your house, and I find the mother's chair. It is very apt to be a rocking chair. She had so many cares and troubles to soothe, that it must have rockers. I remember it well. It was an old chair, and the rockers were almost worn out, for I was the youngest, and the chair had rocked the whole family. It made a creaking noise as it moved, but there was music in the sound. It was just high enough to allow us children to put our heads into her lap. That was the bank where we deposited all our hurts and worries. Oh, what a chair that was! It was different from the father's chair—it was entirely different. Perhaps there was about this chair more gentleness, more tenderness, more grief when we had done wrong. When we were wayward, father scolded, but mother cried. It was a very wakeful chair. In the sick days of children other chairs could not keep awake; that chair always kept awake —kept easily awake. That chair knew all the old lullabies, and all those wordless songs which mothers sing to their-sick children— songs in which all pity and compassion and sympathetic influences are combined. That old chair has stopped rocking for a good many years. It may be set up in the loft or the garret, but it holds a queenly power yet. When at midnight you went into that grog-shop to get the intoxicating draught, did you not hear a voice that said, "My son, why go in there?" and louder than the boisterous encore of the theater, a voice saying, "My son, what do you here?" And when you went into the house of sin, a voice saying, "What would your mother do if she knew you were here?" and you were provoked at yourself, and you charged yourself with superstition and fanaticism, and your head got hot with your own thoughts, and you went home, and you went to bed, and no sooner had you touched the bed than a voice said, "What, a prayerless pillow!" Man! what is the matter? This! You are too near your mother's rocking-chair! "Oh, pshaw!" you say, "there's nothing in that. I'm five hundred miles off from where I was born—I'm three thousand miles off from the Scotch kirk whose bell was the first music I ever heard." I cannot help that; you are too near your mother's rocking-chair. "Oh!" you say, "there can't be anything in that; that chair has been vacant a great while." I cannot help that. It is all the mightier for that; it is omnipotent, that vacant mother's chair. It whispers. It speaks. It weeps. It carols. It mourns. It prays. It warns. It thunders. A young man went off and broke his mother's heart, and while he was away from home his mother died, and the telegraph brought the son, and he came into the room where she lay, and looked upon her face, and cried out, "O, mother, mother! what your life could not do your death shall effect. This moment I give my heart to God." And he kept his promise. Another victory for the vacant chair. With reference to your mother, the words of my text were fulfilled: "Thou shalt be missed because thy seat will be empty."

How Tom Sawyer Whitewashed His Fence.

[Tom Sawyer, having offended his sole guardian, Aunt Polly, is by that sternly affectionate dame punished by being set to whitewash the fence in front of the garden.]

Tom appeared on the sidewalk with a bucket of whitewash and a long-handled brush. He surveyed the fence, and all gladness left him, and a deep melancholy settled down upon his spirit. Thirty yards of board fence nine feet high. Life to him seemed hollow, and existence but a burden. Sighing, he dipped his brush and passed it along the topmost plank; repeated the operation; did it again; compared the insignificant whitewashed streak with the far-reaching continent of unwhitewashed fence, and sat down on a tree-box, discouraged.

He began to think of the fun he had planned for this day, and his sorrows multiplied. Soon the free boys would come tripping along on all sorts of delicious expeditions, and they would make a world of fun of him for having to work—the very thought of it burnt him like fire. He got out his worldly wealth and examined it—bits of toys, marbles, and trash; enough to buy an exchange of *work*, maybe, but not half enough to buy so much as half an hour of pure freedom. So he returned his straitened means to his pocket, and gave up the idea of trying to buy the boys. At this dark and hopeless moment an inspiration burst upon him! Nothing less than a great, magnificent inspiration.

He took up his brush and went tranquilly to work. Ben Rogers hove in sight, presently—the very boy, of all boys, whose ridicule he had been dreading. Ben's gait was the hop-skip-and-jump—proof enough that his heart was light and his anticipations high. He was eating an apple, and giving a long, melodious whoop, at intervals, followed by a deep-toned ding-dong-dong, ding-dong-dong,—for he was personating a steamboat. As he drew near he slackened speed, took the middle of the street, leaned far over to starboard and rounded to, ponderously, and with laborious pomp and circumstance—for he was personating the "Big Missouri," and considered himself to be drawing nine feet of water. He was boat, and captain, and engine-bells combined, so he had to imagine himself standing on his own hurricane-deck giving the orders and executing them:

"Stop her, sir! Ting-a-ling-ling!" The headway ran almost out, and he drew up slowly toward the sidewalk.

"Ship up to back! Ting-a-ling-ling!" His arms straightened and stiffened down his sides.

"Set her back on the stabboard! Ting-a-ling-ling! Chow! ch-chow-wow! Chow!" His right hand, meantime, describing stately circles—for it was representing a forty-foot wheel.

"Let her go back on the labboard! Ting-a-ling-ling! Chow-ch-chow-chow!" The left hand began to describe circles.

"Stop the stabboard! Ting-a-ling-ling! Stop the labboard! Come ahead on the stabboard. Stop her! Let your outside turn over slow! Ting-a-ling-ling! Chow-ow-ow! Get out that head-line. Lively, now! Come—out with your spring line—what're you about there! Take a turn round that stump with the bight of it! Stand by that stage, now—let her go! Done with the engine, sir! Ting-a-ling-ling! Sh't! Sh't! Sh't!" (trying the gauge-cocks.)

Tom went on whitewashing—paid no attention to the steamboat. Ben stared a moment, and then said:

"Hi-*yi!* *you're* a stump, ain't you?"

No answer. Tom surveyed his last touch with the eye of an artist; then he gave his brush another gentle sweep, and surveyed the result as before. Ben ranged up alongside of him. Tom's mouth watered for the apple, but he stuck to his work. Ben said:

"Hello, old chap; you got to work, hey?"

Tom wheeled suddenly, and said:

"Why, it's you, Ben; I warn't noticing."

"Say, I'm going in a-swimming, I am. Don't you wish you could? But, of course, you'd druther *work*, wouldn't you? 'Course you would!"

Tom contemplated the boy a bit, and said:

"What do you call work?"

"Why, ain't *that* work?"

Tom resumed his whitewashing, and answered, carelessly:

"Well, maybe it is, and maybe it ain't. All I know is, it suits Tom Sawyer."

"Oh, come now, you don't mean to let on that you like it?"

"Like it? Well, I don't see why I oughtn't to like it? Does a boy get a chance to whitewash a fence every day?"

That put the thing in a new light. Ben stopped nibbling his apple. Tom swept his brush daintily back and forth—stepped back to note the effect—added a touch here and there—criticised the effect again, Ben watching every move and getting more and more interested, more and more absorbed. Presently he said:

"Say, Tom, let *me* whitewash a little."

Tom considered—was about to consent—but he altered his mind:

"No, no, I reckon it wouldn't hardly do, Ben. You see, Aunt Polly's awful particular about this fence—right here on the street, you know—if it was the back fence I wouldn't mind, and *she* wouldn't. Yes, she's awful particular about this fence; it's got to be done very careful; I reckon there ain't one boy in a thousand, maybe two thousand, that can do it in the way it's got to be done."

"No—is that so? Oh, come, now, lemme just try, only just a little. I'd let *you*, if you was me, Tom."

"Ben, I'd like to, honest Injin; but Aunt Polly—well, Jim wanted to do it, but she wouldn't let him. Sid wanted to do it, but she wouldn't let Sid. Now don't you see how I'm fixed? If you was to tackle this fence and anything was to happen to it—"

"Oh, shucks! I'll be just as careful. Now lemme try. Say—I'll give you the core of my apple."

"Well, here. No, Ben; now don't; I'm afeared—"

"I'll give you *all* of it."

Tom gave up the brush with reluctance in his face, but alacrity in his heart. And while Ben worked and sweated in the sun, the retired artist sat on a barrel in the shade close by, dangled his legs, munched his apple, and planned the slaughter of more innocents. There was no lack of material; boys happened along every little while; they came to jeer, but remained to whitewash. By the time Ben was fagged out, Tom had traded the next chance to Billy Fisher for a kite in good repair; and when *he* played out, Johnny Miller bought in for a dead rat and a string to swing it with; and so on, and so on, hour after hour. And when the middle of the afternoon came, from being a poor, poverty-stricken boy in the morning, Tom was literally rolling in wealth. He had, beside the things before mentioned, twelve marbles, part of a jews-harp, a piece of blue bottle-glass to look through, a spool cannon, a key that wouldn't unlock anything, a fragment of chalk, a glass stopper of a decanter, a tin soldier, a couple of tadpoles, six fire-crackers, a kitten with only one eye, a brass door-knob, a dog-collar—but no dog,—the handle of a knife, four pieces of orange-peel, and a dilapidated old window sash.

Tom had had a nice good idle time all the while—plenty of company—and the fence had three coats of whitewash on it! If he hadn't run out of whitewash he would have bankrupted every boy in the village.

He said to himself that it was not such a hollow world after all. He had discovered a great law of human action without knowing it—namely, that in order to make a man or a boy covet a thing, it is only necessary to make it difficult to attain.

If he had been a great and wise philosopher, like the writer of this, he would now have comprehended that work consists of whatever a body is obliged to do, and that play consists of whatever a body is not obliged to do, and this would help him to understand why constructing artificial flowers or performing on a tread-mill is work, while rolling ten-pins or climbing Mont Blanc is only amusement.

WASHINGTON IRVING.

WASHINGTON IRVING was born in the city of New York, April 3, 1783, and he passed to the higher life on November 28, 1859. He was purely a self-made man, having received only a common-school education. He studied law for a time, but his chief studies were "Robinson Crusoe," collections of voyages, also Chaucer, Spenser and other English classics.

Irving's literary record is as follows:—In 1802 he commenced writing for the newspaper conducted by his brother. His next venture was a publication entitled "Salmagundi," conducted by himself and his brother William, and James K. Paulding. It was filled with satire upon the follies of the day, and it became quite successful. Next followed his *History of New York*, probably the best sustained burlesque ever written. For two years he conducted the "Atlantic Magazine" in Philadelphia. His *Sketch Book* was partly made up of articles from the "Magazine." His *Sketch Book* was published in New York in 1818, and subsequently, in London. This work was at once accepted as classic and the author's reputation was placed upon a permanent basis; it was considered a literary event. In 1822 *Bracebridge Hill*, written in Paris, appeared in London. In 1824 appeared the *Tales of a Traveller;* 1828, *History of the Life and Voyages of Christopher Columbus*, followed by *Voyages and Discoveries of the Companions of Columbus*. While in Spain he collected the materials for *Conquest of Grenada*, *The Alhambra*, *Legends of the Conquest of Spain*, and *Mahomet and His*

WASHINGTON IRVING.

Successors. From his trip beyond the Mississippi came, *A Tour on the Prairies.* This was followed by *Astoria, The Adventures of Captain Bouneville,* and a volume of miscellanies, entitled *Wolfert's Roost.* He also published the *Life of Margaret Davidson,* and his biography of *Oliver Goldsmith.* His last great work is his *Life of Washington,* in five volumes. The words *Rip Van Winkle* and *Sleepy Hollow* and *Knickerbocker* are familiar to all.

For pleasure and for material for his works, Irving traveled quite extensively. In 1804 he started on his tour through Europe. He visited Genoa, Sicily, Naples, Rome, Paris, Brussels, arriving finally at London. In 1814 he went to Europe the second time. He made a tour of the continent, and enjoyed a special literary companionship in London. He also traveled quite extensively in this country.

Irving's civil record is brief but important. He served for a short time as aid-de-camp to Governor Tompkins in 1814. He was commissioned, by Alexander H. Everett, minster to Spain, to make translations of the newly discovered papers in Madrid referring to Columbus. In 1829 he was appointed secretary of legation to the American embassy in London. In 1842 he was appointed minister to Spain.

In closing this sketch we quote from Underwood:

"It is not difficult to assign Irving's place among our authors. Thackeray happily spoke of him as 'the first embassador whom the New World of Letters sent to the Old.' In our lighter literature he is without a rival as an artist. He is equally happy in his delineations of scenery and charater; he moves us to tears or to laughter at his pleasure. His works have all an admirable proportion; nothing necessary is omitted, and needless details are avoided. He never fatigues us by learned antithesis, nor by the parallelism of proverbial grace, and picturesque effect. The vivacity of his youth never wholly deserted him; although he ceased writing humorous works, it served to animate his graver histories, and to give them a charm which the mere annalist could not attain. His life, on the whole, was fortunate; his fame came in season for him to enjoy it; his works brought him his bread, honestly earned, and not merely the monumental stone. Other authors may perhaps excite more of our wonder or reverence, but Irving will be remembered with delight and love. Irving's last years were spent at 'Sunnyside,' near Tarrytown, N. Y. He was never married. Miss Matilda Hoffman, the lady to whom he was betrothed, having died at the age of eighteen, he remained faithful to her memory; and her Bible, kept for so many years, was upon the table at his bedside when he died."

The Grave.

Oh, the grave! the grave! It buries every error, covers every defect, extinguishes every resentment. From its peaceful bosom spring none but fond regrets and tender recollections. Who can look down upon the grave even of an enemy, and not feel a compunctious throb that he should ever have warred with the poor handful of earth that lies moldering before him? But the grave of those we loved,—what a place for meditation! There it is we call up, in long review, the whole history of virtue and gentleness, and the thousand endearments lavished upon us, almost unheeded, in the daily intercourse of intimacy; there it is that we dwell upon the tenderness, the solemn, awful tenderness of the parting scene; the bed of death, with all its stifled griefs, its noiseless attendants, its mute, watchful assiduities; the last testimonies of expiring love; the feeble, fluttering, thrilling—oh, how thrilling!—pressure of the hand; the faint, faltering accents struggling in death to give one more assurance of affection; the last fond look of the glazing eye, turned upon us even from the threshold of existence! Aye, go to the grave of buried love and meditate! There settle the account with thy conscience for every past benefit unrequited, every past endearment unregarded, of that departed being who can never, never, never return, to be soothed by thy contrition.

If thou art a child, and hast ever added a sorrow to the soul, or a furrow to the silvered brow of an affectionate parent, if thou art a husband, and hast ever caused the fond bosom that ventured its whole happiness in thy arms to doubt one moment of thy kindness or thy truth, if thou art a friend, and hast ever wronged in thought, or word, or deed, the spirit that generously confided in thee, if thou art a lover, and hast ever given one unmerited pang to that true heart which now lies cold and still beneath thy feet, then be sure that every unkind look, every ungracious word, every ungentle action, will come thronging back upon thy memory, and knocking dolefully at thy soul; then be sure that thou wilt lie down, sorrowing and repentant on the grave, and utter the unheard groan, and pour the unavailing tear, more deep, more bitter because unheard and unavailing.

Rural Life in England.

The stranger who would form a correct opinion of the English character must not confine his observations to the metropolis. He must go forth into the country; he must sojourn in villages and hamlets; he must visit castles, villas, farmhouses, cottages; he must wander through parks and gardens, along hedges and green lanes; he must loiter about country churches, attend wakes and fairs, and other rural festivals, and cope with the people in all their conditions, and all their habits and humors.

In some countries, the large cities absorb the wealth and fashion of the nation; they are the only fixed abodes of elegant and intelligent society, and the country is inhabited almost entirely by boorish peasantry. In England, on the contrary, the metropolis is a mere gathering-place, or general rendezvous, of the polite classes, where they devote a small portion of the year to a hurry of gayety and dissipation, and having indulged this carnival, return again to the apparently more congenial habits of rural life. The various orders of society are therefore diffused over the whole surface of the kingdom, and the most retired neighborhoods afford specimens of the different ranks.

The English, in fact, are strongly gifted with the rural feeling. They possess a quick sensibility to the beauties of nature, and a keen relish for the pleasures and employments of the country. This passion seems inherent in them. Even the inhabitants of cities, born and brought up among brick walls and bustling streets, enter with facility into rural habits and evince a turn for rural occupation. The merchant has his snug retreat in the vicinity of the metropolis, where he often displays as much pride and zeal in the cultivation of his flower-garden and the maturing of his fruits as he does in the conduct of his business and the success of his commercial enterprises. Even those less fortunate individuals who are doomed to pass their lives in the midst of din and traffic, contrive to have something that shall remind them of the green aspect of nature. In the most dark and dingy quarters of the city, the drawing-room window resembles, frequently, a bank of flowers; every spot capable of vegetation has its grass plot and flower-bed and every square its mimic park, laid out with picturesque taste and gleaming with refreshing verdure.

Those who see the Englishman only in town are apt to form an unfavorable opinion of his social character. He is either absorbed in business or distracted by the thousand engagements that dissipate time, thought and feeling, in this huge metropolis; he has, therefore, too commonly, a look of hurry and abstraction. Wherever he happens to be he is on the point of going somewhere else; at the moment he is talking on one subject his mind is wandering to another; and while paying a friendly visit, he is calculating how he shall economize time so as to pay the other visits allotted to the morning. An immense metropolis like London is calculated to make men selfish and uninteresting. In their casual and transient meetings, they can but deal briefly in common places. They present but the cold superfices of character—its rich and genial qualities have no time to be warmed into a flow.

It is in the country that the Englishman gives scope to his natural feelings. He breaks loose gladly from the cold formalities and negative civilities of town; throws off his habits of shy reserve, and becomes joyous and free-hearted. He manages to collect around him all the conveniences and elegancies of polite life, and to banish its restraint. His country seat abounds with every requisite, either for studious retirement, tasteful gratification, or rural exercise. Books, paintings, music, horses, dogs, and sporting implements of all kinds, are at hand. He puts no constraint either upon his guests or himself, but in the true spirit of hospitality provides the means of enjoyment, and leaves every one to partake according to his inclination.

The taste of the English in the cultivation of land, and in what is called landscape gardening, is unrivaled. They have studied nature intently, and discover an exquisite sense of her beautiful forms and harmonious combinations. Those charms, which in other countries she lavishes in wild solitudes, are here assembled round the haunts of domestic life. They seem to have caught her coy and furtive glances, and spread them, like witchery, about their rural abodes.

Nothing can be more imposing than the magnificence of English park scenery. Vast lawns that extend like sheets of vivid green, with here and there clumps of gigantic trees, heaping up rich piles of foliage. The solemn pomp of groves and woodland glades, with the deer trooping in silent herds across them; the hare, bounding away to the covert; or the pheasant, suddenly bursting upon the wing. The brook, taught to wind in the most natural meanderings, or expand into a glassy lake—the sequestered pool, reflecting the quivering trees, with the yellow leaf sleeping on its bosom, and the trout roaming fearlessly about its limpid waters; while some rustic temple or sylvan statue, grown green and dark with age, gives an air of classic sanctity to the seclusion. These are but a few of the features of park scenery; but what most delights me, is the creative talent with which the English decorate the unostentatious abodes of middle life. The rudest habitation, the most unpromising and scanty portion of land, in the hands of an Englishman of taste, becomes a little paradise. With a nicely discriminating eye he seizes at once upon its capabilities, and pictures in his mind the future landscape. The sterile spot grows into loveliness under his hand; and yet the operations of art which produce the effect are scarcely to be perceived. The cherishing and training of some trees; the cautious pruning of others; the nice distribution of flowers and plants of tender and graceful foliage; the introduction of a green slope of velvet turf; the partial opening to a peep of blue distance, or silver gleam of water; all these are managed with a delicate tact, a prevailing, yet quiet assiduity, like the magic touchings with which a painter finishes up a favorite picture. The residence of people of fortune and refinement in the country has diffused a degree of taste and elegance in rural economy that descends to the lowest class. The very laborer, with his thatched cottage and narrow slip of ground, attends to their embellishment. The trim hedge, the grass-plot before the door, the little flower bed bordered with snug box, the woodbine trained up against the wall, and hanging its blossoms about the lattice, the pot of flowers in the window, the holly providentially planted about the house, to cheat Winter of its dreariness, and throw in a semblance of green Summer to cheer the fireside; all these bespeak the influence of taste, flowing down from high sources and pervading the lowest levels of the public mind. If ever love, as poets sing, delight to visit a cottage, it must be the cottage of an English peasant.

The fondness for rural life among the higher classes of the English has had a great and salutary effect upon the national character. I do not know a finer race of men than the English gentlemen. Instead of the softness and effeminacy which characterizes the men of rank in most countries, they exhibit a union of elegance and strength, a robustness of frame, and freshness of complexion, which I am inclined to attribute to their living so much in the open air, and pursuing so eagerly the invigorating recreations of the country. These hardy exercises produce also a healthful tone of mind and spirits, and a manliness and simplicity of manners, which even the follies and dissipations of the town cannot easily pervert, and can never entirely destroy. In the country, too, the different orders of society seem to approach more freely, to be more disposed to blend and operate favorably upon each other. The distinctions between them do not appear to be so marked and impassable as in the cities. The manner in which property has been distributed into small estates and farms has established a regular gradation from the nobleman, through the classes of gentry, small landed proprietors and substantial farmers, down to the laboring peasantry; and while it has thus banded the extremes of society together, has infused into each intermediate rank a spirit of independence. This, it must be confessed, is not so universally the case at present as it was formerly; the larger estates having, in late years of distress, absorbed the smaller, and, in some parts of the country, almost annihilated the sturdy race of small farmers. These, however, I believe, are but casual breaks in the general system I have mentioned.

In rural occupation there is nothing mean and debasing. It leads a man forth among scenes of natural grandeur and beauty; it leaves him to the workings of his own mind, operated upon by the purest and most elevating of external influences. Such a man may be simple and rough, but he cannot be vulgar. The man of refinement, therefore, finds nothing revolting in an intercourse with the lower orders of rural life, as he does when he casually mingles with the lower orders of cities. He lays aside his distance and reserve, and is glad to waive the distinctions of rank and to enter into the honest, heartfelt enjoyment of common life. Indeed, the very amusements of the country bring men more and more together, and the sound of hound and horn blend all feelings into harmony. I believe this is one great reason why the nobility and gentry are more popular among the inferior orders in England than they are in any other country; and why the latter have endured so many excessive pressures and extremities, without repining more generally at the unequal distribution of fortune and privilege.

To this mingling of cultivated and rustic society may also be attributed the rural feeling that runs through British literature; the frequent use of illustrations from rural life—those incomparable descriptions of nature which abound in the British poets, that have continued down from "The Flower and the Leaf," of Chaucer, and have brought into our closets all the freshness and fragrance of the dewy landscape. The pastoral writers of other countries appear as if they had paid nature an occasional visit, and become acquainted with her general charms; but the British poets have lived and

TREASURES FROM THE PROSE WORLD. 49

reveled with her; they have wooed her in her most secret haunts; they have watched her minutest caprices. A spray could not tremble in the breeze, a leaf could not rustle to the ground, a diamond drop could not patter in the stream, a fragrance could not exhale from the humble violet, nor a daisy unfold its crimson tints to the morning, but it has been noticed by these impassioned and delicate observers, and wrought up into some beautiful morality.

The effect of this devotion of elegant minds to rural occupations has been wonderful on the face of the country. A great part of the island is level, and would be monotonous were it not for the charms of culture; but it is studded and gemmed, as it were, with castles and palaces, and embroidered with parks and gardens. It does not abound in grand and sublime prospects, but rather in little home scenes of rural repose and sheltered quiet. Every antique farm-house and moss-grown cottage is a picture; and as the roads are continually winding, and the view is shut in by groves and hedges, the eye is delighted by a continual succession of small landscapes of captivating loveliness.

The great charm, however, of English scenery is the moral feeling that seems to pervade it. It is associated in the mind with ideas of order, of quiet, of sober, well-established principles, of hoary usage and reverend custom. Everything seems to be the growth of ages of regular and peaceful existence. The old church of remote achitecture, with its low, massive portal, its Gothic tower, its windows rich with tracery and painted glass, its stately monuments of warriors and worthies of the olden time, ancestors of the present lords of the soil, its tombstones, recording successive generations of sturdy yeomanry, whose progeny still plow the same fields and kneel at the same altar. The parsonage, a quaint, irregular pile, partly antiquated, but repaired and altered in the taste of various ages and occupants; the stile and foot-path leading from the churchyard across pleasant fields and along shady hedgerows, according to an immemorial right of way; the neighboring village with its venerable cottages, its public green, sheltered by trees under which the forefathers of the present race have sported;

the antique family mansion, standing apart in some little rural domain, but looking down with a protecting air on the surrounding scene,—all these common features of English landscape evince a calm and settled security, and hereditary transmission of home-bred virtues and local attachments, that speak deeply and touchingly for the moral character of the nation.

It is a pleasing sight on a Sunday morning, when the bell is sending its sober melody across the quiet fields, to behold the peasantry in their best finery, with ruddy faces and modest cheerfulness, thronging tranquilly along the green lanes to church; but it is still more pleasing to see them in the evenings, gathering about their cottage doors, and appearing to exult in the humble comforts and embellishments which their own hands have spread around them.

Our Revolutionary Fathers

[The following address to our Revolutionary Fathers, we take from Webster's "masterpiece as a dedicatory orator;" an address delivered at the laying of the corner-stone of the Bunker Hill Monument, at Charlestown, Mass., June 17, 1825.]

Venerable men! you have come down to us from a former generation. Heaven has bounteously lengthened out your lives that you might behold this joyous day. You are now where you stood fifty years ago this very hour, with your brothers and your neighbors, shoulder to shoulder in the strife of your country. Behold, how altered! The same heavens are indeed over your heads, the same ocean rolls at your feet, but all else how changed! You hear now no roar of hostile cannon, you see no mixed volumes of smoke and flame rising from burning Charlestown. The ground strewed with the dead and the dying, the impetuous charge, the steady and successful repulse, the loud call to repeated assault, the summoning of all that is manly to repeated resistance, a thousand bosoms freely and fearlessly bared in an instant to whatever of terror there may be in war and death,—all these you have witnessed, but you witness them no more. All is peace. The heights of yonder metropolis, its towers and roofs, which you then saw filled with wives and children and countrymen in distress and terror, and looking with unutterable emotions for the issue of the combat, have presented you to-day with the sight of its whole happy population, come out to welcome and greet you with an universal jubilee. Yonder proud ships, by a felicity of position appropriately lying at the foot of this mount, and seeming fondly to cling around it, are not means of annoyance to you, but your country's own means of distinction and defense. All is peace, and God has granted you this sight of your country's happiness ere you slumber forever in the grave. He has allowed you to behold and to partake the reward of your patriotic toils, and he has allowed us, your sons and countrymen, to meet you here, and in the name of the present generation, in the name of your country, in the name of liberty, to thank you!

But, alas! you are not all here! Time and the sword have thinned your ranks. Prescott, Putnam, Stark, Brooks, Read, Pomeroy, Bridge! our eyes seek for you in vain amid this broken band! You are gathered to your fathers, and live only to your country in her grateful remembrance and your own bright example. But let us not too much grieve that you have met the common fate of men. You lived at least long enough to know that your work had been nobly and successfully accomplished. You lived to see your country's independence established and to sheathe your swords from war. On the light of liberty you saw arise the light of peace, like

"Another morn,
Risen on mid-noon;"

and the sky on which you closed your eyes was cloudless.

But, ah! Him! the first great martyr in this great cause! Him! the premature victim of his own self-devoting heart! Him! the head of our civil councils, and the destined leader of our military bands, whom nothing brought hither but the unquenchable fire of his own spirit! Him! cut off by Providence in the hour of overwhelming anxiety and thick gloom, falling ere he saw the star of his country rise, pouring out his generous blood like water, before he knew whether it would fertilize a land of freedom or of bondage! How shall I struggle with the emotions that stifle the utterance of thy name! Our poor work may perish, but thine shall endure! This monument may molder away, the solid ground it rests upon may sink down to a level with the sea, but thy memory shall not fail! Wheresoever among men a heart shall be found that beats to the transports of patriotism and liberty, its aspirations shall be to claim kindred with thy spirit!

But the scene amidst which we stand does not permit us to confine our thoughts or our sympathies to those fearless spirits who hazarded or lost their lives on this consecrated spot. We have the happiness to rejoice here in the presence of a most worthy representation of the survivors of the whole Revolutionary Army.

Veterans! you are the remnant of many a well-fought field. You bring with you marks of honor from Trenton and Monmouth, from Yorktown, Camden, Bennington and Saratoga. Veterans of half a century! when in your youthful days you put everything at hazard in your country's cause, good as that cause was, and sanguine as youth is, still your fondest hopes did not stretch onward to an hour like this! At a period to which you could not reasonably have expected to arrive, at a moment of national prosperity such as you could never have foreseen, you are now met here to enjoy the fellowship of old soldiers and to receive the overflowing of an universal gratitude.

But your agitated countenances and your heaving breasts inform me that even this is not an unmixed joy. I perceive that a tumult of contending feelings rushes upon you. The images of the dead, as well as the persons of the living, throng to your embraces. The scene overwhelms you, and I turn from it. May the Father of all mercies smile upon your declining years and bless them! And when you shall here have exchanged your embraces, when you shall one more have pressed the hands which have been so often extended to give succor in adversity, or grasped in the exultation of victory, then look abroad into this lovely land which your young valor defended, and mark the happiness with which it is filled; yea, look abroad in the whole earth and see what a name you have contributed to give to your country, and what a praise you have added to freedom, and then rejoice in the sympathy and gratitude which beam upon your last days from the improved condition of mankind!

[Here follow a few remarks in which Mr. Webster refers to the effects of the battle of June 17th and its impression upon those who were about to engage in the struggle for equal rights. He sees the colonists standing together and he expresses the hope that this feeling will remain with them forever: "One cause, one country one heart."] Mr. Webster then continues as follows:

Information of these events, circulating through Europe, at length reached the ears of one who now hears me.* He has not forgotten the emotion which the fame of Bunker Hill and the name of Warren excited in his youthful breast.

Sir, we are assembled to commemorate the establishment of great public principles of liberty, and to do honor to the distinguished dead. The occasion is too severe for eulogy to the living. But, sir, your interesting relation to this country, the peculiar circumstances which surround you and surround us, call on me to express the happiness which we derive from your presence and aid in this solemn commemoration.

Fortunate, fortunate man! with what measure of devotion will you not thank God for the circumstances of your extraordinary life! You are connected with both hemispheres, and with two generations. Heaven saw fit to ordain that the electric spark of liberty should be conducted, through you, from the New World to the Old; and, we who are now here to perform this duty of patriotism have all of us long ago received it in charge from our fathers to cherish your name and your virtues. You will account it an instance of your good fortune, sir, that you crossed the seas to visit us at a time which enables you to be present at this solemnity. You now behold the field, the renown of which reached you in the heart of

―――
*General Lafayette

France, and caused a thrill in your ardent bosom. You see the lines of the little redoubt thrown up by the incredible diligence of Prescott; defended, to the last extremity, by his lion-hearted valor; and, within which, the corner-stone of our monument has now taken its position. You see where Warren fell, and where Parker, Gardner, McCleary, Moore, and other early patriots fell with him. Those who survived that day, and whose lives have been prolonged to the present hour, are now around you. Some of them you have known in the trying scenes of the war. Behold! they now stretch forth their feeble arms to embrace you. Behold! they raise their trembling voices to invoke the blessing of God on you and yours forever.

Sir, you have assisted us in laying the foundation of this edifice. You have heard us rehearse, with our feeble commendation, the names of departed patriots. Sir, monuments and eulogy belong to the dead. We give them this day to Warren and his associates. On other occasions, they have been given to your more immediate companions in arms, to Washington, to Greene, to Gates, Sullivan, and Lincoln. Sir, we have become reluctant to grant these, our highest and last honors; further: we would gladly hold them yet back from the little remnant of that immortal band. *Serus in cælum redeas.* Illustrious as are your merits, yet far, Oh, very far distant be the day, when any inscription shall bear your name, or any tongue pronounce its eulogy.

Happiness.

She is deceitful as the calm that precedes the hurricane, smooth as the water on the verge of the cataract, and beautiful as the rainbow, that smiling daughter of the storm; but, like the mirage in the desert, she tantalizes us with a delusion that distance creates and that contiguity destroys. Yet, when unsought, she is often found, and when unexpected, often obtained; while those who seek for her the most diligently fail the most, because they seek her where she is not. Anthony sought her in love; Brutus, in glory; Cæsar, in dominion;—the first found disgrace, the second disgust, the last ingratitude, and each destruction. To some she is more kind, but not less cruel; she hands them her cup and they drink even to stupefaction, until they doubt whether they are men, with Philip, or dream that they are gods, with Alexander. On some she smiles, as on Napoleon, with an aspect more bewitching than an Italian sun; but it is only to make her frown the more terrible, and by one short caress to embitter the pangs of separation. Yet is she, by universal homage and consent, a queen; and the passions are the vassal lords that crowd her court, await her mandate, and move at her control. But, like other mighty sovereigns, she is so surrounded by her envoys, her officers, and her ministers of state, that it is extremely difficult to be admitted to her presence chamber, or to have any immediate communication with herself. Ambition, avarice, love, revenge, all these seek her, and her alone; alas! they are neither presented to her nor will she come to them. She dispatches, however, her envoys unto them,—mean and poor representatives of their queen. To ambition, she sends power; to avarice, wealth; to love, jealousy; to revenge, remorse; alas! what are these, but so many other names for vexation or disappointment? Neither is she to be won by flatteries or by bribes—she is to be gained by waging war against her *enemies*, much sooner than by paying any particular court to herself. Those that conquer her adversaries will find that they need not go to her, for she will come unto them. None bid so high for her as kings; few are more willing, none are more able to purchase her alliance at the fullest price. But she has no more respect for kings than for their subjects; she mocks them, indeed, with the empty show of a visit, by sending to their palaces all her equipage, her pomp, and her train; but she comes not herself. What detains her? She is traveling *incognito* to keep a private appointment with contentment and to partake of a dinner of herbs in a cottage.

The Music of Child Laughter.

The laugh of a child will make the holiest day more sacred still. Strike with hand of fire, O weird musician, thy harp strung with Apollo's golden hair! Fill the vast cathedral aisles with symphonies sweet and dim, deft toucher of the organ keys! Blow, bugle, blow, until thy silver notes do touch and kiss the moonlit waves, charming the wandering lovers on the vine-clad hills; but know your sweetest strains are discord all compared with childhood's happy laugh—the laugh that fills the eyes with light and dimples every cheek with joy. Oh, rippling river of laughter, thou art the blessed boundary line between the beast and man, and every wayward wave of thine doth drown some fretful fiend of care.

VICTOR HUGO.

VICTOR HUGO.

VICTOR HUGO was born at Besançon, on the 26th of February, 1802. His father, General Hugo, distinguished himself in the first French Revolution, under Napoleon. His mother was of the old royalist Vendean stock. Thus we find that Victor Hugo came from a good family. He received an excellent classical education in France, and afterward spent a year in Spain, in a school devoted to the sons of nobles. At the age of fourteen, Victor Hugo distinguished himself in the production of a tragedy called *Irtamene*, and two lyric pieces of excellent qualities.

Besides other remarkable works, he produced in 1822 a volume of *Odes et Ballades,* in which, although the old classic form was not quite thrown aside, may be discovered traces of that romantic spirit which became the prevailing characteristic of Victor Hugo's writings. This volume announced the poet and author in all the strength, richness, and brilliancy of his genius. It raised Victor at once to the highest rank of modern poets, a position which he has since maintained.

His romance, *Notre Dame de Paris,* in which he displayed treasures of style, of imagination, of antiquarian knowledge, and great powers of description, raised him to the very foremost rank of romancers. In addition to the wonderful powers of description, Victor Hugo's writings possess a charm and sonority of language, and a remarkable brilliancy of fancy which make his style very picturesque and attractive.

In the Revolution of 1830, which drove Charles X from his throne, Hugo was on the side of the Revolution. When Louis Philippe was on the throne, he raised Victor Hugo to the peerage. When the monarchy was at an end, Hugo was with the Republic, and received the high compliment of being sent to the Assembly as a representative of the city of Paris. In 1851 Hugo opposed the change in which Louis Napoleon established the throne again in France. For his opposition he was obliged to leave his native land and live in exile. He firmly refused to compromise himself and return to France under the rule of Louis Napoleon. During the greater portion of his absence from his own country he occupied Hauteville House, a pretty residence with a charming garden, standing on the high ground over St. Peter's Port. The house belonged to the Queen of England. In speaking of the matter, Hugo once said: "My position is somewhat anomalous. I am a republican, and also a peer of France; a Frenchman in exile, who is the tenant of a house held by the Queen of England as Duchess of Normandy."

While in exile Hugo wrote quite extensively both in prose and poetry. His *Les Miserables* is sufficient to crown his eminent literary career, and, indeed, it is enough glory for one man to have given birth to what may be considered the greatest work of the imagination which the century has produced.

Upon the overthrow of Louis Napoleon in the war with Prussia, and the consequent return of France to a Republic, Victor Hugo returned to his native land. It was a happy day both to him and his countrymen when the long spell of exile was broken and he returned to his own loved France.

A Paradise on Earth,

OR,

THE BLIND BISHOP AND HIS SISTER.

[The following charming selection is taken from *Les Misérables*. It is written in remembrance of a blind bishop who died in 1821, at the age of eighty-two. He had been prominent in the affairs of his country, and in his old age was satisfied to be blind, as his sister was by his side.]

Let us say, parenthetically, that to be blind and to be loved, is one of the most strangely exquisite forms of happiness upon this earth, where nothing is perfect. To have continually at your side a wife, a sister or a daughter, a charming being, who is there because you have need of her, and because she cannot do without you; to know yourself indispensable to a woman who is necessary to you; to be able constantly to gauge her affection by the amount of her presence which she gives you, and to say to yourself: "She devotes all her time to me because I possess her entire heart;" to see her thoughts in default of her face; to prove the fidelity of a being in the eclipse of the world; to catch the rustling of a dress like the sound of wings; to hear her come and go, leave the room, return, talk, sing, and then to dream that you are the center of those steps, those words, those songs; to manifest at every moment your own attraction, and to feel yourself powerful in proportion to your weakness; to become in darkness and through darkness the planet round which this angel gravitates—but few felicities equal this. The supreme happiness of life is the conviction of being loved for yourself, or more correctly speaking, loved in spite of yourself; and this conviction the blind man has. In this distress to be served is to be caressed. Does he want for anything? No. When you possess love, you have not lost the light. And what a love! a love entirely made of virtues. There is no blindness where there is certainty; the groping soul seeks a soul and finds it, and this fond and tried soul is woman. A hand supports you, it is hers; a mouth touches your forehead, it is hers; you hear a breathing close to you, it is she.

To have everything she has, from her worship to her pity, to be never left, to have this gentle weakness to succor you, to lean on this unbending reed, to touch providence with her hands, and be able to take her in your arms—oh! what rapture this is! The heart, that obscure celestial flower, begins to expand mysteriously, and you would not exchange this shadow for all the light! The angel soul is thus necessarily there; if she go away, it is to return; she disappears like a dream, and reappears like a reality. You feel heat approaching you, it is she. You overflow with serenity, ecstacy, and gayety; you are a sunbeam in the night. And then the thousand little attentions, the nothings which are so enormous in this vacuum! The most ineffable accents of the human voice employed to lull you, and taking the place of the vanished universe! You are caressed with the soul; you see nothing, but you feel yourself adored; it is a paradise of darkness.

Napoleon Buonaparte

[The selection given below occurs in a conversation between two Frenchmen. One, a Republican, holds up his country by saying, "France requires no Corsica to be great. France is great because she is France." The other, one of "The Old Guard," with a strangely tremulous voice, produced by his internal emotion, answers, "Heaven forbid that I should diminish France; but it is not diminishing her to amalgamate Napoleon with her."]

Come, let us talk. I am a new-comer among you, but I confess that you astonish me. * * * * I fancied you young men, but where do you keep your enthusiasm, and what do you do with it? Whom do you admire, if it is not the Emperor, and what more do you want? If you will not have that great man, what great man would you have?

He had everything, he was complete, and in his brain was the cube of human faculties. He made codes like Justinian, and dictated like Cæsar; his conversation blended the lightning of Pascal with the thunder of Tacitus; he made history and wrote it, and his bulletins are Iliads; he combined the figures of Newton with the metaphor of Mahomet.

He left behind him in the east worlds great as the pyramids, at Tilsit he taught majesty to emperors, at the Academy of Science he answered Laplace, at the Council of State he held his own against Merlin, he gave a soul to the geometry of one and to the sophistry of others, for he was a legist with the lawyers, a sidereal with the astronomers. Like Cromwell, blowing out one of two candles, he went to the temple to bargain for a curtain tassel; he saw everything, knew everything, but that did not prevent him from laughing heartily by the cradle of his new-born son. And, all at once, startled Europe listened, armies set out, parks of artillery rolled along, bridges of boats were thrown over rivers, clouds of cavalry galloped in the hurricane, and shouts, bugles, and crashing of thrones could be heard all around. The frontiers of kingdoms oscillated on the map, the sound of a superhuman sword being drawn from its scabbard could be heard, and he was seen, standing erect on the horizon, with a gleam in his hand, and a splendor in his eye, opening in the thunder of his two wings, the Grand Army and the Old Guard. He was the archangel of war.

Let us be just, my friends! What a splendid destiny it is for a people to be the empire of such an emperor, when that people is France and adds its genius to the genius of that man. To appear and reign; to march and triumph; to have as bivouacs every capital; to select grenadiers and make kings of them; to decree the downfall of dynasties; to transfigure Europe at double quick steps; to feel when you threaten that you lay your hand on the sword-hilt of God; to follow in one man Hannibal, Cæsar, and Charlemagne; to be the people of a ruler who accompanies your every day-break with the brilliant announcement of a battle gained; to be aroused in the morning by the guns of the Invalides; to cast into the abysses of light prodigious words which are eternally luminous—Marengo, Arcola, Austerlitz, Jena, and Wagram!—to produce at each moment on the zenith of centuries constellations of victories; to make the French Emperor a pendant of the Roman Empire; to be the great nation, and give birth to the great army; to send legions all over the world, as the mountain sends its eagles in all directions to conquer, rule, and crush; to be in Europe a people gilt by glory; to sound a Titanic flourish of trumpets through history; to conquer the world twice, by conquest and by amazement—all this is sublime.

A Heart Beneath a Stone.

[The sentiments which we copy here are extremely beautiful. A Frenchman, who by his political opinions was obliged to live in secret, communicated with his lady by leaving a letter beneath a stone. The rest is fully explained in the following:]

She raised the stone, which was of some size, and there was something under it that resembled a letter; it was an envelope of white paper. Cosette seized it; there was no address on it, and it was not sealed up. Still the envelope, though open, was not empty, for papers could be seen inside. Cosette no longer suffered from terror, nor was it curiosity: it was a commencement of anxiety. Cosette took out a small quire of paper, each page of which was numbered, and bore several lines written in a very nice and delicate hand, so Cosette thought. She looked for a name, but there was none; for a signature, but there was none, either. For whom was the packet intended? probably for herself, as a hand had laid it on the bench. From whom did it come? An irresistible fascination seized upon her. She tried to turn her eyes away from these pages, which trembled in her hand. She looked at the sky, the street, the acacias all bathed in light, the pigeons circling round an adjoining roof, and then her eyes settled on the manuscript, and she said to herself that she must know what was inside it. This is what she read:

The reduction of the universe to a single being, the dilation of a single being as far as God, such is love.
Love is the salutation of the angels to the stars.

How sad is the soul when it is sad through love! What a void is the absence of the being, who of her own self fills the world. Oh! how true it is that the beloved being becomes God! We might understand how God might be jealous of her, had not the Father of all evidently made creation for the soul, and the soul for love.

God is behind everything, but everything conceals God. Things are black and creatures are opaque, but to love a being is to render her transparent.

Certain thoughts are prayers. There are moments when the soul is kneeling, no matter what the attitude of the body may be.

O love, adoration! voluptuousness of two minds which comprehend each other, of two hearts which are exchanged, of two glances which penetrate one another. You will come to me, O happiness, will you not? Walks with her in the solitudes, blest, and radiant days! I have dreamed that from time to time hours were detached from the lives of angels, and came down here to traverse the destinies of men.

God can add nothing to the happiness of those who love, except giving them endless duration. After a life of love, an eternity of love is in truth an augmentation; but it is impossible even for God to increase in its intensity the ineffable felicity which love gives to the soul in this world. God is the fullness of heaven, love is the fullness of man.

You gaze at a star for two motives: because it is luminous and because it is impenetrable. You have by your side a sweeter radiance and greater mystery—woman.

When love has blended and molded two beings in an angelic and sacred union, they have found the secret of life; henceforth they are only the two terms of the same destiny, the two wings of one mind. Love and soar!

If you are a stone, be a magnet; if you are a plant, be sensitive; if you are a man, be love.

Love is the celestial breathing of the atmosphere of paradise.

I have met in the street a very poor young man who was in love. His hat was old, his coat worn, his coat was out at elbows, the water passed through his shoes, and the stars through his soul.

What a grand thing it is to be loved! What a grander thing still to love! The heart becomes heroic by the might of passion. Henceforth it is composed of nought but what is pure, and is only supported by what is elevated and great. An unworthy thought can no more germinate in it than a nettle on a glacier. The lofty and serene soul, inaccessible to emotions and vulgar passions, soaring above the clouds and shadows of the world, follies, falsehoods, hatreds, vanities, and miseries, dwells in the azure of the sky, and henceforth only feels the profound and subterranean heavings of destiny as the summit of the mountains feels earthquakes.

If there were nobody who loved, the sun would be extinguished.

Advice to a Would-Be Criminal.

[A young man sought to murder an elderly citizen for his money. In the struggle the young man was overcome by his intended victim and held by an iron grasp. While in this situation the citizen gave his intended murderer the following excellent lecture:]

"My boy, you are entering by sloth into the most laborious of existences. Ah! you declare yourself an idler, then prepare yourself for labor. Have you ever seen a formidable machine which is called a flatting-press? You must be on your guard against it, for it is a crafty and ferocious thing, and if it catches you by the skirt of the coat it drags you under it entirely. This machine is indolence. Stop while there is yet time, and save yourself, otherwise it is all over with you, and ere long you will be among the cog-wheels. Once caught, hope for nothing more. You will be forced to fatigue yourself, idler, and no rest will be allowed you, for the iron hand of implacable toil has seized you. You refuse to earn your livelihood, have a calling, and accomplish a duty; it bores you to be like the rest—well, you will be different. Labor is the law, and whoever repulses it as a bore must have it as a punishment. You do not wish to be a laborer, and you will be a slave; toil only lets you loose on one side to seize you again on the other; you do not wish to be its friend, and you will be its negro. Ah, you did not care for the honest fatigue of men, and you are about to know the sweat of the damned; while others sing you will groan. You will see other men working in the distance, and they will seem to you to be resting. The laborer, the reaper, the sailor, the blacksmith, will appear to you in the light, like the blessed inmates of a paradise.

"What a radiance there is in the anvil; what joy it is to guide the plow and tie up the sheaf; what a holiday to fly before the wind in a boat! But you, idler, will have to dig, and drag, and roll, and walk! Pull at your halter, for you are a beast of burden in the service of hell! So your desire is to do nothing? Well, you will not have a week, a day, an hour without feeling crushed. You will not be able to lift anything without agony, and every passing minute will make your muscles crack. What is a feather for others will be a rock for you, and the most simple things will grow scarped. Life will become a monster around you, and coming, going, breathing, will be so many terrible tasks for you. Your lungs will produce in you the effect of a hundred-pound weight, and going there sooner than here will be a problem to solve. Any man who wishes to go out, merely opens his door and finds himself in the street; but if you wish to go out you must pierce through your wall. What do honest men do to reach to street? They go down stairs; but you will tear up your sheets, make a cord of them, fiber by fiber, then pass through your window and hang by this thread over an abyss, and it will take place at night, in the storm, the rain, or the hurricane, and if the cord be too short you will have but one way of descending, by falling—falling hap-hazard into the gulf, and from any height, and on what? On some unknown thing beneath. Or you will climb up a chimney at the risk of burning yourself, or crawl through a sewer at the risk of drowning. I will say nothing of the holes which must be masked, of the stones which you will have to remove and put back twenty times a day, or of the plaster you must hide under your mattress. A lock presents itself, and the citizen has in his pocket the key for it, made by the locksmith. But you, if you wish to go out, are condemned to make a terrible masterpiece; you will take a double sou and cut it asunder with tools of your own invention—that is your business. Then you will hollow out the interior of the two parts, being careful not to injure the outside, and form a thread all round the edge, so that the two parts may fit closely like a box and its cover. When they are screwed together there will be nothing suspicious to the watchers—for you will be watched—it will be a double sou, but for yourself a box. What will you place in this box? A small piece of steel, a watch-spring in which you have made teeth, and which will be a saw. With this saw, about the length of a pin, you will be obliged to cut through the bolt of the lock, the padlock of your chain, the bar at your window, and the fetter on your leg. This masterpiece done, this prodigy accomplished, all the miracles of art, skill, cleverness and patience executed, what will be your reward if you are detected? A dungeon. Such is the future. What precipices are sloth and pleasure! To do nothing is a melancholy resolution; are you aware of that? To live in indolence on the social substance, to be useless, that is to say, injurious! This leads straight to the bottom of the misery. Woe to the man who wishes to be a parasite, for he will be a vermin! Ah! it does not please you to work! Ah! you have only one thought: to drink well, eat well, and sleep well. You will drink water, you will eat black bread, you will sleep on a plank with fetters riveted to your limbs and feel their coldness at night in your flesh! You will break these fetters and fly? Very good. You will drag yourself on your stomach into the shrubs and eat grass like the beasts of the field, and you will be recaptured, and then you will pass years in a dungeon, chained to the wall, groping in the dark for your water-jug, biting at frightful black bread which dogs would refuse, and eating beans which maggots have eaten before you. You will be a wood-louse in a cellar. Ah, ah! take pity on yourself, wretched boy, still so young, who were at your nurse's breast not twenty years ago, and have doubtless a mother still! I implore you to listen to me. You want fine black cloth, polished shoes, to scent your head with fragrant oil, to please creatures and be a pretty fellow; you will have your hair close shaven, and wear a red jacket and wooden shoes. You want a ring on your finger, and will wear a collar on your neck and if you look at a woman you will be beaten; and you will go in there at twenty and come out at fifty years of age; you will go in young, red-cheeked, healthy, with your sparkling eyes, and all your white teeth and your curly locks, and you will come out again broken, bent, wrinkled, toothless, horrible and gray-headed! Ah, my poor boy, you are on the wrong road, and indolence is a bad adviser, for robbery is the hardest of labors. Take my advice, and do not undertake the laborious task of being an idler. To become a rogue

is inconvenient, and it is not nearly so hard to be an honest man
Now go and think over what I have said to you. By the by,
what did you want of me? My purse? Here it is." And the old
man, releasing Montparnasse, placed his purse in his hand, which
Montparnasse weighed for a moment, after which, with the same
mechanical precaution as if he had stolen it, Montparnasse let it
glide gently into the back-pocket of his coat. All this said and
done, the old gentleman turned his back and quietly resumed his
walk.

A Glass of Cold Water.

Where is the liquor which God, the Eternal, brews for all his
children? Not in the simmering still, over smoky fires choked with
poisonous gases, surrounded with the stench of sickening odors
and rank corruptions doth your Father in Heaven prepare the
precious essence of life, the pure cold water. But in the green
glade and grassy dell, where the red deer wanders and the child
loves to play; there God brews it. And down, low down in the lowest valleys, where the fountains murmur and the rills sing; and high
upon the tall mountain tops, where the naked granite glitters like
gold in the sun; where the storm-cloud broods, and the thunder-
storms crash; and away, far out on the wide, wild sea, where the
hurricane howls music, and the big waves roar; the chorus sweeping
the march of God; there He brews it—that beverage of life and
health-giving water. And everywhere it is a thing of beauty,
gleaming in the dew-drop; singing in the summer rain; shining in
the ice-gems till the leaves all seem to turn to living jewels; spreading a golden veil over the setting sun, or a white gauze around the
midnight moon; sporting in the cataract, sleeping in the glacier,
dancing in the hail shower, folding its bright snow curtains softly
about the wintry world, and waving the many-colored iris, that

seraph's zone of the sky, whose warp is the rain-drop of earth, whose woof is the sunbeam of heaven, all checkered over with celestial flowers by the mystic hand of refraction.

Still always it is beautiful, that life-giving water; no poison bubbles on its brink; its foam brings not madness and murder; no blood stains its liquid glass; pale widows and starving orphans weep no burning tears in its depth; no drunken, shrieking ghost from the grave curses it in the words of eternal despair. Speak on, my friends, would you exchange it for demon's drink, alcohol?

The Schoolmaster.

It has been to me a source of pleasure, though a melancholy one, that in rendering this public tribute to the worth of our departed friend, the respectable members of two bodies, one of them most devoted and efficient in its scientific inquiries, the other comprising so many names eminent for philanthropy and learning, have met to do honor to the memory of a schoolmaster.

There are prouder themes for the eulogist than this. The praise of the statesman, the warrior or the orator furnish more splendid topics for ambitious eloquence; but no theme can be more rich in desert or more fruitful in public advantage.

The enlightened liberality of many of our state governments, —amongst which we may claim a proud distinction for our own—by extending the common school system over their whole population, has brought elementary education to the door of every family. In this State, it appears from the annual reports of the secretary of the State, there are, besides the fifty incorporated academies and numerous private schools, about nine thousand school districts, in each of which instruction is regularly given. These contain at present half a million of children taught in the single State of New York. To these may be added nine or ten thousand more youth in the higher seminaries of learning, exclusive of the colleges.

Of what incalculable influence, then, for good or for evil, upon the dearest interests of society, must be the estimate entertained for the character of this great body of teachers, and the consequent respectability of the individuals who compose it!

At the recent general election in this State the votes of above three hundred thousand persons were taken. In thirty years the great majority of these will have passed away; their rights will be exercised and their duties assumed by those very children whose minds are now open to receive their earliest and most durable impressions from the ten thousand schoolmasters of this State.

What else is there, in the whole of our social system, of such extensive and powerful operation on the national character? There is one other influence more powerful, and but one. It is that of the MOTHER. The forms of a free government, the provisions of wise legislation, the schemes of the statesman, the sacrifices of the patriot, are as nothing compared with these. If the future citizens of our republic are to be worthy of their rich inheritance, they must be made so principally through the virtue and intelligence of their mothers. It is in the school of maternal tenderness that the kind affections must be first roused and made habitual, the early sentiment of piety awakened and rightly directed, the sense of duty and moral responsibility unfolded and enlightened. But next in rank and in efficacy to that pure and holy source of moral influence is that of the schoolmaster. It is powerful already. What would it be if in every one of those school districts which we now count by annually increasing thousands, there were to be found one teacher well-informed without pedantry, religious without bigotry or fanaticism, proud and fond of his profession, and honored in the discharge of his duties! How wide would be the intellectual, the moral influence of such a body of men! Many such we have already amongst us—men humbly wise and obscurely useful, whom poverty cannot depress nor neglect degrade. But to raise up a body of such men as numerous as the wants and the dignity of the country demand, their labors must be fitly remunerated and themselves and their calling cherished and honored.

The schoolmaster's occupation is laborious and ungrateful; its rewards are scanty and precarious. He may indeed be, and he ought to be, animated by the consciousness of doing good, that best of all considerations, that noblest of all motives. But that, too, must be often clouded by doubt and uncertainty. Obscure and inglorious as his daily occupation may appear to learned pride or worldly ambition, yet to be truly successful and happy, he must be animated by the spirit of the same great principles which inspired the most illustrious benefactors of mankind. If he bring to his task high talent and rich acquirements, he must be content to look into distant years for the proof that his labors have not been wasted, that the good seed which he daily scatters abroad does not fall on stony ground and wither away; or among thorns, to be choked by the cares, the delusions or the vices of the world. He must solace his toils with the same prophetic faith that enabled the greatest of modern philosophers, amidst the neglect or contempt of his own times, to regard himself as sowing the seeds of truth for posterity and the care of Heaven. He must arm himself against disappointment and mortification with a portion of that same noble confidence which soothed the greatest of modern poets when weighed down by care and danger, by poverty, old age and blindness—still

> "In prophetic dream he saw
> The youth unborn, with pious awe
> Imbibe each virtue from his sacred page."

He must know, and he must love to teach his pupils, not the meager elements of knowledge, but the secret and the use of their own intellectual strength, exciting and enabling them hereafter to raise for themselves the veil which covers the majestic form of Truth. He must feel deeply the reverence due to the youthful mind, fraught with mighty though undeveloped energies and affections, and mysterious and eternal destinies. Thence he must have learnt to reverence himself and his profession and to look upon its otherwise ill-requited toils as their own exceeding great reward.

If such are the difficulties and the discouragements, such the duties, the motives and the consolations of teachers who are worthy of that name and trust, how imperious, then, the obligation upon every enlightened citizen who knows and feels the value of such men to aid them, to cheer them and honor them!

But let us not be content with barren honor to buried merit. Let us prove our gratitude to the dead by faithfully endeavoring to elevate the station, to enlarge the usefulness and to raise the character of the schoolmaster amongst us. Thus shall we best testify our gratitude to the teachers and guides of our own youth, thus best serve our country, and thus most effectually diffuse over our land light, and truth, and virtue.

Admiration of Genius.

There is a certain charm about great superiority of intellect that winds into deep affections, which a much more constant and even amiability of manners in lesser men, often fails to reach. Genius makes many enemies, but it makes sure friends, friends who forgive much, who endure long, who exact little; they partake of the character of disciples as well as friends. There lingers about the human heart a strong inclination to look upward—to revere; in this inclination lies the source of religion, of loyalty, and also of the worship and immortality which are rendered so cheerfully to the great of old. And, in truth, it is a divine pleasure to admire. Admiration seems, in some measure, to appropriate to ourselves the qualities it honors in others. We wed—we root ourselves to the natures we so love to contemplate, and their life grows a part of our own. Thus, when a great man, who has engrossed our thoughts, our conjectures, our homage, dies, a gap seems suddenly left in the world —a wheel in the mechanism of our own being appears abruptly stilled; a portion of ourselves, and not our worst portion—for how many pure, high, generous sentiments it contains—dies with him.

BENJAMINE F. TAYLOR.

BENJAMINE FRANKLIN TAYLOR, one of America's most gifted and entertaining authors and lecturers, was born in Lowville, N. Y., in 1822. He received his education at Madison University, New York, under the tutorship of his father, who was at that time president of the institution. Mr. Taylor has been an active and popular worker in the literary field. *The Attractions of Language* appeared in 1845, and *January and June*, in 1853. From the latter volume of charming essays and poems we have made our selections. No one who admires beautiful word-pictures, fine sentiment, and a clear and entertaining literary style, can afford to be without the volumes of B. F. Taylor.

For many years he was literary editor of the Chicago "Evening Journal." During the late war he was the "Journal's" principal war correspondent. Many of his letters have been gathered together and published under the title of *Pictures in Camp and Field*.

His pictures are so perfect, and his words so admirably selected, that in reading them we live again our soldier life. We hear the rattle of musketry, and the roar of artillery; and we see the advancing columns and the terrible conflict as the armies contest in a hand-to-hand struggle; and when the winds have lifted the black smoke, we see the terrible work of battle, and we again earnestly pray a kind Father to spread the mantled mourning of night over the scene.

Mr. Taylor published *The World on Wheels* in 1873, and

Old Time Pictures and Sheaves of Rhyme in 1874. All of his works have passed through several editions. He has been very popular on the lyceum platform.

It will pay us, kind friends, to read the volumes of Taylor. They contain the beautiful wish that "our lives and his may not be composed of random 'scores,' but be a beautiful anthem, harmony in all its parts, melody in all its tones; not a strain wanting, not a note out of tune; till 'the daughters of music are brought low,' and the life-anthem is ended."

"But isn't it a pleasant thought that *perhaps* somebody may take up the tune, when we are dead—not a note lost, nor a jar, nor a discord, but all swan-like harmony? Perhaps! perhaps! There is something hollow, like a knell, in that word. The veil that hides the future is woven of 'perhaps;' in it the greatest ills have their solace, the brightest joys their cloud."

At the Open Window.

Here I am, to-day, sitting by an open window, the wind as gentle as June, playfully lifting the corners of the paper I write on, and letting them softly down again; while yesterday, or the day before, I was in perihelion, nestled close in the chimney-corner; and wind —could it have been this same wind, now toying with the tassel of the curtain, that in such a mood twisted up a little oak by the roots, that never did any harm, and hollow-voiced and frosty from the dim northwest, made penny-whistles of the huge, old-fashioned chimney-tops? Nature is a good deal of a rhetorician; she loves rapid transitions and startling contrasts.

Time, itself, all through the long-drawn past, is inlaid with day and night—night and day. Suppose it had been all day through the world; it would have been "all day" with us—our happiness, our interests, and life would be "dull" at eighty cents on the dollar. Now, we are like those wandering at leisure from room to room, in some splendid suite of apartments, divided by the dark and marble walls of night. We enter some beautiful day, pearl for its threshold and crimson for its curtains. With what music they rustle as unseen hands lift them to let us through! And what varied surprises keep us on the *qui vive* all along, as we pass through it! And how gorgeous the drapery let down behind us, as we enter the dark opening in the walls of night—those walls God built, and yet, through which, at a thousand points, shine divided days, yesterday, and tomorrow!

And what a lamp—no "Astral," but a true Lunar, is hung in the passage-way; and then, when we have done wandering through this great temple of Time, and pass the last door, and the veil closes down before the last day, and we find ourselves "out doors" in the universe, and free to go whither we will—children again—aye, children "just let loose from school." How we shall scatter away over fields all flowers, and no frosts, where there is no such word as November, and no such thought as death. Life will be life still, but without its struggle, and ourselves still ourselves, but with windows all around the soul. We shall see hearts beat as plainly then, as we now see the movements of delicate chronometers beneath their crystal cases—emotions will be visible—the footfalls of thought audible—the trickery of light and shade by-gone, and things will appear as they are.

And the pleasant surprises that shall meet us there; perhaps the trees will grow by music, and the streams murmur articulate; perhaps we shall meet and recognize those who had gone on before. New scenes, new beauties, new thought—everywhere *"plus ultra"*—more beyond.

And Such a Change.

The glories of twilight have departed, and the gray night of the year has, at last, set in.

The tree by my window has thrown off the red and yellow livery it has worn of late, and with naked arms tossing wildly about, stands shivering in the gusts, dismantled and desolate. Strange to say, I love it better than when song and shadow met in its branches —better than ever; but it is not a love born of pity; it needs none, for its life is locked up safely in the earth beneath, and whistle as it will, the boatswain of a Winter wind cannot pipe up a pulse or a bud. Through its leafless limbs I can see Heaven, now, and there are no stars in the trees in June. The sweet brier creaks uneasily against the wall; the snow is heaped on the window sill; the frost is "castle building" on the panes; the streams are dumb; the woods stand motionless under the weight of white Winter.

It is Saturday—Saturday afternoon; the children "just let loose from school," and Clear Lake is swarming with juvenile skaters.

Grouped here and there in clusters, like swarms of bees or bevies of blackbirds in council, now and then, one and another and a third dash out in graceful circles, with motion as easy as flying. Huge sixes and sweeping eights, and eagles with enormous length of wings, are "cut" upon the "solid water."

Presently the whole cluster breaks and fly in every direction, like a flock of pigeons. There go a brace in a trial of speed; there, a Castor and Pollux, hand in hand; here, a game of goal is going on, and here, a game of "red lion."

Away there lies a little fellow upon his back, taking his first lesson in skater's astronomy. Ask him, and he will tell you he "saw stars" but a moment ago, that never were named.

The sun is going down in the west, and they have been upon the ice since high noon. But what is that to them? What care they for cold, and fatigue, and time? Saturday comes but once a week, and ice hardly once a year. But they'll find ice enough by and by—ice in midsummer—iced hopes, iced friendship, icy hearts. And as for the Saturdays, they'll grow "few and far between"— they'll not come once a week, nor once a month; and happy will he be who has a Saturday afternoon and evening to end his life with. Then who says the boys sha'n't skate? Who grudges them the "rockers?" Look at that little fellow now; on one arm hang his skates, a "brand new" pair, glittering like a couple of scimetars. 'Tis his first appearance on the skater's field. Down he gets upon the ice; his little red and white mittens, tethered with a string, lie beside him, while with his chubby red fingers he dallies and tugs with buckles and straps, every now and then blowing his fingers to keep them in a glow. All right and tight, he's rigged, he's ready, he's up and off! What warrior ever harnessed for the field and the fray with a richer pride mantling his cheek, or a brighter joy lighting his eye! There may have been one or two, but there is no record of them in Froissart.

Musing by the Fire.

Musing here by the sleepy fire, this stormy night, about "one thing and another," the chime of bells, little and big, comes sweetly to my ear through the snowy air.

Those sounds are mnemonic—they are the sweet bells of the past; and in the time of a single note, we are back again into the vanished years in a winter's night, the moon at the full, "somebody very near," and the merry bells ringing as they ring now. How silvery were the laughs that issued then, from beneath the downy mufflers and quilted hoods. How bright were the eyes that glittered through green veils then, like stars through a leafy wood. Bells! There have been *knells* since then, and those who "make no new friends," must journey alone. You who vaunt upon life and station and the permanence of things earthly, return to the scenes of your youthful days of a winter's night. And the "turn-out"— let it be as of old, and call here and there, where dwelt the companions of a brighter time. Here the stranger, there the estranged, and there, echo answers to your impatient rap.

The horses are at the gate, eager to be gone, and shake music from those bells at every toss of the head. But it is not music to you, and turning slowly homeward, you pass in the moonlight a field furrowed with many a drifted heap. It is "God's Field," and many who were your companions on just such a night, lie silent there. Aye! muffle the bells of memory, and pass on, a sadder but a wiser man.

The Old-Fashioned Mother.

Old-fashioned mothers have nearly all passed away with the blue check and homespun woolen of a simpler but purer time. Here and there one remains, truly accomplished in heart and life for the sphere of home.

Old-fashioned mothers—God bless them!—who followed us, with heart and prayer, all over the world—lived in our lives and sorrowed in our griefs; who knew more about patching than poetry; spoke no dialect but that of love; never preached nor wandered; "made melody with their hearts;" and sent forth no books but living volumes, that honored their authors and blessed the world.

If woman have a broader mission now, in Heaven's name let her fulfill it! If she have aught to sing, like the daughters of Judah let her sit down by the waters of Babel, and the world shall weep; like Miriam let her triumph-strain float gloriously over crushed but giant wrong, and the giant wrong and the world shall hear; but let the triumph and lament issue, as did the oracles of old, from behind the veil that cannot be rent, the "inner temple" of sacred Home.

Within it should be enshrined the divinity of the place. Here, and here only, would we find woman; here imprison her—imprison her? Aye, as the light-house ray, that flows out, pure as an angel's pulses, into the night and darkness of the world—*a star beneath the cloud;* but brightest there—warmest there—*always* there where Heaven did kindle it, within the precinct, the very altar-place of home!

It is related of Madame Lucciola, a renowned vocalist, that she ruined a splendid tenor voice by her efforts to imitate male singing. Many a sweet voice and gentle influence in the social harmony has been lost to the world in the same manner. There is nothing more potent than woman's voice, if heard, not in the field or the forum, but at home. The song-bird of Eastern story, borne from its native isle, grew dumb and languished. Seldom did it sing, and only when it saw a dweller from its distant land, or to its drowsy perch there came a tone heard long ago in its own woods. So with the song that woman sings; best heard within Home's sacred temple. Elsewhere, a trumpet-tone—perhaps a clarion-cry, but the lute-like voice has fled: the "mezzo-soprano" is lost in the discords of earth.

The old homestead! I wish I could paint it for you, as it is—no, no, I dare not say, as it is—as it *was;* that we could go together, to-night, from room to room; sit by the old hearth round which that circle of light and love once swept, and there linger till all those simpler, purer times returned, and we should grow young again.

And how can we leave that spot without remembering one form, that occupied, in days gone by, the old arm-chair,—that "old-fashioned MOTHER?"—one, in all the world, the law of whose life was love; one who was the divinity of our infancy, and the sacred presence in the shrine of our first earthly idolatry; one whose heart is far below the frosts that gather so thickly on her brow; one to whom we never grow old, but in "the plumed troop" or the grave council are children still; one who welcomed us coming, blest us going, and never forgets us—never.

And when, in some closet, some drawer, some corner, she finds a garment or a toy that once was yours, how does she weep as she thinks you may be suffering or sad. And when Spring

"Leaves her robe on the trees,"

does she not remember *your* tree, and wish you were there to see it in its glory?

Nothing is "far," and nothing "long," to *her;* she girdles the globe with a cincture of love; she encircles her child, if he be on the face of the earth.

Think you, as she sits in that well remembered corner to-night, she dreams her trembling arm is less powerful to protect him now, stalwart man though he is, than when it clasped him, in infancy, to her bosom?

Does the battle of life drive the wanderer to the old homestead, at last? Her hand is upon his shoulder; her dim and fading eyes are kindled with something of "the light of other days," as she gazes upon his brow: "Be of stout heart, my son! No harm can reach thee here!"

Surely, there is but one Heaven—one Mother—and one God.

But sometimes that arm-chair is set back against the wall, the corner is vacant, or another's, and they seek the dear old occupant in the graveyard. God grant *you* never have! Pray God, I never may!

There are some there, though, whom we loved—there *must* be to make it easy dying; some, perhaps, who were cradled on that mother's bosom; some, perhaps, who had grown fast to our own.

The old graveyard in L—— ——! How the cloudy years clear away from before that little acre in God's fallow field, and the memories return.

Work.

There is a perennial nobleness, and even sacredness, in work. Were he never so benighted, forgetful of his high calling, there is always hope in a man that actually and earnestly works; in idleness alone is there perpetual despair. Work, never so mammonish, mean, is in communication with nature; the real desire to get work done will itself lead one more and more to truth, to Nature's appointments and regulations, which are truth.

The latest gospel in this world is: "Know thy work, and do it." "Know thyself:" long enough has that poor "self" of thine tormented thee; thou wilt never get to "know" it,' I believe! Think it not thy business, this of knowing thyself, thou art an unknowable individual; know what thou canst work at, and work at it like a Hercules! That will be thy better plan.

It has been written "an endless significance lies in work," as man perfects himself by writing. Foul jungles are cleared away,

82   TREASURES FROM THE PROSE WORLD.

fair seed-fields rise instead, and stately cities; and withal the man himself first ceases to be a jungle and foul, unwholesome desert thereby. Consider how, even in the meanest sorts of labor, the whole soul of a man is composed into a kind of real harmony the instant he sets himself to work! Doubt, desire, sorrow, remorse, indignation, despair itself, all these, like hell-dogs, lie beleaguering the soul of the poor day-worker, as of every man, but as he bends himself with free valor against his task, all these are stilled, all these shrink murmuring afar off into their caves. The man is now a man. The blessed glow of labor in him, is it not a purifying fire, wherein all poison is burnt up, and of sour smoke itself there is made bright, blessed flame?

Destiny, on the whole, has no other way of cultivating us. A formless chaos, once set it *revolving*, grows round and ever rounder; ranges itself, by mere force of gravity, into strata, spherical courses; is no longer a chaos, but a round, compacted world. What would become of the earth did she cease to revolve? In the poor old earth, so long as she revolves, all inequalities, irregularities, disperse themselves; all irregularities are incessantly becoming regular. Hast thou looked on the potter's wheel, one of the venerablest objects; old as the prophet Ezekiel, and far older? Rude lumps of clay, how they spin themselves up, by mere quick whirling, into beautiful circular dishes. And fancy the most assiduous potter, but without his wheel, reduced to make dishes, or rather amorphous botches, by mere kneading and baking! Even such a potter were destiny with a human soul that would rest and lie at ease, that would not work and spin! Of an idle, unrevolving man, the kindest destiny, like the most assiduous potter without wheel, can bake and knead nothing other than a botch; let her spend on him what expensive coloring, what gilding and enameling she will, he is but a botch. Not a dish; no, a bulging, kneaded, crooked, shambling, squint-cornered, amorphous botch, a mere enameled vessel of dishonor! Let the idle think of this.

Blessed is he who has found his work; let him ask no other blessedness. He has a work, a life-purpose; he has found it and will follow it! How, as the free-flowing channel, dug and torn by noble force through the sour mud-swamp of one's existence, like an ever-deepening river there, it runs and flows, draining off the sour, festering water gradually from the root of the remotest grass blade, making, instead of pestilential swamp, a green, fruitful meadow with its clear, flowing stream. How blessed for the meadow itself, let the stream and *its* value be great or small!

Labor is life! From the inmost heart of the worker rises his God-given force, the sacred, celestial life-essence breathed into him by Almighty God; from his inmost heart awakens him to all nobleness, to all knowledge, "self-knowledge" and much else, so soon as work fitly begins. Knowledge! the knowledge that will hold good in working, cleave thou to that, for nature herself accredits that, says Yea to that. Properly thou hast no other knowledge but what thou hast got by working,—the rest is yet all an hypothesis of knowledge, a thing to be argued of in schools, a thing floating in the clouds, in endless logic vortices, till we try it and fix it. "Doubt, of whatever kind, can be ended by action alone."

And again, hast thou valued patience, courage, perseverance, openness to light, readiness to own thyself mistaken, to do better next time? All these, all virtues in wrestling with the dim brute powers of fact, in ordering of thy fellows in such wrestle, there, and elsewhere not at all, thou wilt continually learn. Set down a brave Sir Christopher in the middle of black, ruined stone-heaps of foolish unarchitectural bishops, red-tape officials, idle Nell Gwyn defenders of the faith, and see whether he will ever raise a Paul's Cathedral out of all that, yea or no! Rough, rude, contradictory are all things and persons, from the mutinous masons and Irish hod-men, up to the idle Nell Gwyn defenders, to blustering red-tape officials, foolish unarchitectural bishops. All these things and persons are there, not for Christopher's sake and his cathedrals; they are there for their own sake, mainly! Christopher will have to conquer and constrain all these, if he be able. All these are against him.

Equitable nature herself, who carries her mathematics and

architectonics not on the face of her, but deep in the hidden heart of her—nature herself is but partially for him,—will be wholly against him, if he constrain her not! His very money, where is it to come from? The pious munificence of England lies far scattered, distant, unable to speak and say, "I am here;" must be spoken to before it can speak. Pious munificence, and all help, is so silent, invisible like the gods; impediment, contradictions manifold are so loud and near! O brave Sir Christopher, trust thou in those notwithstanding, and front all these; understand all these; by valiant patience, noble effort, insight, vanquish and compel all these, and, on the whole, strike down victoriously the last top-stone of that Paul's edifice, thy monument for certain centuries, the stamp "Great Man" impressed very legibly in Portland stone there!

Yes, all manner of work, and pious response from men or nature, is always what we call silent,—cannot speak or come to light till it be seen, till it be spoken to. Every noble work is at first "impossible." In very truth, for every noble work the possibilities will lie diffused through immensity, inarticulate, undiscoverable except to faith. Like Gideon, thou shalt spread out thy fleece at the door of thy tent; see whether under the wide arch of heaven there be any bounteous moisture, or none. Thy heart and life-purpose shall be a miraculous Gideon's fleece spread out in silent appeal to heaven; and from the kind immensities, what from the poor unkind localities and town and country parishes there never could, blessèd dew-moisture to suffice thee shall have fallen!

Work is of a religious nature: work is of a *brave* nature, which it is the aim of all religion to be. "All work of man's is as the swimmer's," a waste ocean threatens to devour him; if he front it not bravely it will keep its word. By incessant, wise defiance of it, lusty rebuke and buffet of it, behold how it loyally supports him, bears him as its conqueror along. "It is so," says Goethe, "with all things that man undertakes in this world."

Brave sea-captain, Norse sea-king, Columbus, my hero, royalist sea-king of all! it is no friendly environment this of thine in the waste deep waters; around thee mutinous, discouraged souls, behind thee disgrace and ruin, before thee unpenetrated veil of night. Brother, these wild water-mountains, bounding from their deep bases—ten miles deep, I am told,—are not entirely there on thy behalf! Meseems *they* have other work than floating thee forward; and the huge winds that sweep from Ursa Major of the tropics and equator, dancing their giant waltz through the kingdoms of chaos and immensity, they care little about filling rightly or filling wrongly the small shoulder-of-mutton sails in this cockle skiff of thine! Thou art not among articulate speaking friends, my brother; thou art among immeasurable dumb monsters, tumbling, howling wide as the world here. Secret, far-off, invisible to all hearts but thine, there lies a help in them. See how thou wilt get at that. Patiently thou wilt wait until the mad southwester spend itself, saving thyself by dexterous science of defence the while; valiantly, with swift decision, wilt thou strike in when the favoring east, the possible, springs up. Mutiny of men thou wilt sternly repress; weakness, despondency, thou wilt cheerily encourage; thou wilt swallow down complaint, unreason, weariness, weakness of others and thyself—how much wilt thou swallow down! There shall be a depth of silence in thee deeper than this sea which is but ten miles deep; a silence unsoundable, known to God only. Thou shalt be a great man. Yes, my world-soldier, thou of the world marine-service, thou wilt have to be *greater* than this tumultuous, unmeasured world here around thee is; thou in thy strong soul, as with wrestler's arms, shalt embrace it, harness it down, and make it bear thee on to new Americas, or whither God wills!

* * * * * * * * * *

Religion, I said, for, properly speaking, all true work is religion; and whatsoever religion is not work may go and dwell among the Brahmins, Antinomians, spinning dervishes, or where it will; with me it shall have no harbor. Admirable was that of the old monks· *Laborare est orare,* "work is worship."

Older than all preached gospels was this unpreached, inarticulate, but ineradicable, forever-enduring gospel: Work, and therein have well-being. Man, son of earth and of heaven, lies there not, in the innermost heart of thee, a spirit of active method, a force for work;—and burn like a painfully smoldering fire, giving thee no rest till thou unfold it, till thou write it down in beneficent facts around thee! What is immethodic, waste, thou shalt make methodic, regulated, arable; obedient and productive to thee. Wheresoever thou findest disorder, there is thy eternal enemy; attack him swiftly, subdue him; make order of him, the subject, not of chaos, but of intelligence, divinity and thee! The thistle that grows in thy path, dig it out that a blade of useful grass, a drop of nourishing milk may grow there instead. The waste cotton-shrub, gather its waste white down, spin it, weave it, that in place of idle litter there may be folded webs, and the naked skin of man be covered.

But above all, where thou findest ignorance, stupidity, brute-mindedness, attack it, I say; smite it wisely, unweariedly, and rest not while thou livest and it lives, but smite, smite in the name of God! The Highest God, as I understand it, does audibly so command thee—still audibly, if thou have ears to hear. He, even He, with His unspoken voice, fuller than any Sinai thunders or syllabled speech of whirlwinds—for the silence of deep eternities, of worlds from beyond the morning-stars, does it not speak to thee? The unborn ages; the old graves, with their long-moldering dust, the very tears that wetted it, now all dry—do not these speak to thee what ear hath not heard? The deep death—kingdoms, the stars in their never-resting courses, all space and all time proclaim it to thee in continual silent admonition. Thou, too, if ever man should, shalt work while it is called to-day. For the night cometh wherein no man can work.

All true work is sacred. In all true work, were it but true hand-labor, there is something of divineness. Labor, wide as the earth, has its summit in heaven. Sweat of the brow; and up from that to sweat of the brain, sweat of the heart—which includes all Kepler calculations, Newton meditations, all sciences, all spoken epics, all acted heroisms, martyrdoms,—up to that "agony of bloody sweat" which all men have called divine! O brother, if this is not "worship," then I say, the more pity for worship; for this is the noblest thing yet discovered under God's sky. Who art thou that complainest of thy life of toil? Complain not. Look up, my wearied brother; see thy fellow-workmen there in God's eternity; surviving there, they alone surviving; sacred band of the immortals, celestial body-guard of the empire of mankind. Even in the weak human memory they survive so long, as saints, as heroes, as gods; they alone surviving; peopling, they alone, the unmeasured solitudes of time! To thee heaven, though severe, is *not* unkind. Heaven is kind as a noble mother, as that Spartan mother, saying while she gave her son his shield, "With it, my son, or upon it!" Thou, too, shalt return *home* in honor, to thy far-distant home in honor, doubt it not, if in the battle thou keep thy shield! Thou, in the eternities and deepest death kingdoms, art not an alien; thou everywhere art a denizen! Complain not; the very Spartans did not complain.

HENRY WADSWORTH LONGFELLOW.

HENRY WADSWORTH LONGFELLOW was born in Portland, Me., February 27, 1807, and he died at his home in Cambridge, Mass., March 24, 1882, at the age of seventy-five. For some time before his death his home was in the building formerly occupied by Gen. Washington as his headquarters.

Longfellow studied at Bowdoin College, Brunswick, and after three years' travel and study in Europe, became Professor of Modern Languages in his native college. In 1835, he accepted the Chair of Modern Languages and Literature in Harvard University.

The poet's youth was noted for industry and close application to study, While at college, he became somewhat noted for his poems and criticisms contributed to periodicals. Longfellow's literary record is a long one. In 1833, he published translations of Spanish verses called *Coplas de Manrique*, and an essay on Spanish poetry; 1835, *Sketches from Beyond the Sea;* 1839, *Hyperion, a Romance*, and also collections of poems, entitled *Voices of the Night;* 1842, *Poems on Slavery;* 1843, *The Spanish Student*, a tragedy; 1845, *Poets and Poetry of Europe;* 1846, *The Belfry of Bruges;* 1847, *Evangeline;* 1849, *Kavanaugh*, and *The Seaside and Fireside;* 1851, *The Golden Legend;* 1855, *Song of Hiawatha;* 1858, *Miles Standish;* 1863, *Tales of a Wayside Inn.*

He has also published *Three Books of Song*, a divine tragedy; and translations. Thus we see that Longfellow

HENRY WADSWORTH LONGFELLOW.

was a great literary worker. Whipple says that Longfellow idealizes real life, embodies high moral sentiment in beautiful and ennobling forms, and inweaves the golden threads of spiritual being into the texture of common existence. He is the most popular of American poets, and his works are admired throughout the literary world. In speaking of his death, under date of March 24, 1882, the *London Times* says: " News of Longfellow's death will be read with deep regret wherever the English language is spoken. The death of no literary Englishman could excite more general sorrow than that of the much-loved author of *Evangeline*. He will be no more sincerely lamented in America than in this country."

The *News*, *Standard* and *Telegraph* all speak in equally graceful terms of Longfellow.

"All the many sounds of nature
Borrowed sweetness from his singing;
All the hearts of men were softened
By the pathos of his music;

For he sang of peace and freedom,
Sang of beauty, love, and longing;
Sang of death, a life undying
In the Islands of the Blessed."

Rural Life in Sweden.

There is something patriarchal still lingering about rural life in Sweden, which renders it a fit theme for song. Almost primeval simplicity reigns over that northern land—almost primeval solitude and stillness. You pass out from the gate of the city, and, as if by magic, the scene changes to a wild woodland landscape. Around you are forests of fir. Overhead hang the long, fan-like branches, trailing with moss and heavy with red and blue cones. Under foot is a carpet of yellow leaves, and the air is warm and balmy. On a wooden bridge you cross a little silver stream; and anon come forth into a pleasant and sunny land of farms. Wooden fences divide the adjoining fields. Across the road are gates, which are opened by troops of children. The peasants take off their hats as you pass; you sneeze, and they cry, "God bless you!" The houses in the villages and smaller towns are all built of hewn timber, and for the most part painted red. The floors of the taverns are strewed with the fragrant tips of fir boughs. In many villages there are no taverns, and the peasants take turns in receiving travelers. The thrifty housewife shows you into the best chamber, the walls of which are hung round with rude pictures from the Bible; and brings you her heavy silver spoons—an heirloom—to dip the curdled milk from the pan. You have oaten cakes baked some months before, or bread with anise-seed and coriander in it, or perhaps a little pine bark. Meanwhile the sturdy husband has brought his horses from the plow, and harnessed them to your carriage. Solitary travelers come and go in uncouth one-horse chaises. Most of them have pipes in their mouths, and hanging around their necks in front, a leather wallet, in which they carry tobacco, and the great bank notes of the country, as large as your two hands. You meet also groups of Dalekarlian peasant women, traveling homeward or townward in pursuit of work. They walk barefoot, carrying in their hands their shoes, which have high heels under the hollow of the foot, and soles of birch bark.

Frequent, too, are the village churches standing by the roadsides, each in its own little garden of Gethsemane. In the parish register great events are doubtless recorded. Some old king was christened or buried in that church; and a little sexton, with a rusty key, shows you the baptismal font or the coffin. In the churchyard are a few flowers and much green grass; and daily the shadow of the church spire with its long, tapering finger, counts the tombs, representing a dial-plate of human life on which the hours and minutes are the graves of men. The stones are flat, and large, and low, and perhaps sunken, like the roofs of old houses. On some are armorial bearings; on others only the initials of the poor tenants, with a date, as on the roofs of Dutch cottages. They all sleep with their heads to the westward. Each held a lighted taper in his hand when he died, and in his coffin were placed his little heart-treasures, and a piece of money for his last journey. Babes that came lifeless into the world were carried in the arms of gray-haired old men to the only cradle they ever slept in; and in the shroud of the dead mother were laid the little garments of the child that lived and died in her bosom. And over this scene the village pastor looks from his window in the stillness of midnight, and says in his heart, "How quietly they rest, all the departed!"

Near the churchyard gate stands a poor-box, fastened to a post by iron bands, and secured by a padlock, with a sloping wooden roof to keep off the rain. If it be Sunday, the peasants sit on the church steps and con their psalm-books. Others are coming down the road with their beloved pastor, who talks to them of holy things from beneath his broad-brimmed hat. He speaks of fields and harvests, and of the parable of the sower, that went forth to sow. He leads them to the Good Shepherd, and to the pleasant pastures of the Spirit-land. He is their patriarch, and, like Melchizedek, both priest and king, though he has no other throne than the church pulpit. The women carry psalm-books in their hands, wrapped in silk handkerchiefs, and listen devoutly to the good man's words;

but the young men, like Galileo, care for none of these things. They are busy counting the plaits in the kirtles of the peasant girls, their number being an indication of the wearer's wealth. It may end in a wedding.

I will endeavor to describe a village wedding in Sweden. It shall be in Summer time, that there may be flowers, and in a southern province, that the bride may be fair. The early song of the lark and of chanticleer are mingling in the clear morning air, and the sun, the heavenly bridegroom with golden locks, arises in the east, just as our earthly bridegroom, with yellow hair, arises in the south. In the yard there is a sound of voices and trampling of hoofs, and horses are led forth and saddled. The steed that is to bear the bridegroom has a bunch of flowers upon his forehead, and a garland of corn flowers around his neck. Friends from the neighboring farms come riding in, their blue cloaks streaming to the wind; and finally the happy bridegroom, with a whip in his hand, and a monstrous nosegay in the breast of his black jacket, comes forth from his chamber; and then to horse and away toward the village, where the bride already sits and waits.

Foremost rides the spokesman, followed by some half-dozen village musicians. Next comes the bridegroom between his two groomsmen; and then forty or fifty friends and wedding guests, half of them perhaps with pistols and guns in their hands. A kind of baggage wagon brings up the rear, laden with food and drink for these merry pilgrims. At the entrance of every village stands a triumphal arch, adorned with flowers, and ribands, and evergreens; and, as they pass beneath it, the wedding guests fire a salute, and the whole procession stops; and straight from every pocket flies a black-jack, filled with punch or brandy. It is passed from hand to hand among the crowd; provisions are brought from the wagon, and, after eating and drinking and hurrahing, the procession moves forward again, and at length draws near the house of the bride. Four heralds ride forward to announce that a knight and his attendants are in the neighboring forest, and pray for hospitality. "How many are you?" asks the bride's father. "At least three hundred," is the answer; and to this the last replies, "Yes, were you seven times as many, you should all be welcome; and in token thereof receive this cup." Whereupon each herald receives a can of ale; and soon after the whole jovial company comes storming into the farmer's yard, and, riding around the Maypole, which stands in the center, alight amid a grand salute and flourish of music. In the hall sits the bride, with a crown upon her head and a tear in her eye, like the Virgin Mary in old church paintings. She is dressed in a red bodice and kirtle, with loose linen sleeves. There is a gilded belt around her waist, and around her neck strings of golden beads, and a golden chain. On the crown rests a wreath of wild roses, and below it another of cypress. Loose over her shoulders falls her flaxen hair, and her blue innocent eyes are fixed upon the ground. O thou good soul! thou hast hard hands, but a soft heart. Thou art poor. The very ornaments thou wearest are not thine. They have been hired for this great day. Yet thou art rich, rich in health, rich in hope, rich in thy first, young, fervent love. The blessing of Heaven be upon thee! So thinks the parish priest as he joins together the hands of bride and bridegroom, saying in deep, solemn tones, "I give thee in marriage this damsel, to be thy wedded wife in all honor, and to share the half of thy bed, thy lock and key, and every third penny which you two may possess, or may inherit, and all the rights which upland's laws provide, and the holy King Erik gave."

The dinner is now served, and the bride sits between the bridegroom and the priest. The spokesman delivers an oration after the ancient custom of his fathers. He interlards it well with quotations from the Bible, and invites the Savior to be present at this marriage feast, as he was at the marriage feast of Cana of Galilee. The table is not sparingly set forth. Each makes a long arm, and the feast goes cheerily on. Punch and brandy pass round between the courses, and here and there a pipe is smoked while waiting for the next dish. They sit long at table; but, as all things must have an end, so must a Swedish dinner. Then the dance begins. It is led off by the bride and the priest, .. perform a solemn minuet together. Not till after midnight comes the last dance. The girls form a ring around the bride, to keep her from the hands of the married women, who endeavor to break through the magic circle, and seize their new sister. After long struggling they succeed; and the crown is taken from her head and the jewels from her neck, and her bodice is unlaced, and her kirtle taken off, and, like a vestal virgin, clad all in white, she goes,—but it is to her marriage chamber, not to her grave; and the wedding guests follow her with lighted candles in their hands. And this is a village bridal.

Nor must I forget the suddenly changing seasons of the northern clime. There is no long and lingering Spring, unfolding leaf and blossom one by one; no long and lingering Autumn, pompous with many colored leaves and the glow of Indian Summers. But Winter and Summer are wonderful, and pass into each other. The quail has hardly ceased piping in the corn, when Winter, from the folds of trailing clouds, sows broadcast over the land snow, icicles, and rattling hail. The days wane apace. Ere long the sun hardly rises above the horizon, or does not rise at all. The moon and the stars shine through the day; only, at noon, they are pale and wan, and in the southern sky a red, fiery glow, as of sunset, burns along the horizon, and then goes out. And pleasantly under the silver moon, and under the silent, solemn stars, ring the steel shoes of the skaters on the frozen sea, and voices, and the sound of bells.

And now the northern lights begin to burn, faintly at first, like sunbeams playing on the waters of the blue sea. Then a soft crimson glow tinges the heavens. There is a blush on the cheek of night. The colors come and go, and change from crimson to gold, from gold to crimson. The snow is stained with rosy light. Twofold from the zenith, east and west, flames a fiery sword; and a broad band passes athwart the heavens like a Summer sunset. Soft purple clouds come sailing over the sky, and through their vapory folds the winking stars shine white as silver. With such pomp as this is merry Christmas ushered in—though only a single star heralded the first Christmas. And in memory of that day the Swedish peasants dance on straw, and peasant girls throw straws at the timbered roof of the hall, and for every one that sticks in a crack shall a groomsman come to their wedding. Merry Christmas, indeed! For pious souls there shall be church songs and sermons, but for Swedish peasants brandy and nut-brown ale in wooden bowls; and the great Yule-cake, crowned with a cheese, and garlanded with apples, and upholding a three-armed candle-stick over the Christmas feast. They may tell tales, too, of Jons Lundsbracka, and Lunkenfus, and the great Riddar-Finke of Pingsdaga.

And now the glad, leafy Midsummer, full of blossoms and the song of nightingales, is come! Saint John has taken the flowers and festival of heathen Balder; and in every village there is a Maypole fifty feet high, with wreaths and roses, and ribands streaming in the wind, and a noisy weathercock on the top to tell the village whence the wind cometh and whither it goeth. The sun does not set till 10 o'clock at night, and the children are at play in the streets an hour later. The windows and doors are all open, and you may sit and read till midnight without a candle. Oh, how beautiful is the Summer night, which is not night, but a sunless yet unclouded day, descending upon earth with dews and shadows, and refreshing coolness! How beautiful the long, mild twilight, which, like a silver clasp, unites to-day with yesterday! How beautiful the silent hour, when morning and evening thus sit together, hand in hand, beneath the starless sky of midnight! From the church tower in the public square the bell tolls the hour with a soft, musical chime, and the watchman, whose watch-tower is the belfry, blows a blast on his horn for each stroke of the hammer, and four times to the four corners of the heavens, in a sonorous voice he chants:

"Ho! watchman, ho!
Twelve is the clock!
God keep our town
From fire and brand,
And hostile hand!
Twelve is the clock!"

From his swallow's nest in the belfry he can see the sun all night long; and farther north the priest stands at his door in the warm midnight and lights his pipe with a common burning-glass.

Scene at the Natural Bridge.

The scene opens with a view of the great Natural Bridge in Virginia. There are three or four lads standing in the channel below, looking up with awe to that vast arch of unhewn rocks, which the Almighty bridged over those everlasting butments, "when the morning stars sung together." The little piece of sky spanning those measureless piers is full of stars, although it is mid-day.

It is almost five hundred feet from where they stand, up those perpendicular bulwarks of limestone, to the key-rock of that vast arch, which appears to them only the size of a man's hand. The silence of death is rendered more impressive by the little stream that falls from rock to rock down the channel. The sun is darkened, and the boys have unconsciously uncovered their heads, as if standing in the presence-chamber of the Majesty of the whole earth.

At last this feeling begins to wear away; they begin to look around them; they find that others have been there before them. They see the names of hundreds cut in the limestone butments. A new feeling comes over their young hearts, and their knives are in their hands in an instant. "What man has done, man can do," is their watchword, while they draw themselves up and carve their names a foot above those of a hundred full-grown men who have been there before them.

They are all satisfied with this feat of physical exertion, except one, whose example illustrates perfectly the forgotten truth, that there is no royal road to intellectual eminence. This ambitious youth sees a name just above his reach—a name that will be green in the memory of the world, when those of Alexander, Cæsar, and Bonaparte shall be lost in oblivion. It was the name of Washington.

Before he marched with Braddock to that fatal field, he had been there, and left his name a foot above all his predecessors. It was a glorious thought for a boy to write his name side by side with that of the great father of his country. He grasped his knife with a firmer hand, and clinging to a little jutting crag, he cuts a gain into the limestone, about a foot above where he stands; he then reaches up and cuts another for his hands.

'Tis a dangerous adventure; but as he puts his feet and hands into those gains, and draws himself up carefully to his full length, he finds himself a foot above every name chronicled in that mighty wall. While his companions are regarding him with concern and admiration, he cuts his name in rude capitals, large and deep into that flinty album.

His knife is still in his hand, and strength in his sinews, and a new created aspiration in his heart. Again he cuts another niche, and again he carves his name in larger capitals. This is not enough. Heedless of the entreaties of his companions, he cuts and climbs again. The gradations of his ascending scale grow wider apart. He measures his length at every gain he cuts. The voices of his friends wax weaker and weaker, till their words are finally lost on his ear.

He now, for the first time, cast a look beneath him. Had that glance lasted a moment, that moment would have been his last. He clings with a convulsive shudder to his little niche in the rock. He is faint from severe exertion, and trembling from the sudden view of the dreadful destruction to which he is exposed. His knife is worn half way to the haft. He can hear the voices, but not the words, of his terror-stricken companions below! What a moment! What a meager chance to escape destruction! There is no retracing his steps. It is impossible to put his hand into the same niche with his feet, and retain his slender hold a moment.

His companions instantly perceive this new and fearful dilemma, and await his fall with emotions that "freeze their young blood." He is too high, too faint, to ask for his father and mother, and brothers and sisters, to come and witness or avert his destruction. But one of his companions anticipates his desire. Swift as

98   TREASURES FROM THE PROSE WORLD.

the wind, he bounds down the channel, and the situation of the ill-fated boy is told upon his father's hearthstone.

Minutes of almost eternal length roll on, and there are hundreds standing in that rocky channel, and hundreds on the bridge above, all holding their breath, and awaiting the fearful catastrophe. The poor boy hears the hum of new and numerous voices both above and below. He can distinguish the tones of his father, who is shouting, with all the energy of despair, "William! William! don't look down! Your mother, and Henry, and Harriet, are all here, praying for you! Don't look down! Keep your eye towards the top!"

The boy didn't look down. His eye is fixed like a flint towards heaven, and his young heart on Him who reigns there. He grasps again his knife. He cuts another niche, and another foot is added to the hundreds that remove him from the reach of human help from below! How carefully he uses his wasting blade! How anxiously he selects the softest places in that vast pier! How he avoids every flinty grain! How he economizes his physical powers, resting a moment at each gain he cuts! How every motion is watched from below! There stand his father, mother, brother, and sister, on the very spot where, if he falls, he will not fall alone.

The sun is half way down the west. The lad has made fifty additional niches in that mighty wall, and now finds himself directly under the middle of that vast arch of rocks, earth, and trees. He must cut his way in a new direction, to get from under this overhanging mountain. The inspiration of hope is dying in his bosom; its vital heat is fed by the increasing shouts of hundreds, perched upon cliffs and trees, and others who stand with ropes in their hands on the bridge above, or with ladders below.

Fifty more gains must be cut before the longest rope can reach him. His wasting blade strikes again into the limestone. The boy is emerging painfully, foot by foot, from under that lofty arch. Spliced ropes are ready in the hands of those who are leaning over the outer edge of the bridge. Two minutes more and all must be over. The blade is worn to the last half inch. The boy's head reels; his eyes are starting from their sockets. His last hope is dying in his heart; his life must hang on the next gain he cuts. That niche is the last.

At the last faint gash he makes, his knife—his faithful knife—falls from his little nerveless hand, and ringing along the precipice, falls at his mother's feet. An involuntary groan of despair runs like a death-knell through the channel below, and all is still as the grave. At the height of nearly three hundred feet, the devoted boy lifts his hopeless heart, and closes his eyes to commend his soul to God.

'Tis but a moment—there! one foot swings off—he is reeling—trembling—toppling over into eternity! Hark! a shout falls on his ear from above. The man who is lying with half his length over the bridge has caught a glimpse of the boy's head and shoulders. Quick as thought the noosed rope is within reach of the sinking youth. No one breathes. With a faint convulsive effort, the swooning boy drops his arms into the noose. Darkness comes over him, and with the words God—Mother—the tightening rope lifts him out of his last shallow niche. Not a lip moves while he is dangling over that fearful abyss; but when a sturdy Virginian reaches down and draws up the lad, and holds him up in his arms before the tearful, breathless multitude, such shouting—such leaping and weeping for joy—never greeted the ear of a human being so recovered from the yawning gulf of eternity.

The Personality and Uses of a Laugh.

I would be willing to choose my friend by the quality of his laugh, and abide the issue. A glad, gushing outflow, a clear, ringing, mellow note of the soul, as surely indicates a genial and genuine nature as the rainbow in the dew-drop heralds the morning sun, or the frail flower in the wilderness betrays the zephyr-tossed seed of the parterre.

A laugh is one of God's truths. It tolerates no disguises. Falsehood may train its voice to flow in softest cadences, its lips to wreathe into smiles of surpassing sweetness, its face

"———To put on
That look we trust in———,"

but its laugh will betray the mockery. Who has not started and shuddered at the hollow "he-he-he!" of some velvet-voiced Mephistopheles, whose sinuous fascinations, without this note of warning, this premonitory rattle, might have bound the soul with a strong spell!

Leave nature alone. If she is noble, her broadest expression will soon tone itself down to fine accordance with life's earnestness; if she is base, no silken interweavings can keep out of sight her ugly head of discord. If we put a laugh into straight-jacket and leading-strings, it becomes an abortion; if we attempt to refine it, we destroy its pure, mellifluent ring; if we suppress a laugh, it struggles and dies on the heart, and the place where it lies is apt ever after to be weak and vulnerable. No, laugh truly, as you would speak truly, and both the inner and the outer man will rejoice. A full, spontaneous outburst opens all the delicate valves of being, and glides a subtle oil through all its complicated mechanism.

Laugh heartily, if you would keep the dew of your youth. There is no need to lay our girlhood and boyhood so doggedly down upon the altar of sacrifice as we toil up life's mountain. Dear, innocent children, lifting their dewy eyes and fair foreheads to the benedictions of angels, prattling and gamboling because it is a great joy to live, should flit like sunbeams among the stern-faced and stalwart. Young men and maidens should walk with strong, elastic tread, and cheerful voices among the weak and uncertain. White hairs should be no more the insignia of age, but the crown of ripe and perennial youth.

Laugh for your beauty. The joyous carry a fountain of light in their eyes, and round into rosy dimples where the echoes of gladness play at "hide-and-go-seek." Your "lean and hungry Cassius" is never betrayed into a laugh, and his smile is more cadaverous than his despair.

Laugh if you would live. He only exists who drags his days after him like a massive chain, asking sympathy with uplifted eyebrows and weak utterance as the beggar asks alms. Better die, for your own sake and the world's sake, than to pervert the uses and graces and dignities of life.

Make your own sunshine and your own music, keep your heart open to the smile of the good Father, and brave all things.

"Care to our coffin adds a nail, no doubt,
And every laugh so merry draws one out."

Omens.

Poict. I hope we shall have another good day to-morrow, for the clouds are red in the west.

Phys. I have no doubt of it, for the red has a tint of purple.

Hal. Do you know why this tint portends fine weather?

Phys. The air when dry, I believe, refracts more red, or heat-making rays; and as dry air is not perfectly transparent, they are again reflected in the horizon. I have observed generally a coppery or yellow sunset to foretell rain; but, as an indication of wet weather approaching, nothing is more certain than a halo round the moon, which is produced by the precipitated water; and the larger the circle, the nearer the clouds, and, consequently, the more ready to fall.

Hal. I have often observed that the old proverb is correct: "A rainbow in the morning is the shepherd's warning. A rainbow at night is the shepherd's delight." Can you explain this omen?

Phys. A rainbow can only occur when the clouds containing or depositing the rain are opposite to the sun,—and in the evening the rainbow is in the east, and in the morning in the west; and as our heavy rains in this climate are usually brought by the westerly wind, a rainbow in the west indicates that the bad weather is on the road, by the wind, to us; whereas the rainbow in the east proves that the rain in these clouds is passing from us.

Poict. I have often observed that when the swallows fly high, fine weather is to be expected or continued; but when they fly low, and close to the ground, rain is almost surely approaching. Can you account for this?

Hal. Swallows follow the flies and gnats, and flies and gnats usually delight in warm strata of air; and as warm air is lighter, and usually moister than cold air, when the warm strata of air are higher, there is less chance of moisture being thrown down from them by the mixture with cold air; but when the warm and moist air is close to the surface, it is almost certain that, as the cold air flows down into it, a deposition of water will take place.

Poict. I have often seen sea-gulls assemble on the land, and have almost always observed that very stormy and rainy weather was approaching. I conclude that these animals, sensible of a current of air approaching from the ocean, retire to the land to shelter themselves from the storm.

Orn. No such thing. The storm is their element; and the little petrel enjoys the heaviest gale, because, living on the smaller sea insect, he is sure to find his food in the spray of a heavy wave, and you may see him flitting above the edge of the highest surge. I believe that the reason of this migration of sea-gulls and other sea-birds to the land, is their security of finding food; and they may be observed, at this time, feeding greedily on the earthworms and larvæ, driven out of the ground by severe floods; and the fish, on which they prey in fine weather in the sea, leave the surface and go deeper in storms. The search after food, as we agreed on a former occasion, is the principal cause why animals change their places. The different tribes of the wading birds always migrate when rain is about to take place; and I remember once, in Italy, having been long waiting, in the end of March, for the arrival of the double snipe in the Campagne of Rome, a great flight appeared on the 3d of April, and the day after heavy rain set in, which greatly interfered with my sport. The vulture, upon the same principle, follows armies; and I have no doubt that the augury of the ancients was a good deal founded upon the observation of the instincts of birds. There are many superstitions of the vulgar. owing to the same source. For anglers, in Spring, it is always unlucky to see single magpies, but *two* may be always regarded as a favorable omen; and the reason is, that in cold and stormy weather one magpie alone leaves the nest in search of food, the other remaining sitting upon the eggs or the young ones; but when two go out together, it is only when the weather is warm and mild, and favorable for fishing.

Poict. The singular connections of causes and effects, to which you have just referred, make superstition less to be wondered at, particularly amongst the vulgar; and when two facts, naturally unconnected, have been accidentally coincident, it is not singular that this coincidence should have been observed and registered, and that omens of the most absurd kind should be trusted in. In the west of England, half a century ago, a particular hollow noise on the sea-coast was referred to a spirit or goblin called Bucca, and was supposed to foretell a shipwreck; the philosopher knows that sound travels much faster than currents in the air, and the sound always foretold the approach of a very heavy storm, which seldom takes place on that wild and rocky coast without a shipwreck on some part of its extensive shores, surrounded by the Atlantic.

Phys. All the instances of omens you have mentioned are founded on reason; but how can you explain such absurdities as Friday being an unlucky day, the terror of spilling salt, or meeting an old woman? I knew a man of very high dignity who was exceedingly moved by these omens, and who never went out shooting without a bittern's claw fastened to his button-hole by a riband, which he thought insured him good luck.

Poict. These, as well as the omens of death-watches, dreams, etc., are for the most part founded upon some accidental coincidence; but spilling of salt, on an uncommon occasion, may, as I have known it, arise from a disposition to apoplexy, shown by an incipient numbness in the hand, and may be a fatal symptom; and persons dispirited by bad omens sometimes prepare the way for evil fortune, for confidence in success is a great means of insuring it. The dream of Brutus before the field of Pharsalia probably produced a species of irresolution and despondency which was the principal cause of his losing the battle; and I have heard that the illustrious sportsman to whom you referred just now, was always observed to shoot ill, because he shot carelessly, after one of his dispiriting omens.

Hal. I have in life met with a few things which I have found it impossible to explain, either by chance coincidences or by natural connections, and I have known minds of a very superior class affected by them—persons in the habit of reasoning deeply and profoundly.

Phys. In my opinion, profound minds are the most likely to think lightly of the resources of human reason; and it is the pert superficial thinker who is generally strongest in every kind of unbelief. The deep philosopher sees chains of causes and effects so wonderfully and strangely linked together, that he is usually the last person to decide upon the impossibility of any two series of events being made independent of each other; and in science so many natural miracles, as it were, have been brought to light, such as the fall of stones from meteors in the atmosphere, the disarming a thunder-cloud by a metallic point, the production of fire from ice by a metal white as silver, and the referring certain laws of motion of the sea to the moon, that the physical inquirer is seldom disposed to assert confidently on any abstruse subjects belonging to the order of natural things, and still less so those relating to the more mysterious relations of moral events and intellectual natures.

JOHN RUSKIN.

JOHN RUSKIN.

JOHN RUSKIN was born in London, England, February, 1819. Having inherited a large fortune from his father, he was enabled to make complete preparation for his life work and to devote his entire time to art and literature. In 1842, he graduated at Oxford, and further prepared himself by studying art and learning water-color painting. His literary work may be recorded as follows: In 1839, he gained a prize for a poem entitled *Salsetto Elphanta;* in 1843, *Modern Painters: Their Superiority in the Art of Landscape Painting to all the Ancient Masters.* The fifth volume of this treatise was published in 1860.

The Seven Lamps of Architecture appeared in 1849; *Pre-Raphaelitism* and *The King of the Golden River,* in 1851; *The Stones of Venice,* 1851-3; *Lectures on Architecture and Painting,* 1854; *Elements of Drawing,* 1857; *The Political Economy of Art,* 1858; *The Two Paths,* 1859; *Unto This Last,* 1862; *Sesame and Lilies,* 1864; *The Ethics of the Dust,* 1865; *The Crown of Wild Olive,* 1866; and *The Queen of the Air,* 1869. He has also written extensively for periodicals.

In 1867 he was appointed Rede Lecturer at Cambridge, and in 1869 was elected Professor of Fine Arts at Oxford. At Oxford he endowed a chair of drawing. He is also prominent as a popular public speaker.

Those who love the true and beautiful in Nature and Art, and who admire an attractive statement of pure and ennobling thoughts, will be amply repaid for their time in reading Ruskin.

Precipices of the Alps.

Dark in color, robed with everlasting mourning, forever tottering like a great fortress shaken by war, fearful as much in their weakness as in their strength, and yet gathered after every fall into darker frowns and unhumiliating threatening; forever incapable of comfort or healing from herb or flower, nourishing no root in their crevices, touched by no hue of life on buttress or ledge, but to the utmost desolate; knowing no shaking of leaves in the wind, nor of grass beside the stream—no other motion but their own mortal shivering, the dreadful crumbling of atom from atom in their corrupting stones; knowing no sound of living voice or living tread, cheered neither by the kid's bleat nor the marmot's cry; haunted only by uninterrupted echoes from afar off, wandering hither 'and thither among their walls unable to escape, and by the hiss of angry torrents, and sometimes the shriek of a bird that flits near the face of them, and sweeps, frightened, back from under their shadow into the gulf of air; and sometimes, when the echo has fainted, and the wind has carried the sound of the torrent away, and the bird has vanished, and the moldering stones are still for a little time—a brown moth, opening and shutting its wings upon a grain of dust, may be the only thing that moves or feels in all the waste of weary precipice darkening five thousand feet of the blue depth of heaven.

The Fall of the Leaf.

If ever, in Autumn, a pensiveness falls upon us as the leaves drift by in their fading, may we not wisely look up in hope to their mighty monuments? Behold how fair, how far prolonged in arch and aisle, the avenues of the valleys, the fringes of the hills! So stately—so eternal; the joy of man, the comfort of all living creatures, the glory of the earth—they are but the monuments of those poor leaves that flit faintly past us to die. Let them not pass without our understanding their last counsel and example; that we also, careless of monument by the grave, may build it in the world —monument by which men may be taught to remember, not where we died, but where we lived.

The Sky.

Not long ago I was slowly descending the carriage road after you leave Albano. It had been wild weather when I left Rome, and all across the Campagna the clouds were sweeping in sulphurous blue, with a clap of thunder or two, and breaking gleams of sun along the Claudian aqueduct, lighting up its arches like the bridge of chaos. But as I climbed the long slope of the Alban mount, the storm swept finally to the north, and the noble outline of the domes of Albano and the graceful darkness of its ilex grove rose against pure streaks of alternate blue and amber, the upper sky gradually flushing through the last fragments of rain-cloud, in deep palpitating azure, half ether and half dew. The noon-day sun came slanting down the rocky slopes of La Ricca, and its masses of entangled and tall foliage, whose autumnal tints were mixed with the wet verdure of a thousand evergreens, were penetrated with it as with rain. I cannot call it color, it was conflagration. Purple, and crimson and scarlet, like the curtains of God's tabernacle, the rejoicing trees sank into the valley in showers of light, every separate leaf quivering with buoyant and burning life; each, as it turned to reflect or to transmit the sunbeam, first a torch and then an emerald. Far up into the recesses of the valley, the green vistas, arched like the hollows of mighty waves of some crystalline sea, with the arbutus flowers dashed along their flanks for foam, and silver flakes of

108   TREASURES FROM THE PROSE WORLD.

orange spray tossed into the air around them, breaking over the
gray walls of rock into a thousand separate stars, fading and kind-
ling alternately as the weak wind lifted and let them fall. Every
blade of grass burned like the golden floor of heaven opening in
sudden gleams as the foliage broke and closed above it, as sheet
lightning opens in a cloud at sunset the motionless masses of dark
rock—dark, though flushed with scarlet lichen, casting their quiet
shadows across its restless radiance, the fountain underneath them
filling its marble hollow with blue mist and fitful sound, and, over
all,—the multitudinous bars of amber and rose, the sacred clouds
that have no darkness, and only exist to illumine, were seen in intervals between the solemn and orbed repose of the stone pines,
passing to lose themselves in the last, white, blinding luster of the
measureless line where the Campagna melted into the blaze of the sea.

* * * * * * * *

Are not all natural things, it may be asked, as lovely near as
far away? By no means. Look at the clouds and watch the delicate sculpture of their alabaster sides, and the rounded luster of
their magnificent rolling. They are meant to be beheld far away:
they were shaped for their place high above your head: approach
them and they fuse into vague mists, or whirl away in fierce fragments of thunderous vapor. Look at the crest of the Alp from the
far away plains over which its light is cast, whence human souls
have communed with it by their myriads. It was built for its place
in the far off sky: approach it, and as the sound of the voice of man
dies away about its foundations, and the tide of human life is met
at last by the eternal "Here shall thy waves be stayed," the glory
of its aspect fades into blanched fearfulness: its purple walls are
rent into grisly rocks, its silver fret-work saddened into wasting
snow: the storm-brands of ages are on its breast, the ashes of its
own ruin lie solemnly on its white raiment.

If you desire to perceive the great harmonies of the form of a rocky
mountain, you must not ascend upon its sides. All there is disorder
and accident, or seems so. Retire from it, and as your eye commands

it more and more, you see the ruined mountain world with a wider glance; behold! dim sympathies begin to busy themselves in the disjointed mass: line binds itself into stealthy fellowship with line: group by group the helpless fragments gather themselves into ordered companies: new captains of hosts, and masses of battalions become visible one by one; and far away answers of foot to foot and of bone to bone, until the powerless is seen risen up with girded loins, and not one piece of all the unregarded heap can now be spared from the mystic whole.

The Old Churchyard.

The next day, the day of the resurrection, rose glorious from its sepulchre of sea-fog and drizzle. It had poured all night long, but at sunrise the clouds had broken and scattered, and the air was the purer for the cleansing rain, while the earth shone with that peculiar luster which follows the weeping which has endured its appointed night. The larks were at it again, singing as if their hearts would break for joy as they hovered in brooding exultation over the song of the future; for their nests beneath hoarded a wealth of larks for Summers to come. Especially about the old churchyard, half buried in the ancient trees of Lossie House, the birds that day were jubilant; their throats seemed too narrow to let out the joyful air that filled all their hollow bones and quills; they sang as if they must sing or choke with too much gladness. Beyond the short spire and its shining cock rose the balls and stars and arrowy vanes of the house, glittering in gold and sunshine. The inward hush of the resurrection, broken only by the prophetic birds, the poets of the groaning and travailing creation, held time and space as in a trance; and the center from which radiated both the hush and the caroling expectation seemed to Alexander Graham to be the churchyard in which he was now walking in the cool of the

morning. It was more carefully kept than most Scottish church-
yards, and yet was not too trim; nature had a word in the affair—
was allowed her part of mourning in long grass and moss and the
crumbling away of stone. The wholesomeness of decay, which
both in nature and humanity is but the miry road back to life, was
not unrecognized here, there was nothing of the hideous attempt
to hide death in the garments of life. The master walked about
gently, now stopping to read some well-known inscription, and
ponder for a moment over the words; and now wandering across
the stoneless mounds, content to be forgotten by all but those who
loved the departed. At length he seated himself on a slab by the
side of the mound that rose but yesterday; it was sculptured with
symbols of decay—needless, surely, where the originals lay about
the mouth of every newly-opened grave, as surely ill befitting the
precincts of a church whose indwelling gospel is of life victorious
over death! "What are these stones," he said to himself, "but
monuments to oblivion!" They are not memorials of the dead, but
memorials of the forgetfulness of the living. How vain it is to
send a poor forsaken name, like the title-page of a lost book, down
the careless stream of time! Let me serve my generation, and
may God remember me!

Home.

Society is marked by greater and smaller divisions, as into
nations, communities, and families. A man is a member of the
commonwealth, a smaller community, as a hamlet or city, and his
family at the same time; and the more perfectly all his duties to his
family are discharged, the more fully does he discharge his duties
to the community and the nation; for a good member of a family
cannot be a bad member of the commonwealth, for he that is faithful in what is least will also be faithful in what is greater. Indeed,

the more perfectly a man fulfills all his domestic duties, the more perfectly, in that very act, has he discharged his duty to the whole; for the whole is made up of parts, and its health depends entirely upon the health of the various parts. There are, of course, general as well as specific duties; but the more conscientious a man is in the discharge of specific duties, the more ready will he be to perform those that are general; and we believe that the converse of this will be found equally true, and that those who have least regard for home—who have, indeed, no home, no domestic circle—are the worst citizens. This they may not be apparently; they may not break the laws, nor do anything to call down upon them censure from the community, and yet, in the secret and almost unconscious dissemination of demoralizing principles, may be doing a work far more destructive of the public good than if they had committed a robbery.

We always feel pain when we hear a young man speak lightly of home, and talk carelessly, or it may be with sportive ridicule, of the "old man," and the "old woman," as if they were of but little consequence. We mark it as a bad indication, and feel that the feet of that young man are treading upon dangerous ground. His home education may not have been of the best kind, nor may home influences have reached his higher and better feelings; but he is at least old enough now to understand the causes, and to seek rather to bring into his home all that it needs to render it more attractive, than to estrange himself from it, and expose its defects.

Instances of this kind are not of very frequent occurrence. Home has its charms for nearly all, and the very name comes with a blessing to the spirit. This, however, is more the case with those who have been separated from it, than it is with those who yet remain in the old homestead, with parents, brothers, and sisters as their friends and companions.

The earnest love of home, felt by nearly all who have been compelled to leave that pleasant place, is a feeling that should be tenderly cherished, and this love should be kept alive by associations that have in them as perfect a resemblance of home as it is possible to obtain. It is for this reason that it is bad for a young man to board in a large hotel, where there is nothing in which there is even an image of the home circle. Each has his separate chamber; but that is not home; all meet together at the common table; but there is no home feeling there, with its many sweet reciprocations. The meal completed, all separate, each to his individual pursuit or pleasure. There is a parlor, it is true; but there are no family gatherings there. One and another sit there, as inclination prompts; but each sits alone, busy with his own thoughts. All this is a poor substitute for home. And yet it offers its attractions to some. A young man in a hotel has more freedom than in a family or private boarding house. He comes in and goes out unobserved; there is no one to say to him, "why?" or "wherefore?" But this is a dangerous freedom, and one which no young man should desire.

But mere negative evils, so to speak, are not the worst that beset a young man who unwisely chooses a public hotel as a place of boarding. He is much more exposed to temptations there than in a private boarding house or at home. Men of licentious habits, in most cases, select hotels as boarding places; and such rarely scruple to offer to the ardent minds of young men, with whom they happen to fall in company, those allurements that are most likely to lead them away from virtue. And, besides this, there being no evening home circle in a hotel, a young man who is not engaged earnestly in some pursuit that occupies his hours of leisure from business, has nothing to keep him there, but is forced to seek for something to interest his mind elsewhere, and is, in consequence, more open to temptation.

Home is man's true place. Every man should have a home. Here his first duties lie, and here he finds the strength by which he is able successfully to combat in life's temptations. Happy is that young man who is still blessed with a home—who has his mother's counsel and the pure love of sisters to strengthen and cheer him amid life's opening combats.

Parents.

Although the attainment of mature age takes away the obligation of obedience to parents, as well as the right of dependence upon them, it should lessen in no way a young man's deference, respect, or affection. For twenty-one years, or from the earliest period of infancy, through childhood and youth, up to mature age, his parents have felt and thought, and labored for him. They have watched over his pillow, anxiously, in sickness; they have, with the most unselfish love, earnestly sought his good in everything, even to the extent of much self-denial; and can he now offer them less than deference, respect, and affection? No; surely no young man will withhold this.

Let us show you a picture. Do you see that feeble infant asleep on its mother's bosom? How helpless it lies! How dependent it is upon others for everything! The neglect of a moment might cause some fatal injury to a being so entirely powerless. But that mother's love neither slumbers nor sleeps. It is ever around the fragile creature committed to her care, and she is ready to guard its life with her own. You once lay thus in your mother's arms, and she nourished your helpless infancy thus at her bosom. She watched over you, loved you, protected and defended you; and all was from love,—deep, pure, fervent love,—the first love and the most unselfish love that ever has or ever will bless you in this life, for it asked for and expected no return. A *mother's love!*—it is the most perfect reflection of the love of God ever thrown back from the mirror of a human heart.

Here is another picture. A mother sits in grief, and her boy, now no longer an infant, stands in sullen disobedience by her side. She has striven to correct his faults for his own good, and in love reproved him; but he would not regard her admonitions. Again and again she has sought, by gentle urgings, to direct him to good; but all has been in vain, and she now resorts to punishment that is far more painful to her than to her child. The scene is changed. See where she sits now, alone, bitterly weeping. There is an image in her mind, and but one, that obscures all the rest; it is the image of her suffering child—suffering by her hand! Her breast labors heavily, her heart is oppressed—she feels deep anguish of spirit. But she has done her duty, painful though it has been, and that sustains her. You were once a boy like that; and thus your own mother has grieved over your disobedience, and felt the same bitterness of spirit. And love for you was the cause. Can you ever forget this?

Do you see that darkened chamber? By the bed of sickness sits a pale watcher, and there are tears upon her cheek. Day and night, for nearly a week, has she sat by the bed, or moved with noiseless feet about the room. She has not taken off her garments during the time; nor has she joined the family at their regular meals. Who is the object of all this deep solicitude? It is her child. The hand of sickness is upon him, and he has drawn near to the gates of death. In her solicitude she forgets even herself. She has but one thought, and that is for her offspring. Her love, her care, her anxious hopes are at length rewarded. The destroyer passes by and leaves her her child. Thus has your mother watched, day by day and night by night, beside your couch of sickness. Never forget this, young man. Forget every other obligation, but never forget how much you owe your mother! You can never know a thousandth part of what she has endured for your sake; and now, in her old age, all she asks is that you will love her—not with the love she still bears to you; she does not expect that—and care for her, that life's sunshine may, still come through the windows and over the threshold of her dwelling.

And with no less of respect and affection should a young man think of his father. Not until his own life-trials come on will he fully understand how much he owes his father. It is no light task which a man takes upon himself—that of sustaining, by his single efforts, a whole family, and sustaining them in comfort, and perhaps in luxury. You have an education that enables you to take a respectable position in society; you have a groundwork of good principles; habits of industry; in fact, all that a young man need ask for in order that he may rise in the world; and for these you are indebted to your father. To give you such advantages cost him labor, self-denial, and much anxious thought. Many times, during the struggle to sustain his family, has he been pressed down with worldly difficulties, and almost ready to despair. He has seen his last dollar, it may be, leave his hand, without knowing certainly where the next was to come from. But still his love for his children has urged him on, and by new and more vigorous efforts he has overcome the difficulties by which he was surrounded.

A young man should think often of these things, and let them influence his conduct to his parents. There will come a time in life when such thoughts will force themselves upon him; but these thoughts may come too late.

Toward parents the deportment should always be deferential and kind. A young man, who properly reflects upon the new relation now existing between them and himself, will naturally change his manner of address, and be far more guarded than he was before he arrived of age, lest he say or do anything that might cause them to feel that he now considered himself beyond their control. When they advise, he should consider well what they say; and, if compelled to differ from them, he should carefully explain the reason, and show truly his regret at not being able to act from their judgment of the matter. As a general thing, however, he will find their advice better than the counsels of his own scarcely fledged reason, and he will do well seriously to deliberate upon it before taking his own course.

Above all, let no unkind word ever pass your lips. Nothing stings so, nothing so deeply wounds the heart of a parent, as harsh words from his children who have grown up and become men and women. Almost as bad as this is neglect.

The older your father and mother grow, the narrower becomes the sphere of their hopes and wishes until, at length, all thought and all affections are centered on their children. But while this is going on, the children's minds are becoming more and more absorbed in the cares, duties, and new affections of life, until their parents are almost forgotten. Forewarned of this tendency, let every one strive against it, lest he wound by neglect, either seeming or real, a heart that has loved him from life's earliest dawn up to the present moment.

But not alone in deference, respect, and marks of affection lie the limits of a young man's duties to his parents. He should endeavor to take up and bear for them, if too heavy for their declining strength, some of the burdens that oppress them. He should particularly consider his father, and see if the entire support of the family that yet remains upon his hands does not tax his efforts too far; and if such be the case, he should deny himself almost anything, in order to render some aid. For years, he has been receiving all that he required, and it is now but fair that he should begin to make some return.

How often do we see two or three sons, all in the receipt of good salaries, spending their money in self-indulgences, while their father is toiling on for his younger children, broken in health, perhaps disappointed in his worldly prospects, and almost despairing in regard to the final result of all his efforts! They come and go, and never think that anything is due from them. It does not occur to them that if each were to deny himself the gratification of his desires to the extent of one hundred dollars a year, and the aggregate amount were placed in their father's hands to aid in supporting the family, it would take a mountain of care from his shoulders. Why is it that so many young men forget their duty in this important matter? One would think that no prompter was required here to remind them of their part. But it is not so. On the contrary, it is a thing of such rare occurrence for a son to practice self-denial for the sake of his parents, that, wherever it is seen, it forms the subject of remark.

We often see parents who have enjoyed but few advantages themselves, and who, in consequence, are compelled to occupy lower and more laborious positions in the world, denying themselves many comforts and all the luxuries of life, in order to give their children the very best education possible for them to provide. We see these children growing up, and too often the first return they make is in the form of invidious comparisons between themselves and the parents to whom they owe almost everything! In a little while they step into the world as men, and, becoming absorbed in its pursuits from various selfish ends, seem to forget entirely that their parents are still toiling on, enfeebled by years and over-exertion for their sakes, and with the very sweat of their time-worn brows digging out from the hard earth, so to speak, the scanty food and raiment required to sustain nature. Ah! but this is a melancholy sight. Could anything tell the sad tale of man's declension from good so eloquently as this?

It is plainly the duty of every young man, whose parents are poor and compelled to labor beyond their strength, to aid them to the extent of his ability. They have borne the burden for him for many years. From their toil and self-denial he now has the means of rising higher in the world than they had the ability ever to rise; but he is unjust and ungrateful if, in his eager efforts to advance too rapidly, he forget and neglect them. Nothing can excuse conduct so unnatural, so cruel.

The Spider and the Bee.

Upon the highest corner of a large window there dwelt a certain spider, swollen up to the first magnitude by the destruction of infinite numbers of flies, whose spoils lay scattered before the gates of his palace, like human bones before the cave of some giant. The avenues to his castle were guarded with turnpikes and palisadoes. After you had passed several courts you came to the center, wherein you might behold the constable himself, in his own lodgings, which had windows fronting to each avenue, and ports to sally out upon all occasions of prey or defense. In this mansion he had for some time dwelt in peace and plenty, without danger to his person by swallows from above, or to his palace by brooms from below, when it was the pleasure of fortune to conduct thither a wandering bee, to whose curiosity a broken pane in the glass had discovered itself, and in he went, where, expatiating a while, he at last happened to alight upon one of the outer walls of the spider's citadel, which, yielding to the unequal weight, sunk down to the very foundation. Thrice he endeavored to force his passage, and thrice the center shook. The spider within, feeling the terrible convulsion, supposed at first that nature was approaching to her final dissolution, or else that Beelzebub, with all his legions, was come to revenge the death of many thousands of his subjects whom his enemy had slain and devoured. However, he at length valiantly resolved to issue forth and meet his fate. Meanwhile the bee had acquitted himself of his toils, and posted securely at some distance, was employed in cleansing his wings, and disengaging them from the rugged remnants of the cobweb. By this time the spider was adventured out, when beholding the chasms, the ruins and dilapidations of his fortress, he was very near at his wit's end; he stormed and swore like a madman, and swelled till he was ready to burst. At length, casting his eye upon the bee, and wisely gathering causes from events (for they knew each other by sight), "A plague split you," said he, "for a giddy puppy; is it you, with a vengeance, that has made this litter here? Could you not look before you? Do you think I have nothing else to do but to mend and repair after you?"

"Good words, friend," said the bee (having now pruned himself, and being disposed to be droll), "I'll give you my hand and word to come near your kennel no more; I was never in such a confounded pickle since I was born."

"Sirrah," replied the spider, "if it were not for breaking an old custom in our family, never to stir abroad against an enemy, I should come and teach you better manners."

"I pray have patience," said the bee, "or you'll spend your

substance, and for aught I see, you may stand in need of it all toward the repair of your house."

"Rogue, rogue," replied the spider, "yet methinks you should have more respect to a person whom all the world allows to be so much your betters."

"By my troth," said the bee, "the comparison will amount to a very good jest; and you will do me a favor to let me know the reasons that all the world is pleased to use in so hopeful a dispute."

At this the spider, having swelled himself into the size and posture of a disputant, began his argument in the true spirit of controversy, with resolution to be heartily scurrilous and angry; to urge on his own reasons without the least regard to the answers or objections of his opposite; and fully predetermined in his mind against all conviction.

"Not to disparage myself," said he, "by the comparison with such a rascal, what art thou but a vagabond without house or home, without stock or inheritance? born to no possession of your own but a pair of wings and a drone-pipe. Your livelihood is a universal plunder upon nature; a freebooter over fields and gardens; and, for the sake of stealing, will rob a nettle as easily as a violet. Whereas, I am a domestic animal, furnished with a native stock within myself. This large castle (to show my improvements in the mathematics) is all built with my own hands, and the materials extracted altogether out of my own person."

"I am glad," answered the bee, "to hear you grant at least that I come honestly by my wings and my voice; for then, it seems, I am obliged to Heaven alone for my flights and my music; and Providence would never have bestowed on me two such gifts, without designing them for the noblest ends. I visit indeed all the flowers and blossoms of the field and garden; but whatever I collect thence enriches myself, without the least injury to their beauty, their smell, or their taste. Now, for you and your skill in architecture and other mathematics, I have little to say: in that building of yours there might, for aught I know, have been labor and method enough; but, by woeful experience for us both, it is too plain the materials are naught; and I hope you will henceforth take warning, and consider duration and matter, as well as method and art. You boast indeed of being obliged to no other creature, but of drawing and spinning out all from yourself; that is to say, if we may judge of the liquor in the vessel by what issues out, you possess a good plentiful store of dirt and poison in your breast; and though I would by no means lessen or disparage your genuine stock of either, yet I doubt you are somewhat obliged, for an increase of both, to a little foreign assistance. Your inherent portion of dirt does not fail of acquisitions, by sweepings exhaled from below; and one insect furnishes you with a share of poison to destroy another. So that, in short, the question comes all to this: Whether is the nobler being of the two, that which by a lazy contemplation of four inches round, by an overweening pride, feeding and engendering on itself, turns all into excrement and venom, producing nothing at all but flybane and a cobweb; or that which, by a universal range, with long search, much study, true judgment, and distinction of things, brings home honey and wax?"

LORD LYTTON.

LORD LYTTON.

EDWARD LYTTON BULWER, afterward Lord Lytton, was born in May, 1805, and he died at Torquay on the 18th of January, 1873. His remains now rest among England's honored dead in Westminster Abbey. He was the youngest son of General Bulwer, and his mother was of the ancient family of Lytton of Knebworth, in Hertfordshire. Upon his mother's death in 1843, the novelist succeeded to her valuable estate, and took the name Lytton. While our author was prominent in political matters, yet we shall record only his literary work.

His first volume appeared in 1820, the work having been written between the ages of thirteen and fifteen. In his next appearance, he was the successful candidate for a prize poem in Cambridge University; in 1825, he carried off a gold medal for the best English poem. In 1826 appeared a volume of miscellaneous verse, entitled *Weeds and Wild Flowers*, and in 1827, a poetical narrative, called *O'Neill, or, The Rebel*. From this time, his pen was never idle. From the appearance of his first volume till his death, "there was no reposing under the shade of his laurels—no living upon the resources of past reputation; his foot was always in the arena, and his shield hung always in the list." His prominent works may be recorded as follows: In 1827 appeared *Falkland*, his first novel; 1828, *Pelham, or, the Adventures of a Gentleman;* 1828, *The Disowned;* 1829, *Devereux, A Novel*, much more finished than his former works; 1830, *Paul Clifford*,—below the average of his former works; 1831, *The Siamese Twins*, a poem satirical of fashion, of travelers, of politicians, London notoriety, etc. His political satire proved almost a failure, though showing some vigorous thought. Returning to fiction, he was more fortunate in 1831 in *Eugene Aram, a Story of English Life*. In 1833 appeared his *England and the English;* 1834, *The Pilgrims of the Rhine*.

The Last Days of Pompeii, one of his greatest works, and the one from which we have made our chief selection, appeared in 1835. Then followed in quick succession *Rienzi, the Last of the Tribunes, The Crisis, Ernest Maltravers, Alice, or The Mysteries, Athens*, and numerous others, all worthy of mention. We will only record *Night and Morning*, followed by *Day and Night, Lights and Shadows, Glimmer and Gloom*.

The limit of our sketch forbids further notice of Lord Lytton's productions. It would require volumes to make proper mention of his writings, with full notes. "He was at the head of the English literature, with the single exception of Mr. Carlyle; his works were popular over all Europe, and his fertility and industry seemed unabated. His son, the present Lord Lytton, has, with a just pride, said of his father: 'Whether as an author, standing apart from all literary cliques and coteries, or as a politician, never wholly subject to the exclusive dictation of any political party, he always thought and acted in sympathy with every popular aspiration for the political, social and intellectual improvement of the whole national life.'" Lord Lytton left an unfinished romance, *Pausanias, the Spartan*, which was published by his son in 1876.

Last Days of Pompeii.

Lord Lytton's "Historical Romance," from which this selection is taken, is extremely interesting. The description is the work of Lytton's fancy, but is founded upon the destruction of Herculaneum and Pompeii by an eruption of Mt. Vesuvius, A. D. 79. In 1750, nearly seventeen centuries after its destruction, the city of Pompeii was disinterred from its silent tomb, all vivid with undimmed hues; its walls fresh as if painted yesterday.

The scene is located in the amphitheater, when the cloud of fire and destruction was seen rolling toward the city. Glaucus, an Athenian, had been accused of murdering the priest Apaecides, and was doomed to furnish amusement to the spectators by fighting a hungry lion in the amphitheater. As the Athenian entered the arena,—

All evidence of fear—all fear itself—was gone. A red and haughty flush spread over the paleness of his features—he towered aloft to the full of his glorious stature. In the elastic beauty of his limbs and form, in his intent but unfrowning brow, in the high disdain, and in the indomitable soul, which breathed visibly, which spoke audibly, from his attitude, his lip, his eye,—he seemed the very incarnation, vivid and corporeal, of the valor of his land—of the divinity of its worship—at once a hero and a god! * * *

Glaucus had bent his limbs so as to give himself the firmest posture at the expected rush of the lion, with his small and shining weapon raised on high, in the faint hope that one well-directed thrust (for he knew that he should have time but for one), might penetrate through the eye to the brain of his grim foe. But, to the unutterable astonishment of all, the beast seemed not even aware of the presence of the criminal.

At the first moment of its release it halted abruptly in the arena, raised itself half on end, snuffing the upward air with impatient sighs; then suddenly it sprang forward, but not on the Athenian. At half speed it circled round and round the space, turning its vast head from side to side with an anxious and perturbed gaze, as if seeking only some avenue of escape; once or twice it endeavored to leap up the parapet that divided it from the audience, and, on failing, uttered rather a baffled howl than its deep-toned and kingly roar. It evinced no sign, either of wrath or hunger; its tail drooped along the sand instead of lashing its gaunt sides; and its eye, though it wandered at times to Glaucus rolled again listlessly from him. At length, as if tired of attempting to escape, it crept with a moan into its cage, and once more laid itself down to rest.

[Just as the keeper is about to take the goad to urge the lion forth to the conflict, the priest Calenus appears and declares that the Athenian is innocent, and that Arbaces of Egypt is the murderer of Apaecides. It was then thought to be a miracle that the lion had spared the Athenian. In the midst of the confusion, the terrible reality of the eruption of Mt. Vesuvius furnished an explanation of the lion's conduct. Omitting further description, we now quote from "Progress of the Destruction."]

The cloud, which had scattered so deep a murkiness over the day, had now settled into a solid and impenetrable mass. It resembled less even the thickest gloom of a night in the open air than the close and blind darkness of some narrow room. But in proportion as the blackness gathered, did the lightnings around Vesuvius increase in their vivid and scorching glare. Nor was their horrible beauty confined to the usual hues of fire; no rainbow ever rivaled their varying and prodigal dyes. Now brightly blue as the most azure depth of a southern sky—now of a livid and snake-like green, darting restlessly to and fro as the folds of an enormous serpent—now a lurid and intolerable crimson, gushing forth through the columns of smoke, far and wide, and lighting up the whole city from arch to arch—then suddenly dying into a sickly paleness, like the ghost of their own life! In the pauses of the showers, you heard the rumbling of the earth beneath, and the groaning waves of the tortured sea; or lower still, and audible but to the watch of intensest fear, the grinding and hissing murmur of the escaping gases through the chasms of the distant mountain. Sometimes the cloud appeared to break from its solid mass, and, by the lightning, to assume quaint and vast mimicries of human or of monster shapes, striding across the gloom, hurling one upon the other, and vanishing swiftly into the turbulent abyss of shade; so that, to the eyes and fancies of the affrighted wanderers, the unsubstantial vapors were as the bodily forms of gigantic foes—the agents of terror and of death.

The ashes in many places were already knee deep; and the boiling showers which came from the steaming breath of the volcano forced their way into the houses, bearing with them a strong and suffocating vapor. In some places immense fragments of rock, hurled upon the houses' roofs, bore down along the street masses of confused ruin, which yet more and more, with every hour, obstructed the way; and as the day advanced, the motion of the earth was more sensibly felt—the footing seemed to slide and creep—nor could chariot or litter be kept steady, even on the most level ground.

Sometimes the huger stones striking against each other as they fell, broke into countless fragments, emitting sparks of fire, which caught whatever was combustible within their reach; and along the plains beyond the city the darkness was now terribly relieved; for several houses, and even vineyards, had been set on flames; and at various intervals the fires rose sullenly and fiercely against the solid gloom. To add to this partial relief of the darkness, the citizens had, here and there, in the more public places, such as the porticoes of temples and the entrances to the forum, endeavored to place rows of torches; but these rarely continued long; the showers and the wind extinguished them, and the sudden darkness into which their fitful light was converted had something in it doubly impressive on the impotence of human hopes, the lesson of despair.

Frequently, by the momentary light of these torches, parties of fugitives encountered each other, some hurrying towards the sea, others flying from the sea back to the land; for the ocean had retreated rapidly from the shore—an utter darkness lay over it, and, upon its groaning and tossing waves the storm of cinders and rocks fell without the protection which the streets and roofs afforded to the land. Wild—haggard—ghastly with supernatural fears, these groups encountered each other, but without the leisure to speak, to consult, to advise; for the showers fell now frequently, though not continuously, extinguishing the lights which showed to each band the death-like faces of the other, and hurrying all to seek refuge beneath the nearest shelter. The whole elements of civilization were broken up. Ever and anon, by the flickering lights, you saw the thief hastening by the most solemn authorities of the law, laden with, and fearfully chuckling over, the produce of his sudden gains. If, in the darkness, wife was separated from husband, or parent from child, vain was the hope of reunion. Each hurried blindly and confusedly on. Nothing in all the various and complicated machinery of social life was left save the primal law of self-preservation!

Through this awful scene did the Athenian wade his way, accompanied by Ione and the blind girl. Suddenly a rush of hundreds, in their path to the sea, swept by them. Nydia was torn from the side of Glaucus, who, with Ione, was borne rapidly onward; and when the crowd (whose forms they saw not, so thick was the gloom) were gone, Nydia was still separated from their side. Glaucus shouted her name. No answer came. They retraced their steps—in vain: they could not discover her—it was evident she had been swept along in some opposite direction by the human current. Their friend, their preserver, was lost! And hitherto Nydia had been their guide. Her blindness rendered the scene familiar to her alone. Accustomed, through a perpetual night, to thread the windings of the city, she had led them unerringly toward the sea-shore, by which they had resolved to hazard an escape. Now, which way could they wend? All was rayless to them—a maze without a clue. Wearied, despondent, bewildered, they, however, passed along, the ashes falling upon their heads, the fragmentary stones dashing up in sparkles before their feet.

"Alas! alas!" murmured Ione, "I can go no farther; my steps sink among the scorching cinders. Fly, dearest!—beloved, fly! and leave me to my fate!"

"Hush, my betrothed! my bride! Death with thee is sweeter than life without thee! Yet, whither— oh! whither, can we direct ourselves through the gloom? Already, it seems that we have made but a circle, and are in the very spot which we quitted an hour ago."

"Blessed lightning! See, Ione—see! the portico of the Temple of Fortune is before us. Let us creep beneath it; it will protect us from the showers."

He caught his beloved in his arms, and with difficulty and labor gained the temple. He bore her to the remoter and more sheltered part of the portico, and leaned over her, that he might shield her, with his own form, from the lightning and the showers! The beauty and the unselfishness of love could hallow even that dismal time!

"Who is there?" said the trembling and hollow voice of one who had preceded them in their place of refuge. "Yet, what matters? the crush of the ruined world forbids to us friends or foes."

Ione turned at the sound of the voice, and, with a faint shriek, cowered again beneath the arms of Glaucus; and he, looking in the direction of the voice, beheld the cause of her alarm. Through the darkness glared forth two burning eyes—the lightning flashed and lingered athwart the temple—and Glaucus, with a shudder, perceived the pillars;—and, close beside it, unwitting of the vicinity, lay the giant form of him who had accosted them—the wounded gladiator, Niger.

That lightning had revealed to each other the form of beast and man; yet the instinct of both was quelled. Nay, the lion crept near and nearer to the gladiator, as for companionship; and the gladiator did not recede or tremble. The revolution of nature had dissolved her lighter terrors as well as her wonted ties.

While they were thus terribly protected, a group of men and women, bearing torches, passed by the temple. They were of the congregation of the Nazarenes; and a sublime and unearthly emotion had not, indeed, quelled their awe, but it had robbed awe of fear. They had long believed, according to the error of the early Christians that the Last Day was at hand; they imagined now that the Day had come.

"Woe! woe!" cried, in a shrill and piercing voice, the elder at their head. "Behold! the Lord descendeth to judgment! He maketh fire come down from heaven in the sight of men! Woe! woe! ye strong and mighty! Woe to ye of the fasces and the purple! Woe to the idolator and the worshiper of the beast! Woe to ye who pour forth the blood of saints, and gloat over the death pangs of the sons of God! Woe to the harlot of the sea!—woe! woe!"

And with a loud and deep chorus, the troop chanted forth along the wild horrors of the air,—"Woe to the harlot of the sea!—woe! woe!"

The Nazarenes paced slowly on, their torches still flickering in the storm, their voices still raised in menace and solemn warning, till, lost amid the windings in the street, the darkness of the atmosphere and the silence of death again fell over the scene.

The Candid Man.

One bright, laughing day, I threw down my book an hour sooner than usual, and sallied out with a lightness of foot and exhilaration of spirit, to which I had long been a stranger. I had just sprung over a stile that led into one of those green, shady lanes which makes us feel that the old poets who loved and lived for nature were right in calling our island "the merry England," when I was startled by a short quick bark on one side of the hedge. I turned sharply round; and, seated upon the sward was a man, apparently of the peddler profession; a great deal-box was lying open before him; a few articles of linen and female dress were scattered round, and the man himself appeared earnestly occupied in examining the deeper recesses of his itinerant warehouse. A small black terrier flew toward me with no friendly growl.

"Down," said I, "all strangers are not foes, though the English generally think so."

The man hastily looked up; perhaps he was struck with the quaintness of my remonstrance to his canine companion; for, touching his hat civilly, he said, "The dog, sir, is very quiet; he only means to give *me* the alarm by giving it to *you;* for dogs seem to have no despicable insight into human nature, and know well that the best of us may be taken by surprise."

"You are a moralist," said I, not a little astonished in my turn by such an address from such a person. "I could not have expected to stumble upon a philosopher so easily. Have you any wares in your box likely to suit me? If so, I should like to purchase of so moralizing a vendor!"

"No, sir," said the seeming peddler, smiling, and yet at the same time hurrying his goods into his box, and carefully turning the key. "No, sir, I am only a bearer of other men's goods; my morals are all that I can call my own, and those I will sell you at your own price."

"You are candid, my friend," said I, "and your frankness, alone, would be inestimable in this age of deceit, and country of hypocrisy."

"Ah, sir!" said my new acquaintance, "I see already that you are one of those persons who look to the dark side of things; for my part, I think the present age the best that ever existed, and our country the most virtuous in Europe."

"I congratulate you, Mr. Optimist, on your opinions," quoth I; "but your observation leads me to suppose that you are both an historian and a traveler; am I right?"

"Why," answered the box-bearer, "I *have* dabbled a little in books, and wandered *not* a little among men. I am just returned from Germany, and am now going to my friends in London. I am charged with this box of goods. God send me the luck to deliver it safe!"

"Amen," said I; "and with that prayer and this trifle I wish you a good morning."

"Thank you a thousand times, sir, for both," replied the man, "but do add to your favors by informing me of the right road to the town of ———."

"I am going in that direction myself; if you choose to accompany me part of the way, I can insure your not missing the rest.".

"Your honor is too good!" returned he of the box, rising and slinging his fardel across him; "it is but seldom that a gentleman of your rank will condescend to walk three paces with *one* of mine. You smile, sir; perhaps you think I should not class myself among gentlemen; and yet I have as good a right to the name as most of the set. I belong to no trade, I follow no calling; I rove where I list, and rest where I please; in short, I know no occupation but my indolence, and no law but my will. Now, sir, may I not call myself a gentleman?"

"Of a surety," quoth I. "You seem to me to hold a middle rank between a half-pay captain and the king of the gypsies."

"You have it, sir," rejoined my companion with a slight laugh. He was now by my side, and as we walked on, I had leisure more minutely to examine him. He was a middle-sized and rather athletic man; apparently about the age of thirty-eight. He was attired in a dark blue frock-coat, which was neither shabby nor new, but ill-made, and much too large and long for its present possessor; beneath this was a faded velvet waistcoat, that had formerly, like the Persian ambassador's tunic, "blushed with crimson and blazed with gold," but which might now have been advantageously exchanged in Monmouth Street for the lawful sum of two shillings and ninepence; under this was an inner vest of the cashmere shawl pattern, which seemed much too new for the rest of the dress. Though his shirt was of a very unwashed hue, I remarked, with some suspicion, that it was of a very respectable fineness; and a pin, which might be paste, or could be diamond, peeped below a tattered and dingy black kid stock, like a gipsy's eye beneath her hair.

His trousers were of a light gray, and the justice of Providence, or of the tailor, avenged itself upon them for the prodigal length bestowed upon their ill-assorted companion, the coat; for they were much too tight for the muscular limbs they concealed, and, rising far above the ankle, exhibited the whole of a thick Wellington boot, which was the very picture of Italy upon the map.

The face of the man was commonplace and ordinary—one sees a hundred such every day in Fleet Street or on 'Change,—the features were small, irregular, and somewhat flat; yet when you looked twice upon the countenance, there was something marked and singular in the expression, which fully atoned for the commonness of the features. The right eye turned away from the left in that watchful squint which seemed constructed on the same con siderate plan as those Irish guns, made for shooting round a corner; his eyebrows were large and shaggy, and greatly resembled bramble bushes, in which his fox-like eyes had taken refuge. Round these vulpine retreats was a labyrinthean maze of those wrinkles, vulgarly called crow's feet; deep, intricate, and intersected, they seemed for all the world like the web of a chancery suit. Singular enough, the rest of the countenance was perfectly smooth and unindented; even the lines from the nostrils to the corners of the mouth, usually so deeply traced in men of his age, were scarcely more apparent than in a boy of eighteen.

His smile was frank, his voice clear and hearty, his address open, and much superior to his apparent rank of life, claiming somewhat of equality, yet conceding a great deal of respect; but, notwithstanding all these certain favorable points, there was a sly and cunning expression in his perverse and vigilant eye and all the wrinkled demesnes in its vicinity, that made me mistrust even while I liked my companion: perhaps, indeed, he was too frank, too familiar, too *dégagé*, to be quite natural. Your honest men soon buy reserve by experience. Rogues are communicative and open, because confidence and openness costs them nothing. To finish the description of my new acquaintance, I should observe that there was something in his countenance which struck me as not wholly unfamiliar; it was one of those which we have not, in all human probability, seen before, and yet which (perhaps from their very commonness) we imagine we have encountered a hundred times.

We walked on briskly, notwithstanding the warmth of the day; in fact, the air was so pure, the grass so green, the laughing noonday so full of the hum, the motion and the life of creation, that the feeling produced was rather that of freshness and invigoration than of languor and heat.

"We have a beautiful country, sir," said my hero of the box. "It is like walking through a garden, after the more sterile and sullen features of the continent. A pure mind, sir, loves the country; for my part, I am always disposed to burst out in thanksgiving to Providence when I behold its works, and, like the valleys in the Psalm, I am ready to laugh and sing."

"An enthusiast," said I, "as well as a philosopher! perhaps, (and I believe it likely) I have the honor of addressing a poet, also?"

"Why, sir," replied the man, "I have made verses in my life; in short, there is little I have not done, for I was always a lover of variety; but, perhaps, your honor will let me return the suspicion. Are *you* not a favorite of the muse?"

"I cannot say that I am," said I. "I value myself only on my common sense—the very antipodes to genius, you know, according to the orthodox belief."

"Common sense!" repeated my companion, with a singular and meaning smile, and a twinkle with his left eye. "Common sense! Ah, that is not my *forte*, sir. You, I dare say, are one of those gentlemen whom it is very difficult to take in, either passively or actively, by appearance, or in act? For my part, I have been a dupe all my life—a child might cheat me! I am the most unsuspicious person in the world."

"Too candid by half," thought I. "This man is certainly a rascal; but what is that to me? I shall never see him again," and true to my love of never losing an opportunity of ascertaining individual character, I observed that I thought such an acquaintance very valuable, especially if he were in trade; it was a pity, therefore, for my sake, that my companion had informed me that he followed no calling.

"Why, sir," said he, "I *am* occasionally in employment; my nominal profession is that of a broker. I buy shawls and handkerchiefs of poor countesses, and retail them to rich plebeians. I fit up new-married couples with linen at a more moderate rate than the shops, and procure the bridegroom his present of jewels at forty per cent less than the jewelers; nay, I am as friendly to an intrigue as a marriage; and, when I cannot sell my jewels, I will my good offices. A gentleman so handsome as your honor may have an affair upon your hands; if so, you may rely upon my secrecy and zeal. In short, I am an innocent, good-natured fellow, who does harm to no one or nothing, and good to every one for something."

"I admire your code," quoth I, "and whenever I want a mediator between Venus and myself, I will employ you. Have you always followed your present idle profession, or were you brought up to any other?"

"I was intended for a silversmith," answered my friend, "but Providence willed it otherwise. They taught me from childhood to repeat the Lord's prayer. Heaven heard me, and delivered me from temptation,—there is, indeed, something terribly seducing in the face of a silver spoon."

"Well," said I, "you are the honestest knave that ever I met, and one would trust you with one's purse, for the ingenuousness with which you own you would steal it. Pray, think you, is it probable that I have ever had the happiness of meeting you before? I cannot help fancying so—as yet I have never been in the watch-house or the Old Bailey, my reason tells me that I must be mistaken."

"Not at all, sir," returned my worthy; "I remember you well, for I never saw a face like yours that I did *not* remember. I had the honor of sipping some British liquors in the same room with yourself one evening; you were then in company with my friend, Mr. Gordon."

"Ha!" said I, "I thank you for the hint. I now remember well, by the same token, that he told me you were the most ingenious gentleman in England, and that you had a happy propensity of mistaking other people's possessions for your own. I congratulate myself upon so desirable an acquaintance."

My friend smiled with his usual blandness, and made me a low bow of acknowledgment before he resumed:

"No doubt, sir, Mr. Gordon informed you right. I flatter myself few understand better than myself the art of appropriation, though I say it who should not say it. I deserve the reputation I have acquired, sir: I have always had ill-fortune to struggle against, and always have remedied it by two virtues—perseverance and ingenuity. To give you an idea of my ill-fortune, know that I have been taken up twenty-three times on suspicion; of my perseverance, know that I have been taken up *justly*; and, of my ingenuity, know that I have been twenty-three times let off, because there was not a tittle of legal evidence against me!"

"I venerate your talents, Mr. Jonson," replied I, "if by the name of Jonson it pleaseth you to be called, although, like the heathen deities, I presume that you have many titles, whereof some are more grateful to your ears than others."

"Nay," answered the man of two virtues, "I am never ashamed of my name; indeed, I have never done anything to disgrace me. I have never indulged in low company nor profligate debauchery; whatever I have executed by way of profession has been done in a superior and artist-like manner, not in the rude, bungling fashion of other adventurers. Moreover, I have always had a taste for polite literature, and went once as an apprentice to a publishing bookseller, for the sole purpose of reading the new works before they came out. In fine, I have never neglected any opportunity of improving my mind; and the worst that can be said against me is: that I have remembered my catechism, and taken all possible pains to learn and labor truly to get my living, and to do my duty in that state of life to which it has pleased Providence to call me."

"I have often heard," answered I, "that there is *honor* among thieves; I am happy to learn from you that there is also religion; your baptismal sponsors must be proud of so diligent a godson."

"They ought to be, sir," replied Mr. Jonson, "for I gave them the first specimens of my address; the story is long, but, if you ever give me an opportunity, I will relate it."

"Thank you," said I; "meanwhile I must wish you good-morning; your way now lies to the right. I return you my best thanks for your condescension, in accompanying so undistinguished an individual as myself."

"Oh, never mention it, your honor," rejoined Mr. Jonson. "I am always too happy to walk with a gentleman of your 'common sense.' Farewell, sir; may we meet again!" So saying, Mr. Jonson struck into his new road, and we parted.

I went home, musing on my adventure, and delighted with my adventurer. When I was about three paces from the door of my home, I was accosted in a most pitiful tone, by a poor old beggar, apparently in the last extreme of misery and disease. Notwithstanding my political economy, I was moved into alms-giving by a spectacle so wretched. I put my hand into my pocket, my purse was gone; and, on searching the other, lo! my handkerchief, my pocket-book, and a gold locket, which had belonged to Madame D'Anville, had vanished, too.

One does not keep company with men of two virtues and receive compliments upon one's common sense, for nothing!

The beggar still continued to importune me.

"Give him some food and half a crown," said I to my landlady.

Two hours afterward she came up to me: "Oh, sir! my silver teapot—*that villain, the beggar!*"

A light flashed upon me. "Ah, Mr. Job Jonson! Mr. Job Jonson!" cried I, in an indescribable rage; "out of my sight, woman! out of my sight!" I stopped short; my speech failed me. Never tell me that shame is the companion of guilt! The sinful knave is never so ashamed of himself as is the innocent fool who suffers by him.

OLIVER GOLDSMITH.

OLIVER GOLDSMITH was born in 1728; died 1774. He was an Irishman, and his parents were quite poor. At the age of seventeen, Oliver went to Trinity College, Dublin, as a sizar. In this school he had to pay nothing for food and tuition, but he had to perform some menial service. He obtained his bachelor's degree, and left the university. Goldsmith was not a brilliant and attentive student. He became the common butt of boys and master, and was flogged as a dunce in school-room. He tried several professions, but all without success. Eighteen months were spent in studying medicine at Edinburgh, then some time pretending to be studying physic at Leyden. At the age of twenty-seven he left school, with a mere smattering of medical knowledge, and with no property but his clothes and flute.

Next, Goldsmith commenced his wanderings. He rambled on foot through Flanders, France, Switzerland, Italy, " playing tunes which everywhere set the peasantry dancing." His flute frequently gained him meals and bed. Upon his return to England, he obtained a medical appointment in the service of the East India Company, but the appointment was speedily revoked. At last he took a garret, and at thirty commenced to toil like a galley slave.

[" Goldsmith's fame as a poet is secured by the *Traveler*, and the *Deserted Village*."] He wrote the *Vicar of Wakefield*, a novel of much merit. *Good-natured Man, She Stoops to Conquer*, and many other good plays were written by him

OLIVER GOLDSMITH.

for the stage. He also wrote for the use of schools, a *History of Rome*, *History of England*, *of Greece*, and a *Natural History*. His knowledge, however, was not accurate enough to make his histories very valuable. Dr. Johnson says of his *Natural History*: "If he can tell a horse from a cow, that is the extent of his knowledge of zoology." But his ability to select and condense, enabled him to make histories that are models of arrangement and condensation, and in this respect they are valuable.

Although a sloven in his dress and life, yet he has a grace and beauty of style that is chaste and musical and fascinating. Goldsmith is one of the most beloved and brilliant of English writers,—full of tenderness and affection.

Love of Life and Age.

Age, that lessens the enjoyment of life, increases our desire of living. Those dangers, which, in the vigor of youth, we had learned to despise, assume new terrors as we grow old. Our caution increasing as our years increase, fear becomes at last the prevailing passion of the mind, and the small remainder of life is taken up in useless efforts to keep off our end, or provide for a continued existence.

Strange contradiction in our nature, and to which even the wise are liable! If I should judge of that part of life which lies before me by that which I have already seen, the prospect is hideous. Experience tells me that my past enjoyments have brought no real felicity, and sensation assures me that those I have felt are stronger than those which are yet to come. Yet experience and sensation in vain persuade; hope, more powerful than either, dresses out the distant prospect in fancied beauty; some happiness in long perspective, still beckons me to pursue; and, like a losing gamester, every new disappointment increases my ardor to continue the game.

Whence, then, is this increased love of life, which grows upon us with our years? Whence comes it, that we thus make greater efforts to preserve our existence at a period when it becomes scarce worth the keeping? Is it that nature, attentive to the preservation of mankind, increases our wish to live, while she lessens our enjoyments; and, as she robs the senses of every pleasure, equips imagination in the spoil? Life would be insupportable to an old man who, loaded with infirmities, feared death no more than when in the vigor of manhood; the numberless calamities of decaying nature, and the consciousness of surviving every pleasure would at once induce him, with his own hand, to terminate the scene of misery, but happily the contempt of death forsakes him at a time when it could only be prejudicial, and life acquires an imaginary value in proportion as its real value is no more.

Chinwang the Chaste, ascending the throne of China, commanded that all who were unjustly detained in prison during the preceding reigns should be set free. Among the number who came to thank their deliverer on this occasion there appeared a majestic old man, who, falling at the emperor's feet, addressed him as follows: "Great father of China, behold a wretch now eighty-five years old, who was shut up in a dungeon at the age of twenty-two. I was imprisoned though a stranger to crime, or without being confronted by my accusers. I have now lived in solitude and darkness for more than fifty years, and am grown familiar with distress. As yet, dazzled with the splendor of that sun to which you have restored me, I have been wandering the streets to find out some friend who would assist, or relieve, or remember me; but my friends, my family and relations are all dead, and I am forgotten. Permit me, then, O Chinwang, to wear out the wretched remains of life in my former prison; the walls of my dungeon are to me more pleasing than the most splendid palace; I have not long to live, and shall be unhappy except I spend the rest of my days where my youth was passed—in that prison from whence you were pleased to release me."

The old man's passion for confinement is similar to that we all have for life. We are habituated to the prison, we look round with discontent, are displeased with the abode, and yet the length of our captivity only increases our fondness for the cell. The trees we have planted, the houses we have built, or the posterity we have begotten, all serve to bind us closer to earth, and embitter our parting. Life sues the young like a new acquaintance; the companion, as yet unexhausted, is at once instructive and amusing; its company pleases, yet for all this it is but little regarded. To us, who are declined in years, life appears like an old friend; its jests have been anticipated in former conversation; it has no new story to make us smile, no new improvement with which to surprise, yet still we love it; destitute of every enjoyment, still we love it; husband the wasting treasure with increasing frugality, and feel all the poignancy of anguish in the fatal separation.

Sir Philip Mordaunt was young, beautiful, sincere, brave, an Englishman. He had a complete fortune of his own, and the love of the king his master, which was equivalent to riches. Life opened all her treasures before him, and promised a long succession of future happiness. He came, tasted of the entertainment, but was disgusted even at the beginning. He professed an aversion to living, was tired of walking round the same circle; had tried every enjoyment, and found them all grow weaker at every repetition. "If life be in youth so displeasing," cried he to himself, "what will it appear when age comes on? if it be at present indifferent, sure it will then be execrable." This thought embittered every reflection; till at last, with all the serenity of perverted reason, he ended the debate with a pistol! Had this self-deluded man been apprised that existence grows more desirable to us the longer we exist, he would have then faced old age without shrinking; he would have boldly dared to live, and served that society by his future assiduity which he basely injured by his desertion.

Happiness in Solitude.

I can hardly tell you, sir, how concerned I have been to see that you consider me the most miserable of men. The world, no doubt, thinks as you do, and that also distresses me. Oh! why is not the existence I have enjoyed known to the whole universe! every one would wish to procure for himself a similar lot, peace would reign upon the earth, man would no longer think of injuring his fellows, and the wicked would no longer be found, for none would have an interest in being wicked. But what, then, did I enjoy when I was alone? Myself; the entire universe; all that is; all that can be; all that is beautiful in the world of sense; all that is imaginable in the world of intellect. I gathered around me all that could delight my heart; my desires were the limit of my pleasures. No, never have the most voluptuous known such enjoyments; and

I have derived a hundred times more happiness from my chimeras than they from their realities.

When my sufferings make me measure sadly the length of the night, and the agitation of fever prevents me from enjoying a single instant of sleep, I often divert my mind from my present state, in thinking of the various events of my life; and repentance, sweet recollections, regrets, emotions, help to make me for some moments forget my sufferings. What period do you think, sir, I recall most frequently and most willingly in my dreams? Not the pleasures of my youth, they were too rare, too much mingled with bitterness, and are now too distant. I recall the period of my seclusion, of my solitary walks, of the fleeting but delicious days that I have passed entirely by myself, with my good and simple housekeeper, with my beloved dog, my old cat, with the birds of the fields, the hinds of the forest, with all nature and her inconceivable Author. In getting up before the sun to contemplate its rising from my garden, when a beautiful day was commencing, my first wish was that no letters or visits might come to disturb the charm. After having devoted the morning to various duties, that I fulfilled with pleasure, because I could have put them off to another time, I hastened to dine, that I might escape from importunate people, and insure a longer afternoon. Before one o'clock, even on the hottest days, I started in the heat of the sun with my faithful Achates, hastening my steps in the fear that some one would take possession of me before I could escape; but when once I could turn a certain corner, with what a beating heart, with what a flutter of joy, I began to breathe, as I felt that I was safe; and I said, Here now am I my own master for the rest of the day! I went on then at a more tranquil pace to seek some wild spot in the forest, some desert place, where nothing indicating the hand of man announced slavery and power—some refuge to which I could believe I was the first to penetrate, and where no wearying third could step in to interpose between Nature and me. It was there that she seemed to display before my eyes an ever new magnificence. The gold of the broom and the purple of the heath struck my sight with a splendor that touched my heart. The majesty of the trees that covered me with their shadow, the delicacy of the shrubs that flourished around me, the astonishing variety of the herbs and flowers that I crushed beneath my feet kept my mind in a continued alternation of observing and of admiring. This assemblage of so many interesting objects contending for my attention, attracting me incessantly from one to the other, fostered my dreamy and idle humor, and often made me repeat to myself, No, "even Solomon in all his glory was not arrayed like one of these."

The spot thus adorned could not long remain a desert to my imagination. I soon peopled it with beings after my own heart; and dismissing opinion, prejudices, and all factitious passions, I brought to these sanctuaries of nature men worthy of inhabiting them. I formed with these a charming society, of which I did not feel myself unworthy. I made a golden age according to my fancy, and, filling up these bright days with all the scenes of my life that had left the tenderest recollections, and with all that my heart still longed for, I affected myself to tears over the true pleasures of humanity—pleasures so delicious, so pure, and yet so far from men! Oh, if in these moments any ideas of Paris, of the age, and of my little author vanity disturbed my reveries, with what contempt I drove them instantly away, to give myself up entirely to the exquisite sentiments with which my soul was filled. Yet, in the midst of all this, I confess the nothingness of my chimeras would sometimes appear, and sadden me in a moment. If all my dreams had turned to reality, they would not have sufficed—I should still have imagined, dreamed, desired. I discovered in myself an inexplicable void that nothing could have filled—a certain yearning of my heart toward another kind of happiness, of which I had no definite idea, but of which I felt the want. Ah, sir, this even was an enjoyment, for I was filled with a lively sense of what it was, and with a delightful sadness of which I should not have wished to be deprived.

From the surface of the earth I soon raised my thoughts to all the beings of Nature, to the universal system of things, to the incomprehensible Being who enters into all. Then, as my mind was lost in this immensity, I did not think, I did not reason, I did not philosophize. I felt, with a kind of voluptuousness, as if bowed down by the weight of this universe; I gave myself up with rapture to this confusion of grand ideas. I delighted in imagination to lose myself in space; my heart, confined within the limits of the mortal, found not room; I was stifled in the universe; I would have sprung into the infinite. I think that, could I have unveiled all the mysteries of nature, my sensations would have been less delicious than was this bewildering ecstacy, to which my mind abandoned itself without control, and which, in the excitement of my transports, made me sometimes exclaim, " Oh, Great Being! oh, Great Being!" without being able to say or think more.

Thus glided on in a continued rapture the most charming days that ever human creature passed; and when the setting sun made me think of returning, astonished at the flight of time, I thought I had not taken sufficient advantage of my day; I fancied I might have enjoyed it more; and, to regain the lost time, I said,—I will come back to-morrow. I returned slowly home, my head a little fatigued, but my heart content. I reposed agreeably on my return, abandoning myself to the impression of objects, but without thinking, without imagining, without doing anything beyond feeling the calm and the happiness of my situation. I found the cloth laid upon terrace; I supped with a good appetite, amidst my little household. No feeling of servitude or dependence disturbed the good will that united us all. My dog himself was my friend, not my slave. We had always the same wish; but he never obeyed me. My gayety during the whole evening testified to my having been alone the whole day. I was very different when I had seen company. Then I was rarely contented with others, and never with myself. In the evening I was cross and taciturn. This remark was made by my housekeeper; and since she has told me so I have always found it true, when I watched myself. Lastly, after having again taken in the evening a few turns in my garden, or sung an air to my spinnet, I found in my bed repose of body and soul a hundred times sweeter than sleep itself. These were the days that have made the true happiness of my life—a happiness without bitterness, without weariness, without regret, and to which I would willingly have limited my existence. Yes, sir, let such days as these fill up my eternity; I do not ask for others, nor imagine that I am much less happy in these exquisite contemplations than the heavenly spirits. But a suffering body deprives the mind of its liberty; henceforth I am not alone; I have a guest who importunes me; I must free myself of it to be myself. The trial that I have made of these sweet enjoyments serves only to make me with less alarm await the time when I shall taste them without interruption.

Joan of Arc.

What is to be thought of her? What is to be thought of the poor shepherd girl from the hills and forests of Lorraine, that, like the Hebrew shepherd boy from the hills and forests of Judea, rose suddenly out of the quiet, out of the safety, out of the religious inspiration, rooted in deep pastoral solitudes, to a station in the van of armies, and to the more perilous station at the right hand of kings? The Hebrew boy inaugurated his patriotic mission by an act, by a victorious act, such as no man could deny. But so did the girl of Lorraine, if we read her story as it was read by those who saw her nearest. Adverse armies bore witness to the boy as no pretender; but so did they to the gentle girl. Judged by the voices of all who saw them *from a station of good-will*, both were found true and loyal to any promises involved in their first acts. Enemies it was that made the difference between their subsequent fortunes. The boy rose—to a splendor and a noonday prosperity, both personal and public, that rang through the records of his people and became a by-word amongst his posterity for a thousand years, until the scepter was departing from Judah. The poor forsaken girl, on the contrary, drank not herself from that cup of rest which she had secured for France. She never sang together with them the songs that rose in her native Domremy, as echoes to the departing steps of invaders. She mingled not in the festal dances of Vancouleurs which celebrated in rapture the redemption of France. No! for her voice was then silent. No! for her feet were dust. Pure, innocent, noble-hearted girl! whom, from earliest youth, ever I believed in as full of truth and self-sacrifice, this was amongst the strongest pledges for *thy* side, that never once—no, not for a moment of weakness—didst thou revel in the vision of coronets and honors from man. Coronets for thee! Oh, no! Honors, if they come when all is over, are for those that share thy blood. Daughter of Domremy, when the gratitude of thy king shall awaken, thou wilt be sleeping the sleep of the dead. Call her, king of France, but she will not hear thee! Cite her by thy apparitors to come and receive a robe of honor, but she will be found *in contumace*. When the thunders of universal France, as even yet may happen, shall proclaim the grandeur of the poor shepherd girl that gave up all for her country, thy ear, young shepherd girl, will have been deaf for five centuries. To suffer and to do—that was thy portion in this life; to do—never for thyself, always for others; to suffer—never in the persons of generous champions, always in thy own; that was thy destiny; and not for a moment was it hidden from thyself. "Life," thou saidst, "is short, and the sleep which is in the grave is long. Let me use that life, so transitory, for the glory of those heavenly dreams destined to comfort the sleep which is long." This poor creature, pure from every suspicion of even a visionary self-interest, even as she was pure in senses more obvious—never once did this holy child, as regarding herself, relax from her belief in the darkness that was traveling to meet her. She might not prefigure the very manner of her death; she saw not in vision, perhaps, the aerial altitude of the fiery scaffold, the spectators without end on every road pouring into Rouen as to a coronation, the surging smoke, the volleying flames, the hostile faces all around, the pitying eye that lurked but here and there

until nature and imperishable truth broke loose from artificial
restraints; these might not be apparent through the mists of the
hurrying future. But the voice that called her to death, *that* she
heard forever.

Great was the throne of France even in those days, and great
was he that sat upon it; but well Joanna knew that not the throne,
nor he that sat upon it, was for *her;* but, on the contrary, that she
was for *them;* not she by them, but they by her, should rise from
the dust. Gorgeous were the lilies of France, and for centuries had
the privilege to spread their beauty over land and sea, until in another
century the wrath of God and man combined to wither them; but
well Joanna knew, early at Domremy she had read that bitter truth,
that the lilies of France would decorate no garland for *her.* Flower
nor bud, bell nor blossom would ever bloom for *her.*

On the Wednesday after Trinity Sunday in 1431, being then
about nineteen years of age, the Maid of Arc underwent her mar-
tyrdom. She was conducted before midday, guarded by eight
hundred spearmen, to a platform of prodigious height, constructed
of wooden billets, supported by hollow spaces in every direction,
for the creation of air currents. "The pile struck terror," says M.
Michelet, "by its height."

There would be a certainty of calumny rising against her—
some people would impute to her a willingness to recant. No innocence could escape *that.* Now, had she really testified this willingness on the scaffold, it would have argued nothing at all but the
weakness of a genial nature shrinking from the instant approach of
torment. And those will often pity that weakness most, who in
their own persons would yield to it least. Meantime there never
was a calumny uttered that drew less support from the recorded
circumstances. It rests upon no positive testimony, and it has
weight of contradicting testimony to stem.

What else but her meek, saintly demeanor won, from the enemies that till now had believed her a witch, tears of rapturous
admiration? "Ten thousand men," says M. Michelet himself, "ten
thousand men wept;" and of these ten thousand the majority were

political enemies knitted together by cords of superstition. What else was it but her constancy. united with her angelic gentleness, that drove the fanatic English soldier—who had sworn to throw a fagot on her scaffold as *his* tribute of abhorrence, that *did* so, that fulfilled his vow—suddenly to turn away a penitent for life, saying everywhere that he had seen a dove rising upon wings to heaven from the ashes where she had stood? What else drove the executioner to kneel at every shrine for pardon to his share in the tragedy? And if all this were insufficient, then I cite the closing act of her life as valid on her behalf, were all other testimonies against her. The executioner had been directed to apply his torch from below. He did so. The fiery smoke rose up in billowy columns. A Dominican monk was then standing almost at her side. Wrapped up in his sublime office, he saw not the danger, but still persisted in his prayers. Even then when the last enemy was racing up the fiery stairs to seize her, even at that moment did this noblest of girls think only for *him*, the one friend that would not forsake her, and not herself; bidding him with her last breath to care for his own preservation, but to leave *her* to God. That girl, whose latest breath ascended in this sublime expression of self-oblivion, did not utter the word *recant* either with her lips or in her heart. No, she did not, though one should rise from the dead to swear it.

How Curious It Is.

When the life of Daniel Webster—that grand drama—was about drawing to a close, he is represented to have said, "Life—Life—how curious it is!" The word curious was deemed a strange one, but it expressed the very thing. How curious life is, from the cradle to the grave! The forming mind of childhood, busy with the present, and unable to guess the secret of its own existence, is curious. The hopes of youth are curious, reaching forward into the future, and building castles in the perspective for those who entertain them, that will fade away in the sunlight of an older experience. How curious is the first dawning of love; when the young heart surrenders itself to its dreams of bliss, illumined with moonshine! How curious it is, when marriage crowns the wishes, to find the cares of life but begun, and the path all strewn with anxieties that romance had depicted as a road of flowers! How curious it is, says the young mother, as she spreads upon her own the tiny hand of her child, and endeavors to read, in its dim lines, the fortune there hidden! Curious, indeed, would such revealing be. How curious is the greed for gain that controls too much the life of man, leading him away after strange gods, forgetting all the object and good of life in a chase for a phantom light, that ends at last in three-fold Egyptian darkness! How curious is the love of life that clings to the old, and draws them back imploringly to earth, begging for a longer look at time and its frivolities, with eternity and all its joys within their reach! How curious it is, when at length the great end draws nigh,—the glazing eye, the struggle, the groan, proclaiming dissolution, and the still clay—so still!—that lately stood by our side in the pride of health and happiness! How curious it is that the realities of the immortal world should be based upon the crumbling vanities of this, and that the path to infinite life should be through the dark shadow of the grave! How curious it is, in its business and its pleasures, its joys and its sorrows, its hopes and its fears, its temptations and its triumphs; and, as we contemplate life in all its manifestations, we needs must exclaim, "How curious it is!"

The Puritans.

The Puritans were men whose minds had derived a peculiar character from the daily contemplation of superior beings and eternal interests. Not content with acknowledging, in general terms, an over-ruling Providence, they habitually ascribed every event to the will of the Great Being, for whose power nothing was too vast, for whose inspection nothing was too minute. To know him, to serve him, to enjoy him, was with them the great end of existence. They rejected with contempt the ceremonious homage which other sects substituted for the pure worship of the soul. Instead of catching occasional glimpses of the Deity through an obscuring veil, they aspired to gaze full on the intolerable brightness, and to commune with him face to face. Hence originated their contempt for terrestrial distinctions. The difference between the greatest and the meanest of mankind seemed to vanish, when compared with the boundless interval which separated the whole race from him on whom their own eyes were constantly fixed. They recognized no title to superiority but his favor; and, confident of that favor, they despised all the accomplishments and all the dignities of the world. If they were unacquainted with the works of philosophers and poets, they were deeply read in the oracles of God. If their names were not found in the registers of heralds, they felt assured that they were recorded in the Book of Life. If their steps were not accompanied by a splendid train of menials, legions of ministering angels had charge over them. Their palaces were houses not made with hands; their diadems crowns of glory which should never fade away. On the rich and the eloquent, on nobles and priests, they looked down with contempt; for they esteemed them-

selves rich in a more precious treasure, and eloquent in a more
sublime language, nobles by the right of an earlier creation, and
priests by the imposition of a mightier hand. The very meanest
of them was a being to whose fate a mysterious and terrible importance belonged,—on whose slightest actions the spirits of light
and darkness looked with anxious interest,—who had been destined,
before heaven and earth were created, to enjoy a felicity which
should continue when heaven and earth should have passed away.
Events which short-sighted politicians ascribed to earthly causes
had been ordained on his account. For his sake empires had risen,
and flourished, and decayed. For his sake the Almighty had pro-
claimed his will by the pen of the evangelist and the harp of the
prophet. He had been rescued by no common deliverer from the
grasp of no common foe. He had been ransomed by the sweat of
no vulgar agony, by the blood of no earthly sacrifice. It was for
him that the sun had been darkened, that the rocks had been rent,
that the dead had arisen, that all nature had shuddered at the
sufferings of her expiring God.

Thus the Puritan was made up of two different men: the one
all self-abasement, penitence, gratitude, passion; the other proud,
calm, inflexible, sagacious. He prostrated himself in the dust before his Maker; but he set his foot on the neck of his king. In his
devotional retirement, he prayed with convulsions, and groans,
and tears. He was half maddened by glorious or terrible illusions.
He heard the lyres of angels or the tempting whispers of fiends.
He caught a gleam of the Beatific Vision, or woke screaming from
dreams of everlasting fire. Like Vane, he thought himself intrusted
with the scepter of the millennial year. Like Fleetwood, he cried
in the bitterness of his soul that God had hid his face from him.
But when he took his seat in the council, or girt on his sword for
war, these tempestuous workings of the soul had left no perceptible
trace behind them. People who saw nothing of the godly but their
uncouth visages, and heard nothing from them but their groans and
their whining hymns, might laugh at them. But those had little
reason to laugh who encountered them in the hall of debate or on the

field of battle. These fanatics brought to civil and military affairs a coolness of judgment and an immutability of purpose which some writers have thought inconsistent with their religious zeal, but which were, in fact, the necessary effect of it. The intensity of their feeling on one subject made them tranquil on the other. One overpowering sentiment had subjected to itself pity and hatred, ambition and fear. Death had lost its terrors, and pleasure its charms. They had their smiles and their tears, their raptures and their sorrows, but not for the things of this world. Enthusiasm had made them stoics, had cleared their minds from every vulgar passion and prejudice, and raised them above the influence of danger and of corruption. It sometimes might lead them to pursue unwise ends, but never to choose unwise means.

Changes of Matter.

The universe is everywhere in motion. The atmosphere is agitated by winds; the world of waters is in perpetual circulation; plants and animals spring from the earth and air and return to them again; all substances around us are undergoing slow transformation; the stony record of the strata are but histories of past revolutions; our ponderous earth shoots swiftly along its orbit, while the mighty sun, with all its attendant planets, is sweeping on forever through shoreless space. Nothing around or within us is absolutely at rest.

RALPH WALDO EMERSON.

R. W. EMERSON was born in Boston, May 25, 1813. He was graduated at Harvard College in 1821, at the age of 17. He taught school several years, then entered the ministry. From 1829 to 1832 he preached in Boston, but on account of a change in his opinions he left the church and ministry and sailed for Europe. After a year's absence he returned home, took up his residence at Concord and entered the lecture field. Although meeting opposition, yet he advanced steadily to the highest point of excellence in his chosen work. He discussed a subject in his lectures until he had fully matured the plan and matter for a book, when he presented the subject to the public in book form.

The following are Emerson's published volumes: *Nature*, issued in 1836; two series of *Essays*, 1841-4; *Poems*, 1846; *Miscellanies*, 1849; *Representative Men*, 1850; *English Traits*, 1856; *The Conduct of Life*, 1860; *May Day and Other Pieces*, 1867; *Society and Solitude*, 1870. He edited *Parnassus* in 1875. His peculiar philosophy is set forth in *Nature* and *The American Scholar*, an oration published in 1837.

Emerson is not a philosopher solely; he stands rather on the height where poetry and philosophy meet. He never argues and never pursues with strictness a train of thought. He is a disciple of no one master—neither of Plato, Kant, or Comte. He has established no school, intellectual or moral. But with wonderfully sharp perception he has looked into the vast drama of the universe, the mystery of existence, and

RALPH WALDO EMERSON.

the powers of the soul. With equal acuteness he has observed the manifestations of nature in plants and animals. And in a long lifetime he has mastered and assimilated the wisdom of centuries. His vivid imagination supplies him with figures that are as brilliant and enduring as diamonds. But all he sees is with a poet's eye. The course of empires, the development of the arts, the learning of scholars, the beauty of landscapes, furnish hints to his all-absorbing mind; but the separate ideas never coalesce into a system. His essays are full of golden veins and imbedded gems; a whole dictionary of quotations could be made from them. His poems have the same qualities, and sparkle with aphoristic lines: but his sense of melody or his command of meter is limited, and his verses sometimes have a simple and rustic monotony of cadence, like the oft-repeated plaint of a wild bird.

Beauty.

The poets are quite right in decking their mistresses with the spoils of the landscape, flower gardens, gems, rainbows, flushes of morning and stars of night, since all beauty points at identity, and whatsoever thing does not express to me the sea and sky, day and night, is somewhat forbidden and wrong. Into every beautiful object there enters somewhat immeasurable and divine, and just as much bounded by outlines, like mountains on the horizon, as into tones of music or depths of space. Polarized light showed the secret architecture of bodies; and when the second-sight of the mind is opened, now one color, or form, or gesture, and now another, has a pungency, as if a more interior ray had been emitted, disclosing its deep holdings in the frame of things.

The laws of this translation we do not know, or why one feature or gesture enchants, why one word or syllable intoxicates, but the fact is familiar that the fine touch of the eye, or a grace of manners, or a phrase of poetry, plants wings at our shoulders; as if the Divinity, in his approaches, lifts away mountains of obstruction, and designs to draw a truer line, which the mind knows and owns. This is that haughty force of beauty, *vis superba formæ*, which the poets praise—under calm and precise outline, the immeasurable and divine—beauty hiding all wisdom and power in its calm sky.

All high beauty has a moral element in it, and I find the antique sculpture as ethical as Marcus Antoninus, and the beauty ever in proportion to the depth of thought. Gross and impure natures, however decorated, seem impure shambles; but character gives splendor to youth, and awe to wrinkled skin and gray hairs. An adorer of truth we cannot choose but obey, and the woman who has shared with us the moral sentiments—her locks must appear to us sublime. Thus, there is a climbing scale of culture, from the first agreeable sensation which a sparkling gem or a scarlet stain affords the eye, up through fair outlines and details of the landscape, features of the human face and form, signs and tokens of thought and character in manners, up to the ineffable mysteries of the human intellect. Wherever we begin, thither our steps tend; an ascent from the joy of a horse in his trappings up to the perception of Newton, that the globe on which we ride is only a larger apple falling from a larger tree; up to the perception of Plato, that globe and universe are rude and early expression of an all-dissolving unity—the first stair on the scale to the temple of the mind.

Old Age.

When life has been well spent, age is a loss of what it can well spare—muscular strength, organic instincts, gross bulk, and works that belong to these. But the central wisdom, which was old in infancy, is young in fourscore years, and, dropping off obstructions, leaves in happy subjects the mind purified and wise. I have heard that whoever loves is in no condition old. I have heard that whenever the name of man is spoken the doctrine of immortality is announced; it cleaves to his constitution. The mode of it baffles our wit, and no whisper comes to us from the other side. But the inference from the working of intellect, living knowledge, living skill—at the end of life just ready to be born—affirms the inspirations of affection and of the moral sentiment.

Character of Washington.

I think I knew General Washington intimately and thoroughly; and were I called on to delineate his charater, it would be in terms like these:

His mind was great and powerful, without being of the very first order; his penetration strong, though not so acute as that of a Newton, Bacon, or Locke; and as far as he saw, no judgment was ever sounder. It was slow in operation, being little aided by invention or imagination, but sure in conclusion. Hence the common remark of his officers, of the advantage he derived from councils of war, where, hearing all suggestions, he selected whatever was best; and certainly no general ever planned his battles more judiciously. But if deranged during the course of the action, if any member of his plan was dislocated by sudden circumstances, he was slow in a re-adjustment. The consequence was, that he often failed in the field, and rarely against an enemy in station, as at Boston and York. He was incapable of fear, meeting personal dangers with the calmest unconcern. Perhaps the strongest feature in his character was prudence, never acting until every circumstance, every consideration was maturely weighed; refraining, if he saw doubt; but, when once decided, going through with his purpose, whatever obstacles opposed. His integrity was the most pure, his justice the most inflexible I have ever known; no motives of interest or consanguinity, of friendship or hatred, being able to bias his decision. He was, indeed, in every sense of the words, a wise, a good and great man. His temper was naturally irritable and high-toned; but reflection and resolution had obtained a firm and habitual ascendancy over it. If ever, however, it broke its bounds, he was most tremendous in his wrath. In his expenses he was honorable, but exact; liberal in contributions to whatever promised utility; but frowning and unyielding on all visionary projects and all unworthy calls on his charity. His heart was not warm in its affections; but he exactly calculated every man's value, and gave him a solid esteem proportioned to it. His person, you know, was fine; his stature exactly what one would wish; his deportment easy, erect, and noble; the best horseman of his age, and the most graceful figure that could be seen on horseback. Although in the circle of his friends, where he might be unreserved with safety, he took a free share in conversation, his colloquial talents were not above mediocrity, possessing neither copiousness of ideas nor fluency of words. In public, when called on for a sudden opinion, he was unready, short, and embarrassed. Yet he wrote readily, rather diffusely, in an easy and correct style. This he had acquired by conversation with the world, for his education was merely reading, writing, and common arithmetic, to which he added surveying, at a later day. His time was employed in action chiefly, reading little, and that only in agricultural and English history. His correspondence became necessarily extensive, and, with journalizing, his agricultural proceedings occupied most of his leisure hours within doors. On the whole, his character was in its mass, perfect; in nothing bad, in few points indifferent; and it may truly be said, that never did nature and fortune combine more perfectly to make a man great, and to place him in the same constellation with whatever worthies have merited from man an everlasting remembrance. For his was the singular destiny and merit of leading the armies of his country successfully through an arduous war, for the establishment of its independence; of conducting its councils through the birth of a government, new in its forms and principles, until it had settled down into a quiet and orderly train; and of scrupulously obeying the laws through the whole of his career, civil and military, of which the history of the world furnishes no other example.

Poor Richard.

I have heard that nothing gives an author so great pleasure as to find his works respectfully quoted by others. Judge, then, how much I must have been gratified by an incident I am going to relate to you. I stopped my horse, lately, where a great number of people were collected at an auction of merchant's goods. The hour of sale not being come, they were conversing on the badness of the times; and one of the company called to a plain, clean old man, with white locks, "Pray, father Abraham, what think you of the times? Will not those heavy taxes quite ruin the country? How shall we ever be able to pay them? What would you advise us to?" Father Abraham stood up, and replied, "If you would have my advice, I will give it you in short, 'for a word to the wise is enough,' as poor Richard says." They joined in desiring him to speak his mind, and gathering round him, he proceeded as follows:—

"Friends," says he, "the taxes are indeed very heavy; and, if those laid on by the Government were the only ones we had to pay, we might more easily discharge them; but we have many others, and much more grievous to some of us. We are taxed twice as much by our idleness, three times as much by our pride, and four times as much by our folly; and from these taxes the commissioners cannot ease or deliver us by allowing an abatement. However, let us hearken to good advice, and something may be done for us; 'God helps them that helps themselves,' as poor Richard says.

"I. It would be thought a hard Government that should tax its people one-tenth part of their time to be employed in its service; but idleness taxes many of us much more; sloth, by bringing on diseases, absolutely shortens life. 'Sloth, like rust, consumes faster than labor wears, while the used key is always bright,' as poor Richard says. 'But dost thou love life, then do not squander time, for that is the stuff life is made of,' as poor Richard says. How much more than is necessary do we spend in sleep; forgetting that 'the sleeping fox catches no poultry, and that there will be sleeping enough in the grave,' as poor Richard says.

"If time be of all things the most precious, wasting time must be, as poor Richard says, 'the greatest prodigality;' since, as he elsewhere tells us, 'Lost time is never found again; and what we call time enough, always proves little enough.' Let us then up and be doing, and doing to the purpose, so by diligence shall we do more with less perplexity. 'Sloth makes all things difficult, but industry all easy, and he that riseth late, must trot all day and shall scarce overtake his business at night; while laziness travels so slowly, that poverty soon overtakes him. Drive thy business, let not that drive thee; and 'early to bed, and early to rise, makes a man healthy, wealthy, and wise,' as poor Richard says.

"So what signifies wishing and hoping for better times? We may make these times better, if we bestir ourselves. 'Industry need not wish, and he that lives upon hope will die fasting. There are no gains without pains; then help hands for I have no lands, or if I have, they are smartly taxed. 'He that hath a trade hath an estate; and he that hath a calling, hath an office of profit and honor,' as poor Richard says; but then the trade must be worked at, and the calling well followed, or neither the estate nor the office will enable us to pay our taxes. If we are industrious, we shall never starve; for 'at the workingman's house hunger looks in but dares not enter.' Nor will the bailiff or the constable enter, for 'industry pays debts, while despair increaseth them.' What though you have found no treasure, nor has any rich relation left a legacy, 'Diligence is the mother of good luck, and God gives all things to industry. Then plow deep, while sluggards sleep, and you shall have corn to sell and to keep.' Work while it is called to-day, for you know not how much you may be hindred to-morrow. 'One to-day is worth two to-morrows,' as poor Richard says; and further, 'Never leave that till to-morrow which you can do to-day.' If you were a servant, would you not be ashamed that a good master should catch you idle? Are you then your own master? Be ashamed to catch yourself idle, when there is so much to be done for yourself, your family, your country, and your king. 'Handle your tools without mittens; remember that 'the cat in gloves catches no mice,' as poor Richard says. It is true there is much to be done, and, perhaps, you are weak-handed; but stick to it steadily, and you will see great effects; for 'constant dropping wears away stones;' and 'by diligence and patience the mouse ate in two the cable;' and 'little strokes fell great oaks.'

"Methinks I hear some of you say, 'Must a man afford himself no leisure?' I will tell thee, my friend, what poor Richard says: 'Employ thy time well, if thou meanest to gain leisure; and, since thou art not sure of a minute, throw not away an hour.' Leisure is time for doing something useful; this leisure the diligent man will obtain, but the lazy man never; for, 'A life of leisure and a life of laziness are two things. Many, without labor, would live by their wits only, but they break for want of stock;' whereas industry gives comfort, and plenty, and respect. 'Fly pleasures and they will follow you. The diligent spinner has a large shift, and now I have a sheep and a cow, everybody bids me good-morrow.'

"II. But with our industry we must likewise be steady, settled and careful, and oversee our own affairs with our own eyes, and not trust too much to others, for, as poor Richard says—

> 'I never saw an oft removed tree,
> Nor yet an oft removed family,
> That throve so well as those that settled be.

And again, 'Three removes are as bad as a fire;' and again, 'Keep thy shop, and thy shop will keep thee;' and again, 'If you would have your business done, go; if not, send;' and again—

> 'He that by the plow would thrive,
> Himself must either hold or drive.'

And again, 'The eye of the master will do more work than both his hands;' and again, 'Want of care does more damage than want of knowledge;' and again, 'Not to oversee workmen, is to leave them your purse open.' Trusting too much to others' care is the ruin of many; for 'In the affairs of this world, men are saved, not by faith, but by the want of it;' but a man's own care is profitable, for 'If you would have a faithful servant, and one that you like, serve yourself. A little neglect may breed great mischief; for want of a nail the shoe was lost; for want of a shoe the horse was lost; for want of a horse the rider was lost,' being overtaken and slain by the enemy; all for the want of a little care about a horse-shoe nail.

"III. So much for industry, my friends, and attention to one's own business; but to these we must add frugality, if we would make our industry more certainly successful. A man may, if he knows not how to save as he gets, 'keep his nose all his life to the grindstone, and die not worth a groat at last. A fat kitchen makes a lean will;' and—

> 'Many estates are spent in the getting,
> Since women for tea forsook spinning and knitting,
> And men for punch forsook hewing and splitting.'

'If you would be wealthy, think of saving, as well as of getting. The Indies have not made Spain rich, because her outgoes are greater than her incomes.'

"Away, then, with your expensive follies, and you will not then have so much cause to complain of hard times, heavy taxes, and chargeable families; for—

> 'Women and wine, game and deceit,
> Make the wealth small, and the want great.'"

And further, 'What maintains one vice, would bring up two children.' You may think, perhaps, that a little tea or a little punch now and then, diet a little more costly, clothes a little finer, and a little entertainment now and then, can be no great matter; but remember, 'Many a little makes a mickle.' Beware of little expenses; 'A small leak will sink a great ship,' as poor Richard says; and again, 'Who dainties love, shall beggars prove;' and moreover, 'Fools make feasts, and wise men eat them.' Here you are all got together to this sale of fineries and nicknacks. You call them goods; but, if you do not care, they will prove evils to some of you. You expect they will be sold cheap, and, perhaps, they may for less than they cost; but, if you have no occasion for them, they must be dear to you. Remember what poor Richard says: 'Buy those that thou hast no need of, and ere long thou shalt sell thy necessaries.' And again, 'At a great pennyworth pause a while;' he means, that perhaps the cheapness is apparent only, and not real; or the bargain, by straitening thee in thy business, may do thee more harm than good. For in another place he says, 'Many have been ruined by buying good pennyworths.' Again, 'It is foolish to lay out money in a purchase of repentance;' and yet this folly is practiced every day at auctions, for want of minding the Almanack. Many a one, for the sake of finery on the back, have gone with a hungry belly, and half starved their families; 'silks and satins, scarlet and velvets put out the kitchen fire,' as poor Richard says. These are not the necessaries of life; they can scarcely be called the conveniences; and yet, only because they look pretty, how many want to have them! By these and other extravagances, the greatest are reduced to poverty, and forced to borrow of those whom they formerly despised, but who, through industry and frugality, have maintained their standing; in which case it appears plainly, that 'A plowman on his legs is higher than a gentleman on his knees,' as poor Richard says. Perhaps they have had a small estate left them, which they knew not the getting of; they think, 'It is day, and will never be night;' 'that a little to be spent out of so much is not worth minding; but 'Always taking out of the meal-tub and never putting in soon comes to the bottom,' as poor Richard says; and then 'When the well is dry, they know the worth of water.' But this they might have known before, if they had taken his advice. 'If you would know the value of money, go and try to borrow some; for he that goes a borrowing goes a sorrowing,' as poor Richard says; and, indeed, so does he that lends to such people, when he goes to get it in again. Poor Dick further advises, and says,—

'Fond pride of dress is sure a very curse;
Ere fancy you consult, consult your purse.'

And again, 'Pride is as loud a beggar as want, and a great deal more saucy.' When you have bought one fine thing, you must buy ten more, that your appearance may be all of a piece; but poor Dick says, 'It is easier to suppress the first desire, than to satisfy all that follow it.' And it is as truly folly for the poor to ape the rich, as for the frog to swell, in order to equal the ox.

> 'Vessels large may venture more,
> But little boats should keep near shore.'

"It is, however, a folly soon punished; for, as poor Richard says, 'Pride that dines on vanity sups on contempt; pride breakfasted with plenty, dined with poverty, and supped with infamy.' And after all, of what use is this pride of appearance, for which so much is risked, so much is suffered? It cannot promote health, nor ease pain; it makes no increase of merit in the person; it creates envy, it hastens misfortune.

"But what madness it must be to run in debt for these superfluities! We are offered, by the terms of this sale, six months credit; and that, perhaps, has induced some of us to attend it, because we cannot spare the ready money, and hope now to be fine without it. But, ah! think what you do when you run in debt; you give to another power over your liberty. If you cannot pay at the time, you will be ashamed to see your creditor; you will be in fear when you speak to him; you will make poor, pitiful, sneaking excuses, and, by degrees, come to lose your veracity, and sink into base, downright lying; for 'The second vice is lying: the first is running in debt,' as poor Richard says: and again, to the same purpose, 'Lying rides upon debt's back;' whereas a freeborn Englishman ought not to be ashamed nor afraid to see or speak to any man living. But poverty often deprives a man of all spirit and virtue. 'It is hard for an empty bag to stand upright.' What would you think of that Prince, or of that Government, who should issue an edict forbidding you to dress like a gentleman or gentlewoman, on pain of imprisonment or servitude? Would you not say that you were free, have a right to dress as you please, and that such an edict would be a breach of your privileges, and such a government tyrannical? and yet you are about to put yourself under that tyranny, when you run in debt for such dress! Your creditor has authority, at his pleasure, to deprive you of your liberty, by confining you in gaol for life, or by selling you for a servant, if you should not be able to pay him. When you have got your bargain, you may, perhaps, think little of payment; but, as poor Richard says, 'creditors have better memories than debtors; creditors are a superstitious sect, great observers of days and times.' The day comes round before you are aware, and the demand is made before you are prepared to satisfy it; or, if you bear your debt in mind, the term which at first seemed so long, will as it lessens, appear extremely short: Time will seem to have added wings to his heels as well as his shoulders. 'Those have a short Lent, who owe money to be paid at Easter.' At present, perhaps, you may think yourselves in thriving circumstances, and that you can bear a little extravagance without injury; but,

'For age and want save while you may,
No morning sun lasts a whole day.'

'Gain may be temporary and uncertain; but ever, while you live, expense is constant and certain; and 'It is easier to build two chimneys than to keep one in fuel,' as poor Richard says: so, 'Rather go to bed supperless than rise in debt.'

'Get what you can, and what you get hold,
'Tis the stone that will turn all your lead into gold.'

And, when you have got the philosopher's stone, sure you will no longer complain of bad times, or the difficulty of paying taxes.

"IV. This doctrine, my friends, is reason and wisdom; but, after all, do not depend too much upon your own industry and frugality, and prudence, though excellent things; for they may all be blasted without the blessing of Heaven; and therefore, ask that blessing humbly, and be not uncharitable to those that at present seem to want it, but comfort and help them. Remember, Job suffered, and was afterward prosperous.

"And now to conclude, 'Experience keeps a dear school, but

fools will learn in no other,' as poor Richard says, and scarce in that; for it is true, 'we may give advice, but we cannot give conduct.' However, remember this, 'They that will not be counseled, cannot be helped:' and further, that, 'If you will not hear reason, she will surely rap your knuckles,' as poor Richard says."

Thus the old gentleman ended his harangue. The people heard it, and approved the doctrine, and immediately practiced the contrary, just as if it had been a common sermon; for the auction opened, and they began to buy extravagantly. I found the good man had thoroughly studied Almanack, and digested all I had dropped on these topics during the course of twenty-five years. The frequent mention he made of me must have tired any one else; but my vanity was wonderfully delighted with it, though I was conscious that not a tenth part of the wisdom was my own which he ascribed to me; but rather the gleanings that I had made of the sense of all ages and nations. However, I resolved to be the better for the echo of it; and though I had at first determined to buy stuff for a new coat, I went away, resolved to wear my old one a little longer. Reader, if thou wilt do the same, thy profit will be as great as mine. I am, as ever, thine to serve thee.

Putting Up Stoves.

One who has had considerable experience in the work of putting up stoves says the first step to be taken is to put on a very old and ragged coat, under the impression that when he gets his mouth full of plaster it will keep his shirt-bosom clean. Next he gets his hands inside the place where the pipe ought to go, and blacks his fingers, and then he carefully makes a black mark down one side of his nose. It is impossible to make any headway, in doing this work, until this mark is made down the side of the nose. Having got his face properly marked, the victim is ready to begin the ceremony. The head of the family, who is the big goose of the sacrifice, grasps one side of the bottom of the stove, and his wife and the hired girl take hold of the other side. In this way the load is started from the wood-shed toward the parlor. Going through the door, the head of the family will carefully swing his side of the stove around, and jamb his thumb-nail against the door-post. This part of the ceremony is never omitted. Having got the stove comfortably in place, the next thing is to find the legs. Two of these are left inside the stove since the Spring before; the other two must be hunted after for twenty-five minutes. They are usually found under the coal. Then the head of the family holds up one side of the stove while his wife puts two of the legs in place, and next he holds up the other side while the other two are fixed, and one of the first two falls out. By the time the stove is on its legs he gets reckless, and takes off his coat, regardless of his linen. Then he goes off for the pipe, and gets a cinder in his eye. It don't make any difference how well the pipe was put up last year, it will be found a little too short or a little too long. The head of the family jambs his hat over his eyes, and, taking a pipe under each arm, goes to the tin-shop to have it fixed. When he gets back he steps up on one of the best parlor chairs to see if the pipe fits, and his wife makes him get down for fear he will scratch the varnish off from the chair with the nails in his boot-heel. In getting down he will surely step on the cat, and may thank his stars if it is not the baby. Then he gets an old chair, and climbs up to the chimney again, to find that in cutting the pipe off, the end has been left too big for the hole in the chimney. So he goes to the wood-shed and splits one end of the pipe with an old axe, and squeezes it in his hands to make it smaller. Finally he gets the pipe in shape, and finds that the stove does not stand true. Then himself and wife and the hired girl move the stove to the left, and the legs fall out again. Next it is to move to the right. More difficulty with the legs. Moved to the front a little. Elbow not even with the hole in the chimney, and he goes to the wood-shed after some little blocks. While putting the blocks under the legs the pipe comes out of the chimney. That remedied, the elbow keeps tipping over, to the great alarm of the wife. Head of the family gets the dinner-table out, puts the old chair on it, gets his wife to hold the chair, and balances himself on it, to drive some nails into the ceiling. Drops the hammer onto wife's head. At last gets the nails driven, makes a wire swing to hold the pipe, hammers a little here, pulls a little there, takes a long breath and announces the ceremony completed. Job never put up any stoves. It would have ruined his reputation if he had.

NATHANIEL HAWTHORNE.

NATHANIEL HAWTHORNE was born in Salem, Mass., July 4, 1804, and he died in Plymouth, N. H., May 19, 1864. His father died when Nathaniel was six years of age. At ten, on account of feeble health, he was taken to live on a farm in Maine. He studied at Bowdoin College, and received his degree in 1825. This gifted author was a classmate of our loved and lamented Longfellow. Hawthorne's first work was a collection of stories entitled *Twice Told Tales*, which, though praised by Longfellow, produced no special impression upon the public.

His reputation was fully established by the picturesque and powerful romance, *The Scarlet Letter*, published in 1850. This work carried his name across the waters, and gave him prominence in England. In 1851 appeared *The House of the Seven Gables*. In 1852 he wrote the biography of his college friend, Franklin Pierce, then a candidate for the presidency.

He published an Italian romance, called *The Marble Faun*, in 1860; and his impressions of England, under the title of *Our Old Home*, in 1863. *The Wonder Book*, *The Snow Image*, *Tanglewood Tales*, and *True Stories from History and Biography* are among his excellent works. Six volumes of his *Note Books* have been published since his death, and *Septimus Felton*, a posthumous romance, has appeared in the [*Atlantic Monthly*.] Hawthorne's literary works fill twenty-one volumes.

In addition to his literary work, he held important po-

NATHANIEL HAWTHORNE.

sitions under our government. In 1846 he was appointed surveyor of the port of Salem. He was removed from office in 1849, when the Whigs returned to power. His college friend, Franklin Pierce, upon his accession to the presidency, gave Hawthorne the place of consul to Liverpool, a position worth about $25,000 per year. In 1857 Hawthorne resigned, and spent several years with his family in traveling in France and Italy.

In the Spring of 1864, being in feeble health, he started with Ex-President Pierce for a tour in the White Mountains. They stopped over night at Plymouth, N. H., and in the morning Pierce found his friend, the subject of our sketch, dead in his bed.

It is claimed that "he wrote the cleanest and most effective English of any American who has ever put pen to paper."

Underwood, in his *Handbook of English Literature*, thus closes his sketch of Hawthorne: "The judicious critic in time comes to hesitate about giving estimates of greater and less. It is not easy to compare the dissimilar, but convenient rather to take refuge in the saying of Paul: 'One star differeth from another star in glory.' The genius of Hawthorne was unique; as the Germans say of Jean Paul Richter, he was *Hawthorne the Only*; his niche in the temple of fame will not be claimed by another."

Buds and Bird Voices.

The lilac-shrubs under my study windows are almost in leaf; in two or three days more I may put forth my hand and pluck the topmost bough in its freshest green. These lilacs are very aged, and have lost the luxuriant foliage of their prime. The heart, or the judgment, or the moral sense, or the taste, is dissatisfied with their present aspect. Old age is not venerable when it embodies itself in lilacs, rose bushes, or any other ornamental shrub; it seems as if such plants, as they grow only for beauty, ought to flourish always in immortal youth, or at least to die before their sad decrepitude. Trees of beauty are trees of paradise, and therefore not subject to decay by their original nature, though they have lost that precious birthright by being transplanted to an earth soil. There is a kind of ludicrous unfitness in the idea of a time-stricken and grandfatherly lilac bush. The analogy holds good in human life. Persons who can only be graceful and ornamental—who can give the world nothing but flowers—should die young and never be seen with gray hair and wrinkles, any more than the flower shrubs with mossy bark and blighted foliage, like the lilacs under my window. Not that beauty is worthy of less than immortality; no, the beautiful should live forever,—and thence, perhaps, the sense of impropriety when we see it triumphed over by time. Apple-trees, on the other hand, grow old without reproach. Let them live as long as they may, and contort themselves into whatever perversity of shape they please, and deck their withered limbs with a spring-time gaudiness of pink blossoms; still they are respectable, even if they afford us only an apple or two in a season. Those few apples,—or, at all events, the remembrance of apples in by-gone years—are the atonement which utilitarianism inexorably demands for the privilege of lengthened life. Human flower-shrubs, if they grow old on earth, should, besides their lovely blossoms, bear some kind of fruit that will satisfy earthly appetites; else neither man nor the decorum of nature will deem it fit that the moss should gather on them.

One of the first things that strikes the attention when the white sheet of Winter is withdrawn, is the neglect and disarray that lay hidden beneath it. Nature is not cleanly according to our prejudices. The beauty of preceding years, now transformed to brown and blighted deformity, obstructs the brightening loveliness of the present hour. Our avenue is strewn with the whole crop of autumn's withered leaves. There are quantities of decayed branches which one tempest after another has flung down, black and rotten, and one or two with the ruin of a bird's nest clinging to them. In the garden are the dried bean vines, the brown stalks of the asparagus bed, and melancholy old cabbage, which were frozen into the soil before their unthrifty cultivator could find time to gather them. How invariably, throughout all the forms of life, do we find these intermingled memorials of death! On the soil of thought and in the garden of the heart, as well as in the sensual world, lie withered leaves,—the ideas and feelings that we have done with. There is no wind strong enough to sweep them away; infinite space will not garner them from our sight. What mean they? Why may we not be permitted to live and enjoy, as if this were the first life and our own the primal enjoyment, instead of treading always on these dry bones and moldering relics, from the aged accumulation of which springs all that now appears so young and new? Sweet must have been the Spring-time of Eden, when no earlier year had strewn its decay upon the virgin turf, and no former experience had ripened into Summer and faded into Autumn in the hearts of its inhabitants! That was a world worth living in. O thou murmurer, it is out of the very wantonness of such a life that thou feignest these idle lamentations. There is no decay. Each human soul is the first-created inhabitant of its own Eden. We dwell in an old moss-covered mansion, and tread in the worn foot-prints of the past, and have a gray clergyman's ghost for our daily and nightly inmate; yet all these outward circumstances are made less than visionary by the renewing power of the spirit. Should the spirit ever lose this power,—should the withered leaves and rotten branches, and the moss-covered house, and the ghost of the gray past ever become its realities, and the verdure and the freshness merely its faint dream,—then let it pray to be released from earth. It will need the air of heaven to revive its pristine energies.

What an unlooked-for flight was this from our shadowy avenue of black ash and balm-of-Gilead trees into the infinite! Now we have our feet again upon the turf. Nowhere does the grass spring up so industriously as in this homely yard, along the base of the stone wall, and in the sheltered nooks of the buildings; and especially around the southern doorstep,—a locality which seems particularly favorable to its growth, for it is already tall enough to bend over and wave in the wind. I observe that several weeds, and most frequently a plant that stains the fingers with its yellow juice—have survived and retained their freshness and sap throughout the Winter. One knows not how they have deserved such an exception from the common lot of their race. They are now the patriarchs of the departed year, and may preach mortality to the present generation of flowers and weeds.

Among the delights of Spring, how is it possible to forget the birds? Even the crows were welcome as the sable harbingers of a brighter and livelier race. They visited us before the snow was off, but seem mostly to have betaken themselves to remote depths of the woods, which they haunt all summer long. Many a time shall I disturb them there, and feel as if I had intruded among a company of silent worshipers, as they sit in Sabbath stillness among the tree tops. Their voices, when they speak, are in admirable accordance with the tranquil solitude of a summer afternoon; and resounding so far above the head, their loud clamor increases the religious quiet of the scene instead of breaking it. A crow, however, has no real pretentions to religion, in spite of his gravity of mien and black attire; he is certainly a thief, and probably an infidel. The gulls are far more respectable, in a moral point of view. These denizens of sea-beaten rocks and haunters of the lonely beach come up our inland river at this season, and soar high overhead, flapping their broad wings in the upper sunshine. They are among the most picturesque of birds, because they so float and rest upon the air as to become almost stationary parts of the landscape. The imagination has time to grow acquainted with them; they have not flitted away in a moment. You go up among the clouds and greet these lofty-flighted gulls, and repose confidently with them upon the sustaining atmosphere. Ducks have their haunts along the solitary places of the river, and alight in flocks upon the broad bosom of the overflowed meadows. Their flight is too rapid and determined for the eye to catch enjoyment from it, although it never fails to stir up the heart with the sportsman's ineradicable instinct. They have now gone farther northward, but will visit us again in Autumn.

The smaller birds,—the little songsters of the woods, and those that haunt man's dwellings and claim human friendship by building their nests under the sheltering eaves or among the orchard trees,—these require a touch more delicate and a gentler heart than mine to do them justice. Their outburst of melody is like a brook let loose from wintry chains. We need not deem it a too high and solemn word to call it a hymn of praise to the Creator, since Nature, who pictures the reviving year in so many sights of beauty, has expressed the sentiments of renewed life in no other sound save the notes of these blessed birds. Their music, however, just now, seems to be incidental, and not the result of a set purpose. They are discussing the economy of life and love, and the site and architecture of their Summer residences, and have no time to sit on a twig and pour forth solemn hymns, or overtures, operas, symphonies, and waltzes. Anxious questions are asked; grave subjects are settled in quick and animated debate; and only by occasional accident, as from pure ecstacy, does a rich warble roll its tiny waves of golden sound through the atmosphere. Their little bodies are as busy as their voices; they are in constant flutter and restlessness. Even when two or three retreat to a tree top to hold council, they wag their tails and heads all the time with the irrepressible activity of their nature, which perhaps renders their brief span of life in reality as long as the patriarchal age of sluggish man. The black-birds, three species of which consort together, are the noisiest of all our feathered citizens. Great companies of them—more than the famous "four-and-twenty" whom Mother Goose has immortalized—congregate in contiguous tree tops, and vociferate with all the clamor and confusion of a turbulent political meeting. Politics, certainly, must be the occasion of such tumultuous debates; but still, unlike all other politicians, they instill melody into their individual utterances, and produce harmony as a general effect. Of all bird voices, none are more sweet and cheerful to my ear than those of swallows, in the dim, sun-streaked interior of a lofty barn; they address the heart with even a closer sympathy than robin-redbreast. But, indeed, all these winged people, that dwell in the vicinity of homesteads, seem to partake of human nature, and possess the germ, if not the development, of immortal souls. We hear them saying their melodious prayers at morning's blush and eventide. A little while ago, in the deep of night, there came the lively thrill of a bird's note from a neighboring tree,—a real song, such as greets the purple dawn or mingles with the yellow sunshine. What could the little bird mean by pouring it forth at midnight? Probably the music gushed out of the midst of a dream in which he fancied himself in paradise with his mate, but suddenly awoke on a cold, leafless bough, with a New England mist penetrating through his feathers. That was a sad exchange of imagination for reality.

Spring.

Thank Providence for Spring! The earth and man himself, by sympathy with his birthplace, would be far other than we find them if life toiled wearily onward without this periodical infusion of the primal spirit. Will the world ever be so decayed that Spring may not renew its greenness? Can man be so dismally age-stricken that no faintest sunshine of his youth may revisit him once a year? It is impossible. The moss on our time-worn mansion brightens into beauty; the good old pastor who once dwelt here renewed his prime, regained his boyhood, in the genial breezes of his ninetieth spring. Alas for the worn and heavy soul if, whether in youth of age, it has outlived its privilege of Spring-time sprightliness! From such a soul the world must hope no reformation of its evil, no sympathy with the lofty faith and gallant struggles of those who contend in its behalf. Summer works in the present, and thinks not of the future; Autumn is a rich conservative; Winter has utterly lost its faith, and clings tremulously to the remembrance of what has been; but Spring, with its outgushing life, is the true type of movement.

Autumn at Concord, Massachusetts.

Alas for the Summer! The grass is still verdant on the hills and in the valleys; the foliage of the trees is as dense as ever, and as green; the flowers are abundant along the margin of the river, and in the hedge-rows, and deep among the woods; the days, too, are as fervid as they were a month ago; and yet, in every breath of wind and in every beam of sunshine, there is an Autumnal influence. I know not how to describe it.' Methinks there is a sort of coolness amid all the heat, and a mildness in the brightest of the sunshine. A breeze cannot stir without thrilling me with the breath of Autumn; and I behold its pensive glory in the far, golden gleams among the huge shadows of trees.

The flowers, even the brightest of them, the golden-rod and the gorgeous cardinals—the most glorious flowers of the year—have this gentle sadness amid their pomp. Pensive Autumn is expressed in the glow of every one of them. I have felt this influence earlier in some years than in others. Sometimes Autumn may be perceived even in the early days of July. There is no other feeling like that caused by this faint, doubtful, yet real perception, or rather prophecy of the year's decay, so deliciously sweet and sad at the same time.

I scarcely remember a scene of more complete and lovely seclusion than the passage of the river through this wood (North Branch). Even an Indian canoe, in olden times, could not have floated onward in deeper solitude than my boat. I have never elsewhere had such an opportunity to observe how much more beautiful reflection is than what we call reality. The sky and the clustering foliage on either hand, and the effect of sunlight as it found its way through the shade, giving lightsome hues in contrast with the quiet depth of the prevailing tints—all these seemed unsurpassably beautiful when beheld in upper air. But on gazing downward, there they were, the same even to the minutest particular, yet arrayed in ideal beauty, which satisfied the spirit incomparably more than the actual scene. I am half convinced that the reflection is indeed the reality, the real thing which nature imperfectly images to our grosser sense. At any rate the disembodied shadow is nearest to the soul. There were many tokens of Autumn in this beautiful picture. Two or three of the trees were actually dressed in their coats of many colors—the real scarlet and gold which they wear before they put on mourning.

There is a pervading blessing diffused over all the world. I look out of the window, and think: O perfect day! O beautiful world! O good God! And such a day is the promise of a blissful eternity. Our Creator would never have made such weather, and given us the deep heart to enjoy it, above and beyond all thought, if he had not meant us to be immortal. It opens the gates of heaven, and gives us glimpses far inward.

A Plea For the Erring.

There are few subjects upon which men are so likely to err in forming their judgments as in estimating the degrees of guilt involved in the conduct of their erring and depraved fellow men. Especially is this the case when the judgments are passed upon the poor and the outcast,—the unhappy persons who from infancy have lived in daily communion with wretchedness and vice. In spite of Cannings's sneer at the nice judge who

> "—— found with keen, discriminating sight,
> Black's not so black, nor white so very white."

the doctrine thus ridiculed is nevertheless true in morals, if not in physics; and not to recognize it is to incur the risk of undue harshness in our estimates of our fellow men. If there is any one lesson which frequent intercourse with them teaches, it is the folly of attempting nicely to classify their characters, so as to place them distinctly among the sheep or the goats. Here and there a man is found who is almost wholly bad, and another who is almost wholly good; but, in the infinite majority of cases, the problem is so complex as to defy all our powers of analysis. A young men's debating society may easily enough resolve that some famous man or woman was worthy of approbation or of reprobation; but men of experience, who have learned the infinite complexity of human nature, know that a just judgment of human beings is not to be packed into any such summary formula. Even in judging our friends, whom we see daily, we make the grossest mistakes; they are constantly startling us by acts which show us how little we know of the fathomless depths of their moral being. How, then, can we expect to judge accurately of those who are utter strangers to us, and by what right do we presume to place them irrevocably in our moral pigeon-holes?

It is difficult to say how far in our judgments of the vilest men, —or those who seem to be such,—allowance should be made for perplexing circumstances, for temptations which we have never experienced, and for motives which we can but partially analyze. Certain it is that they who, from their earliest years, have lived always in affluence—who have never known the cravings of a hunger that they knew not how to satisfy,—who have been supplied with a constant succession of innocent pleasure to relieve the monotony of life, and with all the appliances of art to cheat pain of its sting,—have but a faint conception of the privations and anxieties, the irritating and maddening thoughts, that torture the victim of poverty, and drive him, with an impulse dreadfully strong, to deeds of darkness and blood.

Well did Maggie Mucklebacket, in Scott's novel, retort to the Laird of Monkbarns, when he expressed a hope that the distilleries would never work again: "Ay, it is easy for your honor, and the like o' you gentle folks, to say sae, that hae stouth and routh and fire and fending, and meat and claith, and sit dry and canny by the fireside; but an ye wanted fere, and meat and dry claise, and were deeing o' cauld, and had a sair heart into the bargain, which is warst ava, wi' just tippence in your pouch, wadna ye be glad to buy a dram wi't, to be eilding, and claise, and a supper, and heart's ease into the bargain, till the morn's morning?" We may not admit the strict logic of this appeal, for the dram is too often the cause, as well as the effect, of the absence of fire, and meat, and heart's ease; but the fact upon which the poly-petticoated philosopher insists so pathetically is unquestionably a key, not only to nine-tenths of the vices, but also to many of the darkest crimes, that stain the annals of the poor.

Easy, indeed, is it, for such persons as Maggie describes,—those for whom a serene and quiet life has been provided by fortune,—who are free from all harrassing cares,—their livelier and more errant feelings all settled down into torpidity,—with not even any tastes to lead astray,—nothing, in short, to do but to live a life of substantial comfort within the easy bounds which worldly wisdom prescribes,—easy is it for all these sleek and well-fed members of the venerable corps of "excessively good and rigidly righteous people," as Burns calls them,—

"Whose life is like a weel gaun mill,—
Supplied wi' store o' water,
The heapet happer's ebbing still,
And still the clap plays clatter,"—

to abstain from vice and crime; for were they to be guilty of the outrageous sins of the distressed and tempted, they would be monsters indeed. But, before such sit in judgment on their fellow men,

"Their dousie tricks, their black mistakes,
Their failings and mischances,"

or boast of keeping their own feet within the prescribed bounds of virtue, would they not do well to ask themselves how many inward struggles this negative merit has cost them, or whether their circumstances were not such as to render temptation to any glaring error impossible?

It is said that John Bunyan, seeing a drunkard staggering along the street, exclaimed, "There, but for the grace of God, goes John Bunyan!" "Tolerance," says Goethe, "comes with age. I see no fault committed that I myself could not have committed at some time or other." Truly, we have but to look into our own hearts to find the germ of many a crime which only our more favored circumstances have prevented us from committing, and would we ponder on this thought with a wise humility, it might teach us, not to palliate or excuse, but "more gently to scan our fellow man,"—to judge mercifully of the sinner while we hate the sin,—and, above all, meekly to thank God, not that we are better than other men, but that we, too, have not been brought into temptations too fiery for our strength. "No man," says the large-hearted poet, Burns, "can say in what degree any other persons, besides himself, can be with strict justice called wicked. Let any of the strictest character for regularity of conduct among us examine impartially how many vices he has not been guilty of, not from any care or vigilance, but for want of opportunity, or some accidental circumstance intervening; how many of the weaknesses of mankind he has escaped because he was out of the line of such temptation; and what often, if not always, weighs more than all the rest, how much he is indebted to the world's good opinion, because the world does not know all; I say, any man who can thus think, may view the faults and crimes of mankind around him with a brother's eye."

It was in a land of harsh moralists, and in an age when little pity was shown to the erring, that Burns wrote these words; but, though in these days a great advance has been made, it is doubtful if we yet have sufficient sympathy for those who stray from the paths of virtue. We need again and again to be reminded that the bad are not all bad; that there is "a soul of goodness in things evil;" and that in balancing the ledger of human conduct, we should make a large subtraction from the bad man's debit side, as from the good man's credit side, of the account. Not more true is it that there are many "mute, inglorious Miltons," or "village Hampdens," whose lofty intellectual powers, like the music of an untouched instrument, have remained dormant for the want of circumstances to call them forth, than that there sleep in the breast of many an innocent man impulses and tendencies of a wicked character, which need but the breath of occasion to start them into a giant life. The pregnant story of Hazel furnishes not the only instance of a nature which, in ordinary circumstances, was shocked at the very imputation of wrong, and yet, when clothed with despotic authority, exhibited all the odious features of the oppressor and the tyrant. "Nature," says the sententious Bacon, "may be buried a great while, and yet revive on the occasion of temptation; like as it was with Æsop's damsel, turned from a cat to a woman, who sat very demurely at the board's end till a mouse ran before her."

It is a striking fact, noted by Sir Arthur Helps, that the man in all England whose duty it is to know most about crime has been heard to say that he finds more and more to excuse in men, and thinks better of human nature, even after tracking it through the most perverse and intolerable courses. It is the man who has seen most of his fellows, who is most tolerant of his fellow man. In the great Battle of Life, we may see many a fellow creature fall beneath a temptation which from our own shield would have glanced harmless; but let us reflect that, though we might have been adamant to this, there are a thousand other darts of Satan, better suited to our natures, by which, though pressing with less crushing force, we might have perished without a struggle. Only the All-Seeing Eye can discern how far the virtues of any one are owing to a happy temperament, or from how many vices he abstains, not from any care or vigilance, but, as Burns says, "for want of opportunity, or some accidental circumstances intervening."

When Henry Martyn was in college he was such a slave to anger that he one day hurled a knife with all his force at a fellow student, which might have killed or fearfully mutilated him, had it not missed the mark, and stuck in the wainscot of the room. "Martyn," exclaimed his friend, in consternation, "if you do not learn to govern your temper, you will one day be hanged for murder!" He *did* learn to govern it; became meek and humble; won high honors in college; went to India as a missionary; distinguished himself as a linguist; translated the Testament into several languages; and died, after doing and enduring a vast deal to rescue the East from the darkness of paganism. What if, with his sensitive and fiery organism, he had been born amid the squalor and vice of St. Giles? Or who can say what Martin Luther would have become, if, born as he was with organs of destructiveness like those of a bull-dog, he had not been led by his religious training to employ his destructive energies in killing error instead of in killing human beings? An English writer was so struck with the prodigious energy, the native feral force of Chalmers, that he declared that had it not been intellectualized and sanctified it would have made him, who was the greatest of orators, the strongest of ruffians, a mighty murderer upon the earth. On the other hand, who does not remember that even Nero, at one time of his life, could lament that he knew how to read or write, when called on to sign a death warrant. The colliers of Bristol had been noted for ages as among the most hardened and profligate of beings, till Whitefield touched them one day with the wand of his magic eloquence. Even a Nancy Sykes, amid the grossest degradation, could do many virtuous actions; and the stern Milton has said that "it was from the rind of one apple that the knowledge of good and evil, as two twins cleaving together, leaped forth into the world." Moderate, then, O thou stern moralist! thy harsh and unrelenting views of human guilt: —

> "Still mark if vice or nature prompt the deed;
> Still mark the strong temptation or the need;
> On pressing want, on famine's powerful call,
> At least more lenient let thy justice fall;
> For him, who, lost to every hope of life,
> Has long with fortune held unequal strife,
> Known to no human love, no human care,
> The friendless, homeless object of despair;
> For the poor vagrant feel, while he complains,
> Nor from sad freedom send to sadder chains.
> Alike if fortune or misfortune brought
> Those last of woes his evil days have wrought;
> Believe, with social mercy and with me,
> Folly's misfortune in the first degree."

Shakespere's Style.

Words in a master's hands seem more than words; he seems to double or quadruple their power by skill in using, giving them a force and significance which in the dictionary they never possessed. Yet, mighty as is the sorcery of these wizards of words, that of Shakespere is still greater. The marvel of his diction is its immense suggestiveness,—the mysterious synthesis of sound and sense, of meaning and association, which characterizes his verse; a necromancy to which Emerson alludes in a passage which is itself an illustration almost of the thing it describes. Speaking of the impossibility of acting or reciting Shakespere's plays, he says: "The recitation begins, when lo! one golden word leaps out immortal from all this painted pedantry, and sweetly torments us with invitations to its own inaccessible homes."

Hardly less surprising than this suggestiveness of Shakespere, is the variety of rhythm in his ten-syllable verse. We speak sometimes of Shakespere's style; but we might as well speak of the style of "Rumor with her hundred tongues.". Shakespere has a multiplicity of styles, varying with the ever varying character of his themes. The Proteus of the dramatic art, he identifies himself with each of his characters in turn, passing from one to another like the same soul animating different bodies. Like a ventriloquist, he throws his voice into other men's larynxes, and makes every word appear to come from the person whose character he for the moment assumes. The movement and measure of Othello and The Tempest, Macbeth and the Midsummer Night's Dream, Lear and Coriolanus, are almost as different from each other as the rhythm of them all from that of Beaumont and Fletcher; and yet in every case the music or melody is a subtle accompaniment to the sentiment that ensouls the play. Whoever would know the exhaustless riches of our many-tongued language, its capability of expressing the daintiest delicacies and subtlest refinements of thought, as well as the grandest emotions that can thrill the human brain, should give his days and nights to the study of the myriad-souled poet. It may be doubted whether there is any inflection of harmony, any witchery of melody, from the warble of the flute and the low thrill of the flageolet to the trumpet-peal or the deep and dreadful sub-bass of the organ, which is not brought out in the familiar or the passionate tones of this imperial master.

DR. SAMUEL JOHNSON.

SAMUEL JOHNSON was born at Litchfield, Sept. 18, 1709. After having fought the early battles of life in feeble health and poverty, and without patronage, he gained a complete victory, placed himself at the head of English literature, and died in a serene and happy frame of mind on the 13th of December, 1784.

Johnson had attended school at Oxford fourteen months when his father, a bookseller, met with misfortunes in trade, thereby forcing Samuel to leave school. In his short college life, he distinguished himself by translating Pope's *Messiah* into Latin verse. To do Johnson justice in a brief sketch is impossible, but the plan of this book forbids more than the following summary of his work. Upon failure to found a private academy at Edial, near his native city, he determined to make authorship his profession. His first tragedy, *Irene*, was refused by stage managers, but his contributions to the *Gentleman's Magazine* were quite popular. He next wrote monthly reports of the proceedings of Parliament, taking care to give the Tories the advantage over the Whigs. In 1738, appeared his poem of *London*, for which Dodsley gave him ten guineas. No name was signed to this poem, but Pope made inquiries after the author, saying such a man would soon be known. In 1744, he published the *Life of Savage*, late editor of the *Gentleman's Magazine*. "This admirable specimen of biography was published anonymously, but it was known to be Johnson's."

His reputation was so well established by this time that the chief booksellers of London engaged him, for 1500 guineas, to prepare a *Dictionary of the English Language*. The

DR. SAMUEL JOHNSON.

work was completed in about seven years. *Johnson's Dictionary* became at once the standard authority in England. His *Vanity of Human Wishes* appeared in 1748; *Irene*, formerly refused, was brought out by Garrick in 1749. Johnson's other works were the *Rambler*, 1750-52 ; the *Idler*, 1758-60 ; the tale of *Rasselas*, 1759. The last named was written to pay a debt, and also to pay the funeral expenses of his mother, who had died at the age of ninety.

In 1765 appeared his edition of Shakspere, and in 1775 appeared his *Lives of the Poets*, the most interesting and valuable of his last works.

Johnson is also numbered among the great poets. Sir Walter Scott has termed his poem, *The Vanity of Human Wishes*, a satire, the deep and pathetic morality of which has often extracted tears from those whose eyes wander dry over pages professedly sentimental.

At the age of twenty-seven, he married Mrs. Porter, a widow who was in her forty-eighth year. In 1762, through the influence of Lord Bute, the then all-potent minister of England, a pension of £300 was settled upon Johnson. In 1773, at the age of sixty-four, he commenced his celebrated journey to the Hebrides. The greater part of the journey he performed on horseback. His narrative of his travels is one of his most interesting works. His Tory principles led him to write two pamphlets in defense of the ministry and in bitter opposition to the claims of the Americans. In the literary club, including Burke, Reynolds, Goldsmith, Gibbon, Murphy, and others, Johnson " reigned supreme, the most brilliant conversationalist of his age." " In massive force of understanding, multifarious knowledge, sagacity, and moral intrepidity, no writer of the eighteenth century surpasses *Dr. Samuel Johnson.*"

On Revenge.

A wise man will make haste to forgive, because he knows the true value of time, and will not suffer it to pass away in unnecessary pain. He that willingly suffers the corrosions of inveterate hatred, and gives up his days and nights to the gloom and malice and perturbations of strategem, cannot surely be said to consult his ease. Resentment is a union of sorrow with malignity, a combination of a passion which all endeavor to avoid, with a passion which all concur to detest. The man who retires to meditate mischief, and to exasperate his own rage—whose thoughts are employed only on means of distress and contrivances of ruin—whose mind never pauses for the remembrance of his own sufferings, but to indulge some hope of enjoying the calamities of another—may justly be numbered among the most miserable of human beings, among those who are guilty without reward, who have neither the gladness of prosperity nor the calm of innocence. Whoever considers the weakness both of himself and others, will not long want persuasives to forgiveness. We know not to what degree of malignity any injury is to be imputed; or how much its guilt, if we were to inspect the mind of him that committed it, would be extenuated by mistake, precipitance, or negligence; we cannot be certain how much more we feel than was intended to be inflicted, or how much we increase the mischief to ourselves by voluntary aggravations. We may charge to design the effects of accident; we may think the blow violent only because we have made ourselves delicate and tender; we are on every side in danger of error and of guilt which we are certain to avoid only by speedy forgiveness.

From this pacific and harmless temper, thus propitious to others and ourselves, to domestic tranquility and to social happiness, no man is withheld but by pride, by the fear of being insulted by his adversary, or despised by the world. It may be laid down as an unfailing and universal axiom, that 'all pride is abject and mean.' It is always an ignorant, lazy, or cowardly acquiescence in a false appearance of excellence, and proceeds not from consciousness of our attainments, but insensibility of our wants.

Nothing can be great which is not right.

Nothing which reason condemns can be suitable to the dignity of the human mind.

To be driven by external motives from the path which our own heart approves, to give way to anything but conviction, to suffer the opinion of others to rule our choice or overpower our resolves, is to submit tamely to the lowest and most ignominious slavery and to resign the right of directing our own lives.

The utmost excellence at which humanity can arrive is a constant and determinate pursuit of virtue without regard to present dangers or advantages; a continual reference of every action to the divine will; a habitual appeal to everlasting justice; and an unvaried elevation of the intellectual eye to the reward which perseverance can only obtain. But that pride which many, who presume to boast of generous sentiments, allow to regulate their measures, has nothing nobler in view than the approbation of men; of beings whose superiority we are under no obligation to acknowledge, and who, when we have courted them with the utmost assiduity, can confer no valuable or permanent reward; of beings who ignorantly judge of what they do not understand, or partially determine what they have never examined, and whose sentence is therefore of no weight, till it has received the ratification of our own conscience.

He that can descend to bribe suffrages like these at the price of his innocence—he that can suffer the delight of such acclamations to withhold his attention from the commands of the universal sovereign—has little reason to congratulate himself upon the greatness of his mind; whenever he awakes to seriousness and reflection, he must become despicable in his own eyes, and shrink with shame from the remembrance of his cowardice and folly.

Of him that hopes to be forgiven, it is indispensably required that he forgive. It is therefore superfluous to urge any other motive. On this great duty eternity is suspended; and to him that refuses to practice it, the throne of mercy is inaccessible, and the Saviour of the world has been born in vain.

Old Age.

I cannot tell where childhood ends, and manhood begins; nor where manhood ends, and old age begins. It is a wavering and uncertain line, not straight and definite, which borders betwixt the two. But the outward characteristics of old age are obvious enough. The weight diminishes. Man is commonly heaviest at forty; woman at fifty. After that, the body shrinks a little; the height shortens as the cartilages become thin and dry. The hair whitens and falls away. The frame stoops, the bones become smaller, feebler, have less animal and more mere earthy matter. The senses decay, slowly and handsomely. The eye is not so sharp, and while it penetrates further into space, it has less power clearly to define the outlines of what it sees. The ear is dull; the appetite less. Bodily heat is lower; the breath produces less carbonic acid than before. The old man consumes less food, water, air. The hands grasp less strongly; the feet less firmly tread. The lungs suck the breast of heaven with less powerful collapse. The eye and ear take not so strong a hold upon the world:—

> And the big manly voice;
> Turning again to childish treble, pipes
> And whistles in his sound.

The animal life is making ready to go out. The very old man loves the sunshine and the fire, the arm chair and the shady nook. A rude wind would jostle the full-grown apple from its bough, full-ripe, full-colored, too. The internal characteristics correspond. General activity is less. Salient love of new things and of new persons, which bit the young man's heart, fades away. He thinks the old is better. He is not venturesome; he keeps at home. Passion once stung him into quickened life; now that gad-fly is no more buzzing in his ears. Madame de Staël finds compensation in Science for the decay of the passion that once fired her blood; but Heathen Socrates, seventy years old, thanks the gods that he is now free from that "ravenous beast," which had disturbed his philosophic meditations for many a year. Romance is the child of Passion and Imagination;—the sudden father that, the long protracting mother this. Old age has little romance. Only some rare man, like Wilhelm von Humboldt, keeps it still fresh in his bosom.

In intellectual matters, the venerable man loves to recall the old times, to revive his favorite old men,—no new ones half so fair. So in Homer, Nestor, who is the oldest of the Greeks, is always talking of the old times, before the grandfathers of men then living had come into being; "not such as live in these degenerate days." Verse-loving John Quincy Adams turns off from Byron and Shelley and Wieland and Goethe, and returns to Pope,

Who pleased his childhood and informed his youth.

The pleasure of hope is smaller; that of memory greater. It is exceedingly beautiful that it is so. The venerable man loves to set recollection to beat the roll-call, and summon up from the grave the old time, "the good old time,"—the old places, old friends, old games, old talk; nay, to his ear the old familiar tunes are sweeter than anything that Mendelssohn, or Strauss, or Rossini can bring to pass. Elder Brewster expects to hear St. Martins and Old Hundred chanted in Heaven. Why not? To him Heaven comes in the long used musical tradition, not in the neologies of sound. * * * * * * *

Then the scholar becomes an antiquary; he likes not young men unless he knew their grandfathers before. The young woman looks in the newspaper for the marriages, the old man, for the deaths. The young man's eye looks forward; the world is "all before him where to choose." It is a hard world; he does not know it; he works a little, and hopes much. The middle-aged man looks around at the present; he has found out that it is a hard world; he hopes less and works more. The old man looks back on the field he has trod; "this is the tree I planted; this is my footstep," and he loves his old house, his old carriage, cat, dog, staff, and friend. In lands where the vine grows, I have seen an old man sit all day long, a sunny autumn day, before his cottage door, in a great arm-chair, his old dog crouched at his feet in the genial sun. The autumn wind played with the old man's venerable hairs; above him on the wall, purpling in the sunlight, hung the full cluster of the grape, ripening and maturing yet more. The two were just alike; the wind stirred the vine leaves and they fell; stirred the old man's hair and it whitened yet more. Both were waiting for the spirit in them to be fully ripe. The young man looks forward; the old man looks back. How long the shadows lie in the setting sun, the steeple a mile long reaching across the plain, as the sun stretches out the hills in grotesque dimensions. So all the events of life in the old man's consciousness.

The Progress of Sin.

I have seen the little purls of a spring sweat through the bottom of a bank, and intenerate the stubborn pavement till it hath made it fit for the impression of a child's foot; and it was despised, like the descending pearls of a misty morning, till it had opened its way and made a stream large enough to carry away the ruins of the undermined strand, and to invade the neighboring gardens; but then the despised drops had grown into an artificial river, and an intolerable mischief. So are the first entrances of sin, stopped with the antidotes of a hearty prayer, and checked into sobriety by the eye of a reverend man, or the counsels of a single sermon; but when such beginnings are neglected, and our religion hath not in it so much philosophy as to think anything evil as long as we can endure it, they grow up to ulcers and pestilential evils; they destroy the soul by their abode, who at their first entry might have been killed with the pressure of a little finger. He that hath passed many stages of a good life, to prevent his being tempted to a single sin, must be very careful that he never entertain his spirit with the remembrances of his past sin, nor amuse it with the fantastic apprehensions of the present. When the Israelites fancied the sapidness and relish of the flesh pots, they longed to táste and to return.

So when a Libyan tiger, drawn from his wilder foragings, is shut up and taught to eat civil meat, and suffer the authority of a man, he sits down tamely in his prison and pays to his keeper fear and reverence for his meat; but if he chance to come again and taste a draught of warm blood, he presently leaps into his natural cruelty. He scarce abstains from eating those hands that brought him discipline and food. · · · ·

The Pannonian bears, when they have clasped a dart in the region of their liver, wheel themselves upon the wound, and with anger and malicious revenge strike the deadly barb deeper, and cannot be quit from that fatal steel, but, in flying, bear along that which themselves make the instrument of a more hasty death; so, in every vicious person struck with a deadly wound, and his own hands force it into the entertainments of the heart; and because it is painful to draw it forth by a sharp and salutary repentance, he still rolls and turns upon his wound, and carries his death in his bowels, where it first entered by choice, and then dwelt by love, and at last shall finish the tragedy by divine judgments and an unalterable decree.

Marriage.

They that enter in the state of marriage cast a die of the greatest contingency and yet of the greatest interest in the world, next to the last throw for eternity. Life or death, felicity or a lasting sorrow, are in the power of marriage. A woman, indeed, ventures most, for she has no sanctuary to retire to from an evil husband; she must dwell upon her sorrow, and hatch the eggs which her own folly or infelicity hath produced; and she is more under it, because her tormentor hath a warrant of prerogative, and the woman may complain to God, as subjects do of tyrant princes; but otherwise she has no appeal in the causes of unkindness. And though the man can run from many hours of his sadness, yet he must return to it again; and when he sits among his neighbors he remembers the objection that lies in his bosom, and he sighs deeply. The boys and the pedlers, and the fruiterers, shall tell of this man when he is carried to his grave, that he lived and died a poor wretched person.

The stags in the Greek epigram, whose knees were clogged with frozen snow upon the mountains, came down to the brooks of the valleys, hoping to thaw their joints with the waters of the stream; but there the frost overtook them, and bound them fast in ice, till the young herdsmen took them in their stranger snare. It is the unhappy chance of many men; finding many inconveniences upon the mountains of single life, they descend into the valleys of marriage to refresh their troubles; and there they enter into fetters, and are bound to sorrow by the chords of a man or woman's peevishness.

Man and wife are equally concerned to avoid all offences of each other in the beginning of their conversation; every little thing can blast an infant blossom, and the breath of the South can shake the little rings of the vine, when first they begin to curl like the locks of a new weaned boy; but when by age and consolidation they stiffen in the hardness of a stem, and have, by the warm embraces of the sun and the kisses of the heaven, brought forth their clusters, they can endure the storms of the North, and the loud noises of a tempest, and yet never be broken: so are the early unions of an unfixed marriage; watchful and observant, jealous and busy, inquisitive and careful, and apt to take alarm at every unkind word. After the hearts of the man and the wife are endeared and hardened by a mutual confidence and experience, longer than artifice and pretense can last, there are a great many remembrances, and some things present, that dash all unkindnesses in pieces. · · · ·

There is nothing can please a man without love; and if a man be weary of the wise discourses of the apostles, and of the innocency of an even and a private fortune, or hates peace, or a fruitful year, he hath reaped thorns and thistles from the choicest flowers of Paradise, for nothing can sweeten felicity itself but love; but when a man dwells in love, then the breasts of his wife are pleasant as the droppings upon the hill of Hermon; her eyes are fair as the light of heaven; she is a fountain sealed, and he can quench his thirst, and ease his cares, and lay his sorrows down upon her lap, and can retire home to his sanctuary and refectory, and his gardens of sweetness and chaste refreshments. No man can tell but he that loves his children, how many delicious accents make a man's heart dance in the pretty conversation of those dear pledges; their childishness, their stammering, their little angers, their innocence, their imperfections, their necessities, are so many little emanations of joy and comfort to him that delights in their persons and society. · · · · It is fit that I should infuse a bunch of myrrh into the festival goblet, and, after the Egyptian manner, serve up a dead man's bones at a feast; I will only shew it, and take it away again; it will make the wine bitter, but wholesome. But those married pairs that live as remembering that they must part again, and give an account how they treat themselves and each other, shall, at that day of their death, be admitted to glorious espousals; and when they shall live again, be married to their Lord, and partake of his glories with Abraham and Joseph, St. Peter and St. Paul, and all the married saints. All those things that now please us shall pass from us, or we from them; but those things that concern the other life are permanent as the numbers of eternity. And although at the resurrection there shall be no relation of husband and wife, and no marriage shall be celebrated but the marriage of the Lamb, yet then shall be remembered how men and women passed through this state, which is a type of that; and from this sacramental union all holy pairs shall pass to the spiritual and eternal, where love shall be their portion, and joys shall crown their heads, and they shall lie in the bosom of Jesus, and in the heart of God, to eternal ages.

The Skylark.

For so I have seen a lark rising from his bed of grass, and soaring upwards, singing as he rises, and hopes to get to heaven and climb above the clouds; but the poor bird was beaten back with the loud sighings of an eastern wind, and his motion made irregular and inconstant, descending more at every breath of the tempest than it could recover by the vibration and frequent weighing of his wings, till the little creature was forced to sit down and pant, and stay till the storm was over; and then it made a prosperous flight, and did rise and sing, as if it had learned music and motion from an angel, as he passed sometimes through the air, about his ministries here below.

The Blind Preacher.

I have been, my dear S——, on an excursion through the counties which lie along the eastern side of the Blue Ridge. A general description of that country and its inhabitants may form the subject of a future letter. For the present, I must entertain you with an account of a most singular and interesting adventure, which I met with, in the course of the tour.

It was one Sunday, as I traveled through the county of Orange, that my eye was caught by a cluster of horses tied near a ruinous, old, wooden house, in the forest, not far from the roadside. Having frequently seen such objects before, in traveling through these states, I had no difficulty in understanding that this was a place of religious worship.

Devotion alone should have stopped me, to join in the duties of the congregation; but I must confess that curiosity to hear the preacher of such a wilderness was not the least of my motives. On entering, I was struck with his preternatural appearance. He was a tall and very spare old man; his head, which was covered with a white linen cap, his shriveled hands, and his voice, were all shaking under the influence of a palsy; and a few moments ascertained to me that he was perfectly blind.

The first emotions which touched my breast, were those of mingled pity and veneration. But ah! sacred God! how soon were all my feelings changed! The lips of Plato were never more worthy of a prognostic swarm of bees, than were the lips of this holy man! It was a day of the administration of the sacrament; and his subject, of course, was the passion of our Saviour. I had heard the subject handled a thousand times; I had thought it exhausted long ago. Little did I suppose that in the wild woods of America I was to meet with a man whose eloquence would give the topic a new and more sublime pathos than I had ever before witnessed.

As he descended from the pulpit, to distribute the mystic symbols, there was a peculiar, a more than human solemnity in his air and manner which made my blood run cold and my whole frame shiver.

He then drew a picture of the sufferings of our Saviour; his trial before Pilate; his ascent up Calvary; his crucifixion, and his death. I knew the whole history; but never, until then, had I heard the circumstances so selected, so arranged, so colored! It was all new, and I seemed to have heard it for the first time in my life. His enunciation was so deliberate, that his voice trembled on every syllable; and every heart in the assembly trembled in unison. His peculiar phrases had that force of description that the original scene appeared to be, at that moment, acting before our eyes. We saw the very faces of the Jews: the staring, frightful distortions of malice and rage. We saw the buffet; my soul kindled with a flame of indignation; and my hands were involuntarily and convulsively clinched.

But when he came to touch on the patience, the forgiving meekness of our Saviour; when he drew, to the life, his blessed eyes streaming in tears to Heaven; his voice breathing to God, a soft and gentle prayer of pardon on his enemies.—"Father, forgive them, for they know not what they do"—the voice of the preacher, which had all along faltered, grew fainter and fainter, until his utterance being entirely obstructed by the force of his feelings; he raised his handkerchief to his eyes, and burst into a loud and irrepressible flood of grief. The effect is inconceivable. The whole house resounded with the mingled groans, and sobs, and shrieks of the congregation.

It was some time before the tumult had subsided, so far as to permit him to proceed. Indeed, judging by the usual but fallacious standard of my own weakness, I began to be very uneasy for the situation of the preacher. For I could not conceive how he would be able to let his audience down from the height to which he had wound them without impairing the solemnity and dignity of his subject, or perhaps shocking them by the abruptness of the fall.

But—no; the descent was as beautiful and sublime as the elevation had been rapid and enthusiastic.

The first sentence which broke the awful silence, was a quotation from Rousseau, "Socrates died like a philosopher, but Jesus Chirst, like a God!"

I despair of giving you any idea of the effect produced by this short sentence, unless you could perfectly conceive the whole manner of the man, as well as the peculiar crisis in the discourse. Never before did I completely understand what Demosthenes meant by laying such stress on *delivery*. You are to bring before you the venerable figure of the preacher; his blindness, constantly recalling to your recollection old Homer, Ossian, and Milton, and associating with his performance the melancholy grandeur of their geniuses; you are to imagine you hear his slow, solemn, well accented enunciation, and his voice of affecting, trembling melody; you are to remember the pitch of passion and enthusiasm to which the congregation were raised; and then, the few minutes of portentous, death-like silence which reigned throughout the house; the preacher removing his white handkerchief from his aged face (even yet wet from the recent torrent of his tears), and slowly stretching forth the palsied hand which holds it, begins the sentence, "Socrates died like a philosopher"—then pausing, raising his other hand, pressing them both clasped together, with warmth and energy to his breast, lifting his "sightless balls" to heaven, and pouring his whole soul into his tremulous voice—"but Jesus Christ—like a God!" If he had been indeed and in truth an angel of light, the effect could scarcely have been more divine.

Whatever I had been able to conceive of the sublimity of Massillon, or the force of Bourdalone, had fallen far short of the power which I felt from the delivery of this simple sentence. The blood, which just before had rushed in a hurricane upon my brain, and, in the violence and agony of my feelings had held my whole system in suspense, now ran back into my heart, with a sensation which I cannot describe—a kind of shuddering, delicious horror! The paroxysm of blended pity and indignation, to which I had been transported, subsided into the deepest self-abasement, humility and adoration. I had just been lacerated and dissolved by sympathy for our Saviour as a fellow creature; but now, with fear and trembling, I adored him as—"a God!"

If this description gives you the impression that this incomparable minister had anything of shallow, theatrical trick in his manner, it does him great injustice. I have never seen in any other orator, such a union of simplicity and majesty. He has not a gesture, an attitude or an accent, to which he does not seem forced, by the sentiment which he is expressing. His mind is too serious, too earnest, too solicitous, and, at the same time too dignified, to stoop to artifice. Although as far removed from ostentation as a man can be, yet it is clear from the train, the style and substance of his thoughts, that he is not only a very polite scholar, but a man of extensive and profound erudition. I was forcibly struck with a short, yet beautiful character which he drew of our learned and amiable countryman, Sir Robert Boyle; he spoke of him, as if "his noble mind had, even before death, divested herself of all influence from his frail tabernacle of flesh;" and called him in his peculiarly emphatic and impressive manner, "a pure intelligence; the link between men and angels."

This man has been before my imagination almost ever since. A thousand times, as I rode along, I dropped the reins of my bridle, stretched forth my hand, and tried to imitate his quotation from Rousseau; a thousand times I abandoned the attempt in despair, and felt persuaded that his peculiar manner and power arose from an energy of soul, which nature could give, but which no human being could justly copy. In short, he seems to be altogether a being of a former age, or of a totally different nature from the rest of men. As I recall, at this moment, several of his awfully striking attitudes, the chilling tide with which my blood begins to pour along my arteries reminds me of the emotions produced by the first sight of Gray's introductory picture of his bard:

"On a rock, whose haughty brow
Frowns o'er old Conway's foaming flood,

> Robed in the sable garb of woe,
> With haggard eyes the poet stood;
> (Loose his beard and hoary hair
> Streamed, like a meteor, to the troubled air);
> And with a poet's hand and a prophet's fire,
> Struck the deep sorrows of his lyre."

Guess my surprise, when, on my arrival at Richmond, and mentioning the name of this man, I found not one person who had ever before heard of *James Waddell!* Is it not strange, that such a genius as this, so accomplished a scholar, so divine an orator, should be permitted to languish and die in obscurity, within eighty miles of the metropolis of Virginia?

Order in Nature.

How marvelous is this order! The stones and soil beneath our feet, and the ponderous mountains, are not mere confused masses of matter; they are pervaded through their innermost constitution by the harmony of numbers. The elements of the wood we burn are associated in fixed mathematical ratios. In the violence of combustion, the bond that held them together is destroyed; they break away and rush into new combinations, but they cannot escape the law of numerical destiny. The burning candle gradually wastes away before us, dissolves in air, and passes beyond the reach of sight; but in that invisible region, forces are playing among its unseen particles with the same exactitude and harmony as among those which rule the constellations. And so is it with all chemical mutations. In the gradual growth of living structures, in the digestion of food, and in the slow decay of organic matter, no less than in its quick combustion, the transposition of elements takes place in rigorous accordance with the law of quantitative proportion.

EDWARD EVERETT.

EDWARD EVERETT was born in Dorchester, Mass., April 11, 1794, and he died in Boston, Jan. 15, 1865. "At the age of thirteen he entered Harvard College, and he was graduated with the highest honors." He also studied divinity and settled in Boston as pastor of Brattle Street Church. His scholarly discourses attracted great public attention. He was appointed professor of Greek literature at Cambridge in 1814. "He spent four years in Europe, visiting the principal cities and seats of learning, and extending his researches into a wide range of subjects. On his return, he gave a brilliant series of college lectures, and, beside, conconducted the "North American Review." From his lecture delivered in 1824 before the *Phi Beta Kappa Society* of Harvard, we have taken the article entitled *Welcome to La Fayette*. He served in Congress for ten years from 1824, then served his State as governor for four terms. In 1841, President Harrison appointed him minister to England. He returned to the United States in 1845, and was made president of Harvard College. Upon the death of Daniel Webster, President Fillmore appointed Everett Secretary of State. In 1853, he was chosen United States senator, but, at the close of one year, he resigned. For the purpose of purchasing Mount Vernon, he visited the principal cities of the United States, and delivered his lecture upon Washington. In this way he raised more than fifty thousand dollars.

"It is evident from this brief summary that Mr. Everett was a man of rare powers and rarer culture. He might

EDWARD EVERETT.

truly say, 'What could I have done unto my vineyard that I have not done unto it?' From his infancy he seemed to have been marked out for a scholar, and through his life he enjoyed exceptional advantages in acquiring knowledge, and the best use of his naturally brilliant faculties. His orations were composed for widely differing occasions, but in each case the treatment is so masterly that one would think the subject then in hand had been the special study of his life. But his care did not cease with the preparation; his voice, gestures, and cadences were always in harmony with his theme, so that he was absolute master of his audience. It is seldom that the literary annalist has to record a career in which the preacher and essayist is developed by natural growth into the statesman and diplomatist, while his scholastic tastes and habits grow in parallel lines, and the man at threescore is an epitome of the knowledge and an exemplar of the eloquence of his generation.

"Everett's works are always interesting to the reader. Open a volume at random, and the thought at once engages attention. It is true we do not find passages, like those in Webster's speeches, which come upon us like thunder strokes; but, on the other hand, there are fewer arid spaces. Webster is often uninteresting, if not dull, for pages together. Everett, if he never astonishes, never fails to delight.

"Mr. Everett's works are comprised in four vols. 8 vo. He edited also the works of Webster, and wrote an introductory biography."

Welcome to La Fayette.

Meantime the years are rapidly passing away, and gathering importance in their course. With the present year will be completed the half century from that most important era in human history, the commencement of our Revolutionary War. The jubilee of our national existence is at hand. The space of time that has elapsed from that momentous date, has laid down in the dust, which the blood of many of them had already hallowed, most of the great men to whom, under Providence, we owe our national existence and privileges. A few still survive among us, to reap the rich fruits of their labors and sufferings; and one has yielded himself to the united voice of a people, and returned in his age to receive the gratitude of the nation to whom he devoted his youth. It is recorded on the pages of American history, that when this friend of our country applied to our commissioners at Paris, in 1776, for a passage to America, they were obliged to answer him (so low and abject was then our dear native land), that they possessed not the means nor the credit sufficient for providing a single vessel, in all the ports of France. "Then," exclaimed the youthful hero, "I will provide my own;" and it is a literal fact, that when all America was too poor to offer him so much as a passage to our shores, he left, in his tender youth, the bosom of home, of happiness, of wealth, of rank, to plunge in the dust and blood of our inauspicious struggle.

Welcome, Friend of our Fathers, to our shores! Happy are our eyes that behold those venerable features. Enjoy a triumph such as never conqueror or monarch enjoyed—the assurance that throughout America there is not a bosom which does not beat with joy and gratitude at the sound of your name. You have already met and saluted, or will soon meet the few that remain of the ardent patriots, prudent counselors, and brave warriors, with whom you were associated in achieving our liberty. But you have looked around in vain for the faces of many who would have lived years of pleasure on a day like this, with their old companion in arms and brother in peril. Lincoln, and Greene, and Knox, and Hamilton are gone; the heroes of Saratoga and Yorktown have fallen before the only foe they could not meet. Above all, the first of heroes and of men, the friend of your youth, the more than friend of his country, rests in the bosom of the soil he redeemed. On the banks of his Potomac he lies in glory and peace. You will revisit the hospitable shades of Mount Vernon, but him whom you venerated as we did, you will not meet at its door. His voice of consolation, which reached you in the Austrian dungeons, cannot now break its silence, to bid you welcome to his own roof. But the grateful children of America will bid you welcome in his name. Welcome, thrice welcome, to our shores; and whithersoever throughout the limits of the continent your course shall take you, the ear that hears you shall bless you, the eye that sees you shall bear witness to you, and every tongue exclaim, with heartfelt joy, Welcome, Welcome, Lafayette!

Penn's Advice to His Children.

Next, betake yourself to some honest, industrious course of life, and that not of sordid covetousness, but for example, and to avoid idleness. And if you change your condition and marry, choose with the knowledge and consent of your mother, if living, or of guardians, or of those that have the charge of you. Mind neither beauty nor riches, but the fear of the Lord, and a sweet and amiable disposition, such as you can love above all this world, and that may make your habitations pleasant and desirable to you.

And being married, be tender, affectionate, patient and meek. Live in the fear of the Lord, and He will bless you and your offspring. Be sure to live within compass; borrow not, neither be beholden to any. Ruin not yourself by kindness to others; for that exceeds the due bonds of friendship, neither will a true friend expect it. Small matters I heed not.

Let your industry and parsimony go no further than for a sufficiency for life, and to make a provision for your children, and that in moderation, if the Lord gives you any. I charge you help the poor and needy; let the Lord have a voluntary share of your income for the good of the poor, both in our society and others—for we are all his creatures—remembering that "he that giveth to the poor lendeth to the Lord."

Know well your incomings, and your outgoings may be better regulated. Love not money nor the world; use them only, and they will serve you; but if you love them, you serve them, which will debase your spirits as well as offend the Lord. Pity the distressed, and hold out a hand of help to them; it may be your case, and as you mete to others, God will mete to you again. Be humble and gentle in your conversation, of few words, I charge you; but always pertinent when you speak, hearing out before you attempt to answer, and then speaking as if you would persuade, not impose. Affront none, neither revenge the affronts that are done to you; but forgive, and you shall be forgiven of your Heavenly Father.

In making friends, consider well first; and when you are fixed, be true, not wavering by reports, nor deserting in affliction, for that becomes not good and virtuous. Watch against anger; neither speak nor act in it; for, like drunkenness, it makes a man a beast, and throws people into desperate inconveniences. Avoid flatterers, for they are thieves in disguise; their praise is costly, designing to get by those they bespeak; they are the worst of creatures; they lie to flatter and flatter to cheat; and which is worse, if you believe them, you cheat yourselves most dangerously. But the virtuous, though poor, love, cherish, and prefer. Remember David, who, asking the Lord: "Who shall abide in thy tabernacle? who shall dwell in thy holy hill?" answers: "He that walketh uprightly, and worketh righteousness, and speaketh the truth in his heart; in whose eyes a vile person is contemned, but he honoreth them that fear the Lord."

Next, my children, be temperate in all things: in your diet, for that is physic by prevention; it keeps, nay, it makes people healthy, and their generation sound. This is exclusive of the spiritual advantage it brings. Be also plain in your apparel; keep out that lust which reigns too much over some; let your virtues be your ornaments, remembering life is more than food, and the body than raiment. Let your furniture be simple and cheap. Avoid pride, avarice, and luxury. Read my "No Cross, No Crown." There is instruction. Make your conversation with the most eminent for wisdom and piety, and shun all wicked men as you hope for the blessing of God and the comfort of your father's living and dying prayers. Be sure you speak no evil of any, no, not of the meanest, much less of your superiors, as magistrates, guardians, tutors, teachers and elders in Christ.

Be no busy-bodies; meddle not with other folks' matters, but when in conscience and duty pressed; for it procures trouble, and is ill manners, and very unseemly to wise men. In your families remember Abraham, Moses and Joshua, their integrity to the Lord, and do as you have them for your example. Let the fear and service of the living God be encouraged in your houses, and that plainness, sobriety and moderation in all things, as becometh God's people; and as I advise you, my beloved children, do you counsel yours, if God should give you any. Yea, I counsel and command them as my posterity, that they love and serve the Lord God with an upright heart, that he may bless you and yours from generation to generation.

And as for you, who are likely to be concerned in the government of Pennsylvania and my part of East Jersey, especially the first, I do charge you before the Lord God and his holy angels, that you be lowly, diligent, and tender, fearing God, loving the people, and hating covetousness. Let justice have its impartial course, and the law free passage. Though to your loss, protect no man against it; for you are not above the law, but the law above you. Live, therefore, the lives yourselves, you would have the people live, and then you have right and boldness to punish the transgressor.

Keep upon the square, for God sees you; therefore, do your duty, and be sure you see with your own eyes, and hear with your own ears. Entertain no lurchers, cherish no informers for gain or revenge, use no tricks, fly to no devices to support or cover injustice; but let your hearts be upright before the Lord, trusting in him above the contrivances of men, and none shall be able to hurt or supplant.

Christianity.

Taken from a speech of Charles Phillips, the Irish orator, delivered at Cheltenham England, on the 7th of October, 1819, at the fourth anniversary of the Gloucester Missionary Society.

When I consider the source from whence Christianity springs—the humility of its origin—the poverty of its disciples—the miracles of its creation—the mighty sway it has acquired not only over the civilized world, but which your missions are hourly extending over lawless, mindless, and imbruted regions—I own the awful presence of the Godhead—nothing less than a Divinity could have done it! The powers, the prejudices, the superstitions of the earth were all in arms against it; it had nor sword nor sceptre—its founder was in rags—its apostles were lowly fishermen—its inspired prophets, lowly and uneducated—its cradle was a manger—its home a dungeon—its earthly diadem a crown of thorns! And yet, forth it went—that lowly, humble, persecuted spirit—and the idols of the heathen fell; and the thrones of the mighty trembled; and paganism saw her peasants and her princes kneel down and worship the unarmed Conqueror! If this be not the work of the Divinity, then I yield to the reptile ambition of the atheist. I see no God above—I see no government below, and I yield my consciousness of an immortal soul to his boasted fraternity with the worm that perishes! But, sir, even when I thus concede to him the divine origin of our Christian faith, I arrest him upon worldly principles—I desire him to produce, from all the wisdom of the earth, so pure a system of practical morality—a code of ethics more sublime in its conception—more simple in its means—more happy and more powerful in its operation; and, if he cannot do so, I then say to him, Oh! in the name of your own darling policy filch not its guide from youth, its shield from manhood, and its crutch from age! Though the light I follow may lead me astray, still I think it is light from Heaven! The good, and great, and wise, are my companions—my delightful hope is harmless, if not holy; and wake me not to a disappointment, which in *your tomb of annihilation*, I shall not taste hereafter!

The following extract we take from Mr. Phillip's speech delivered at the annual meeting of the British and Foreign Auxiliary Society, London.

My Lord, I will abide by the precepts, admire the beauty, revere the mysteries, and as far as in me lies, practice the mandates of this sacred volume; and should the ridicule of earth, and the blasphemy of hell assail me, I shall console myself by the contemplation of those blessed spirits, who, in the same holy cause, have toiled, and shone, and suffered. In the "goodly fellowship of the saints"—in the "noble army of the martyrs"—in the society of the great, and good, and wise of every nation, if my sinfulness be not cleansed, and my darkness illuminated, at least my pretensionless submission may be excused. If I err with the luminaries I have chosen for my guides, I confess myself captivated by the loveliness of their aberrations. If they err it is in an heavenly region; if they wander, it is in fields of light; if they aspire, it is at all events a glorious daring; and rather than sink with infidelity into the dust, I am content to cheat myself with their vision of eternity. It may, indeed, be nothing but delusion, but then I err with the disciples of philosophy and of virtue—with men who have drank deep at the fountain of human knowledge, but who dissolved not the pearl of their salvation in the draught. I err with Bacon, the great Bacon, the great confidant of nature, fraught with all the learning of the past, and almost prescient of the future; yet too wise not to know his weakness, and too philosophic not to feel his ignorance. I err with Milton, rising on an angel's wings to heaven, and like the bird of morn, soaring out of light, amid the music of his grateful piety. I err with Locke, whose pure philosophy only taught him to adore its source, whose warm love of genuine liberty was never chilled into rebellion with its author. I err with Newton, whose star-like spirit shooting athwart the darkness of the sphere, too soon to re-ascend to the home of his nativity. With men like these, my lord, I shall remain in error. * * *

Holding opinions such as these, I should consider myself culpable, if, at such a crisis, I did not declare them. A lover of my country, I yet draw a line between patriotism and rebellion. A warm friend of liberty of conscience, I will not confound toleration with infidelity. With all its ambiguity, I shall die in the doctrines of the Christian faith; and, with all its errors, I am contented to live under the safeguards of the British Constitution.

Eleonora.

I am come of a race noted for vigor of fancy and ardor of passion. Men have called me mad, but the question is not yet settled whether madness is or is not the loftiest intelligence—whether much that is glorious—whether all that is profound—does not spring from disease of thought, from *moods* of mind exalted at the expense of the general intellect. They who dream by day are cognizant of many things which escape those who dream only by night. In their gray visions they obtain glimpses of eternity, and thrill, in waking, to find that they have been upon the verge of the great secret. In snatches, they learn something of the wisdom which is of good, and more of the mere knowledge which is of evil. They penetrate, however rudderless or compassless, into the vast ocean of the "light ineffable;" and again, like the adventures of the Nubian geographer, *agressi sunt mare tenebrarum quid in eo esset exploraturi.* We will say, then, that I am mad. I grant, at least, that there are two distinct conditions of my mental existence—the condition of a lucid reason, not to be disputed, and belonging to the memory of events forming the first epoch of my life—and a condition of shadow and doubt, appertaining to the present, and to the recollection of what constitutes the second great era of my being. Therefore, what I shall tell of the earlier period, believe; and to what I may relate of the later time, give only such credit as may seem due, or doubt it altogether; or if doubt it ye cannot, then play unto its riddle the Œdipus.

She whom I loved in youth, and of whom I now pen calmly and distinctly these remembrances, was the sole daughter of the only sister of my mother long departed. Eleonora was the name of my cousin. We had always dwelled together, beneath a tropical sun, in the Valley of the Many-Colored Grass. No unguided footstep ever came upon that vale; for it lay far away up among a range of giant hills that hung beetling around about it, shutting out the sunlight from its sweetest recesses. No path was trodden in its vicinity; and to reach our happy home, there was need of putting back, with force, the foliage of many thousands of forest trees, and of crushing to death the glories of many millions of fragrant flowers. Thus it was that we lived all alone, knowing nothing of the world without the valley,—I, and my cousin, and her mother.

From the dim regions beyond the mountains at the upper end of our encircled domain, there crept out a narrow and deep river, brighter than all save the eyes of Eleonora; and, winding stealthily about in mazy courses, it passed away, at length, through a shadowy gorge, among hills still dimmer than those whence it had issued. We called it the "River of Silence;" for there seemed to be a hushing influence in its flow. No murmur arose from its bed, and so gently it wandered along, that the pearly pebbles upon which we loved to gaze, far down within its bosom, stirred not at all, but lay in a motionless content, each in its own old station, shining on gloriously forever.

The margin of the river, and of the many dazzling rivulets

that glided through devious ways into its channel, as well as the spaces that extended from the margins away down into the depths of the streams until they reached the bed of pebbles at the bottom,—these spots, not less than the whole surface of the valley, from the river to the mountains that girdled it in, were carpeted all by a soft green grass, thick, short, perfectly even, and vanilla perfumed, but so besprinkled throughout with the yellow buttercup, the white daisy, the purple violet, and the ruby-red asphodel, that its exceeding beauty spoke to our hearts in loud tones, of the love and of the glory of God.

And, here and there, in groves about this grass, like wildernesses of dreams, sprang up fantastic trees, whose tall, slender stems stood not upright, but slanted gracefully toward the light that peered at noon-day into the center of the valley. Their bark was speckled with the vivid alternate splendor of ebony and silver, and was smoother than all save the cheeks of Eleonora; so, that but for the brilliant green of the huge leaves that spread from their summits in long, tremulous lines, dallying with the zephyrs, one might have fancied them giant serpents of Syria doing homage to their sovereign, the sun.

Hand in hand about this valley, for fifteen years, roamed I with Eleonora before Love entered within our hearts. It was one evening at the close of the third lustrum of her life, and of the fourth of my own, that we sat, locked in each other's embrace, beneath the serpent-like trees, and looked down within the waters of the River of Silence at our images therein. We spoke no words during the rest of that sweet day, and our words even upon the morrow were tremulous and few. We had drawn the god Eros from that wave, and now we felt that he had enkindled within us the fiery souls of our forefathers. The passions which had for centuries distinguished our race came thronging with the fancies for which they had equally noted and together breathed a delirious bliss over the Valley of the Many-Colored Grass. A change fell upon all things. Strange, brilliant flowers, star-shaped, burst out upon the trees where no flowers had been known before. The tints

of the green carpet deepened; and when, one by one, the white
daisies shrank away, there sprang up in place of them ten by ten
of the ruby-red asphodel, and life arose in our paths; for the tall
flamingo, hitherto unseen, with all gay glowing birds, flaunted his
scarlet plumage before us. The golden and silver fish haunted the
river, out of the bosom of which issued, little by little, a murmur
that swelled, at length, into a lulling melody more divine than that
of the harp of Æolus—sweeter than all save the voice of Eleonora.
And now, too, a voluminous cloud, which we had long watched in
the regions of Hesper, floated out thence, all gorgeous in crimson
and gold, and settling in peace above us, sank, day by day, lower
and lower, until its edges rested upon the tops of the mountains,
turning all their dimness into magnificence, and shutting us up,
as if forever, within a magic prison-house of grandeur and of glory.

The loveliness of Eleonora was that of the Seraphim; but she
was a maiden artless and innocent as the brief life she had led among
the flowers. No guile disguised the fervor of love which animated
her heart, and she examined with me its inmost recesses as we
walked together in the Valley of the Many-Colored Grass, and dis-
coursed of the mighty changes which had lately taken place therein.

At length, having spoken one day, in tears, of the last, sad
change which must befall Humanity, she thenceforward dwelt only
upon this one sorrowful theme, interweaving it into all our converse,
as, in the songs of the bard of Schiraz the same images are found
occurring, again and again, in every impressive variation of phrase.

She had seen that the finger of Death was upon her bosom—
that, like the ephemeron, she had been made perfect in loveliness
only to die; but the terrors of the grave, to her, lay solely in a consideration which she revealed to me, one evening at twilight, by the
banks of the River of Silence. She grieved to think that, having
entombed her in the Valley of the Many-Colored Grass, I would
quit forever its happy recesses, transferring the love which now was
so passionately her own to some maiden of the outer and every-day
world. And, then and there, I threw myself hurriedly at the feet
of Eleonora, and offered up a vow to herself and to Heaven, that

I would never bind myself in marriage to any daughter of Earth—that I would in no manner prove recreant to her dear memory, or to the memory of the devout affection with which she blessed me. And I called the Mighty Ruler of the Universe to witness the pious solemnity of my vow. And the curse which I invoked of *Him* and of her, a saint in Helusion, should I prove traitorous to that promise, involved a penalty the exceeding great horror of which will not permit me to make a record of it here. And the bright eyes of Eleonora grew brighter at my words; and she sighed as if a deadly burthen had been taken from her breast, and she trembled and very bitterly wept; but she made acceptance of the vow, (for what was she but a child?) and it made easy to her the bed of her death. And she said to me, not many days afterward, tranquilly dying, that, because of what I had done for the comfort of her spirit, she would watch over me in that spirit when departed, and, if so it were permitted her, return to me visibly in the watches of the night; but, if this thing were, indeed, beyond the power of the souls in Paradise, that she would, at least, give me frequent indications of her presence; sighing upon me in the evening winds, or filling the air which I breathed with perfume from the censers of the angels. And, with these words upon her lips, she yielded up her innocent life, putting an end to the first epoch of my own.

Thus far I have faithfully said. But as I pass the barrier in Time's path, formed by the death of my beloved, and proceed with the second era of my existence, I feel that a shadow gathers over my brain, and I mistrust the perfect sanity of the record. But let me on. Years dragged themselves along heavily and still I dwelled within the Valley of the Many-Colored Grass; but a second change had come upon all things. The star-shaped flowers shrank into the stems of the trees, and appeared no more. The tints of the green carpet faded, and one by one ruby-red asphodels withered away; and there sprang up, in place of them, ten by ten, dark, eye-like violets, that writhed uneasily and were ever encumbered with dew. And Life departed from our paths; for the tall flamingo flaunted no longer his scarlet plumage before us, but flew sadly from the vale into the hills, with all the gay glowing birds that had arrived in his company. And the golden and silver fish swam down through the gorge at the lower end of our domain, and bedecked the sweet river never again. And the lulling melody that had been softer than the wind-harp of Æolus, and more divine than all save the voice of Eleonora, it died little by little away, in murmurs growing lower and lower, until the stream returned at length utterly into the solemnity of its original silence. And then, lastly, the voluminous cloud uprose, and, abandoning the tops of the mountains to the dimness of old, fell back into the regions of Hesper, and took away all its manifold golden and gorgeous glories from the Valley of the Many-Colored Grass.

Yet the promises of Eleonora were not forgotten; for I heard the sounds of the swinging of the censers of the angels; and streams of a holy perfume floated ever and ever about the valley; and at lone hours, when my heart beat heavily, the winds that bathed my brow came unto me laden with soft sighs; and indistinct murmurs filled often the night air; and once—oh, but once only! I was awakened from a slumber, like the slumber of death, by the pressing of spiritual lips upon my own.

But the void within my heart refused, even then, to be filled. I longed for the love which had before filled it to overflowing. At length the valley pained me through its memories of Eleonora, and I left it forever for the vanities and the turbulent triumphs of the world.

* * * * * * * * *

I found myself within a strange city, where all things might have served to blot from recollection the sweet dreams I had dreamed so long in the Valley of the Many Colored Grass. The pomps and pageantries of a stately court, and the mad clangor of arms, and the radiant loveliness of woman, bewildered and intoxicated my brain. But as yet my soul had proved true to its vows, and the indications of the presence of Eleonora were still given me in the silent hours of the night. Suddenly, these manifestations ceased; and the world grew dark before mine eyes; and I stood aghast at the burning thoughts which possessed—at the terrible temptations which beset me; for there came from some far, far distant and unknown land, into the gay court of the king I served, a maiden to whose beauty my whole recreant heart yielded at once —at whose footstool I bowed down without a struggle, in the most ardent, in the most abject worship of love. What, indeed, was my passion for the young girl of the valley in comparison with the fervor, and the delirium, and the spirit-lifting ecstacy of adoration with which I poured out my whole soul in tears at the feet of the ethereal Ermengarde? Oh, bright was the seraph Ermengarde! and in that knowledge I had room for none other. Oh, divine was the angel Ermengarde! and as I looked down into the depths of her memorial eyes, I thought only of them—and *of her* I wedded; nor dreaded the curse I had invoked; and its bitterness was not visited upon me. And once—but once again in the silence of the night, there came through my lattice the soft sighs which had forsaken me; and they modeled themselves into familiar and sweet voice, saying:

"Sleep in peace!—for the Spirit of Love reigneth and ruleth, and in taking to thy passionate heart her who is Ermengarde, thou art absolved, for reasons which shall be made known to thee in Heaven, of thy vows unto Eleonora."

English Language.

The language which, at the very beginning of its full organization, could produce the linked sweetness of Sidney and the "mighty line" of Marlowe, the voluptuous beauty of Spenser and the oceanic melody of Shakespere, and which, at a riper age, could show itself an adequate instrument for the organ-like harmonies of Milton and the matchless symphonies of Sir Thomas Browne; which could give full and fit expression to the fiery energy of Dryden and the epigrammatic point of Pope, to the forest-like gloom of Young and the passionate outpourings of Burns; which sustained and supported the tremulous elegance and husbanded strength of Campbell, the broad-winged sweep of Coleridge, the deep sentiment and all-embracing humanities of Wordsworth and the gorgeous emblazonry of Moore; and which to-day, in the plenitude of its powers, responds to every call of Tennyson, Ruskin, Newman, and Froude,—is surely equal to the demands of any genius that may yet arise to tax its powers. Spoken in the time of Elizabeth by a million fewer persons than to-day speak it in London alone, it now girdles the earth with its electric chain of communication, and voices the thoughts of a hundred million of souls. It has crossed the peaks of the Rocky Mountains, and has invaded South America and the Sandwich Islands; it is advancing with giant strides through Africa and New Zealand, and on the scorching plains of India; it is penetrating the wild waste of Australia, making inroads upon China and Japan, and bids fair to become the dominant language of the civilized world. Let us jealously guard its purity, maintain its ancient idioms, and develop its inexhaustible resources, that it may be even more worthy than it now is to be the mother tongue, not only of the two great brother nations whose precious legacy it is, but of the whole family of man.

OLIVER WENDELL HOLMES.

OLIVER WENDELL HOLMES was born at Cambridge, Mass., August 29, 1809, and at this time (1882) he occupies the chair of Anatomy and Physiology in Harvard University. At the age of twenty, Holmes graduated at Harvard and commenced the study of law. Law was soon abandoned for medicine. He studied in Europe, and in 1836 graduated at Cambridge as *Doctor of Medicine*. In 1838 he became professor of Anatomy and Physiology in Dartmouth College, and in 1847 accepted the same position at Harvard.

The following are among his literary works: *Poetry, a Metrical Essay; Terpsichore; Urania; Astræa*. The above poems were delivered before college and literary societies. He is also author of three excellent works, entitled: *Autocrat of the Breakfast Table; The Professor at the Breakfast Table*, and *The Poet at the Breakfast Table*. Three other well known works of his are *Elsie Venner*, published in 1861; *The Guardian Angel*, in 1868; *Mechanism in Thought and Morals*, in 1872.

Besides his excellent literary works already noted, he is author of valuable medical works.

Although not a literary man by profession, yet he has written extensively, and has gained a high position in the literary world. His composition is always smooth and graceful, and many of his sayings are among the finest specimens of American humor.

Holmes combines science and philosophy, wit and hu-

Oliver Wendell Holmes

mor, in poetry and prose, in a most happy and brilliant manner. His poems, written for class reunions and other special occasions, are so happy that they make Holmes "the fountain of perpetual youth" in American literature.

Autocrat of the Breakfast-Table.

[The "Atlantic" obeys the moon, and its *luniversary* has come round again. I have gathered up some hasty notes of my remarks made since the last high tides, which I respectfully submit. Please to remember this is *talk*; just as easy and just as formal as I choose to make it.]

I never saw an author in my life—saving, perhaps, one—that did not purr as audibly as a full grown domestic cat, on having his fur smoothed in the right way by a skilful hand.

But let me give you a caution. Be very careful how you tell an author he is *droll*. Ten to one he will hate you; and if he does, be sure he can do you a mischief, and very probably will. Say you *cried* over his romance or his verses, and he will love you and send you a copy. You can laugh over that as much as you like—in private.

Wonder why authors and actors are ashamed of being funny? Why, there are obvious reasons, and deep philosophical ones. The clown knows very well that the women are not in love with him, but with Hamlet, the fellow in black cloak and plumed hat. Passion never laughs. The wit knows that his place is at the tail of a procession.

If you want the deep, underlying reason, I must take more time to tell it. There is a perfect consciousness in every form of wit—using that term in its general sense—that its essence consists in a partial and incomplete view of whatever it touches. It throws a single ray, separated from the rest—red, yellow, blue, or any intermediate shade,—upon an object; never white light; that is the province of wisdom. We get beautiful effects from wit,—all the prismatic colors,—but never the object as it is in fair daylight. A pun, which is a kind of wit, is a different and much shallower trick in mental optics, throwing the *shadows* of two objects so that one overlies the other. Poetry uses the rainbow tints for special effects, but always keeps its essential object in the purest white light of truth. Will you allow me to pursue this subject a little further?

[They didn't allow me at that time, for somebody happened to scrape the floor with his chair just then; which accidental sound, as all must have noticed, has the instantaneous effect that the cutting of the yellow hair by Iris had upon inflexible Dido. It broke the charm, and that breakfast was over].

Don't flatter yourselves that friendship authorizes you to say disagreeable things to your intimates. On the contrary, the nearer you come into relation with a person, the more necessary do tact and courtesy become. Except in cases of necessity, which are rare, leave your friend to learn unpleasant truths from his enemies; they are ready enough to tell them. Good breeding never forgets *amour propre* is universal. When you read the story of the Archbishop and Gil Blas, you may laugh, if you will, at the poor old man's delusion; but don't forget that the youth was the greater fool of the two, and that his master served such a booby rightly in turning him out of doors.

You need not get up a rebellion against what I say, if you find everything in my sayings is not exactly new. You can't possibly mistake a man who means to be honest, for a literary pickpocket. I once read an introductory lecture that looked to me too learned for its latitude. On examination, I found all its erudition was taken ready made from D'Israeli. If I had been ill-natured, I should have shown up the little great man, who had once belabored me in his feeble way. But one can generally tell these wholesale thieves easily enough, and they are not worth the trouble of putting them in the pillory. I doubt the entire novelty of my remarks just made on telling unpleasant truths, yet I am not conscious of any larceny.

Neither make too much of flaws and occasional over statements. Some persons seem to think that absolute truth, in the form of rigidly stated propositions, is all that conversation admits. This is precisely as if a musician should insist on having nothing but perfect chords and simple melodies,—no diminished fifths, no flat sevenths, no flourishes, on any account. Now it is fair to say, that, just as music must have all these, so conversation must have its partial truths, its embellished truths, its exaggerated truths. It is in its higher forms an artistic product, and admits the deal element as much as pictures or statues. One man who is a little too literal can spoil the talk of a whole table full of men of esprit. "Yes," you say, "but who wants to hear fanciful people's nonsense? Put the facts to it, and then see where it is!" Certainly, if a man is too fond of paradox,—if he is flighty and empty,—if, instead of striking those fifths and sevenths, those harmonious discords, often so much better than the twinned octaves, in the music of thought, if, instead of striking these, he jangles the chords, stick a fact into him like a stiletto. But remember that talking is one of the fine arts,—the noblest, the most important, and the most difficult,—and that its fluent harmonies may be spoiled by the intrusion of a single harsh note. Therefore conversation which is suggestive rather than argumentative, which lets out the most of each talker's results of thoughts, is commonly the pleasantest and the most profitable. It is not easy, at the best, for two persons talking together to make the most of each other's thoughts, there are so many of them.

[The company looked as if they wanted an explanation].

When John and Thomas, for instance, are talking together, it is natural enough that among the six there should be more or less confusion and misapprehension.

[Our landlady turned pale; no doubt she thought there was a screw loose in my intellect,—and that involved the probable loss of a boarder. A severe looking person, who wears a Spanish cloak and a sad cheek, fluted by the passions of the melodrama, whom I understand to be the professional ruffian of the neighboring theater, alluded, with a certain lifting of the brow, drawing down the corners of the mouth, and somewhat rasping *voce di petto*, to Falstaff's nine men in buckram. Everybody looked up; I believe the old gentleman opposite was afraid I should seize the carving-knife; at any rate, he slid it to one side, as it were carelessly.]

I think, I said, I can make it plain to Benjamin Franklin here, that there are at least six personalities distinctly to be recognized as taking part in that dialogue between John and Thomas.

Three Johns.
1. The real John; known only to his Maker.
2. John's ideal John; never the real one, and often very unlike him.
3. Thomas's ideal John; never the real John, nor John's John, but often very unlike either.

Three Thomases.
1. The real Thomas.
2. Thomas's ideal Thomas.
3. John's ideal Thomas.

Only one of the three Johns is taxed; only one can be weighed on a platform balance; but the other two are just as important in the conversation. Let us suppose the real John to be old, dull, and ill-looking. But as the Higher Powers have not conferred on men the seeing themselves in the true light, John very possibly conceives himself to be youthful, witty, and fascinating, and talks from the point of view of this ideal. Thomas, again, believes him to be an artful rogue, we will say; therefore he *is*, so far as Thomas's attitude in the conversation is concerned, an artful rogue, though really simple and stupid. The same conditions apply to the three Thomases. It follows, that, until a man can be found who knows himself as his Maker knows him, or who sees himself as others see him, there must be at least six persons engaged in every dialogue between two. Of these, the least important, philosophically speaking, is the one that we have called the real person. No wonder two disputants often get angry, when there are six of them talking and listening all at the same time.

[A very unphilosophical application of the above remarks was made by a young fellow, answering to the name of John, who sits near me at the table. A certain basket of peaches, a rare vegetable, little known to boarding-houses, was on its way to me *via* this unlettered Johannes. He appropriated the three that remained in the basket, remarking that there was just one piece for him. I convinced him that his practical inference was hasty and illogical, but in the meantime he had eaten the peaches.]

The opinions of relatives as to a man's powers are very commonly of little value; not merely because they sometimes overrate their own flesh and blood, as some may suppose; on the contrary, they are quite as likely to underrate those whom they have grown into the habit of considering like themselves. The advent of genius is like what florists style the *breaking* of a seedling tulip into what we may call high-caste colors,—ten thousand dingy flowers, then one with the divine streak; or, if you prefer it, like the coming up in old Jacob's garden of that most gentlemanly little fruit, the seckel pear, which I have sometimes seen in shop windows. It is a surprise,—there is nothing to account for it. All at once we find that twice two make *five.* Nature is fond of what is called "gift enterprises." This little book of life which she has given into the hands of its joint possessors is commonly one of the old story books bound over again. Only once in a great while there is a stately poem in it, or its leaves are illuminated with the glories of art, or they enfold a draft for untold values signed by the millionfold millionaire old mother herself. But strangers are commonly the first to find the "gift" that came with the little book.

Jerusalem.

The broad noon lingers on the summit of Mount Olivet, but its beam has long left the garden of Gethsemane and the tomb of Absalom, the waters of Kedron and the dark abyss of Jehosaphat. Full falls its splendor, however, on the opposite city, vivid and defined in its silver blaze. A lofty wall, with turrets and towers and frequent gates, undulates with the unequal ground which it covers, as it encircles the lost capital of Jehovah. It is a city of hills far more famous than those of Rome; for all Europe has heard of Zion and of Calvary, while the Arab and the Assyrian, and the tribes and nations beyond, are as ignorant of the Capitolan and Aventine Mounts as they are of the Malvern or the Chiltern Hills.

The broad steep of Sion crowned with the tower of David; nearer still, Mount Moriah, with the gorgeous temple of the God of Abraham, but built, alas! by the child of Hagar, and not by Sarah's chosen one; close to its cedars and its cypresses, its lofty spires and airy arches, the moonlight falls upon Bethesda's pool; further on, entered by the gate of St. Stephen, the eye, though 'tis the noon of night, traces with ease the Street of Grief, a long, winding ascent to a vast cupolaed pile that now covers Calvary—called the Street of Grief because there the most illustrious of the human, as well as of the Hebrew race, the descendant of King David, and the divine son of the favored of women, twice sank under that burden of suffering and shame which is now throughout all Christendom the emblem of triumph and of honor; passing over groups and masses of houses built of stone, with terraced roofs, or surmounted with small domes, we reach the hill of Salem, where Melchisedek built his mystic citadel; and still remains the hill of Scopas, where Titus gazed upon Jerusalem on the eve of his final assault. Titus destroyed the temple. The religion of Judea has in turn subverted the fanes which were raised to his father and to himself in their imperial capital; and the God of Abraham, of Isaac, and of Jacob, is now worshiped before every altar in Rome. Jerusalem by moonlight! 'Tis a fine spectacle, apart from all its indissoluble associations of awe and beauty. The mitigating hour softens the austerity of a mountain landscape magnificent in outline, however harsh and severe in detail; and, while it retains all its sublimity, removes much of the savage sternness of the strange and unrivaled scene.

A fortified city, almost surrounded by ravines, and rising in the center of chains of far-spreading hills, occasionally offering, through their rocky glens, the gleams of a distant and richer land!

The moon has sunk behind the Mount of Olives, and the stars in the darker sky shine doubly bright over the sacred city. The all-pervading stillness is broken by a breeze that seems to have traveled over the plain of Sharon from the sea. It wails among the tombs and sighs among the cypress groves. The palm-tree trembles as it passes, as if it were a spirit of woe. Is it the breeze that has traveled over the plains of Sharon from the sea? Or is it the haunting voice of prophets mourning over the city that they could not save? Their spirits surely would linger on the land where their Creator had deigned to dwell, and over whose impending fate Omnipotence had shed human tears. From this mount who can but believe that, at the midnight hour, from the summit of the Ascension, the great departed of Israel assemble to gaze upon the battlements of their mystic city? There might be counted heroes and sages, who need shrink from no rivalry with the brightest and wisest of other lands; but the lawgiver of the time of the Pharaohs, whose laws are still obeyed; the monarch whose reign has ceased for three thousand years, but whose wisdom is a proverb in all nations of the earth; the teacher, whose doctrines have modeled civilized Europe—the greatest of legislators, the greatest of administrators, and the greatest of reformers—what race, extinct or living, can produce three such men as these?

The last light is extinguished in the village of Bethany. The wailing breeze has become a moaning wind; a white film spreads over the purple sky; the stars are veiled; the stars are hid; all becomes as dark as the waters of Kedron and the valley of Jehosaphat. The tower of David merges into obscurity; no longer glitter the minarets of the mosque of Omar; Bethesda's angelic waters, the gate of Stephen, the street of sacred sorrow, the hill of Salem, and the heights of Scopas, can no longer be discerned. Alone in the increasing darkness, while the line of the very walls gradually eludes the eye, the church of the Holy Sepulcher is a beacon light.

And why is the church of the Holy Sepulcher a beacon light? Why, when it is already past the noon of darkness, when every soul slumbers in Jerusalem, and not a sound disturbs the deep repose except the howl of the wild dog crying to the wilder wind—why is the cupola of the sanctuary illumined, though the hour has long since been numbered when the pilgrims there kneel and the monks pray?

An armed Turkish guard are bivouacked in the court of the church; within the church itself two brethren of the convent of

Terra Santa keep holy watch and ward, while at the tomb beneath there kneels a solitary youth, who prostrated himself at sunset, and who will there pass unmoved the whole of the sacred night.

Yet the pilgrim is not in communion with the Latin church; neither is he of the Church Armenian, or the Church Greek; Maronite, Coptic, or Abyssinian—these also are Christian churches which cannot call him child. He comes from a distant and a northern isle to bow before the tomb of a descendant of the kings of Israel, because he, in common with all the people of that isle, recognizes in that sublime Hebrew incarnation the presence of a Divine Redeemer. Then why does he come alone? It is not that he has availed himself of the inventions of modern science, to repair first to a spot which all his countrymen may equally desire to visit, and thus anticipate their hurrying arrival. Before the inventions of modern science, all his countrymen used to flock hither. Then why do they not now? Is the Holy Land no longer hallowed? Is it not the land of sacred and mysterious truths? The land of heavenly messages and earthly miracles? The land of prophets and apostles? Is it not the land upon whose mountains the Creator of the universe parleyed with man, and the flesh of whose anointed race He mystically assumed when he struck the last blow at the powers of evil? Is it to be believed that there are no peculiar and eternal qualities in a land thus visited, which distinguished it from all others—that Palestine is like Normandy, or Yorkshire, or even Attica or Rome?

There may be some who maintain this; there have been some, and those, too, among the wisest and the wittiest of the northern and western races, who, touched by a presumptuous jealousy of the long predominance of that oriental intellect to which they owed their civilization, would have persuaded themselves and the world that the traditions of Sinai and Calvary were fables. Half a century ago Europe made a violent and apparently successful effort to disembarrass itself of its Asian faith. The most powerful and the most civilized of its kingdoms, about to conquer the rest, shut up its churches, desecrated its altars, massacred and persecuted their

sacred servants, and announced that the Hebrew creeds which
Simon Peter brought from Palestine, and which his successors
revealed to Clovis, were a mockery and a fiction. What has been
the result? In every city, town, village and hamlet of that great
kingdom, the divine image of the most illustrious of Hebrews has
been again raised amid the homage of kneeling millions; while in
the heart of its bright and witty capital the nation has erected the
most gorgeous of modern temples, and consecrated its marble and
golden walls to the name, and memory, and celestial efficacy of a
Hebrew woman. The country of which the solitary pilgrim, kneeling at this moment at the Holy Sepulchre, was a native, had not
actively shared in that insurrection against the first and second Testament which distinguished the end of the eighteenth century. But
more than six hundred years before, it had sent its king and the
flower of its peers and people, to rescue Jerusalem from those whom
they considered infidels! and now, instead of the third crusade,
they expand their superfluous energies in the construction of rail-
roads.

The failure of the European kingdom of Jerusalem, on which
such vast treasure, such prodigies of valor and such ardent belief
had been wasted, has been one of those circumstances which have
tended to disturb the faith of Europe, although it should have carried convictions of a very different character. The Crusaders looked
upon the Saracens as infidels, whereas the children of the desert
bore a much nearer affinity to the sacred corpse that had, for a brief
space, consecrated the Holy Sepulchre, than any of the invading
host of Europe. The same blood flowed in their veins, and they
recognized the divine missions both of Moses and of his greater successor. In an age so deficient in physiological learning as the
twelfth century, the mysteries of race were unknown. Jerusalem,
it cannot be doubted, will ever remain the appendage either of Israel
or of Ishmael; and if, in the course of those great vicissitudes
which are no doubt impending for the East, there be any attempt to
place upon the throne of David a prince of the House of Coburg or
Deuxponts, the same fate will doubtless await him, as, with all

their brilliant qualities and all the sympathy of Europe, was the final doom of the Godfreys, the Baldwins, and the Lusignans.

Pictures of Swiss Scenery and of the City of Venice.

It was in Switzerland that I first felt how constantly to contemplate sublime creation develops the poetic power. It was here that I first began to study nature. Those forests of black, gigantic pines rising out of the deep snows; those tall, white cataracts, leaping like headstrong youth into the world, and dashing from their precipices as if allured by the beautiful delusion of their own rainbow mist; those mighty clouds sailing beneath my feet, or clinging to the bosoms of the dark green mountains, or boiling up like a spell from the invisible and unfathomable depths; the fell avalanche, fleet as a spirit of evil, terrific when it suddenly breaks upon the almighty silence, scarcely less terrible when we gaze upon its crumbling and pallid frame, varied only by the presence of one or two blasted firs; the head of a mountain loosening from its brother peak, rooting up, in the roar of its rapid rush, a whole forest of pines, and covering the earth for miles with elephantine masses; the supernatural extent of landscape that opens to us new worlds; the strong eagles and the strange wild birds that suddenly cross you in your path, and stare, and shrieking fly—and all the soft sights of joy and loveliness that mingle with these sublime and savage spectacles, the rich pastures and the numerous flocks, and the golden bees and the wild flowers, and the carved and painted cottages, and the simple manner and the primeval grace—wherever I moved, I was in turn appalled or enchanted; but whatever I beheld, new images ever sprang up in my mind, and new feelings ever crowded on my fancy. · · · ·

If I were to assign the particular quality which conduces to that dreamy and voluptuous existence which men of high imagination experience in Venice, I should describe it as the feeling of abstraction, which is remarkable in that city, and peculiar to it. Venice is the only city which can yield the magical delights of solitude. All is still and silent. No rude sound disturbs your reveries; fancy, therefore, is not put to flight. No rude sound distracts your self-consciousness. This renders existence intense. We feel everything. And we feel thus keenly in a city not only eminently beautiful, not only abounding in wonderful creations of art, but each step of which is hallowed ground, quick with associations, that in their more various nature, their nearer relation to ourselves, and perhaps their more picturesque character, exercise a greater influence over the imagination than the more antique story of Greece and Rome. We feel all this in a city, too, which, although her luster be indeed dimmed, can still count among her daughters, maidens fairer than the orient pearls with which her warriors once loved to deck them. Poetry, Tradition, and Love—these are the Graces that invested with an ever charming cestus this Aphrodite of cities.

A Good Man's Day.

Every day is a little life; and our whole life is but a day repeated; whence it is that old Jacob numbers his life by days; Moses desires to be taught this point of holy arithmetic, to number not his years, but his days. Those, therefore, that dare lose a day, are dangerously prodigal; those that dare misspend it, desperate. We can best teach others by ourselves; let me tell your lordship how I would pass my days, whether common or sacred, that you (or whosoever others overhearing me,) may either approve my thriftiness, or correct my errors; to whom is the account of my hours either more due, or more known. All days are His who gave time a beginning and continuance; yet some He hath made ours, not to command, but to use.

In none may we forget him; in some we must forget all besides Him. First, therefore, I desire to wake at those hours, not when I will, but when I must; pleasure is not a fit rule for rest, but health; neither do I consult so much with the sun, as mine own necessity, whether of body or in that of mind. If this vassal could well serve me waking, it should never sleep; but now it must be pleased, that it may be serviceable. Now, when sleep is rather driven away than leaves me, I would ever awake with God; my first thoughts are for Him who hath made the night for rest and the day for travel; and as He gives, so blesses both. If my heart be early seasoned with His presence, it will savor of Him all day after. While my body is dressing, not with an effeminate curiosity, nor yet with rude neglect, my mind addresses itself to her ensuing task, bethinking what is to be done, and in what order, and marshalling (as it may) my hours with my work; that done, after some while's meditation, I walk up to my masters and companions, my books, and sitting down amongst them with the best contentment, I dare not reach forth my hand to salute any of them, till I have first looked up to heaven, and craved favor of Him to whom all my studies are duly referred; without whom I can neither profit nor labor. After this, out of no over great variety, I call forth those which may best fit my occasions, wherein I am not too scrupulous of age. Sometimes I put myself to school to one of those ancients whom the Church hath honored with the name of Fathers, whose volumes I confess not to open without a secret reverence of their holiness and gravity; sometimes to those later doctors, which want nothing but age to make them classical; always to God's Book. That day is lost whereof some hours are not improved in those divine monuments; others I turn over out of choice; these out of duty. Ere I can have sat unto weariness, my family, having now overcome all household distractions, invites me to our common devotions; not without some short preparation. These, heartily performed, send me up with a more strong and cheerful appetite to my former work, which I find made easy to me by intermission and variety; now, therefore, can I deceive the hours with change of pleasures, that is, of labors. One while mine eyes are busied, another while my hand, and sometimes my mind takes the burden from them both; wherein I would imitate the skilfullest cooks, which make the best dishes with manifold mixtures; one hour is spent in textual divinity, another in controversy; histories relieve them both. Now, when the mind is weary of others' labors, it begins to undertake her own; sometimes it meditates and winds up for future use; sometimes it lays forth her conceits into present discourse; sometimes for itself, after for others. Neither know I whether it works or plays in these thoughts. I am sure no sport hath more pleasure, no work more use; only the decay of a weak body makes me think these delights insensibly laborious. Thus could I all day (as singers use) make myself music with changes, and complain sooner of the day for shortness than of the business for toil, were it not that this faint monitor interrupts me still in the midst of my busy pleasures, and enforces me both to respite and repast. I must yield to both; while my body and mind are joined together in these unequal couples, the better must follow the weaker. Before my meals, therefore, and after, I let myself loose from all thoughts, and now would forget that I ever studied; a full mind takes away the body's appetite, no less than a full body makes a dull and unwieldly mind; company, discourse, recreations, are now seasonable and welcome; these prepare me for a diet, not gluttonous, but medicinal. The palate may not be pleased, but the stomach, nor that for its own sake; neither would I think any of these comforts worth respect in themselves but in their use, in their end, so far as they may enable me to better things. If I see any dish to tempt my palate, I fear a serpent in that apple, and would please myself in a wilful denial; I rise capable of more, not desirous; not now immediately from my trencher to my book, but after some intermission. Moderate speed is a sure help to all proceedings; where those things which are prosecuted with violence of endeavor or desire, either succeed not or continue not.

After my later meal, my thoughts are slight, only my memory may be charged with her task of recalling what was committed to her custody in the day; and my heart is busy in examining my

hands and mouth, and all other senses of that day's behavior.
And now the evening is come; no tradesman doth more carefully
take in his wares, clear his shopboard, and shut his window,
than I would shut up my thoughts and clear my mind. That
student shall live miserably, which like a camel lies down under
his burden. All this done, calling together my family, we end
the day with God; thus do we rather drive away the time before
us than follow it. I grant neither is my practice worthy to be
exemplary, neither are our callings proportionable. The life of
a nobleman, of a courtier, of a scholar, of a citizen, of a countryman, differ no less than their dispositions; yet must all conspire in
honest labor.

Sweat is the destiny of all trades, whether of the brows or of
the mind. God never allowed any man to do nothing. How miserable is the condition of those men who spend the time as if it
were given them, and not lent; as if hours were waste creatures,
and such as should never be accounted for; as if God would take
this for a good bill of reckoning: *Item*, spent upon my pleasures
forty years! These men shall once find that no blood can privilege
idleness, and that nothing is more precious to God than that which
they desire to cast away—time. Such are my common days; but
God's day calls for another respect. The same sun arises on this
day, and enlightens it; yet because that Sun of Righteousness
arose on it, and drew the strength of God's moral precept unto it,
therefore justly do we sing with the Psalmist, "This is the day
which the Lord hath made." Now I forget the world, and in a
sort myself; and deal with my wonted thoughts, as great men use,
who, at some times of their privacy, forbid the access of all suitors.
Prayer, meditation, reading, hearing, preaching, singing, good conference, are the businesses of this day, which I dare not bestow on
any work, or pleasure, but heavenly.

I hate superstition on the one side, and looseness on the other;
but I find it hard to offend in too much devotion, easy in profane-
ness. The whole week is sanctified by this day; and according to
my care of this is my blessing on the rest. I show your lordship

what I would do, and what I ought; I commit my desires to the imitation of the weak, my actions to the censures of the wise and holy, my weaknesses to the pardon and redress of my merciful God.

Silent Forces.

I have seen the wild stone avalanches of the Alps, which smoke and thunder down the declivities with a vehemence almost sufficient to stun the observer. I have also seen snowflakes descending so softly as not to hurt the fragile spangles of which they were composed; yet to produce from aqueous vapor a quantity of that tender material which a child could carry, demands an exertion of energy competent to gather up the shattered blocks of the largest stone avalanche I have ever seen, and pitch them to twice the height from which they fell.

JOSIAH GILBERT HOLLAND.

JOSIAH GILBERT HOLLAND.

J. G. HOLLAND was born in Belchertown, Mass., July 24, 1819, and died October 12, 1881.
He practiced medicine for a short time, superintended the schools in Vicksburg, Mass., for a year, and in 1849, became associate editor of the Springfield, Mass., *Republican*. For the columns of this paper he wrote several of his popular works. In 1870, he became editor of *Scribner's Monthly*, in New York. The following are his published works: *The Bay Path*, published in 1857; *Timothy Titcomb's Letters to the Young*, 1858; *Bitter Sweet*, a dramatic poem, 1858; *Gold Foil, Hammered from Popular Proverbs*, 1859; *Miss Gilbert's Career*, 1860; *Lessons in Life*, 1861; *Letters to the Joneses*, 1863; *Plain Talk on Familiar Subjects*, 1865; *Life of Abraham Lincoln*, 1866; *Kathrina, Her Life and Mine*, a narrative poem, 1867.

His novels are his best and most artistic works. His poems are filled with fine sentiment, but they lack the smoothness and poetic finish of a truly great poet. *Bitter Sweet* and *Kathrina* have been immensely popular. They gained a circulation which has been awarded to but few American works.

Holland is known as the popular editor of *Scribner's Monthly*. His lessons of life are truly noble, and the religious tone given to many of his works is specially commendable.

To Goodrich Jones, Jr.

[Concerning his disposition to be content with the respectability and wealth which his father has acquired for him.]

Your father, by a life of integrity and close and skilful application to business, has made for himself a good reputation in the world, and become what the world calls rich. He lives in a good house, moves in good society, commands for his family all desirable luxuries of dress and equipage, and holds a position which places him upon an equality with the greatest and best. He began humbly, if I am correctly informed, and has won his eminence by the force of his own life and character. I honor him. I count him worthy of the respect of every man, and I find myself disposed to treat his family with respect on his account—for his sake. This feeling toward his family, which I find springing up spontaneously within' myself seems to be quite universal. The world bows to the family of the venerable Goodrich Jones—bows, not to Mrs. Jones, particularly, as a respectable woman, but to the wife of Goodrich Jones—bows not to his children, as young men and women of intelligence and good morals, but as young people who are to be treated with more than ordinary courtesy because they are the children of the rich and respectable Goodrich Jones.

This feeling of the world toward Mr. Goodrich Jones' family is very natural. It is a tribute of respect to a worthy old gentleman, and, so far as he is concerned, is one of the natural rewards of his life of industry and integrity. I notice, however, that the family of Mr. Jones have come to look upon these tributes of respect to them, on account of Mr. Jones, as quite the proper and regular thing, and to feel that *they* are really worthy of special attention, because Mr. Jones commands it for himself. Instead of feeling a little humiliated by the consciousness that they are treated with special politeness, not because they are particularly brilliant, or rich, or well bred, but because they are the family of a rich and respectable man, they are inclined to feel proud of it. How they manage to be vain of respectability and wealth won for them by somebody beside themselves, I do not know; but I suppose their case is not singular. Indeed, I know that the world is full of such cases, many of which would be ridiculous were they not pitiful.

The thought that you, Goodrich Jones, Jr., are the son of Goodrich Jones, and that you bear his name, seems to form the basis of your estimate of yourself. I have already given the reason why the world treats you respectfully, but that reason need not necessarily be identical with that which leads you to respect yourself. If, owing to some circumstances or agency beyond your control, you were to be suddenly stripped of all your ready money and other resources, and set down in some distant city among strangers, what would be your first impulse? Would you go to work, and try to make a place for yourself? Would you be willing to pass for just what you are—to be estimated for just what there is in you of the elements of manhood, or would you endeavor to convince everybody that you were the son of a certain very rich and respectable Goodrich Jones, and try to secure consideration for yourself by such representation? I presume you would pursue the same policy among strangers that you pursue among friends. You have never made an effort to be respected for works or personal merits of your own. You push yourself forward everywhere as the son of Goodrich Jones—indeed, as Goodrich Jones, Jr. You have not only been content to live in the shadow of your father's name, but you have been apparently anxious to invite public attention to the fact that you do. You have not only been content to live upon money which your father has made, but you seem delighted to have it understood that you can draw upon him for all you want. You seem to have no ambition to make either reputation or money for yourself. On the contrary, I think you would look upon it as disgraceful for you to engage in business for the purpose of winning wealth by labor.

Now, will you permit one who has bowed to you frequently for your father's sake, to talk very plainly to you for your own? Let me assure you, in the first place, that all this respect which the world shows to you is unsubstantial and unreliable. The man who treats you with respect because your father is rich would cease to treat you with respect if you were to become poor. The man who bows to you because your father occupies a high social position, would pass you without recognition were your father, for any reason, to lose that position. Let me assure you that the world does not care for you any further than you are the partaker of the money and the respectability which have been achieved by your father. Nay, I will go further, and say that, side by side with the deference which it shows for you on your father's account, it cherishes contempt for one who is willing to receive his position at second hand. You cannot complain of this, for you place your claims for social consideration entirely on your father's position. The negro slave is proud of the superior wealth of his master, and among his fellow slaves, assumes a superior position in consequence of wealth which is not his own. He belongs to a splendid establishment, and, in his own eyes, wins importance from the association. When his master fails, the slave sinks. No, sir, there is nothing reliable in this consideration of the world for you. You are only treated as a representative of the wealth and respectability of another man, and if he were to be displeased with you, and were to disown and disinherit you, you would find yourself without a friend in the world.

In the second place, your position is an unmanly one. None but a mean man can be willing to hold his position at second hand. I count him fortunate who is born to pleasant and good social relations, and all the advantages which they bring him for the development of his personal character; but I count him most unfortunate who, born to such relations, is willing to hold them as a birthright alone. A man who is willing to keep a place in society which his father has given him, through his father's continued influence, is necessarily mean spirited and contemptible. Every young man of a manly spirit who finds himself in good society, through the influences of others, will prove his right to the place and hold the place by his own merits. No man of your age can consent to hold his social position solely through the influence of his father without convicting himself either of imbecility or meanness. If you had any genuine self-respect, you would feel that to owe to others what you are capable of winning for yourself, and to be considered only as a portion of a rich and respectable man's belongings, is a disgrace to your manhood.

I suppose the thought has never occurred to you that you owe something to your father for what he has done for you. He gave you position. His name shielded you through all your childhood and youth from many of the dangers and disadvantages which other young men are forced to encounter. He gave you great vantage ground in the work of life, and you owe it to him to improve it. If your name helps you, you ought to do something for your name. If your father honors you, you ought to honor him, and to do as much for his name as he has done for yours. You have no moral right to disgrace one who has done so much for you; for his reputation is partly in your keeping. It would be an everlasting disgrace to him to bring up a boy who relied solely upon his father for respectability. It would be a blot upon his reputation to have a son so mean as to be content with a name and fortune at second hand I tell you, sir, that you must change your plan and course of life, or people will talk more and more of your unworthiness to stand in your father's shoes, and express their wonder more and more that so sensible and industrious a father could train a son so inefficiently as he has trained you. When this good father of yours shall die, you will be thrown more upon yourself. You will have money, I presume, and you will still sit in the comfortable shadows of your father's name; but the world changes, and strangers will estimate you at your true value, and those who knew your father will only talk of the sad contrast between his character and your own.

I suppose you are not above the desire for the good will of the world. Well, the world is made up of workers. The great masses of men—and your father is among the number—are obliged to depend upon their own labor and their own force and excellence of character for wealth and position. People do not envy him, because he won all that he possesses by his own skill and industry. He is universally admired and esteemed, and you are enjoying some of the fruits of this admiration and esteem in the politeness of the world toward yourself; but this will not always last. You must mingle in the world's work, and cast in your lot with your fellows, contributing your share of labor, and taking what comes of it in pelf and position, or else you will be voted out of the pale of popular sympathy. The world does not love drones, and you must cease to be a drone or it will never love you.

I suppose it is hard for you to realize that you are not the object of envy among men, but I wish you could for once feel the contempt which your parasitic position excites even among men whom you deem beneath your notice. There are many young men who have been compelled to labor all their lives for bread, that would shrink from exchanging places with you as from a loathsome disgrace. They would not take your idle habits, your foppish tastes, your childish spirit, and your reputation, for all your father's money; and these men, strange as it may seem to your mean spirit, are more respected and better loved by the world than yourself. I say that you are not above the desire for the good will of the world; but, if you would get it, you must be a man. You must show that you have a man's spirit, and that you are willing to do a man's work. No idle man ever yet lived upon the wealth won for him by others and at the same time enjoyed the love of the world.

All this you will find out by-and-by without my telling you, but then it may be too late for remedy. You are now young, but, if you live, you will come at length to realize that instead of being envied, you are despised. You will make a sadder discovery, too, than this. You will discover that you have as little basis for self-respect as for popular regard. Years cannot fail to reveal to you some things which youth hides from you. You will find that the world is busy, that you have no one to spend your time with, and that the men who have power and public consideration are men who have something to do besides killing time and spending money.

You will find that you are without sympathy and companionship among the best people, and when you ascertain the reason—for it will be so obvious that you will not fail to see it—you will learn that you are not worthy of their sympathy and companionship. In short, you will learn to despise yourself.

I have already spoken to you of the debt which you owe to your father for what he has done for you. There are some further considerations relating to your family which I wish to offer. A family name and reputation are things of life and growth. The character which your father has made is a product of life, so grand and far-spreading that his family sits beneath, and is sheltered by it. It is the law of all vital products that they shall grow, or hold their ground against encroachment, by what they feed upon. Food must be constant, or death is sure to come, soon or late. The character of your family—its power, position and high relations—is the product of your father's vital force, working in various ways. Not many years hence, that force must stop its work. Your father will die, and unless you take up his work and do it, this family character will pine and dwindle, and ultimately sink in utter decay.

Look around you and see how some of the rich and influential old families have died out, because there was no man in them to keep them alive. The founder of the family did what he could, raised his family to the highest social position, gave them wealth, bequeathed to them a good name, and died. The sons who followed were not worthy of him. They were not men. They were babies, who were willing to live upon their family name, and who did live upon it until they consumed it. It is sad to see a family name fade out as it often does, through the failure of its men to feed it with the blood of a worthy life; and yours will fade out in a single generation, if you do not immediately prepare yourself to take up your father's work, and carry it on. It is always pleasant and inspiring to see young men who expect to inherit money entering with energy upon the work of life, as if they had their fortunes to make. It proves that they are men, and proves that they are preparing to handle usefully the money that is to come into their hands. It proves that they intend to win respect for themselves, and to lay at least the foundation of their own fortune. When I see such men, I feel that the name of their families is safe in their keeping, and that, for at least one generation, those families cannot sink. The desire to be somebody besides somebody's son, shows a manly disposition, which the world at once recognizes, and to which it freely opens its heart.

I am aware that a young man in your position has great temptations, and labors under great disadvantages. We are in the habit of regarding a poor young man, who has neither family name nor influence, as laboring under disadvantages, and in some aspects of his case, we regard him rightly. But he has certainly the advantage of the stimulus which obstacles to be overcome afford. The poor man sees that he must make his own fortune, or that his fortune will not be made at all; and the obstacles that lie before him only stimulate him to labor with the greater efficiency. When I see a poor young man bravely accepting his lot, and patiently and heroically applying himself to the work of building a fortune and achieving a position, I am moved to thank God for his poverty, for I know that in that poverty he will ultimately discover the secret of his best successes.

Your disadvantage is that position and wealth have already been won for you. It is not necessary for you to labor to get bread and clothing and a comfortable home. These have already been won for you by other hands. I do not deny that this condition of things is naturally enervating. I confess that it takes much good sense and an unusual degree of manliness to resist the temptations to idleness which it brings; but you must resist them or suffer the saddest consequences. You must labor in a steady, manly way to make your own place in the world, as a fitting preparation for the husbandry and enjoyment of the wealth which will some day be yours. If you have not those considerations in your favor which stimulate the poor man to exertion, then you must adopt those which I have tried to present to you. You must remember that to be content with a position received at second hand, and to live simply to spend the money earned by others is most unmanly. You must remember that you owe it to your father and to your family name and fame, to keep your family in the position of consideration and influence in which he has placed it, and that it is certain to recede from that position unless you do. You must remember that only by work can you win the good will of the world around you, or win and retain respect for yourself.

If the disadvantages of your position are great, your reward for worthy work is also great. The world always recognizes the strength of the temptations which attach to the position of a rich young man, and awards to him a peculiar honor for that spirit which refuses to be respected for anything but his own manliness. I know of no young men who hold the good-will of the public more thoroughly than those who set aside all the temptations to indolence and indulgence which attend wealth, and put themselves heartily to the work of deserving the social position to which they are born, and of earning the bread which a father's wealth has already secured. You have but to will and to work, and this beautiful reward will be yours.

Tramp, Tramp, Tramp.

Tramp, tramp, tramp, the boys are marching; how many of them? Sixty thousand! Sixty full regiments, every man of which will, before twelve months shall have completed their course, lie down in the grave of a drunkard! Every year during the past decade has witnessed the same sacrifice; and sixty regiments stand behind this army ready to take its place. It is to be recruited from our children and our children's children. Tramp, tramp, tramp—the sounds come to us in the echoes of the army just expired; tramp, tramp, tramp—the earth shakes with the tread of the host now passing; tramp, tramp, tramp—comes to us from the camp of the recruits. A great tide of life flows resistlessly to its death. What in

God's name are they fighting for? The privilege of pleasing an appetite, of conforming to a social usage, of filling sixty thousand homes with shame and sorrow, of loading the public with the burden of pauperism, of crowding our prison-houses with felons, of detracting from the productive industries of the country, of ruining fortunes and breaking hopes, of breeding disease and wretchedness, of destroying both body and soul in hell before their time.

The prosperity of the liquor interest, covering every department of it, depends entirely on the maintenance of this army. It cannot live without it. It never did live without it. So long as the liquor interest maintains its present prosperous condition, it will cost America the sacrifice of sixty thousand men every year. The effect is inseparable from the cause. The cost to the country of the liquor traffic is a sum so stupendous that any figures which we should dare to give would convict us of trifling. The amount of life absolutely destroyed, the amount of industry sacrificed, the amount of bread transformed into poison, the shame, the unavailing sorrow, the crime, the poverty, the pauperism, the brutality, the wild waste of vital and financial resources, make an aggregate so vast,—so incalculably vast,—that the only wonder is that the American people do not rise as one man and declare that this great curse shall exist no longer.

A hue-and-cry is raised about woman suffrage, as if any wrong which may be involved in woman's lack of the suffrage could be compared to the wrongs attached to the liquor interest.

Does any sane woman doubt that women are suffering a thousand times more from rum than from political disability?

The truth is, that there is no question before the American people to-day that begins to match in importance the temperance question. The question of American slavery was never anything but a baby by the side of this; and we prophecy that within ten years, if not within five, the whole country will be awake to it, and divided upon it. The organizations of the liquor interest, the vast funds at its command, the universal feeling of those whose business is pitted against the national prosperity and public morals—these are enough to show that, upon one side of this matter, at least, the present condition of things and the social and political questions that lie in the immediate future are apprehended. The liquor interest knows there is to be a great struggle, and is preparing to meet it. People both in this country and in Great Britain are beginning to see the enormity of the business—are beginning to realize that Christian civilization is actually poisoned at its fountain, and that there can be no purification of it until the source of the poison is dried up.

Temperance laws are being passed by the various Legislatures, which they must sustain, or go over, soul and body, to the liquor interest and influences. Steps are being taken on behalf of the public health, morals and prosperity, which they must approve by voice and act, or they must consent to be left behind and left out. There can be no concession and no compromise on the part of temperance men, and no quarter to the foe. The great curse of our country and our race must be destroyed.

Meantime, the tramp, tramp, tramp, sounds on,—the tramp of sixty thousand yearly victims. Some are besotted and stupid, some are wild with hilarity and dance along the dusty way, some reel along in pitiful weakness, some wreak their mad and murderous impulses on one another, or on the helpless women and children whose destinies are united to theirs, some stop in wayside debaucheries and infamies for a moment, some go bound in chains from which they seek in vain to wrench their bleeding wrists, and all are poisoned in body and soul, and all are doomed to death.

My Mother's Bible.

On one of the shelves in my library, surrounded by volumes of all kinds on various subjects, and in various languages, stands an old book, in its plain covering of brown paper, unprepossessing to the eye, and apparently out of place among the more pretentious volumes that stand by its side. To the eye of a stranger it has certainly neither beauty nor comeliness. Its covers are worn; its leaves marred by long use; yet, old and worn as it is, to me it is the most beautiful and most valuable book on my shelves. No other awakens such associations, or so appeals to all that is best and noblest within me. It is, or rather it *was*, my mother's Bible —companion of her best and holiest hours, source of her unspeakable joy and consolation. From it she derived the principles of a truly Christian life and character. It was the light to her feet, and the lamp to her path. It was constantly by her side; and, as her steps tottered in the advancing pilgrimage of life, and her eyes grew dim with age, more and more precious to her became the well worn pages.

One morning, just as the stars were fading into the dawn of the coming Sabbath, the aged pilgrim passed on beyond the stars and beyond the morning, and entered into the rest of the eternal Sabbath—to look upon the face of Him of whom the law and the prophets had spoken, and whom, not having seen, she had loved. And now, no legacy is to me more precious than that old Bible. Years have passed; but it stands there on its shelf, eloquent as ever, witness of a beautiful life that is finished, and a silent monitor to the living. In hours of trial and sorrow it says, "Be not cast down, my son; for thou shalt yet praise Him who is the health of thy countenance and thy God." In moments of weakness and fear it says, "Be strong, my son; and quit yourself manfully." When sometimes, from the cares and conflicts of external life, I come back to the study, weary of the world and tired of men —of men that are so hard and selfish, and a world that is so unfeeling—and the strings of the soul have become untuned and discordant, I seem to hear that Book saying, as with the well remembered tones of a voice long silent, "Let not your heart be troubled. For what is your life? It is even as a vapor." Then my troubled spirit becomes calm; and the little world, that had grown so great and so formidable, sinks into its true place again. I am peaceful, I am strong.

There is no need to take down the volume from the shelf, or open it. A glance of the eye is sufficient. Memory and the law of association supply the rest. Yet there are occasions when it is otherwise; hours in life when some deeper grief has troubled the heart, some darker, heavier cloud is over the spirit and over the dwelling, and when it is comfort to take down that old Bible and search its pages. Then, for a time, the latest editions, the original languages, the notes and commentaries, and all the critical apparatus which the scholar gathers around him for the study of the Scriptures, are laid aside; and the plain old English Bible that was my mother's is taken from the shelf.

The Wonders of an Atom.

All things visible around us are aggregations of atoms. From particles of dust, which under the microscope could scarcely be distinguished one from the other, are all the varied forms of nature created. This grain of dust, this particle of sand, has strange properties and powers. Science has discovered some, but still more truths are hidden within this irregular molecule of matter which we now survey than even philosophy dares dream of. How strangely it obeys the impulses of heat—mysterious are the influences of light upon it—electricity wonderfully excites it—and still more curious is the manner in which it obeys the magic of chemical force. These are phenomena which we have seen; we know them and we can reproduce them at our pleasure. We have advanced a little way into the secrets of nature, and from the spot we have gained we look forward with a vision somewhat brightened by our task; but we discover so much yet unknown that we learn another truth —our vast ignorance of many things relating to this grain of dust.

It gathers around it other particles; they cling together, and each acting upon every other one, and all of them arranging themselves around the little center, according to some law, a beautiful crystal results, the geometric perfection of its form being a source of admiration.

It quickens with yet undiscovered energies; it moves with life; dust and vital force combine; blood and bone, nerve and muscle result from the combination. Forces which we can not, by the utmost refinements of our philosophy detect, direct the whole, and from the same dust which formed the rock and grew in the tree, is produced a living and a breathing thing, capable of receiving a divine illumination, of bearing in its new state the gladness and the glory of a soul.

The Mocking Bird.

The plumage of the mocking bird, though none of the homeliest, has nothing gaudy or brilliant in it; and, had he nothing else to recommend him, would scarcely entitle him to notice, but his figure is well proportioned and even handsome. The ease, elegance, and rapidity of his movements, the animation of his eye, and the intelligence he displays in listening and laying up lessons from almost every species of the feathered creation within his hearing, are really surprising, and mark the peculiarity of his genius. To these qualities we may add that of a voice full, strong, and musical, and capable of almost every modulation, from the clear mellow tones of the wood thrush to the savage scream of the bald eagle. In measure and accent he faithfully follows his originals. In force and sweetness of expression he greatly improves upon them. In his native groves, mounted on the top of a tall bush or half-grown tree, in the dawn of a dewy morning, while the woods are already vocal with a multitude of warblers, his admirable song rises preeminent over every competitor. The ear can listen to *his* music alone, to which that of all the others seems a mere accompaniment. Neither is this strain altogether imitative. His own native notes, which are easily distinguishable by such as are well acquainted with those of our various song birds, are bold and full, and varied seemingly beyond all limits. They consist of short expressions of two, three, or at the most, five or six syllables; generally interspersed with imitations, and all of them uttered with great emphasis and rapidity, and continued with undiminished ardor, for half an hour or an hour at a time, his expanded wings and tail, glistening with white, and the buoyant gayety of his action, arresting the eye, as his song most irresistibly does the ear. He sweeps round with enthusiastic ecstacy—he mounts and descends as his song swells or dies away; and, as my friend Mr. Bartram has beautifully expressed it, "He bounds aloft with the celerity of an arrow, as if to recover or recall his very soul, expired in the last elevated strain." While thus exerting himself, a by-stander, destitute of sight, would suppose that the whole feathered tribe had assembled together, on a trial of skill, each striving to produce his utmost effect, so perfect are his imitations. He many times deceives the sportsman, and sends him in search of birds that perhaps are not within miles of him, but whose notes he exactly imitates. Even birds themselves are frequently imposed on by this admirable mimic, and are decoyed by the fancied call of their mates, or dive, with precipitation, into the depths of thickets, at the scream of what they suppose to be the sparrow hawk.

The mocking bird loses little of the power and energy of his song by confinement. In his domesticated state, when he commences his career of song, it is impossible to stand by uninterested. He whistles for the dog; Cæsar starts up, wags his tail, and runs to meet his master. He squeaks out like a hurt chicken, and the hen hurries about with hanging wings, and bristled feathers, clucking to protect its injured brood. The barking of the dog, the mewing of the cat, the creaking of a passing wheelbarrow, follow with great truth and rapidity. He repeats the tune taught him by his master, though of considerable length, fully and faithfully. He runs over the quaverings of the canary, and the clear whistlings of the Virginian nightingale, or red-bird, with such superior execution and effect, that the mortified songsters feel their own inferiority, and become altogether silent; while he seems to triumph in their defeat by redoubling his exertions.

This excessive fondness for variety, however, in the opinion of some, injures his song. His elevated imitations of the brown thrush are frequently interrupted by the crowing of cocks; and the warblings of the blue-bird, which he exquisitely manages, are mingled with the screaming of swallows, or the cackling of hens; amidst the simple melody of the robin we are suddenly surprised by the shrill reiterations of the whip-poor-will; while the notes of the kildeer, bluejay, martin, Baltimore, and twenty others, succeed with such imposing reality, that we look round for the originals, and discover, with astonishment, that the solo performer in this singular concert is the admirable bird now before us. During this exhibition of his powers he spreads his wings, expands his tail, and throws himself around the cage in all the ecstasy of enthusiasm, seeming not only to sing, but to dance, keeping time to the measure of his own music. Both in his native and domesticated state, during the solemn stillness of night, as soon as the moon rises in silent majesty, he begins his delightful solo; and serenades us the livelong night with a full display of his vocal powers, making the whole neighborhood ring with his inimitable medley.

WALTER SCOTT.

WALTER SCOTT.

SIR WALTER SCOTT was born in the city of Edinburgh on the 15th of August, 1771. After an unusually busy and successful literary life, he died on the 21st of September, 1832. The poet and novelist was well related and he came from good ancient Scottish families. Delicate health, arising chiefly from lameness, led to his being placed under charge of some relations in the country. His early impressions from country life and Border stories, he received while residing with his grandfather at Sandy-Knowe, an extremely romantic situation near Kelso. At an early age, he had tried his hand at verse with considerable success. He passed through the High School and University of Edinburgh. Although he made some proficiency in Latin, and in classes of ethics, moral philosophy and history, "he had an aversion to Greek, and we may regret, with Lord Lytton, 'that he refused to enter into that chamber in the magic palace of literature in which the sublimest relics of antiquity are stored.'" Being a great reader, he had gathered a vast variety of miscellaneous knowledge. Romances and stories were his chief delight.

His earliest literary labors were translations. "In 1796, he published translations of Burger's *Lenore* and *The Wild Huntsman*, ballads of singular wildness and power." In 1799, appeared his translation of Goethe's tragedy, *Goetz von Berlichingen*. In 1799, he was appointed sheriff of Selkirkshire at a salary of £300 per annum. Scott now visited the country for the purpose of collecting the ballad poetry of Scotland. As a result, *Minstrelsy of the Scottish Border* appeared in 1802. After other work of importance, his *Lay of the Last Minstrel* appeared in 1805, "which instantly stamped him as one of the greatest poets of the age." The tide of his popularity had now fully set in, and as of Burns, the people murmured of him from shore to shore.

In 1808 appeared the great poem *Marmion*, and also his edition of Dryden. *Lady of the Lake* was published in 1810. In 1811, *The Vision of Don Roderick;* in 1813, *Rokeby,* and *The Bridal of Triermain;* 1814, *The Lord of the Isles;* 1815, *The Field of Waterloo;* and in 1817, *Harold the Dauntless.*

"So early as 1805, before his great poems were produced, Scott had entered on the composition of *Waverly,* the first of his illustrious progeny of tales." *Waverly* appeared in 1814, and was received with "unmingled applause." For fear that he would compromise his reputation as a poet, Scott did not prefix his name to the work. In 1815 appeared *Guy Mannering;* in 1816, *The Antiquary,* and also *The Black Dwarf,* and *Old Mortality.* "The year 1818 witnessed two other coinages from *Waverly* mint, *Rob Roy* and *The Heart of Mid-Lothian.*" *The Bride of Lammermoor,* a story of sustained and overwhelming pathos, appeared in 1819.

Ivanhoe, from which we have taken our selection, appeared in 1820. For want of space, we must omit mention of Scott's other excellent works, and pass to a brief sketch of his life.

He studied law, and was admitted to the bar at the age of twenty-one. He joined the Tory party, and became one of a band of volunteers to defend his country. After his first love disappointment, he was finally married to Charlotte Margaret Carpenter in 1797. "Miss Carpenter had some fortune and the young couple retired to a cottage at Lasswade, where they seem to have enjoyed sincere and unalloyed happiness."

The success of Scott's works gained for him a large fortune. At a princely outlay, he purchased land and fitted up a home known now by the immortal name of Abbotsford. Princes, peers and poets—men of all grades—were his constant visitors. Failure of his publishers left him heavily in debt. In his old age, Scott undertook the task of paying a debt of £120,000. " The fountain was awakened from its inmost recess, as if the spirit of affliction had troubled it in his passage," and before his death, the commercial debt was reduced to £54,000.

"In six years, Scott had nearly reached the goal of his ambition. He had ranged the wide fields of romance, and the public had liberally rewarded their illustrious favorite. The ultimate prize was within view, and the world cheered him on, eagerly anticipating his triumph; but the victor sank exhausted on the course. He had spent his life in the struggle. The strong man was bowed down, and his living honor, genius, and integrity were extinguished by delirium and death.

"About half past one, p. m.," says Mr. Lockhart, "on the 21st of September, 1832, Sir Walter breathed his last, in the presence of all his children. It was a beautiful day —so warm that every window was wide open—and so perfectly still that the sound of all others most delicious to his ear, the gentle ripple of the Tweed over its pebbles, was distinctly audible as we knelt around the bed, and his eldest son kissed and closed his eyes."

Rebecca's Description of the Siege.

In the "Passage of Arms" on the memorable field of Ashby-de-la-Zouche, Ivanhoe, known as the disinherited knight, was named by Prince John as the champion of the day. Although the head of a lance had penetrated his breastplate, and inflicted a wound, yet he bore up till he had been named Champion, and had received the Chaplet of Honor, from the Queen of Love and Beauty. Ivanhoe was taken to the castle commanded by the Templar Bois-Guilbert and the Baron Front-de-Boeuf. While lodged within the castle, Ivanhoe's friends, under the leadership of the Black Knight, advanced to the rescue. The rest is fully explained in the text, in the conversation between Rebecca and Ivanhoe. But Ivanhoe was like the war-horse of that sublime passage, glowing with impatience at his inactivity, and with his ardent desire to mingle in the affray of which these sounds were the introduction. "If I could but drag myself," he said, "to yonder window, that I might see how this brave game is like to go. If I had but bow to shoot a shaft, or battle-axe to strike, were it but a single blow for our deliverance! It is in vain—it is in vain—I am alike nerveless and weaponless."

"Fret not thyself, noble knight," answered Rebecca, "the sounds have ceased of a sudden—it may be they join not battle."

"Thou knowest nought of it," said Wilfred, impatiently; "this dead pause only shows that the men are at their posts on the walls, and expecting an instant attack; what we have heard was but the distant muttering of the storm—it will burst anon in all its fury. Could I but reach yonder window!" "Thou wilt but injure thyself by the attempt, noble knight," replied his attendant. Observing his extreme solicitude, she firmly added, "I myself will stand at the lattice, and describe to you as I can what passes without."

"You must not—you shall not!" exclaimed Ivanhoe; "each lattice, each aperture, will be soon a mark for the archers; some random shaft—" "It shall be welcome!" muttered Rebecca, as with firm pace she ascended two or three steps which led to the window of which they spoke. "Rebecca, dear Rebecca!" exclaimed Ivanhoe, "this is no maiden's pastime—do not expose thyself to wounds and death, and render me forever miserable for having given thee occasion; at least, cover thyself with yonder ancient buckler, and show as little of your person at the lattice as may be." Following with wonderful promptitude the directions of Ivanhoe, and availing herself of the protection of the large ancient shield, which she placed against the lower part of the window, Rebecca, with tolerable security to herself, could witness part of what was passing without the castle, and report to Ivanhoe the preparations which the assailants were making for the storm. Indeed, the situation which she thus obtained was peculiarly favorable for this purpose, because, being placed on an angle of the main building, Rebecca could not only see what passed beyond the precincts of the castle, but also commanded a view of the out-work likely to be the first object of the meditated assault. It was an exterior fortification of no great height, or strength, intended to protect the postern-gate, through which Cedric had been recently dismissed by Front-de-Boeuf. The castle moat divided this species of barbican from the rest of the fortress, so that, in case of its being taken, it was easy to cut off the communication with the main building, by withdrawing the temporary bridge. In the out-work was a sally-port corresponding to the postern of the castle, and the whole was surrounded by a strong palisade. Rebecca could observe from the number of men placed for the defence of this post, that the besieged entertained apprehension for its safety; and from the mustering of the assailants in a direction nearly opposite to the out-work, it seemed no less plain that it had been selected as a vulnerable point of attack. These appearances she hastily communicated to Ivanhoe, and added, "The skirts of the wood seemed lined with archers, although only a few are advanced from its dark shadow."

"Under what banner?" asked Ivanhoe. "Under no ensign of war which I can observe," answered Rebecca.

"A singular novelty," muttered the Knight, "to advance to storm such a castle without pennon or banner displayed! Seest thou who they be that act as leaders? "A knight, clad in sable armor, is the most conspicuous," said the Jewess; "he alone is armed from head to heel, and seems to assume the direction of all round him."

"What device does he bear on his shield?" inquired Ivanhoe.

"Something resembling a bar of iron, and a padlock painted blue on the black shield."

"A fetterlock and shackle-bolt azure," said Ivanhoe; "I know not who may bear the device, but well I ween it might now be mine own. Canst thou not see the motto?"

"Scarce the device itself, at this distance," replied Rebecca; "but when the sun glances fair upon his shield, it shows as I tell you."

"Seem there no other leaders?" exclaimed the anxious inquirer. "None of mark and distinction that I can behold from this station," said Rebecca, "but, doubtless, the other side of the castle is also assailed. They appear even now preparing to advance,—God of Zion, protect us!—What a dreadful sight!—Those who advanced first bear huge shields, and defences made of plank; the others follow, bending their bows as they come on. They raise their bows! God of Moses, forgive the creatures thou hast made!"

Her description was here suddenly interrupted by the signal for assault, which was given by the blast of a shrill bugle, and at once answered by a flourish of the Norman trumpets from the battlements, which mingled with the deep and hollow clang of the nakers (a species of kettle-drum,) retorted in notes of defiance the challenge of the enemy. The shouts of both parties augmented the fearful din, the assailants crying, "Saint George for merry England!" and the Normans answering them with loud cries of "*En-avant de Bracy!—Beau seant!—Front-de-Boeuf a la rescousse!*" according to the war cries of their different commanders.

It was not, however, by clamor that the contest was to be decided, and the desperate efforts of the assailants were met by an equally vigorous defence on the part of the besieged. The archers, trained by their woodland pastimes to the most effective use of the long-bow, shot, to use the appropriate phrase of the time, so "wholly together," that no point at which a defender could show the least part of his person escaped their cloth-yard shafts. By this heavy discharge, which continued as thick and sharp as hail, while, notwithstanding, every arrow had its individual aim, and flew by scores together against each embrasure and opening in the parapets, as well as at every window where a defender either occasionally had post, or might be suspected to be stationed,—by this sustained discharge, two or three of the garrison were slain, and several others wounded. But, confident in their armor of proof, and in the cover which their situation afforded, the followers of Front-de-Boeuf, and his allies, showed an obstinacy in defence proportioned to the fury of the attack, and replied with the discharge of their large cross-bows as well as with their long-bows, slings, and other missile weapons, to the close and continued shower of arrows; and, as the assailants were necessarily but indifferently protected, did considerably more damage than they received at their hand. The whizzing of shafts and of missiles, on both sides, was only interrupted by the shouts which arose when either side inflicted or sustained some notable loss.

"And I must lie here like a bed-ridden monk," exclaimed Ivanhoe, "when the game that gives me freedom or death is played out by the hand of others!—Look from the window once again, kind maiden, but beware that you are not marked by the archers beneath! Look out once more, and tell me if they yet advance to the storm." With patient courage, strengthened by the interval which she had employed in mental devotion, Rebecca again took post at the lattice, sheltering herself, however, so as not to be visible from beneath. "What dost thou see, Rebecca?" again demanded the wounded knight.

"Nothing but the cloud of arrows flying so thick as to dazzle mine eyes, and to hide the bowmen who shoot them."

"That cannot endure," said Ivanhoe; "if they press not right on to carry the castle by pure force of arms, the archery may avail but little against stone walls and bulwarks. Look for the knight of the fetterlock, fair Rebecca, and see how he bears himself; for as the leader is, so will his followers be." "I see him not," said Rebecca.

"Foul craven!" exclaimed Ivanhoe; "does he blench from the helm when the wind blows highest?"

"He blenches not! he blenches not!" said Rebecca, "I see him now; he leads a body of men close under the outer barrier of the barbican. They pull down the piles and palisades; they hew down the barriers with axes. His high black plume floats abroad over the throng, like a raven over the field of the slain. They have made a breach in the barriers—they rush in—they are thrust back! Front-de-Boeuf heads the defenders, I see his gigantic form above the press. They throng again to the breach, and the pass is disputed hand to hand and man to man. God of Jacob! it is the meeting of two fierce tides—the conflict of two oceans moved by adverse winds!" She turned her head from the lattice, as if unable longer to endure a sight so terrible.

"Look forth again, Rebecca," said Ivanhoe, mistaking the cause of her retiring; "the archery must in some degree have ceased, since they are now fighting hand to hand. Look again, there is now less danger."

Rebecca again looked forth, and almost immediately exclaimed, "Holy prophets of the law! Front-de-Boeuf and the Black Knight fight hand to hand on the breach, amid the roar of their followers who watch the progress of the strife—Heaven strike with the cause of the oppressed and of the captive!" She then uttered a loud shriek, and exclaimed, "He is down! he is down!"

"Who is down?" cried Ivanhoe; "for our dear Lady's sake, tell me which has fallen?"

"The Black Knight," answered Rebecca, faintly; then instantly again shouted with joyful eagerness, "But no—but no!—the name of the Lord of Hosts be blessed!—he is on foot again, and fights as if there were twenty men's strength in his single arm. His sword is broken—he snatches an ax from a yeoman—he presses Front-de-Boeuf with blow on blow. The giant stoops and totters like an oak under the steel of the woodman. He falls—he falls!"

"Front-de-Boeuf?" exclaimed Ivanhoe.

"Front-de-Boeuf!" answered the Jewess; "his men rush to the rescue, headed by the haughty Templar—their united force compels the champion to pause. They drag Front-de-Boeuf within the walls."

"The assailants have won the barriers, have they not?" said Ivanhoe.

"They have—they have!" exclaimed Rebecca—"and they press the besieged hard upon the outer wall; some plant ladders, some swarm like bees, and endeavor to ascend upon the shoulders of each other—down go stones, beams, and trunks of trees upon their heads, and as fast as they bear the wounded to the rear, fresh men supply their places in the assault. Great God! hast thou given men thine own image, that it should be thus cruelly defaced by the hands of their brethren!"

"Think not of that," said Ivanhoe; "this is no time for such thoughts.—Who yield? who push their way?"

"The ladders are thrown down," replied Rebecca, shuddering; "the soldiers lie groveling under them like crushed reptiles. The besieged have the better."

"Saint George strike for us!" exclaimed the Knight; "do the false yeomen give way?"

"No!" exclaimed Rebecca, "they bear themselves right yeomanly—the Black Knight approaches the postern with his huge ax—the thundering blows which he deals, you may hear them above all the din and shouts of the battle. Stones and beams are hailed down on the bold champion—he regards them no more than if they were thistledown or feathers!"

"By Saint John of Acre," said Ivanhoe, raising himself joyfully on his couch, "methought there was but one man in England that might do such a deed."

"The postern gate shakes," continued Rebecca; "it crashes—it is splintered by his blows—they rush in—the out-work is won. Oh, God!—they hurl the defenders from the battlements—they throw them into the moat. O men, if ye be indeed men, spare them that can resist no longer!"

"The bridge—the bridge which communicates with the castle—have they won that pass?" exclaimed Ivanhoe.

"No," replied Rebecca, "the Templar has destroyed the plank on which they crossed—few of the defenders escaped with him into the castle—the shrieks and cries which you hear, tell the fate of the others. Alas! I see it is still more difficult to look upon victory than upon battle."

"What do they now, maiden?" said Ivanhoe; "look forth yet again—this is no time to faint at bloodshed." "It is over for the time," said Rebecca; "our friends strengthen themselves within the out-work which they have mastered, and it affords them so good a shelter from the foemen's shot, that the garrison only bestow a few bolts on it from interval to interval, as if rather to disquiet than effectually to injure them."

"Our friends," said Wilfred, "will surely not abandon an enterprise so gloriously begun and so happily attained. Oh, no! I will put my faith in the good knight whose ax hath rent heart of oak and bars of iron,—singular," he again muttered to himself, "if there be two who can do a deed of such *derring—do!*—a fetterlock, and a shackle-bolt on a field sable—what may that mean—seest thou nought else, Rebecca, by which the Black Knight may be distinguished?"

"Nothing," said the Jewess; "all about him is black as the wing of the night raven. Nothing can I spy that can mark him further; but having once seen him put forth his strength in battle, methinks I could know him again among a thousand warriors. He rushes to the fray as if he were summoned to a banquet. There is more than mere strength—there seems as if the whole soul and spirit of the champion were given to every blow which he deals upon his enemies. God assoilzie him of the sin of blood-shed!—it is fearful, yet magnificent, to behold how the arm and heart of one man can triumph over hundreds."

"Rebecca," said Ivanhoe, "thou hast painted a hero; surely they rest but to refresh their force, or to provide the means of crossing the moat. Under such a leader as thou hast spoken this knight to be, there are no craven fears, no cold-blooded delays, no yielding up a gallant emprize; since the difficulties which render it arduous render it also glorious. I swear by the honor of my house —I vow by the name of my bright lady-love, I would endure ten years captivity to fight one day by that good knight's side in such a quarrel as this!"

"Alas!" said Rebecca, leaving her station at the window, and approaching the couch of the wounded knight, "this impatient yearning after action—this struggling with and repining at your present weakness, will not fail to injure your returning health. How couldst thou hope to inflict wounds on others, ere that be healed which thyself hast received?"

"Rebecca," he replied, "thou knowest not how impossible it is for one trained to actions of chivalry, to remain passive as a priest, or a woman, when they are acting deeds of honor around him. The love of battle is the food upon which we live—the dust of the mellay is the breath of our nostrils! We live not—we wish not to live, longer than while we are victorious and renowned. Such, maiden, are the laws of chivalry to which we are sworn and to which we offer all that we hold dear."

"Alas!" said the fair Jewess, "and what is it, valiant knight, save an offering of sacrifice to a demon of vain glory, and a passing through the fire to Moloch? What remains to you as the prize of all the blood you have spilled—of all the travel and pain you have endured—of all the tears which your deeds have caused, when death hath broken the strong man's spear and overtaken the speed of his war-horse?"

"What remains?" cried Ivanhoe. "Glory, maiden, glory! which gilds our sepulchre and embalms our name."

"Glory?" continued Rebecca; "alas! is the rusted mail which hangs as a hatchment over the champion's dim and moldering tomb—is the defaced sculpture of the inscription which the ignorant monk can hardly read to the inquiring pilgrim—are these sufficient rewards for the sacrifice of every kindly affection, for a life spent miserably that ye may make others miserable? Or is there such virtue in the rude rhymes of a wandering bard, that domestic love, kindly affection, peace and happiness, are so widely bartered, to become the hero of those ballads which vagabond minstrels sing to drunken churls over their evening ale?"

The Works of Creation.

I was yesterday, about sunset, walking in the open fields, until the night insensibly fell upon me. I at first amused myself with all the richness and variety of colors which appeared in the western parts of heaven. In proportion as they faded away and went out, several stars and planets appeared one after another, until the whole firmament was in a glow. The blueness of the ether was exceedingly heightened and enlivened by the season of the year, and by the rays of all those luminaries that passed through it. The galaxy appeared in its most beautiful white. To complete the scene, the full moon rose at length in that clouded majesty which Milton takes notice of, and opened to the eye a new picture of nature, which was more finely shaded and disposed among softer lights, than that which the sun had before discovered to us.

As I was surveying the moon walking in her brightness, and taking her progress among the constellations, a thought rose in me which I believe very often perplexes me and disturbs men of serious and contemplative nature. David himself fell into it in that reflection: "When I consider the heavens the work of thy fingers, the moon and the stars which thou hast ordained, what is man that thou art mindful of him, and the son of man that thou regardest him?" In the same manner, when I considered that infinite host of stars, or, to speak more philosophically, of suns, which were then shining upon me, with those innumerable sets of planets or worlds which were moving round their respective suns—when I still enlarged the idea, and supposed another heaven of suns and worlds rising still above this which we discovered, and these still enlightened by a superior firmament of luminaries, which are planted at so great a distance that they may appear to the inhabitants of the former as the stars do to us—in short, while I pursued this thought I could not but reflect on that little insignificant figure which I myself bore amidst the immensity of God's works.

Were the sun which enlightens this part of the creation, with all the host of planetary worlds that move about him, utterly extinguished and annihilated, they would not be missed more than a grain of sand upon the sea shore. The space they possess is so exceedingly little in comparison with the whole, that it would scarcely make a blank in the creation. The chasm would be imperceptible to an eye that could take in the whole compass of nature, and pass from one end of the creation to the other; as it is possible there may be such a sense in ourselves hereafter, or in creatures which are at present more exalted than ourselves. We see many stars by the help of glasses which we do not discover with our naked eyes; and the finer our telescopes are, the more still are our discoveries.

Huygenius carries this thought so far, that he does not think it impossible there may be stars whose light has not yet traveled down to us since their first creation. There is no question but the universe has certain bounds set to it; but when we consider that it is the work of infinite power prompted by infinite goodness, with an infinite space to exert itself in, how can our imagination set any bounds to it?

To return, therefore, to my first thought; I could not but look upon myself with secret horror as a being that was not worth the smallest regard of one who had so great a work under his care and superintendency. I was afraid of being overlooked amidst the immensity of nature, and lost among that infinite variety of creatures which in all probability swarm through all these immeasurable regions of matter.

In order to recover myself from this mortifying thought, I considered that it took its rise from those narrow conceptions which we are apt to entertain of the divine nature. We ourselves cannot attend to many different objects at the same time. If we are careful to inspect some things, we must of course neglect others. This imperfection which we observe in ourselves is an imperfection that cleaves in some degree to creatures of the highest capacities, as they are creatures; that is, beings of finite and limited natures. The presence of every created being is confined to a certain measure of space, and consequently his observation is stinted to a certain number of objects. The sphere in which we move, and act, and understand, is of a wider circumference to one creature than another, according as we rise one above another in the scale of existence. But the widest of these, our spheres, has its circumference. When, therefore, we reflect on the divine nature, we are so used and accustomed to this imperfection in ourselves, that we cannot forbear in some measure ascribing it to Him in whom there is no shadow of imperfection. Our reason indeed assures us that his attributes are infinite, but the poorness of our conceptions is such, that it cannot forbear setting bounds to everything it contemplates, until our reason comes again to our succor, and throws down all those little prejudices which rise in us unawares, and are natural to the mind of man.

We shall, therefore, utterly extinguish this melancholy thought of our being overlooked by our Maker, in the multiplicity of his works and the infinity of those objects among which he seems to be incessantly employed, if we consider, in the first place, that he is omnipresent; and in the second, that he is omniscient.

If we consider him in his omnipresence, his being passes through, actuates, and supports, the whole frame of nature. His creation, and every part of it, is full of him. There is nothing he has made that is either so distant, so little, or so inconsiderable, which he does not essentially inhabit. His substance is within the substance of every being, whether material or immaterial, and as intimately present to it as that being is to itself. It would be an imperfection in him were he able to remove out of one place into another, or to withdraw himself from anything he has created, or from any part of that space which is diffused and spread abroad to infinity. In short, to speak of him in the language of the old philosopher, he is a being whose center is everywhere, and his circumference nowhere.

In the second place, he is omniscient as well as omnipresent. His omniscience, indeed, necessarily and naturally flows from his omnipresence; he cannot but be conscious of every motion that arises in the whole material world, which he thus essentially pervades, and of every thought that is striving in the intellectual world, to every part of which he is thus intimately united. Several moralists have considered the creation as the temple of God, which he has built with his own hands, and which is filled with his presence. Others have considered infinite space as the receptacle, or rather the habitation, of the Almighty. But the noblest and most exalted way of considering this infinite space is that of Sir Isaac Newton, who calls it the sensorium of the Godhead. Brutes and men have their sensoriola, or little sensoriums, by which they apprehend the presence and perceive the actions of a few objects that lie contiguous to them. Their knowledge and observation turn within a very narrow circle. But as God Almighty cannot but perceive and know everything in which he resides, infinite space gives room to infinite knowledge, and is, as it were, an organ to omniscience.

Were the soul separate from the body, and with one glance of thought should start beyond the bounds of the creation—should it for millions of years continue its progress through infinite space with the same activity—it would still find itself within the embrace of its Creator, and encompassed round with the immensity of the Godhead. While we are in body, he is not less present with us because he is concealed from us. "Oh, that I knew where I might find him!" says Job. "Behold I go forward, but he is not there; and backward, but I cannot perceive him; on the left hand where he does work, but I cannot behold him; he hideth himself on the right hand that I cannot see him." In short, reason as well as revelation assures us that he cannot be absent from us, notwithstanding he is undiscovered by us.

In the consideration of God Almighty's omnipresence and omniscience, every uncomfortable thought vanishes. He cannot but regard everything that has being, especially such of his creatures who fear they are not regarded by him. He is privy to all their thoughts, and to that anxiety of heart in particular which is apt to trouble them on this occasion; for as it is impossible he should overlook any of his creatures, so we may be confident that he regards with an eye of mercy those who endeavor to recommend themselves to his notice, and in an unfeigned humility of heart think themselves unworthy that he should be mindful of them.

We have just religion enough to make us hate, but not enough to make us love one another.

When we desire or solicit anything, our minds run wholly on the good side or circumstances of it; when it is obtained, our mind runs only on the bad ones.

When a true genius appeareth in the world, you may know him by this infallible sign, that the dunces are all in confederacy against him.

I am apt to think that, in the day of judgment, there will be small allowance given to the wise for their want of morals, or to the ignorant for their want of faith, because both are without excuse; this renders the advantages equal of ignorance and knowledge. But some scruples in the wise, and some vices in the ignorant, will perhaps be forgiven upon the strength of temptation to each.

HARRIET BEECHER STOWE.

HARRIET BEECHER STOWE.

HARRIET ELIZABETH BEECHER STOWE was born in Litchfield, Conn., June 15, 1812. Her father was Dr. Lyman Beecher, a distinguished clergyman. In 1833, with her father, she removed to Cincinnati, where, in 1836, she was married to the Rev. Calvin E. Stowe, who afterward became professor at Bowdoin College and at Andover Theological School.

Several stories which she had written for the Cincinnati *Gazette* and other periodicals, were collected and published in a volume entitled *The Mayflower*. In 1851, she commenced *Uncle Tom's Cabin*, in the Washington *National Era*. The story was afterward published in Boston in two volumes. "Its success was without a parallel in the literature of any age. Nearly half a million copies were sold in this country, and a considerably larger number in England. It was translated into every language of Europe, and into Arabic and Armenian. It was dramatized and acted in nearly every theater in the world." In 1853 she visited Europe and was received with gratifying attention. *Sunny Memories of Foreign Lands* was published upon her return from Europe. In 1856 appeared *Dred, a Tale of the Great Dismal Swamp*. This work produced but a slight impression. The success of *Uncle Tom's Cabin* probably removed the charm of novelty in the subject of her new story. *The Minister's Wooing* appeared in book form in 1859. *Agnes of Sorrento* and *The Pearl of Orr's Island* were published in 1862; *House and Home Papers*, in 1864; *The Chimney Corner*, in 1865; *Little Foxes*, 1865; *Queer Little People*, 1867; *Oldtown Folks*, 1869; *Pink and White Tyranny*, 1871; *My Wife and I*, 1872. Probably the great mistake in her literary work was made in publishing *True Story of Lady Byron's Life*. If true it should not have been told, but the story is thought not to be true.

Mrs. Stowe has written very extensively, and her published works entitle her to a place among the greatest authors of fiction. While her fame rests upon her first great book, yet all of her works contain excellent qualities. Her genius is rare and original. For several years, she has spent the greater part of her time in her Florida home, in company with her husband and daughters.

It is customary with most authors to classify female writers as the wife or sister, or some other relative of some man. Mrs. Stowe, however, needs not the name of her husband, nor the world-wide fame of the Beechers, to give her a place in the front ranks of literature. The world knows her as well as it knows her relatives, and its admiration for her is richly merited.

Little Eva.

Her form was the perfection of childish beauty, without its usual chubbiness and squareness of outline. There was about it an undulating and aerial grace such as one might dream of for some mythical and allegorical being. Her face was remarkable, less for its perfect beauty of feature than for a singular and dreamy earnestness of expression, which made the ideal start when they looked at her, and by which the dullest and most literal were impressed, without exactly knowing why. The shape of her head and the turn of her neck and bust were peculiarly noble, and the long, golden-brown hair that floated like a cloud around it, the deep, spiritual gravity of her violet-blue eyes, shaded by heavy fringes of golden-brown—all marked her out from other children, and made every one turn and look after her, as she glided hither and thither on the boat. Nevertheless, the little one was not what you would have called either a grave child or a sad one. On the contrary, an airy and innocent playfulness seemed to flicker like the shadow of Summer leaves over her childish face, and around her buoyant figure. She was always in motion, always with half a smile on her rosy mouth, flying hither and thither, with an undulating and cloud-like tread, singing to herself as she moved as in a happy dream. Her father and female guardian were incessantly busy in pursuit of her—but, when caught, she melted from them again like a Summer cloud; and as no word of chiding or reproof ever fell on her ear for whatever she chose to do, she pursued her own way all over the boat. Always dressed in white, she seemed to move like a shadow through all sorts of places, without contracting spot or stain; and there was not a corner or nook, above or below, where those fairy footsteps had not glided, and that visionary golden head, with its deep blue eyes, fleeted along.

The fireman, as he looked up from his sweaty toil, sometimes found those eyes looking wonderingly into the raging depths of the furnace, and fearfully and pityingly at him, as if she thought him in some dreadful danger. Anon the steersman at the wheel paused and smiled, as the picture-like head gleamed through the window of the round house, and in a moment was gone again. A thousand times a day rough voices blessed her, and smiles of unwonted softness stole over hard faces as she passed; and when she tripped fearlessly over dangerous places, rough, sooty hands were stretched involuntarily out to save her, and smooth her path.

Tom, who had the soft, impressible nature of his kindly race, ever yearning towards the simple and child-like, watched the little creature with daily increasing interest. To him she seemed something almost divine; and whenever her golden head and deep blue eyes peered out upon him from behind some dusky cotton-bale, or looked down upon him over some ridge of packages, he half believed he saw one of the angels stepped out of the New Testament.

Uncle Tom Reads His Testament.

Is it strange, then, that some tears fall on the pages of his Bible as he lays it on the cotton-bale, and with patient finger threading his slow way from word to word, traces out its promises? Having learned late in life, Tom was but a slow reader, and passed on laboriously from verse to verse. Fortunate for him was it that the book he was intent on was one which slow reading cannot injure—nay, one whose words, like ingots of gold seem often to need to be weighed separately, that the mind may take in their priceless value. Let us follow him a moment, as, pointing to each word, and pronouncing each half aloud, he reads,—

"Let—not—your—heart—be—troubled. In—my—Father's— house—are—many—mansions. I—go—to—prepare—a—place— for—you."

Cicero, when he buried his darling and only daughter, had a heart as full of honest grief as poor Tom's—perhaps no fuller, for both were only men; but Cicero could pause over no such sublime words of hope, and looked to no such future reunion; and if he had seen them, ten to one he would not have believed,—he must fill his head first with a thousand questions of authenticity of manuscript, and correctness of translation. But, to poor Tom, there it lay, just what he needed, so evidently true and divine that the possibility of a question never entered his simple head. It must be true, for, if not true, how could he live?

As for Tom's Bible, though it had no annotations and helps in the margin from learned commentators, still it had been embellished with certain way-marks and guide-boards of Tom's own invention, and which helped him more than the most learned expositions could have done. It had been his custom to get the Bible read to him by his master's children, in particular by young Master George; and as they read, he would designate, by bold, strong mark and dashes, with pen and ink, the passages which more particularly gratified his ear or affected his heart. His Bible was thus marked through, from one end to the other, with a variety of styles and designations, so he could in a moment seize upon his favorite passages, without the labor of spelling out what lay between them; and while it lay there before him, every passage breathing of some old home scene, and recalling some past enjoyment, his Bible seemed to him all of this life that remained, as well as the promise of a future one.

Pledge With Wine.

"Pledge with wine—pledge with wine!" cried the young and thoughtless Harry Wood. "Pledge with wine," ran through the brilliant crowd.

The beautiful bride grew pale—the decisive hour had come,—she pressed her white hands together, and the leaves of her bridal wreath trembled on her pure brow; her breath came quicker, her heart beat wilder. From her childhood she had been most solemnly opposed to the use of all wines and liquors.

"Yes, Marion, lay aside your scruples for this once," said the Judge, in a low tone, going toward his daughter, "the company expect it; do not so seriously infringe upon the rules of etiquette; in your own house act as you please; but in mine, for this once please me."

Every eye was turned toward the bridal pair. Marion's principles were well known. Henry had been a convivialist, but of late his friends noticed the change in his manners, the difference in his habits—and to-night they watched him to see, as they sneeringly said, if he was tied down to a woman's opinion so soon.

Pouring a brimming beaker, they held it with tempting smiles toward Marion. She was very pale, though more composed, and her hand shook not, as smiling back, gratefully accepted the crystal tempter and raised it to her lips. But scarcely had she done so when every hand was arrested by her piercing exclamation of "Oh, how terrible!"

"What is it?" cried one and all, thronging together, for she had slowly carried the glass at arm's length, and was fixedly regarding it as though it were some hideous object.

"Wait," she answered, while an inspired light shone from her dark eyes, "wait and I will tell you. I see," she added, slowly pointing one jewelled finger at the sparkling ruby liquid, " a sight that beggars all description; and yet listen; I will paint it for you if I can: It is a lonely spot; tall mountains, crowned with verdure, rise in awful sublimity around; a river runs through, and bright flowers grow to the water's edge. There is a thick, warm mist that the sun seeks vainly to pierce; trees, lofty and beautiful, wave to the airy motions of the birds; but there a group of Indians gather; they flit to and fro with something like sorrow upon their dark brows; and in their midst lies a manly form, but his cheek, how deathly; his eye wild with the fitful fire of fever. One friend stands beside him, nay, I should say kneels, for he is pillowing that poor head upon his breast.

"Genius in ruins. Oh! the high, holy looking brow! Why should death mark it, and he so young? Look how he throws the damp curls! see him clasp his hands! hear his thrilling shrieks for life! mark how he clutches at the form of his companion, imploring to be saved. Oh! hear him call piteously his father's name; see him twine his fingers together as he shrieks for his sister—his only sister—the twin of his soul—weeping for him in his distant native land.

"See!" she exclaimed, while the bridal party shrank back, the untasted wine trembling in their faltering grasp, and the Judge fell, overpowered, upon his seat; "see! his arms are lifted to heaven; he prays, how wildly, for mercy! hot fever rushes through his veins. The friend beside him is weeping; awe-stricken, the dark men move silently, and leave the living and dying together."

There was a hush in that princely parlor, broken only by what seemed a smothered sob, from some manly bosom. The bride stood yet upright, with quivering lip, and tears stealing to the outward edge of her lashes. Her beautiful arm had lost its tension, and the glass, with its little, troubled red waves, came slowly toward the range of her vision. She spoke again; every lip was mute. Her voice was low, faint, yet awfully distinct: she still fixed her sorrowful glance upon the wine cup.

"It is evening now; the great white moon is coming up, and her beams lay gently on his forehead. He moves not; his eyes are set in their sockets; dim are their piercing glances; in vain his friend whispers the name of father and sister—death is there.

Death! and no soft hand, no gentle voice to bless and soothe him. His head sinks back! one convulsive shudder! he is dead!"

A groan ran through the assembly, so vivid was her description, so unearthly her look, so inspired her manner, that what she described seemed actually to have taken place then and there. They noticed, also, that the bridegroom hid his face in his hands and was weeping.

"Dead!" she repeated again, her lips quivering faster and faster, and her voice more and more broken: "and there they scoop him a grave; and there without a shroud, they lay him down in the damp, reeking earth. The only son of a proud father, the only idolized brother of a fond sister. And he sleeps to-day in that distant country, with no stone to mark the spot. There he lies—my father's son—my own twin brother! a victim to this deadly poison. Father," she exclaimed, turning suddenly, while the tears rained down her beautiful cheeks, "father, shall I drink it now?"

The form of the old Judge was convulsed with agony. He raised his head, but in a smothered voice he faltered—"No, no, my child, in God's name, no."

She lifted the glittering goblet, and letting it suddenly fall to the floor it was dashed into a thousand pieces. Many a tearful eye watched her movements, and instantaneously every wine glass was transferred to the marble table on which it had been prepared. Then as she looked at the fragments of crystal, she turned to the company, saying, "Let no friend, hereafter, who loves me, tempt me to peril my soul for wine. Not firmer the everlasting hills than my resolve, God helping me, never to touch or taste that terrible poison. And he to whom I have given my hand; who watched over my brother's dying form in that last solemn hour, and buried the dear wanderer there by the river in that land of gold, will, I trust, sustain me in that resolve. Will you not, my husband?"

His glistening eyes, his sad sweet smile, was her answer.

The Judge left the room, and when an hour later he returned, and with a more subdued manner took part in the entertainment of the bridal guests, no one could fail to read that he, too, had determined to dash the enemy at once and forever from his princely rooms.

Those who were present at that wedding can never forget the impression so solemnly made. Many from that hour foreswore the social glass.

The Two Races of Men.

The human species, according to the best theory I can form of it, is composed of two distinct races, the men who borrow, and the men who lend. To these two original diversities may be reduced all those impertinent classifications of Gothic and Celtic tribes, white men, black men, red men. All the dwellers upon earth, "Parthians, and Medes, and Elamites," flock hither, and do naturally fall in the one or the other of these primary distinctions. The infinite superiority of the former, which I choose to designate as the great race, is discernable in their figure, port, and a certain instinctive sovereignty. The latter are born degraded.

"He shall serve his brethren." There is something in the air of one of this cast, lean and suspicious; contrasting with the open, trusting, generous manners of the other.

Observe who have been the greatest borrowers of all ages—Alcibiades—Falstaff—Sir Richard Steele—our late incomparable Brinsley—what a family likeness in all four!

What a careless, even deportment hath your borrower! what rosy gills! what a beautiful reliance on Providence doth he manifest—taking no more thought than lilies! What contempt for money,—accounting it (yours and mine, especially,) no better than dross! What a liberal confounding of those pedantic distinctions of *meum* and *tuum*! or rather, what a noble simplification of language (beyond Tooke) resolving these supposed opposites into one clear, intelligible pronoun adjective!—What near approaches doth he make to the primitive *community*,—to the extent of one-half of the principle, at least.

He is the true taxer who "calleth all the world up to be taxed;" and the distance is as vast between him and *one* of *us*, as subsisted between the Augustan Majesty and the poorest obolary Jew that paid it tribute pittance at Jerusalem! His exactions, too, have such a cheerful, voluntary air! So far removed from your sour parochial or State gatherers,—those ink horn varlets, who carry their want of welcome in their faces! He cometh to you with a smile, and troubleth you with no receipt; confining himself to no set season. Every day is his candlemas, or his Feast of Holy Michael. He applieth the *lene tormentum* of a pleasant look to your purse,—which to that gentle warmth expands her silken leaves, as naturally as the cloak of the traveler, for which sun and wind contended! He is the true Propontic which never ebbeth! The sea which taketh handsomely at each man's hand. In vain the victim, whom he delighteth to honor, struggles with destiny; he is in the net. Lend, therefore, cheerfully; O man ordained to lend—that thou lose not in the end, with thy worldly penny, the reversion promised. Combine not preposterously in thine own person the penalties of Lazarus and of Dives! but, when thou seest the proper authority coming, meet it smilingly, as it were half way. Come, a handsome sacrifice! See how light *he* makes of it! Strain not courtesies with a noble enemy.

Reflections like the foregoing were forced upon my mind by the death of my old friend, Ralph Bigod, Esq., who parted this life on Wednesday evening; dying, as he had lived, without much trouble. He boasted himself a descendant from mighty ancestors of that name, who heretofore held ducal dignities in this realm. In his actions and sentiments he belied not the stock to which he pretended. Early in life he found himself invested with ample revenues; which, with that noble disinterestedness which I have noticed as inherent in men of the *great race*, he took almost immediate measures entirely to dissipate and bring to nothing; for there is something revolting in the idea of a king holding a private purse; and the thoughts of Bigod were all regal. Thus furnished by the very act of disfurnishment; getting rid of the cumbersome luggage of riches, more apt (as one sing) to slacken virtue, and abate her edge—than prompt her to do aught may merit praise—he set forth, like some Alexander, upon his great enterprise, "borrowing and to borrow!"

In his pereigesis, or triumphant progress throughout this island, it has been calculated that he laid a tithe part of the inhabitants under contribution. I reject this estimate as greatly exaggerated; but having the honor of accompanying my friend divers times, in his perambulations about this vast city, I own I was greatly struck at first with the prodigious number of faces we met, who claimed a sort of respectful acquaintance with us. He was one day so obliging as to explain the phenomenon. It seems, these were his tributaries; feeders of his exchequer; gentlemen, his good friends (as he was pleased to express himself) to whom he had occasionally been beholden for a loan. Their multitudes did no way disconcert him. He rather took a pride in numbering them; and, with Comus, seemed pleased to be "stocked with so fair a herd." With such sources, it was a wonder how he contrived to keep his treasury always empty. He did it by force of an aphorism, which he had often in his mouth, that "money kept longer than three days, stinks." So he made use of it while it was fresh. A good part he drank away (for he was an excellent toss-pot); some he gave away, the rest he threw away, literally tossing and hurling it violently from him—as boys do burrs, or as if it had been infectious,—into ponds, or ditches, or deep holes, inscrutable cavities of the earth; or he would bury it (where he would never seek it again) by a river's side under some bank, which (he would facetiously observe) paid no interest—but out away from him it must go peremptorily, as Hagar's offspring into the wilderness, while it was sweet. He never missed it. The streams were perennial which fed his fisc. When new supplies became necessary, the first person that had the felicity to fall in with him, friend or stranger, was sure to contribute to the deficiency. For Bigod had an *undeniable* way with him. He had a cheerful, open exterior, a quick jovial eye, a bald forehead, just touched with gray (*cana fides*).

He anticipated no excuse and found none. And, waiving for a while my theory as to the *great race*, I would put it to the most untheorizing reader, who may at times have disposable coin in his pocket, whether it is not more repugnant to the kindliness of his nature to refuse such a one as I am describing, than to say *no* to a poor petitionary rogue (your bastard borrower,) who, by his mumping visnomy, tells you that he expects nothing better; and, therefore, whose preconceived notions and expectations you do in reality so much less shock in the refusal.

When I think of this man; his fiery glow of heart, his swell of feeling; how magnificent, how *ideal* he was; how great at the midnight hour; and when I compare with him the companions with whom I have associated since, I grudge the saving of a few idle ducats, and think that I am fallen into the society of *lenders* and *little* men.

To one like Elia, whose treasures are rather cased in leather covers than closed in iron coffers, there is a class of alienators more formidable than that which I have touched upon; I mean your *borrowers of books*—those mutilators of collections, spoilers of the symmetry of shelves, and creators of odd volumes. There is Comberbatch, matchless in his depredations!

That foul gap in the bottom shelf facing you, like a great eyetooth knocked out—(you are now with me in my little back study in Bloomsbury, reader!)—with the huge Switzer-like tomes on each side (like the Guildhall giants, in their reformed posture, guardant of nothing) once held the tallest of my folios, *Opera Bonaventurae*, choice and massy divinity, to which its two supporters (school divinity also, but of a lesser caliber,—Bellarmine, and Holy Thomas,)— showed but as dwarfs,—itself an Ascapart!—that Comberbatch abstracted upon the faith of a theory he holds, which is more easy, I confess, for me to suffer by than to refute, namely, that "the title to property in a book (my Bonaventure, for instance,) is in exact ratio to the claimant's powers of understanding and appreciating the same." Should he go on acting upon this theory, which of our shelves is safe?

The slight vacuum in the left hand case—two shelves from the ceiling—scarcely distinguishable but by the quick eye of a loser—was whilom the commodious resting place of Brown on Urn Burial. C. will hardly allege that he knows more about that treatise than I do, who introduced it to him, and was indeed, the first (of the moderns) to discover its beauties—but so have I known a foolish lover to praise his mistress in the presence of a rival more qualified to carry her off than himself. Just below, Dodsley's dramas want their fourth volume, where Vittoria Corombona is. The remaining nine are as distasteful as Priam's refuse sons, when the Fates *borrowed* Hector. Here stood the Anatomy of Melancholy, in sober state. There loitered the Complete Angler, quiet as in life, by some stream side. In yonder nook, John Buncle, a widower-volume, with "eyes closed," mourns his ravished mate.

One justice I must do my friend, that if he sometimes, like the sea, sweeps away a treasure, at another time, sea-like, he throws up as rich an equivalent to match it. I have a small under-collection of this nature (my friend's gatherings in his various calls), picked up, he has forgotten at what odd places, and deposited with as little memory at mine. I take in these orphans, the twice deserted. These proselytes of the gate are welcome as the true Hebrews. There they stand in conjunction, natives, and naturalized. The latter seem as little disposed to inquire out their true lineage as I am. I charge no warehouse-room for these deodands, nor shall ever put myself to the ungentlemanly trouble of advertising a sale of them to pay expenses.

To lose a volume to C. carries some sense and meaning in it. You are sure that he will make one hearty meal on your viands, if he can give no account of the platter after it. But what moved thee, wayward, spiteful K., to be so importune to carry off with thee, in spite of tears and adjurations to thee to forbear, the Letters of that princely woman, the thrice noble Margaret Newcastle?—knowing at the time, and knowing that I knew also, thou most assuredly wouldst never turn over one leaf of the illustrious folio; what but the mere spirit of contradiction, and childish love of getting the better of thy friend? Then, worst cut of all! to transport it with thee to the Gallican land. Unworthy land to harbor such a sweetness. A virtue in which all ennobling thoughts dwelt.

Pure thoughts, kind thoughts, high thoughts, her sex's wonder!

Hadst thou not thy play-books, and books of jests and fancies, about thee, to keep thee merry, even as thou keepest all companies with thy quips and mirthful tales? Child of the Green-room, it was unkindly done of thee. Thy wife, too, that part French, better part English woman!—that *she* could fix upon no other treatise to bear away, in kindly token of remembering us, than the works of Fulke Greville, Lord Brook—of which no Frenchman, nor woman of France, Italy, or England, was ever by nature constituted to comprehend a title! *Was there not "Zimmerman on Solitude?"*

Reader, if haply thou art blessed with a moderate collection, be shy of showing it; or if thy heart overfloweth to lend them, lend thy books; but let it be to such a one as S. T. C.— he will return them (generally anticipating the time appointed) with usury; enriched with annotations tripling their value. I have had experience. Many are these precious MSS. of his—(in *matter* oftentimes, and almost, in *quantity*, not unfrequently, vying with the originals) in no very clerkly hand legible in my Daniel; in old Burton; in Sir Thomas Browne; and those abstruser cogitations of the Greville, now, alas! wandering in Pagan lands. I counsel thee, shut not thy heart, nor thy library, against S. T. C.

Studies.

Studies serve for delight, for ornament, and for ability. Their chief use for delight, is in privateness and retiring; for ornament, is in discourse; and for ability, is in the judgment and disposition of business; for expert men can execute, and perhaps judge of, particulars, one by one; but the general councils, and the plots and marshalling of affairs, come best from those that are learned. To spend too much time in studies, is sloth; to use them too much for ornament, is affectation; to make judgment wholly by their rules, is the humor of a scholar; they perfect nature, and are perfected by experience—for natural abilities are like natural plants, that need pruning by study; and studies themselves do give forth directions too much at large, except they be bounded in by experience. Crafty men contemn studies, simple men admire them, and wise men use them; for they teach not their own use; but that is a wisdom without them, and above them, won by observation. Read not to contradict and confute, nor to believe and take for granted, nor to find talk and discourse, but to weigh and consider. Some books are to be tasted, others to be swallowed, and some few to be chewed and digested; that is, some books are to be read only in parts; others to be read, but not curiously; and some few to be read wholly, and with diligence and attention. Some books also may be read by deputy, and extracts made of them by others; but that would be only in the less important arguments, and the meaner sort of books; else distilled books are, like common distilled waters, flashy things. Reading maketh a full man, conference a ready man, and writing an exact man; and therefore if a man write little, he had need have a great memory; if he confer little, he had need have a present wit; and if he read little, he had need have much cunning to seem to know that he doth not.

Of Beauty.

Virtue is like a rich stone, best plain set; and surely virtue is best in a body that is comely, though not of delicate features, and that hath rather dignity of presence than beauty of aspect; neither is it always seen, that very beautiful persons are otherwise of great virtue; as if nature were rather busy not to err, than in labor to produce excellency; and therefore they prove accomplished, but not of great spirit; and study rather behavior than virtue. But this holds not always; for Augustus Cæsar, Titus Vespasianus, Philip le Bel of France, Edward IV of England, Alcibiades of Athens, Ismael, the sophi of Persia, were all high and great spirits, and yet the most beautiful men of their times. In beauty, that of favor is more than that of color; and that of decent and gracious motion more than that of favor. That is the best part of beauty which a picture cannot express; no, nor the first sight of the life. There is no excellent beauty that hath not some strangeness in the proportion. A man cannot tell whether Appelles or Albert Durer were the more trifler; whereof one would make a personage by geometrical proportions; the other, by taking the best parts out of divers faces to make one excellent. Such personages, I think, would please nobody but the painter that made them; not but I think a painter may make a better face than ever was; but he must do it by a kind of felicity (as a musician that maketh an excellent air in music), and not by rule.

A man shall see faces, that, if you examine them part by part, you shall find never a good; and yet altogether do well. If it be true that the principal part of beauty is in decent motion, certainly it is no marvel though persons in years seem many times more amiable; *pulchrorum autumnus pulcher;* for no youth can be comely but by pardon, and considering the youth as to make up the comeliness. Beauty is as Summer fruits, which are easy to corrupt and cannot last; and, for the most part, it makes a dissolute youth, and an age a little out of countenance; but yet certainly again, if it light well, it maketh virtues shine, and vices blush.

Lily's Ride; or, A Race Against Time.

The sketch which we give below is one of the finest in our language. Lily had been notified that her father's life was in danger. In order to give him warning, she must be at the station when his train arrived. This would prevent his intended visit to a friend in the country, and probably save his life.

"William," said Lily, as the stable-boy appeared, "put my saddle on Young Lollard, and bring him round as quick as possible."

"But, Miss Lily, you know dat hoss—" the servant began to expostulate.

"I know all about him, William. Don't wait to talk. Bring him out."

"All right, Miss Lily," he replied with a bow and a scrape. But, as he went toward the stable, he soliloquized angrily: "Now, what for Miss Lily want to ride dat pertikerler hoss, you spose? Never did afore. Nobody but de kunnel ebber on his back, and *he* hab his hands full wid him sometimes. Dese furrer-bred hosses jes' de debbil anyhow! Dar's dat Young Lollard now, it's jest 'bout all a man's life's wuth ter rub him down an' saddle him. Why can't she take de ole un! Here you, Lollard, come outen dat!"

He threw open the door of the log stable where the horse had his quarters as he spoke, and almost instantly, with a short, vicious whinny, a powerful, dark brown horse leaped into the moonlight, and with ears laid back upon his sinuous neck, white teeth bare, and thin, blood-red nostrils distended, rushed toward the servant, who, with a loud, "Dar now! Look at him! Whoa! See de dam rascal!" retreated quickly behind the door. The horse rushed once or twice around the little stable-yard, and then stopped suddenly beside his keeper, and stretched out his head for the bit, quivering in every limb with that excess of vitality which only the thoroughbred horse ever exhibits. He was anxious for the bit and saddle, because they meant exercise, a race, an opportunity to show his speed, which the thoroughbred recognizes as the one great end of his existence.

Before the horse was saddled, Lily had donned her riding habit, put a revolver in her belt, as she very frequently did when riding alone, swallowed a hasty supper, scrawled a short note to her mother on the envelope of the letter she had received—which she charged William at once to carry to her—and was ready to start on a night-ride to Glenville. She had only been there across the country once; but she thought she knew the way, or at least was so familiar with the "lay" of the country that she could find it.

The brawny groom with difficulty held the restless horse by the bit; but the slight girl, who stood upon the block with pale face and set teeth, gathered the reins in her hand, leaped fearlessly into the saddle, found the stirrup, and said, "Let him go!" without a quiver in her voice. The man loosed his hold. The horse stood upright, and pawed the air for a moment with his feet, gave a few mighty leaps to make sure of his liberty, and then, stretching out his neck, bounded forward in a race which would require all the mettle of his endless line of noble sires. Almost without words, her errand had become known to the household of servants; and as she flew down the road, her bright hair gleaming in the moonlight, old Maggie, sobbing and tearful, was yet so impressed with admiration, that she could only say:—

"De Lor' bress her! 'Pears like dat chile ain't 'fear'd o' noffin!"

As she was borne like an arrow down the avenue, and turned into the Glenville road, Lily heard the whistle of the train as it left the depot at Verdenton, and knew that upon her coolness and resolution alone depended the life of her father. It was, perhaps, well for the accomplishment of her purpose, that, for some time after setting out on her perilous journey, Lily Servosse had enough to do to maintain her seat and guide and control her horse. Young Lollard, whom the servant had so earnestly remonstrated against her taking, added to the noted pedigree of his sire the special excellence of the Glencoe strain of his dam, from whom he inherited also a darker coat, and that touch of native savageness which characterizes the stock of Emancipator. Upon both sides his blood was as pure as that of the great kings of the turf, and what we have termed his savagery was more excess of spirit than any inclination to do mischief. It was that uncontrollable desire of the thoroughbred horse to be always doing his best, which made him restless of the bit and curb, while the native sagacity of his race had led him to practice somewhat on the fears of his groom. With that care which only the true lover of the horse can appreciate, Colonel Servosse had watched over the growth and training of Young Lollard, hoping to see him rival, if he did not surpass, the excellencies of his sire. In everything but temper, he had been gratified at the result. In build, power, speed, and endurance, the horse offered all that the most fastidious could desire. In order to prevent the one defect of a quick temper from developing into a vice, the colonel had established an inflexible rule that no one should ride him but himself. His great interest in the colt had led Lily, who inherited all her father's love for the noble animal, to look very carefully during his enforced absences after the welfare of his favorite. Once or twice she had summarily discharged grooms who were guilty of disobeying her father's injunctions, and had always made it a rule to visit his stall every day; so that although she had never ridden him, the horse was familiar with her person and voice.

It was well for her that this was the case; for, as she dashed away with the speed of the wind, she felt how powerless she was to restrain him by means of the bit. Nor did she attempt. Merely feeling his mouth, and keeping her eye upon the road before him, in order that no sudden start to right or left should take her by surprise, she coolly kept her seat, and tried to soothe him by her voice.

With head outstretched and sinewy neck strained to its uttermost, he flew over the ground in a wild, mad race with the evening wind, as it seemed. Without jerk or strain, but easily and steadily as the falcon flies, the high-bred horse skimmed along the ground. A mile, two, three miles were made, in time that would have done honor to the staying quality of his sires, and still his pace had not slackened. He was now nearing the river into which fell the creek that ran by Warrington. As he went down the long slope that led to the ford, his rider tried in vain to check his speed. Pressure upon the bit but resulted in an impatient shaking of the head, and laying back of the ears. He kept up his magnificent stride until he had reached the very verge of the river. There he stopped, threw up his head in inquiry, as he gazed upon the fretted waters lighted up by the full moon, glanced back at his rider, and with a word of encouragement from her marched proudly into the waters, casting up a silver spray at each step. Lily did not miss this opportunity to establish more intimate relations with her steed. She patted his neck, praised him lavishly, and took occasion to assume control of him while he was in the deepest part of the channel, turning him this way and that much more than was needful, simply to accustom him to obey her will.

When he came out on the other bank, he would have resumed his gallop almost at once, but she required him to walk to the top of the hill. The night was growing chilly by this time. As the wind struck her at the hill-top, she remembered that she had thrown a hooded waterproof about her before starting. She stopped her horse, and taking off her hat, gathered her long hair into a mass, and thrust it into the hood, which she threw over her head and pressed her hat down on it; then she gathered the reins, and they went on in that long, steady stride which marks the high-bred horse when he gets thoroughly down to his work. Once or twice she drew rein to examine the landmarks, and determine which road to take. Sometimes her way lay through the forest, and she was startled by the cry of the owl; anon it was through the reedy bottom land, and the half-wild hogs, starting from their lairs, gave her an instant's fright. The moon cast strange shadows around her, but still she pushed on, with this one only thought in her mind, that her father's life was at stake, and she alone could save him. *   *   *   *   *   *   *

She glanced at her watch as she passed from under the shade of the oaks, and, as she held the dial up to the moonlight, gave a scream of joy. It was just past the stroke of nine. She had still an hour, and half the distance had been accomplished in half that time. She had no fear of her horse. Pressing on now in the swinging fox walk which he took whenever the character of the road or the mood of his rider demanded, there was no sign of weariness. As he threw his head upon one side and the other, as if asking to be allowed to press on, she saw his dark eye gleam with the fire of the inveterate racer. His thin nostrils were distended, but his breath came regularly and full. She had not forgotten, even in her haste and fright, the lessons her father had taught; but, as soon as she could control her horse, she had spared him, and compelled him to husband his strength. Her spirits rose at the prospect. She even caroled a bit of exultant song as Young Lollard swept on through a forest of towering pines, with a white sand-cushion stretched beneath his feet. The fragrance of the pines came to her nostrils, and with it the thought of frankincense, and that brought up the hymns of her childhood. The Star in the East, the Babe of Bethlehem, the Great Deliverer—all swept across her rapt vision; and then came the priceless promise, "I will not leave thee, nor forsake thee."

Still on and on the brave horse bore her with untiring limb. Half the remaining distance is now consumed, and she comes to a place where the road forks, not once, but into four branches. It is in the midst of a level, old field covered with a thick growth of scrubby pines. Through the masses of thick green are white lanes which stretch away in every direction, with no visible difference save in the density or frequency of the shadows which fall across them. She tries to think which of the many intersecting paths lead to her destination. She tries this, and then that, for a few steps, consults the stars to determine in what direction Glenville lies, and has almost decided upon the first to the right, when she hears a sound which turns her blood to ice in her veins. * *

Hardly had she placed herself in hiding, before the open space around the intersecting roads was alive with disguised horsemen. She could catch glimpses of their figures as she gazed through the clustering pines. * * * * (From a conversation among the horsemen, she learns which road leads to Glenville.) Lily, with her revolver ready cocked in her hand, turned, and cautiously made her way to the road which had been indicated as the one which led to Glenville. Just as her horse stepped into the path, an overhanging limb caught her hat, and pulled it off, together with the hood of her waterproof, so that her hair fell down again upon her shoulders. She hardly noticed the fact in her excitement, and, if she had, could not have stopped to repair the accident. She kept her horse upon the shady side, walking upon the grass as much as possible to prevent attracting attention, watching on all sides for any scattered members of the clan. She had proceeded thus about a hundred and fifty yards, when she came to a turn in the road, and saw, sitting before her in the moonlight, one of the disguised horsemen, evidently a sentry who had been stationed there to see that no one came upon the camp unexpectedly. He was facing the other way, but just at that instant turned, and, seeing her indistinctly in the shadow, cried out at once—

"Who's there? Halt!"

They were not twenty yards apart. Young Lollard was trembling with excitement under the tightly drawn rein. Lily thought of her father half prayerfully, half fiercely, bowed close over her horse's neck, and braced herself in the saddle, with every muscle as tense as those of the tiger waiting for his leap. Almost before the words were out of the sentry's mouth, she had given Young Lollard the spur, and shot like an arrow into the bright moonlight, straight toward the black, muffled horseman.

"My God!" he cried, amazed at the sudden apparition.

She was close upon him in an instant. There was a shot; his startled horse sprang aside, and Lily, urging Young Lollard to his utmost speed, was flying down the road toward Glenville. She heard an uproar behind—shouts, and one or two shots. On, on. she sped. She knew now every foot of the road beyond. She looked back, and saw her pursuers swarming out of the wood into the moonlight. Just then she was in a shadow. A mile, two miles, were passed. She drew in her horse to listen. There was the noise of a horse's hoofs coming down a hill she had just descended, as her gallant steed bore her, almost with undiminished stride, up the opposite slope. She laughed, even in her terrible excitement, at the very thought that any one should attempt to overtake her.

"They'll have fleet steeds that follow, quoth young Lochinvar," she hummed as she patted Young Lollard's outstretched neck. She turned when they reached the summit, her long hair streaming backward in the moonlight like a golden banner, and saw the solitary horseman on the opposite slope; then turned back, and passed over the hill. * * * *

The train from Venderton had reached and left Glenville. The incomers had been divided between the rival hotels, the porters had removed the luggage, and the agent was just entering his office, when a foam-flecked horse with bloody nostrils, and fiery eyes, ridden by a young girl with a white, set face, and fair, flowing hair, dashed up to the station.

"Judge Denton!" the rider shrieked. The agent had but time to motion with his hand, and she had swept on toward a carriage which was being swiftly driven away from the station, and which was just visible at the turn of the village street.

"Papa, Papa!" shrieked the girlish voice as she swept on.

A frightened face glanced backward from the carriage, and in an instant Comfort Servosse was standing in the path of the rushing steed.

"Ho, Lollard!" he shouted, in a voice which rang over the sleepy town like a trumpet-note.

The amazed horse veered quickly to one side, and stopped as if stricken to stone, while Lily fell insensible into her father's arms.

When she recovered, he was bending over her with a look in his eyes which she will never forget.

Prosperity and Adversity.

The virtue of prosperity is temperance; the virtue of adversity is fortitude. Prosperity is the blessing of the Old Testament; adversity is the blessing of the New, which carrieth the greater benediction, and the clearer revelation of God's favor. Yet even in the Old Testament, if you listen to David's harp, you shall hear as many hearse-like airs as carols; and the pencil of the Holy Ghost has labored more in describing the afflictions of Job than the felicities of Solomon. Prosperity is not without many fears and distastes; and adversity is not without comforts and hopes. We see in needleworks and embroideries, it is more pleasing to have a lively work upon a sad and solemn ground, than to have a dark and melancholy work upon a lightsome ground; judge, therefore, of the pleasure of the heart by the pleasure of the eye. Certainly, virtue is like precious odors, most fragrant where they are incensed or crushed; for prosperity doth best discover vice, but adversity doth best discover virtue.

HORACE MANN.

HORACE MANN was born in Franklin, Mass., May 4, 1796, and he died August 2, 1859. His parents being poor, his early life was given to hard work. At the age of twenty-one he entered Brown University. Having studied law, he settled in Dedham, but soon moved to Boston.

We admire Horace Mann chiefly for the part he has taken in the educational interests of the United States. The present efficiency of the school system of Massachusetts is due almost wholly to his work. In 1837, he was chosen secretary of the State Board of Education. He continued in this office for twelve years. In 1853, he became president of Antioch College, at Yellow Springs, Ohio. His work as a teacher closed here, but his writing will ever continue to teach and to inspire those engaged in educational matters.

His political record is important. In 1836, he was elected to the Massachusetts State Senate, where his prominence placed him at the head of the educational interests of his State.

Upon the death of John Quincy Adams, he was chosen to represent his district in Congress, a position he occupied for six years. While in Congress he took an active part in all true reform measures. His remains rest in a burying-ground at Providence, R. I., and his bronze statue stands in the State House yard, Boston, opposite to that of Webster.

Children and Their Education.

The following we take from Horace Mann's lecture, entitled—"What God Does, and What He Leaves for Man to do, in the Work of Education." It is one of the finest productions in print, and should be read with careful thought.

The entire helplessness of children, for a long period after birth, is another circumstance not within our control, and one deserving of great moral consideration. In one respect, children may be said to possess their greatest power, at this, the feeblest period of their existence;—a power which,—however paradoxical it may seem,—originates in helplessness, and therefore diminishes just in proportion as they gain strength. It was most beautifully said by Dr. Thomas Brown, that after a child has grown to manhood, "he cannot, even then, by the most imperious order, which he addresses to the most obsequious slave, exercise an authority more commanding than that which, in the very first hours of his life, when a few indistinct cries and tears were his only language, he exercised irresistibly over hearts, of the very existence of which he was ignorant." It may be added that, under no terror of a despot's rage; under no bribe of honors, or of wealth; under no fear of torture, or of death, have greater struggles been made, or greater sacrifices endured, than for those helpless creatures, who, for all purposes of immediate availability, are so utterly worthless. All, unless it be the lowest savages, fly to the succor, and melt at the sufferings of infancy. God has so adapted their unconscious pleadings to our uncontrollable impulse, that they, in their weakness, have the prerogative of command, and we, in our strength, the instinct of obedience. It was the highest wisdom, then, not to intrust the fate of infancy to any volitions or notions of expediency, on our part; but, at once, by a sovereign law of the constitution, to make our knowledge and power submissive to their inarticulate commands.

In proportion as this power of helplessness wanes, the child begins to excite our interest and sympathy, by a thousand personal attractions and forms of loveliness. The sweetness of lips that never told a lie; the smile that celebrates the first-born emotions of love; the intense gaze at bright colors and striking forms, gathering together the elements from whose full splendor and gorgeousness Raphael painted and Homer wrote; the plastic imagination, fusing the solid substances of the earth, to be re-cast into shapes of beauty;—what Rothschild, what Crœsus has wealth that can purchase these!

How cheap and how beautiful, too, are the joys of childhood! Paley, in speaking of the evidences of the goodness of God, says there is always some "bright spot in the prospect;"—some "single example," "by which each man finds himself more convinced than by all others put together. I seem, for my own part," he adds, "to see the benevolence of the Deity more clearly in the pleasure of young children, than many things in the world. The pleasures of grown persons may be reckoned partly of their own procuring, especially if there has been any industry, or contrivance, or pursuit to come at them; or, if they are founded, like music, painting, etc., upon any qualifications of their own acquiring. But the pleasures of a healthy infant are so manifestly provided for it by another, and the benevolence of the provision is so unquestionable, that every child I see at its sport, affords to my mind a kind of sensible evidence of the finger of God, and of the disposition which directs it." At the age of two or three years, before a child has ever seen a jest-book, whence comes his glad and gladdening laughter,—at once costless and priceless? Whence comes that flow of joy, that gurgles and gushes up from his heart, like water flung from a spouting spring? That bright-haired boy, how came he as full of music and poetry as a singing-book? Who imprisoned a dancing-school in each of his toes, which sends him from the earth with bounding and rebounded step? What an Æolian harp the wind finds in him! Nor music alone does it awaken in his bosom; for, let but its feathery touch play upon his locks, or fan his cheek, and gravitation lets go of him,—he floats and sails away, as though his body were a feather and his soul the zephyr that played with it.

Indeed, half his discords come, because the winds, the buds, the flowers, the light,—so many fingers of the hand of nature,—are all striving to play different tunes upon him at the same time. These delights are born of the exquisite workmanship of the Creator, before the ignorance and wickedness of men have had time to mar it;—and they flow out spontaneously and unconsciously, like a bird's song, or a flower's beauty.

Even to those who have no children of their own,—unless they are, as the apostle expresses it, "without natural affection,"—even to those, the wonderful growth of a child in knowledge, in power, in affection, makes all other wonders tame. Who ever saw a wretch so heathenish, so dead, that the merry song or shout of a group of gleeful children did not galvanize the misanthrope into an exclamation of joy? What orator or poet has eloquence that enters the soul with such quick and subtle electricity, as a child's tear of pity or suffering, or his frown of indignation at wrong? A child is so much more than a miracle that its growth and future blessedness re the only things worth working miracles for. God did not make ...e child for the sake of the earth, nor for the sake of the sun, as a footstool and a lamp, to sustain his steps and to enlighten his path, during a few only of the earliest years of his immortal existence.

You perceive, my friends, that in speaking of the loveliness of children, and their power to captivate and subdue all hearts to a willing bondage, I have used none but masculine pronouns,—referring only to the stronger and hardier sex; for by what glow and melody of speech can I sketch the vision of a young and beautiful daughter, with all her bewildering enchantments? By what cunning art can the coarse material of words be refined and subtilized into color and motion and music, till they shall paint the bloom of health, "celestial, rosy red;" till they shall trace those motions that have the grace and the freedom of flame, and echo the sweet and affectionate tones of a spirit yet warm from the hand that created it? What less than a divine power could have strung the living chords of her voice to pour out unbidden and exulting harmonies? What fount of sacred flame kindles and feeds the light that gleams from the pure depths of her eye, and flushes her cheek with the hues of a perpetual morning, and shoots auroras from her beaming forehead? O, profane not this last miracle of heavenly workmanship with sight or sound of earthly impurity! Keep vestal vigils around her inborn modesty; and let the quickest lightnings blast her tempter. She is Nature's mosaic of charms. Looked upon as we look upon an object in natural history,—upon a gazelle or a hyacinth,—she is a magnet to draw pain out of a wounded breast. While we gaze upon her, and press her in ecstacy to our bosom, we almost tremble, lest suddenly she should unfurl a wing and soar to some better world.

But, my friend, with what emotions ought we to tremble, when our thoughts pass from the present to the future,—when we ponder on the possibilities of evil as well as of good, which now, all unconsciously to herself, lie hidden in her spirit's coming history,—now hidden, but to be revealed soon as her tiny form shall have expanded to the stature, and her spirit to the power, of womanhood? When we reflect, on the one hand, that this object, almost of our idolatry, may go through life solacing distress, ministering to want, redeeming from guilt, making vice mourn the blessedness it has lost because it was not virtue; and, as she walks, holy and immaculate before men, some aerial anthem shall seem to be forever hymning peaceful benedictions around her; or, on the other hand, that, from the dark fountains of a corrupted heart, she shall send forth a secret, subtle poison, compared with which all earthly venoms are healthful;—when we reflect that, so soon, she may become one or the other of all this, the pen falls, the tongue falters and fails, while the hopeful, fearful heart rushes from thanksgiving to prayer and from prayer to thanksgiving.

But the most striking and wonderful provision which is made, in the accustomed course of nature and providence, for the welfare of children, remains to be mentioned.

Reflect, for a moment, my friends, how it has come to pass, that the successive generations of children, from Adam to ourselves,—each one of which was wholly incapable of providing for itself for a single day—how has it come to pass, that these successive generations have been regularly sustained and continued to the present day, without intermission or failure? The Creator did not leave these ever-returning exigencies without adequate provision; —for how universal and how strong is the love of offspring in the parental breast! This love is the grand resource,—the complement of all other forces. We are accustomed to call the right of self-preservation the first law of nature; yet how this love of offspring overrules and spurns it. To rescue her child, the mother breaks through a wall of fire, or plunges into the fathomless flood;—or, if it must be consumed in the flames, or lie down in the deep, she clasps it to her bosom and perishes with it. This maternal impulse does not so much subjugate self, as forget that there is any such thing as self; and were the mother possessed of a thousand lives, for the welfare of her offspring she would squander them all. Mourning, disconsolate mothers, bewailing lost children! Behold the vast procession, which reaches from the earliest periods of the race to those who now stand bending and weeping over the diminutive graves which swallow up their hopes; and what a mighty attestation do they give to the strength of that instinct which God has implanted in the maternal breast. Nor is it in the human race only that this love of offspring bears sway. All the higher orders of animated nature are subjected to its control. It inspires the most timid races of the brute creation with boldness, and melts the most ferocious of them into love. To express its strength and watchfulness, the hare is said to sleep with ever-open eye on the form where her young repose; and the pelican to tear open her breast with her own beak, and pour out her life-blood to feed her nestlings. The famishing eagle grasps her prey in her talons and carries it to her lofty nest; and though she screams with hunger, yet she will not taste it until her young are satisfied; and the gaunt lioness bears the spoils of the forest to her cavern, nor quenches the fire of her own parched lips until her whelps have feasted. And thus, from the parent stock,—from the Adam and Eve, whether of animals or of men, who came into life full-formed from the hand of their Creator,—down through all successive generations, to the present dwellers upon earth, has this invisible but mighty instinct of the parent's heart brooded and held its zealous watch over their young, nurturing their weakness and instructing their ignorance, until the day of their maturity, when it became their turn to re-affirm this great law of nature toward their offspring.

This, my friend, is not sentimentality. It is the contemplation of one of the divinest features in the economy of Providence. It was for the wisest ends that the Creator ordained, that as the offspring of each "after its kind" should be brought into life,—then, in that self-same hour, without volition or forethought on their part,—there should flame up in the breast of the parent, as from the innermost recesses of nature, a new and overmastering impulse,—an impulse which enters the soul like a strong invader, conquering, revolutionizing, transforming old pains into pleasures and old pleasures into pains, until its great mission should be accomplished. On this link the very existence of the races was suspended. Hence Divine foreknowledge made it strong enough to sustain them all;—for, in vain would the fountain of life have been opened in the maternal breast, if a deeper fountain of love had not been opened in her heart.

Would you more adequately conceive what an insupportable wretchedness and torment the rearing of children would be, if, instead of being rendered delightful by these endearments of parental love, it had been merely commanded by law, and enforced by pains and penalties,—would you, I say, more fully conceive this difference,—contrast the feelings of a slave-breeder (a wretch abhorred by God and man),—contrast, I say, the feelings of a slave-breeder who raises children for the market, with the feelings of the slave-mother, in whose person this sacred law of parental love is outraged. If one of these doomed children, from what cause soever, becomes puny and sickly, and gives good promise of defeating the cupidity that called it into life, with what bitter emotions does the master behold it! He thinks of investments sunk, of unmerchantable stock on hand, of the profit and loss account; and perhaps he is secretly meditating schemes for preventing further expenditures by bringing the hopeless concern to a violent close. But what an inexpressible joy does the abused mother find in watching over and caressing it, and cheating the hostile hours;—and (for such is the impartiality of nature) if she can beguile it of one note of gladness from its sorrow-stricken frame, her dusky bosom thrills with as keen a rapture as ever dilated the breast of a royal mother, when, beneath a canopy and within curtains of silk and gold, she nursed the heir of a hundred kings.

In civilized and Christianized man, this natural instinct is exalted into a holy sentiment. At first, it is true, there springs up this blind passion of parental love, yearning for the good of the child, delighted by its pleasures, tortured by its pains. But this vehement impulse, strong as it is, is not left to do its work alone. It summons and supplicates all the nobler faculties of the soul to become its counselors and allies. It invokes the aid of conscience, and conscience urges to do all and suffer all, for the child's welfare. For every default, conscience expostulates, rebukes, mourns, threatens, chastises. That is selfishness, and not conscience, in the parent, which says to the child, "You owe your being and your capacities to me." Conscience makes the parent say, "I owe my being and my capacities to you. It is I who have struck out a spark which is to burn with celestial effulgence, or glare with baleful fires. It is I, who have worked out of nothingness, unknown and incalculable capacities of happiness and of misery; and all that can be done by mortal means is mine to do."

Nor does this love of offspring stop with conscience. It enlists, in its behalf, the general feeling of benevolence,—benevolence, that godlike sentiment which rejoices in the joys and suffers in the sufferings of others. The soul of the truly benevolent man does not seem to reside much in its own body. Its life, to a great extent, is the mere reflex of the lives of others. It migrates into their bodies, and, identifying its existence with their existence, finds its own happiness in increasing and prolonging their pleasures, in extinguishing or solacing their pains. And of all places into which the whole heart of benevolence ever migrates, it is in the child where it finds the readiest welcome, and where it loves best to prolong its residence.

So the voice of another sentiment,—a sentiment whose commands are more authoritative than those of any other which ever startles the slumbering faculties from their guilty repose,—I mean the religious sentiment, the sense of duty to God,—this, too, comes in aid of the parental affection; and it appeals to the whole nature, in language awful as that which made the camp of the Israelites tremble, at the foot of Sinai. The sense of duty to God compels the parent to contemplate the child in his moral and religious relations. It says, "However different you may now be from your child,—you strong, and he weak; you learned, and he ignorant; your mind capacious of the mighty events of the past and the future, and he alike ignorant of yesterday and to-morrow,—yet in a few short years, all this difference will be lost, and one of the greatest remaining differences between yourself and him will be that which your own conduct toward him shall have caused or permitted. If, then, God is Truth, if God is Love, teach the child above all things to seek for Truth, and to abound in Love."

So much, then, my friends, is done in the common and established course of nature, for the welfare of our children. Nature supplies a perennial force, unexhausted, inexhaustible, reappearing whenever and wherever the parental relation exists. We, then, who are engaged in the sacred cause of education, are entitled to look upon all parents as having given hostages to our cause; and, just as soon as we can make them see the true relation in which they and their children stand to this cause, they will become advocates for its advancement, more ardent and devoted than ourselves. We hold every parent by a bond more strong and faithful than promises or oaths,—by a Heaven-established relationship, which no power on earth can dissolve. Would parents furnish us with a record of their secret consciousness, how large a portion of those solemn thoughts and emotions, which throng the mind in the solitude of the night watches and fill up their hours of anxious contemplation, would be found to relate to the welfare of their offspring. Doubtless the main part of their most precious joys come from the present or prospective well-being of their children;—and oh! how often would they account all gold as dross, and fame as vanity, and life as nothing, could they bring back the look of the cradle's innocence upon the coffined reprobate!

With some parents, of course, these pleasures and pains constitute a far greater share of the good or ill of life than with others;—and with mothers generally far more than with fathers. We have the evidence of this superior attachment of the mother, in those supernatural energies which she will put forth to rescue her child from danger; we know it by the vigils and fasting she will endure to save it from the pangs of sickness, or to ward off the shafts of death; when, amid all the allurements of the world, her eye is fastened and her heart dwells upon one spot in it; we know it by her agonies, when, at last, she consigns her child to an early grave; we know it by the tear in her eye, when, after the lapse of years, some stranger repeats, by chance, its beloved name; and we know it by the crash and ruin of the intellect sometimes produced by the blow of bereavement;—all these are signatures written by the finger of God upon human nature itself, by which we know that parents are constituted and predestined to be the friends of education. They will, they must, be its friends, as soon as increasing intelligence shall have demonstrated to them the indissoluble relation which exists between Education and Happiness.

I have now spoken, my friends, of what is done for us, in the accustomed course of nature and providence, as it regards the well-being of our children. But here I come to the point of divergence. Here I must speak of our part of the work; of those duties which the Creator has devolved upon ourselves. Here, therefore, it becomes my duty to expose the greatest of all mistakes, committed in regard to the greatest of all subjects, and followed by proportionate calamities.

Two grand qualifications are equally necessary in the education of children,—Love and Knowledge. Without love, every child would be regarded as a nuisance, and cast away as soon as born. Without knowledge, love will ruin every child. Nature supplies the love, but she does not supply the knowledge. The love is spontaneous; the knowledge is to be acquired by study and toil, by the most attentive observation and the profoundest reflection. Here, then, lies the fatal error:—parents rest contented with the feeling of love; they do not devote themselves to the acquisition of that knowledge which is necessary to guide it. Year after year, thousands and tens of thousands indulge the delightful sentiment, but never spend an hour in studying the conditions which are indispensable to its gratification.

In regard to the child's physical condition,—its growth and health and length of life—these depend, in no inconsiderable degree, on the health and self-treatment of the mother before its birth. After birth, they depend not only on the vitality and temperature of the air it breathes, on dress and diet and exercise, but on certain proportions and relations which these objects bear to each other. Now the tenderest parental love,—a love which burns, like incense upon an altar, for an idolized child, for a quarter of a century, or for half a century—will never teach the mother that there are different ingredients in the air we breathe, that one of them sustains life, that another of them destroys life, that every breath we draw changes the life-sustaining element into the life-destroying one; and therefore that the air which is to be respired must be perpetually renewed. Love will never instruct the mother what materials or textures of clothing have the proper conducting or non-conducting qualities for different climates, or for different seasons of the year. Love is no chemist or physiologist, and therefore will never impart to the mother any knowledge of the chemical or vital qualities of different kinds of food, of the nature or functions of the digestive organs, of the susceptibilities of the nervous system, nor, indeed, of any other of the various functions on which health and life depend. Hence, the most affectionate but ignorant mother, during the cold nights of Winter, will visit the closet-like bed-chamber of her darling, calk up every crevice, cranny, smother him with as many integuments as encase an Egyptian mummy, close the door of his apartment, and thus inflict upon him a consumption,—born of love. Or she will wrap nice comforters about his neck, until, in some glow of perspiration, he flings them off, and dies of the croup. Or she will consult the infinite desires of a child's appetite, instead of the finite powers of his stomach, and thus pamper him until he languishes into a life of suffering and imbecility, or becomes stupefied and besotted by one of sensual indulgence.

A mother has a first-born child, whom she dotes upon to distraction, but, through some fatal error in its management, occasioned by her ignorance, it dies in the first, beautiful, budding hour of childhood—nipped like the sweet blossoms of Spring by an untimely frost. Another is committed to her charge, and in her secret heart she says, "I will love this better than the first." But it is not better love that the child needs; it is more knowledge.

It is the vast field of ignorance pertaining to these subjects, in which quackery thrives and fattens. No one who knows anything of the organs and functions of the human system, and of the properties of those objects in nature to which that system is related, can hear a quack descant upon the miraculous virtues of his nostrums, or can read his advertisements in the newspapers—wherein, fraudulently toward man, and impiously toward God, he promises to sell an "Elixir of Life," or "The Balm of Immortality," or "Resurrection Pills"—without contempt for his ignorance, or detestation of his guilt. Could the quack administer his nostrums to the great enemy, death, then, indeed, *we* might expect to live forever. * * * * * *

If the vehement, but blind love of offspring, which comes by nature, is not enlightened and guided by knowledge and study and reflection, it is sure to defeat its own desires. Hence, the frequency and the significance of such expressions as are used by plain, rustic people, of strong common sense: "There were too many peacocks where that boy was brought up;" or, "The silly girl is not to blame, for she was dolled up, from a doll in the cradle to a doll in the parlor." All children have foolish desires, freaks, caprices, appetites, which they have no power or skill to gratify; but the foolish parent supplies all the needed skill, time, money, to gratify them; and thus the greater talent and resource of the parent foster the propensities of the child into excess and predominance. The parental love, which was designed by Heaven to be the guardian angel of the child, is thus transformed into a cruel minister of evil.

Think, my friends, for one moment, of the marvelous nature with which we have been endowed,—of its manifold and diverse capacities, and of their attributes of infinite expansion and duration. Then cast a rapid glance over this magnificent temple of the universe into which we have been brought. The same Being created both by His omnipotence, and by His wisdom. He has adapted the dwelling-place to the dweller. The exhaustless variety of natural objects by which we are surrounded; the relations of the family, of society, and of the race; the adorable perfections of the Divine mind,—these are means for the development, and spheres for the activity, and objects for the aspiration of the immortal soul. For the sustentation of our physical natures God has created the teeming earth, and tenanted the field and the forest, the ocean and the air, with innumerable forms of life; and He has said to us, "have dominion" over them. For the education of the perceptive intellect there have been provided the countless multitude and diversity of substances, forms, colors, motions,—from a drop of water to the ocean; from the tiny crystal that sparkles upon the shore, to the sun that blazes in the heavens, and the sun-strown firmament. For the education of the reflecting intellect we have the infinite relations of discovered and undiscovered sciences,—the encyclopædias of matter and of spirit, of which all the encyclopædias of man, as yet extant, are but the alphabet. We have domestic sympathies looking backward, around, and forward; and answering to these, are the ties of filial, conjugal, and parental relations. Through our inborn sense of melody and harmony, all joyful and plaintive emotions flow out into spontaneous music; and, not friends and kindred only, but even dead nature echoes back our sorrows and our joys. To give a costless delight to our sense of beauty, we have the variegated landscape, the rainbow, the ever-renewing beauty of the moon, the glories of the rising and the setting sun, and the ineffable purity and splendor of that celestial vision when the northern and the southern auroras shoot up from the horizon, and overspread the vast concave with their many-colored flame, as though it were a reflection caught from the waving banner of angels, when the host of heaven rejoices over some sinner that has repented. And finally, for the amplest development, for the eternal progress of those attributes that are proper to man, —for conscience, for the love of truth, for that highest of all emotions, the love and adoration of our Creator,—God, in his unsearchable riches, has made full provision. And here, on the one hand, is the subject of education,—the child, with its manifold and wonderful powers—and, on the other hand, this height and depth, and boundlessness of natural and of spiritual instrumentalities to build up the nature of that child into a capacity for the intellectual comprehension of the universe, and into a spiritual similitude to its Author. And who are they that lay their rash hands upon this holy work? Where or when have they learned, or sought to learn, to look at the unfolding powers of the child's soul, and to see what it requires, and then to run their eye and hand over this universe of material and of moral agencies, and to select and apply whatever is needed, at the time needed, and in the measure needed? Surely, in no other department of life is knowledge so indispensable; surely, in no other is it so little sought for. In no other navigation is there such danger of wreck; in no other is there such blind pilotage. * * * * * * * * * *

You all recollect, my friends, that memorable fire which befell the city of New York, in the year 1835. It took place in the heart of that great emporium,—a spot where merchants whose wealth was like princes' had gathered their treasures. In but few places or the surface of the globe was there accumulated such a mass of riches. From each continent and from all the islands of the sea, ships had brought thither their tributary offerings, until it seemed like a magazine of the nations,—the coffer of the world's wealth. In the midst of these hoards, the fire broke out. It raged between two and three days. Above, the dome of the sky was filled with appalling blackness; below, the flames were of an unapproachable intensity of light and heat; and such were the inclemency of the season and the raging of the elements, that all human power and human art seemed as vanity and nothing. Yet, situated in the very midst of that conflagration, there was one building, upon which the storm of fire beat in vain. All around, from elevated points in the distance, from steeples and the roofs of houses, thousands of the trembling inhabitants gazed upon the awful scene; and thought—as well they might—that it was one of universal and undistinguishing havoc. But, as some swift cross-wind furrowed athwart that sea of flame, or a broad blast beat down its aspiring crests, there, safe amidst ruin, erect amongst the falling walls, was seen that single edifice. And when, at last, the ravage ceased, and men again walked those streets in sorrow, which so lately they had walked in pride, there stood that solitary edifice, unharmed amid surrounding desolation; from the foundation to the cope-stone, unscathed; and over the treasure which had been confided to its keeping, the smell of fire had not passed. There it stood, like an honest man in the streets of Sodom. Now, why was this? It was constructed from the same materials, of brick and mortar, of iron and slate, with the thousands around it whose substance was now rubbish and their contents ashes. Now, why was this? *It was built by a workman.* It was BUILT BY A WORKMAN. The man who erected that surviving, victorious structure knew the nature of the materials he used; he *knew* the element of fire; he *knew* the power of combustion. Fidelity seconded his knowledge. He did not put in stucco for granite, nor touch-wood for iron. He was not satisfied with outside ornaments, with finical cornices and gingerbread work; but deep in all its hidden foundations—in the interior of its walls, and in all its secret joints—where no human eye should ever see the compact masonry—he consolidated, and cemented, and closed it in, until it became impregnable to fire —insoluble in that volcano. And thus, my hearers, must parents become workmen in the education of their children. They must know that, from the very nature and constitution of things, a lofty and enduring character cannot be formed by ignorance and chance. They must know that no skill or power of man can ever lay the imperishable foundations of virtue, by using the low motives of fear, and the pride of superiority, and the love of worldly applause or of worldly wealth, any more than they can rear a material edifice, storm-proof and fire-proof, from bamboo and cane-brake!

Until, then, this subject of education is far more studied and far better understood than it has ever yet been, there can be no security for the formation of pure and noble minds; and though the child that is born to-day may turn out an Abel, yet we have no assurance that he will not be a Cain. Until parents will learn to train up children in the way they should go—until they will learn what that way is—the paths that lead down to the realms of destruction must continue to be thronged; the doting father shall feel the pangs of a disobedient and profligate son, and the mother shall see the beautiful child whom she folds to her bosom turn to a coiling serpent and sting the breast upon which it was cherished. Until the thousandth and the ten thousandth generation shall have passed away the Deity may go on doing his part of the work, but unless we do our part also, the work will never be done—and until it is done, the river of parental tears must continue to flow. Unlike Rachael, parents shall weep for their children *because they are*, and not because they *are not*; nor shall they be comforted, until they will learn that God in His infinite wisdom has pervaded the universe with immutable laws—laws which may be made productive of the highest forms of goodness and happiness; and, in His infinite mercy, has provided the means by which those laws can be discovered and obeyed; but that He has left it to us to learn and to apply them, or to suffer the unutterable consequences of ignorance. But when the immortal nature of the child shall be brought within the action of those influences—each at its appointed time—which have been graciously prepared for training it up in the way it should go, then may we be sure, that God will clothe its spirit in garments of *amianthus*, that it may not be corrupted, and of *asbestos*, that it may not be consumed, and that it will be able to walk through the pools of earthly pollution, and through the furnace of earthly temptation, and come forth white as linen that has been washed by the fuller and pure as the golden wedge of Ophir that has been refined in the refiner's fire.

Pictures.

We don't care whether pictures abound in a house from pride, fashion, or taste, so that they be there. If there is insensibility in the proprietor, he may be the means of gratifying taste in others, or of awakening a taste where it was lying inactive before. It is more delightful, of course, where good taste prompts their supply; then the pleasure of the exhibitor is added to the gazer, be he never so humble, and the two realize a better brotherhood—not before recognized, perhaps—in the broad avenue of natural taste. How cheerful the walls of a home look with them; and, by the rule of opposites, how cheerless without them! It is a garden without flowers, a family without children. Let an observing man enter a house, and ten times in ten he can decide the character of the proprietor. If he is a mean man, there will be no pictures; if rich and ostentatious, they will be garish and costly, brought from over the water, with expensive frames, and mated with mathematical exactness; if a man of taste, the quality is observable, and, whatever their number or arrangement, regard has evidently been had to the beauty of subject and fitness, with just attention to light and position. In humble homes, when this taste exists, it still reveals itself, though cheaply, but the quick eye detects it and respects it. We have seen it in a prison, where a judicious placing of a wood-cut or a common lithograph has given almost cheerfulness to the stone walls on which it hung.

Maxims of George Washington.

The biographer of George Washington has stated that when but thirteen years old, Washington drew up for his future conduct a series of maxims which he called "Rules of Civility and Decent Behavior in Company." We give these rules, as they are worthy of diligent study and cannot fail to both interest and profit the youth of our land:

Every action in company ought to be some sign of respect to those present.

In the presence of others sing not to yourself with a humming voice, nor drum with your fingers or feet.

Speak not when others speak, sit not when others stand, and walk not when others stop.

Turn not your back to others, especially in speaking; jog not the table or desk on which another reads or writes; lean not on any one.

Be no flatterer; neither play with any one that delights not to be played with.

Read no letters, books, or papers in company; but when there is a necessity for doing it you must not leave; come not near the books or writings of any one so as to read them unasked; also look not nigh when another is writing a letter.

Let your countenance be pleasant, but in serious matters somewhat grave.

Show not yourself glad at the misfortune of another, though he were your enemy.

They that are in dignity or office have in all places precedency; but whilst they are young they ought to respect those that are their equals in birth or other qualities, though they have no public charge. It is good manners to prefer them to whom we speak before ourselves, especially if they be above us, with whom in no sort we ought to begin.

Let your discourse with men of business be short and comprehensive.

In writing or speaking give to every person his due title according to his degree and the custom of the place.

Strive not with your superiors in argument, but always submit your judgment to others with modesty.

When a man does all he can, though succeeds not well, blame not him that did it.

Being to advise or reprehend any one, consider whether it ought to be in public or in private, presently or at some other time, also in what terms to do it; and in reproving show no signs of choler, but do it with sweetness and mildness.

Mock not nor jest at anything of importance; break no jests that are sharp and biting; and if you deliver anything witty or pleasant, abstain from laughing thereat yourself.

Wherein you reprove another be unblamable yourself, for example is more prevalent than precept.

Use no reproachful language against any one, neither curses nor revilings.

Be not hasty to believe flying reports to the disparagement of any one.

In your apparel be modest, and endeavor to accommodate nature rather than procure admiration. Keep to the fashion of your equals, such as are civil and orderly with respect to time and place.

Play not the peacock, looking everywhere about you to see if you be well decked, if your shoes fit well, if your stockings set neatly and clothes handsomely.

Associate yourself with men of good quality if you esteem your own reputation, for it is better to be alone than in bad company.

Let your conversation be without malice or envy, for it is a sign of a tractable and commendable nature; and in all causes of passion admit reason to govern.

Be not immodest in urging your friend to discover a secret.

Utter not base and frivolous things amongst grown and learned men, nor very difficult questions or subjects amongst the ignorant, nor things hard to be believed.

Speak not of doleful things in time of mirth nor at the table; speak not of melancholy things, as death and wounds; and if others mention them, change, if you can, the discourse. Tell not your dreams but to your intimate friends.

Break not a jest when none take pleasure in mirth. Laugh not aloud, nor at all without occasion. Deride no man's misfortunes, though there seem to be some cause.

Speak not injurious words, neither in jest nor earnest. Scoff at none, although they give occasion.

Be not forward, but friendly and courteous; the first to salute, hear and answer; and be not pensive when it is time to converse.

Detract not from others, but neither be excessive in commending.

Go not thither where you know not whether you shall be welcome or not. Give not advice without being asked; and when desired, do it briefly.

If two contend together, take not the part of either unconstrained, and be not obstinate in your opinion; in things indifferent be of the major side.

Reprehend not the imperfections of others, for that belongs to parents, masters and superiors.

Gaze not on the marks or blemishes of others, and ask not how they came. What you may speak in secret to your friend deliver not before others.

Speak not in an unknown tongue in company, but in your own language; and that as those of quality do, and not as the vulgar. Sublime matters treat seriously.

Think before you speak; pronounce not imperfectly, nor bring out your words too hastily, but orderly and distinctly. When another speaks, be attentive yourself, and disturb not the audience. If any hesitate in his words, help him not, nor prompt him without being desired; interrupt him not, nor answer him till his speech be ended.

Treat with men at fit times about business, and whisper not in the company of others.

Make no comparisons; and if any of the company be commended for any brave act of virtue, commend not another for the same.

Be not apt to relate news if you know not the truth thereof. In discoursing of things you have heard, name not your author always. A secret discover not.

Be not curious to know the affairs of others, neither approach to those that speak in private.

Undertake not what you cannot perform, but be careful to keep your promise.

When you deliver a matter, do it without passion and indiscretion, however mean the person may be you do it to.

When your superiors talk to anybody, hear them; neither speak nor laugh.

In disputes be not so desirous to overcome as not to give liberty to each one to deliver his opinion, and submit the judgment of the major part, especially if they are judges of the dispute.

Be not tedious in discourse, make not many digressions, nor repeat often the same matter of discourse.

Speak no evil of the absent, for it is unjust.

Let your recreations be manful, not sinful.

Labor to keep alive in your breast that little spark of celestial fire called conscience.

Be not angry at table, whatever happens; and if you have reason to be so show it not; put on a cheerful countenance, especially if there be strangers, for good humor makes one dish a feast.

When you speak of God or his attributes, let it be seriously in reverence and honor, and obey your natural parents.

The Little Woman.

There was a little woman on board, with a little child; and both little woman and little child were cheerful, good-looking, bright-eyed, and fair to see. The little woman had been passing a long time with her sick mother in New York. The child was born in her mother's house, and she had not seen her husband, to whom she was now returning, for twelve months, having left him a month or two after their marriage. Well, to be sure, there never was a little woman so full of hope and tenderness and love and anxiety, as this little woman was; and all day long she wondered whether "he" would be at the wharf; and whether "he" had got her letter; and whether, if she sent the child ashore by somebody else, "he" would know it, meeting it in the street; which, seeing that he had never set eyes upon it in his life, was not very likely in the abstract, but was probable enough to the young mother.

She was such an artless little creature, and was in such a sunny, beaming, hopeful state, and let out all the matter clinging closely about her heart so freely, that all the other lady passengers entered into the spirit of it as much as she; and the captain, who heard all about it from his wife, was wondrous sly, I promise you, inquiring, every time we met at table, as if in forgetfulness, whether she expected anybody to meet her at St. Louis, and cutting many other dry jokes of that nature. There was one little weazen, dried-apple-faced old woman, who took occasion to doubt the constancy of husbands, in such circumstances of bereavement; and there was another lady, with a lap-dog, old enough to moralize on the lightness of human affections, and yet not so old that she could help nursing the child now and then, or laughing with the rest, when the little woman called it by its father's name, and asked it all manner of fantastic questions concerning him, in the joy of her heart.

It was something of a blow to the little woman, that, when

we were within twenty miles of our destination, it became clearly necessary to put this child to bed. But she got over it with the same good humor, tied a handkerchief around her head, and came out into the little gallery with the rest. Then such an oracle as she became in reference to the localities! and such facetiousness as was displayed by the married ladies, and such sympathy as was shown by the single ones, and such peals of laughter as the little woman herself, who would just as soon have cried, greeted every jest with!

At last, there were the lights of St. Louis, and here was the wharf, and those were the steps; and the little woman, covering her face with her hands, and laughing, or seeming to laugh, more than ever, ran into her own cabin, and shut herself up. I have no doubt but, in the charming inconsistency of such excitement, she stopped her ears, lest she should hear "him" asking for her; but I did not see her do it. Then a great crowd of people rushed on board, though the boat was not yet made fast, but was wandering about among the other boats, to find a landing-place; and everybody looked for the husband, and nobody saw him, when, in the midst of us all, Heaven knows how she ever got there, there was the little woman, clinging with both arms tight around the neck of a fine, good-looking, sturdy young fellow, and clapping her little hands for joy as she dragged him through the small door of her small cabin, to look at the child, as he lay asleep.

DONALD G. MITCHELL.

DONALD GRANT MITCHELL was born in April, 1822, in Norwich, Conn. In 1841, at the age of nineteen, he was graduated at Yale College. Having passed three years on a farm, he sailed for Europe. In 1846 Mitchell returned to this country, and studied law in New York. In 1847 he published *Fresh Gleanings; or A New Sheaf from the Old Fields of Continental Europe*. This work he published under the *nom de plume* of "Ik Marvel," a name which he had used in his agricultural articles in the Albany *Cultivator*. In 1848, he went to Europe again, and while there, wrote *The Battle Summer*, which was published in 1849 in New York. A series of sketches called *The Lorgnette*, satirical of city life, appeared anonymously, in 1850; *Dream Life* in 1851. He served as United States consul at Venice from 1853 to 1855. Upon returning to this country, he took up his home on his model farm, "Edgewood," near New Haven, Conn. Besides the works named, he published *Fudge Doings* in 1854; *My Farm of Edgewood*, 1863; *Wet Days at Edgewood*, 1864; *Seven Stories, with Basement and Attic*, 1864; *Doctor Johns*, a novel, 1866; *Rural Studies*, 1867; and *Pictures of Edgewood*, 1869.

Mr. Mitchell has been popular upon the lyceum platform.

His writings are very interesting. His style is pure and worthy of careful study. His *Reveries of a Bachelor*, from which we have taken "Letters," contains a "contemplative view of life," in which are many "pathetic scenes tenderly narrated."

DONALD G. MITCHELL.

Letters.

Blessed be letters!—they are the monitors, they are also the comforters, and they are the only true heart-talkers. Your speech, and their speeches, are conventional; they are molded by circumstances; they are suggested by the observation, remark, and influence of the parties to whom the speaking is addressed, or by whom it may be overheard.

Your truest thought is modified half through its utterance by a look, a sign, a smile, or a sneer. It is not individual; it is not integral; it is social and mixed, half of you, and half of others. It bends, it sways, it multiplies, it retires, and it advances, as the talk of others presses, relaxes, or quickens. But it is not so with letters:—there you are, with only the soulless pen, and the snow-white, virgin paper. Your soul is measuring itself by itself, and saying its own sayings: there are no sneers to modify its utterance, —no scowl to scare,—nothing is present but you and your thought.

Utter it then freely—write it down—stamp it—burn it in the ink!—There it is, a true soul-print!

Oh, the glory, the freedom, the passion of a letter! It is worth all the lip-talk of the world. Do you say, it is studied, made up, acted, rehearsed, contrived, artistic? Let me see it then; let me run it over; tell me age, sex, circumstances, and I will tell you if it be studied or real; if it be the merest lip-slang put into words, or heart-talk blazing on the paper. I have a little *paquet*, not very large, tied up with narrow crimson ribbon, now soiled with frequent handling, which far into some Winter's night I take down from its nook upon my shelf, and untie, and open, and run over, with such sorrow and such joy,—such tears and such smiles, as I am sure make me for weeks after, a kinder and holier man.

There are in this little *paquet*, letters in the familiar hand of a mother—what gentle admonition—what tender affection!—God have mercy on him who outlives the tears that such admonitions and such affection call up to the eye! There are others in the budget, in the delicate and unformed hand of a loved and lost sister;—written when she and you were full of glee and the best mirth of youthfulness; does it harm you to recall that mirthfulness? or to trace again, for the hundredth time, that scrawling postscript at the bottom, with its *i*'s so carefully dotted and its gigantic *t*'s so carefully crossed, by the childish hand of a little brother?

I have added latterly to that *paquet* of letters; I almost need a new and larger ribbon; the old one is getting too short. Not a few of these new and cherished letters, a former Reverie has brought to me; not letters of cold praise, saying it was well done, artfully executed, prettily imagined—no such thing: but letters of sympathy—of sympathy which means sympathy.

It would be cold and dastardly work to copy them; I am too selfish for that. It is enough to say that they, the kind writers, have seen a heart in the Reverie—have felt that it was real, true. They know it; a secret influence has told it. What matters it, pray, if literally there was no wife, and no dead child, and no coffin, in the house? Is not feeling, feeling and heart? Are not these fancies thronging on my brain, bringing tears to my eyes, bringing joy to my soul, as living as anything human can be living? What if they have no material type—no objective form? All that is crude,—a mere reduction of ideality to sense,—a transformation of the spiritual to the earthly,—a leveling of soul to matter.

Are we not creatures of thought and passion? Is anything about us more earnest than that same thought and passion? Is there anything more real,—more characteristic of that great and dim destiny to which we are born, and which may be written down in that terrible word—Forever?

Let those who will, then, sneer at what in their wisdom they call untruth—at what is false, because it has no material presence: this does not create falsity; would to Heaven that it did!

And yet, if there was actual, material truth, superadded to

Reverie, would such objectors sympathize the more? No! a thousand times, no; the heart that has no sympathy with thoughts and feelings that scorch the soul, is dead also—whatever its mocking tears and gestures may say—to a coffin or a grave!

Let them pass, and we will come back to these cherished letters.

A mother who has lost a child, has, she says, shed a tear—not one, but many—over the dead boy's coldness. And another, who has not, but who trembles lest she lose, has found the words failing as she reads, and a dim, sorrow-borne mist, spreading over the page.

Another, yet rejoicing in all those family ties that make life a charm, has listened nervously to careful reading, until the husband is called home and the coffin is in the house—"Stop!" she says; and a gush of tears tells the rest.

Yet the cold critic will say—"It was artfully done." A curse on him!—it was not art: it was nature.

Another, a young, fresh, healthful girl-mind, has seen something in the love-picture—albeit so weak—of truth; and has kindly believed that it must be earnest. Aye, indeed is it, fair and generous one, earnest as life and hope! Who, indeed, with a heart at all, that has not yet slipped away irreparably and forever from the shores of youth—from that fairy land which young enthusiasm creates, and over which bright dreams hover—but knows it to be real? And so such things will be real, till hopes are dashed, and Death is come. Another, a father, has laid down the book in tears.—God bless them all! How far better this, than the cold praise of newspaper paragraphs, or the critically contrived approval of colder friends!

Let me gather up these letters carefully,—to be read when the heart is faint, and sick of all that there is unreal and selfish in the world. Let me tie them together, with a new and longer bit of ribbon—not by a love-knot, that is too hard—but by an easy slipping knot, that so I may get at them the better. And now they are all together, a snug *paquet*, and we will label them, not sentimentally (I pity the one who thinks it), but earnestly, and in the best meaning of the term—*Souvenirs du Cœur.*

Thanks to my first Reverie, which has added to such a treasure!

Happiness of Temper.

Writers of every age have endeavored to show that pleasure is in *us*, and not in the *objects* offered for our amusement. If the *soul* be happily disposed, everything becomes capable of affording entertainment, and distress will almost want a name. Every occurrence passes in review, like the figures of a procession; some may be awkward, others ill-dressed, but none but a *fool* is, on that account, enraged with the master of ceremonies.

I remember to have once seen a slave, in a fortification in Flanders. who appeared no way touched with his situation. He was maimed, deformed, and chained; obliged to toil from the appearance of day till night-fall, and condemned to this for life; yet with all these circumstances of apparent wretchedness, he sang, would have danced, but that he wanted a leg, and appeared the merriest, happiest man of all the garrison. What a practical philosopher was here! A happy constitution supplied philosophy; and, though seemingly destitute of wisdom, he was really wise. No reading or study had contributed to disenchant the fairy-land around him. Everything furnished him with an opportunity of mirth; and though some thought him, from his insensibility, a fool, he was *such* an idiot as philosophers should wish to imitate.

They, who, like that slave, can place themselves on that side of the world in which everything appears in a pleasant light, will find something in every occurrence to excite their good humor. The most calamitous events, either to themselves or others, can bring no new affliction; the world is to them a theater, on which only comedies are acted. All the bustle of heroism or the aspirations of ambition seem only to heighten the absurdity of the scene, and make the humor more poignant. They feel, in short, as little anguish at their own distress or the complaints of others, as the *undertaker*, though dressed in black, feels sorrow at a funeral.

Of all the men I ever read of, the famous Cardinal de Retz possessed this happiness in the highest degree. When fortune wore her angriest look, and he fell into the power of Cardinal Mazarin, his most deadly enemy (being confined a close prisoner in the castle of Valenciennes), he never attempted to support his distress by wisdom or philosophy, for he pretended to neither. He only laughed at himself and his persecutor, and seemed infinitely pleased at his new situation. In this mansion of distress, though denied all amusements and even the conveniences of life, and entirely cut off from all intercourse with his friends, he still retained his good humor, laughed at the little spite of his enemies, and carried the jest so far as to write the life of his jailer.

All that the wisdom of the proud can teach is to be stubborn or sullen under misfortunes. The Cardinal's example will teach us to be good-humored in circumstances of the highest affliction. It matters not whether our good humor be construed by others into insensibility or idiotism; it is happiness to ourselves, and none but a fool could measure his satisfaction by what the *world* thinks of it.

The happiest fellow I ever knew was of the number of those good-natured creatures that are said to do no harm to any body but themselves. Whenever he fell into any misery, he called it "seeing life." If his head was broken by a chairman, or his pocket picked by a sharper, he comforted himself by imitating the Hibernian dialect of the one, or the more fashionable cant of the other. Nothing came amiss to him. His inattention to money matters had *concerned* his father to such a degree, that all intercession of friends was fruitless. The old gentleman was on his death-bed. The whole family (and Dick among the number) gathered around him.

"I leave my second son, Andrew," said the expiring miser,

"my whole estate; and desire him to be frugal." Andrew, in a sorrowful tone (as is usual on such occasions), prayed heaven to prolong his life and health, to enjoy it himself. "I recommend Simon, my third son, to the care of his elder brother, and leave him, beside, four thousand pounds." "Ah, father!" cried Simon (in great affliction, to be sure), "may heaven give you life and strength to enjoy it yourself!" At last, turning to poor Dick: "As for you, you have always been a sad dog; you'll never come to good, you'll never be rich; I leave you a shilling to buy a *halter*." "Ah, father!" cries Dick, without any emotion, *"may heaven give you life and health to enjoy it yourself!"*

Our Old Grandmother.

There is an old kitchen somewhere in the past, and an old-fashioned fire-place therein, with its smooth old jambs of stone; smooth with many knives that have been sharpened there; smooth with many little fingers that have clung there. There are andirons with rings in the top, wherein many temples of flame have been builded with spires and turrets of crimson. There is a broad, worn hearth; broad enough for three generations to cluster on; worn by feet that have been torn and bleeding by the way, or been made "beautiful," and walked upon floors of tessellated gold. There are tongs in the corner, wherewith we grasped a coal, and "blowing for a little life," lighted our first candle; there is a shovel, wherewith were drawn forth the glowing embers in which we saw our first fancies and dreamed our first dreams; the shovel with which we stirred the logs, until the sparks rushed up the chimney as if a forge was in blast below, and wished we had so many lambs, or so many marbles, or so many somethings that we coveted; and so it was that we wished our first wishes.

There is a chair, a low, rush-bottomed chair; there is a little wheel in the corner, a big wheel in the garret, a loom in the chamber. There are chestfuls of linen and yarn, and quilts of rare patterns and samplers in frames.

And everywhere and always, is the dear old wrinkled face of her whose firm, elastic step mocks the feeble saunter of her children's children, the old-fashioned grandmother of twenty years ago; she, the very Providence of the old homestead; she, who loved us all and said she wished there were more of us to love, and took all the school in the hollow for grandchildren besides. A great expansive heart was hers, beneath the woolen gown, or that more stately bombazine, or that sole heirloom of silken texture.

We can see her to-day,—those mild, blue eyes, with more of beauty in them than time could touch, or death could do more than hide; those eyes that held both smiles and tears within the faintest call of every one of us, and soft reproof that seemed not passion but regret. A white tress has escaped from beneath her snowy cap; she lengthened the tether of a vine that was straying over a window, as she came in, and plucked a four-leaf clover for Ellen. She sits down by the little wheel; a tress is running through her fingers from the distaff's disheveled head, when a small voice cries, "Grandma," from the old red cradle, and "Grandma," Tommy shouts from the top of the stairs. Gently she lets go the thread, for her patience is almost as beautiful as her charity, and she touches the little red bark a moment, till the young voyager is in a dream again, and then directs Tommy's unavailing attempts to harness the cat.

The tick of the clock runs fast and low, and she opens the mysterious door and proceeds to wind it up. We are all on tiptoe, and we beg, in a breath, to be lifted up, one by one, and look in, the hundredth time, upon the tin cases of the weights, and the poor lonely pendulum, which goes to and fro by its little dim windows; and our petitions are all granted, and we are all lifted up, and we all touch with the finger the wonderful weights, and the music of the wheel is resumed.

Was Mary to be married, or was Jane to be wrapped in a shroud? So meekly did she fold the white hands of the one upon her still bosom that there seemed to be a prayer in them there; and so sweetly did she wreathe the white rose in the hair of the other that one would not have wondered had more roses budded for company. How she stood between us and apprehended harm; how the rudest of us softened beneath the gentle pressure of her faded and tremulous hand! From her capacious pocket, that hand was ever withdrawn closed, only to be opened in our own with the nuts she had gathered, with the cherries she had plucked, the little egg she had found, the "turn-over" she had baked, the trinkets she had purchased for us as the products of her spinning, the blessings she had stored for us, the offspring of her heart.

What treasures of story fell from those old lips of good fairies and evil; of the old times when she was a girl; but we wonder if ever she *was* a girl—but then she couldn't be handsomer or dearer—she was ever little. And then, when we begged her to sing: "Sing us one of the old songs you used to sing for mother, grandma."

"Children, I can't sing," she always said, and mother used always to lay her knitting softly down, and the kitten stopped playing with the yarn on the floor, and the clock ticked lower in the corner, and the fire died down to a glow, like an old heart that is neither chilled nor dead, and grandmother sang. To be sure, it would not do for the parlor and concert-room nowadays; but then it was the old kitchen and the old-fashioned grandmother, and the old ballad, in the dear old times, and we can hardly see to write for the memory of them, though it is a hand's breadth to the sunset.

Well, she sang. Her voice was feeble and wavering, like a fountain just ready to fail; but then how sweet-toned it was, and it became deeper and stronger; but it could nct grow sweeter. What "joy of grief" it was to sit there around the fire, all of us, excepting Jane, and her we thought we saw when the door was opened a moment by the wind; but then we were not afraid, for was not it her old smile she wore—to sit there around the fire, and weep over the woes of the babes in the woods, who laid down side by side in the great solemn shadows! and how strangely glad we felt, when the robin redbreast covered them with leaves, and last of all, when the angel took them out of night into day everlasting!

We may think what we will of it now, but the song and the story, heard around the kitchen fire, have colored the thoughts and the lives of most of us, have given the germs of whatever poetry blesses our hearts, whatever of memory blooms in our yesterdays. Attribute whatever we may to the school and the schoolmaster, the rays which make that little day we call life, radiate from the God-swept circle of the hearthstone.

Then she sings an old lullaby, the song of her mother; her mother sang it to her; but she does not sing it through, and falters ere it is done. She rests her head upon her hands, and is silent in the old kitchen. Something glitters down between her fingers in the firelight, and it looks like rain in the soft sunshine. The old grandmother is thinking when she first heard the song, and of voices that sang it, when, a light-haired and light-hearted girl, she hung round that mother's chair, nor saw the shadows of the years to come. Oh! the days that are no more! What words unsay, what deeds undo, to set back just this once the ancient clock of time?

So our little hands were forever clinging to her garments, and staying her as if from dying; for long ago she had done living for herself, and lived alone in us.

How she used to welcome us when we were grown, and came back once more to the homestead! We thought we were men and women, but we were children there; the old-fashioned grandmother was blind in her eyes, but she saw with her heart, as she always did. We threw out long shadows through the open door, and she felt them as they fell over her form, and she looked dimly up, and she said: "Edward I know, and Lucy's voice I can hear, but whose is that other? It must be Jane's," for she had almost forgotten the folded hands. "Oh, no, not Jane's, for she—let me see, she is waiting for me, isn't she?" and the old grandmother wandered and wept.

"It is another daughter, grandmother, that Edward has

brought," says some one, "for your blessing." "Has she blue eyes, my son? Put her hands in mine, for she is my late-born, the child of my old age. Shall I sing you a song, children?" and she is idly fumbling for a toy, a welcome gift for the children that have come again.

One of us, men as we thought we were, is weeping; she hears the half-suppressed sobs, and she says, as she extends her feeble hands, "Here, my poor child, rest upon your grandmother's shoulder; she will protect you from all harm." "Come, my children, sit around the fire again. Shall I sing you a song or tell you a story? Stir the fire, for it is cold; the nights are growing colder."

The clock in the corner struck nine, the bedtime of those old days. The song of life was indeed sung, the story told. It was bedtime at last. Good-night to thee, grandmother. The old-fashioned grandmother is no more, and we shall miss her forever. The old kitchen wants a presence to-day, and the rush-bottomed chair is tenantless. But we will set up a tablet in the midst of the heart, and write on it only this:

SACRED TO THE MEMORY
OF THE
GOOD OLD-FASHIONED GRANDMOTHER.
GOD BLESS HER FOREVER.

Our Burdens.

It is a celebrated thought of Socrates, that if all the misfortunes of mankind were cast into a public stock, in order to be equally distributed among the whole species, those who now think themselves the most unhappy, would prefer the share they are already possessed of, before that which would fall to them by such a division. Horace has carried this thought a great deal further: he says that the hardships or misfortunes which we lie under, are more easy to us than those of any other person would be, in case we could change conditions with him.

As I was ruminating on these two remarks, and seated in my elbow-chair, I insensibly fell asleep; when, on a sudden, I thought there was a proclamation made by Jupiter, that every mortal should bring in his griefs and calamities, and throw them together in a heap. There was a large plain appointed for this purpose. I took my stand in the center of it, and saw, with a great deal of pleasure, the whole human species marching one after another, and throwing down their several loads, which immediately grew up into a prodigious mountain, that seemed to rise above the clouds.

There was a certain lady of a thin, airy shape, who was very active in this solemnity. She carried a magnifying glass in one of her hands, and was clothed in a loose, flowing robe, embroidered with several figures of fiends and spectres, that discovered themselves in a thousand chimerical shapes, as her garments hovered in the wind. There was something wild and distracted in her looks. Her name was Fancy. She led up every mortal to the appointed place, after having very officiously assisted him in making up his pack, and laying it upon his shoulders. My heart melted within me, to see my fellow-creatures groaning under their respective burdens, and to consider that prodigious bulk of human calamities which lay before me.

There, were, however, several persons, who gave me great

diversion upon this occasion. I observed one bringing in a fardel very carefully concealed under an old embroidered cloak, which, upon his throwing it into the heap, I discovered to be poverty. Another, after a great deal of puffing, threw down his luggage, which, upon examining, I found to be his wife.

There were multitudes of lovers saddled with very whimsical burdens composed of darts and flames; but, what was very odd, though they sighed as if their hearts would break under these bundles of calamities, they could not persuade themselves to cast them into the heap, when they came up to it; but, after a few faint efforts, shook their heads, and marched away as heavy laden as they came. I saw multitudes of old women throw down their wrinkles, and several young ones who stripped themselves of a tawny skin. There were very great heaps of red noses, large lips, and rusty teeth. The truth of it is, I was surprised to see the greatest part of the mountain made up of bodily deformities. Observing one advancing toward the heap, with a larger cargo than ordinary upon his back, I found, upon his near approach, that it was only a natural hump, which he disposed of, with great joy of heart, among this collection of human miseries. There were likewise distempers of all sorts; though I could not but observe that there were many more imaginary than real. One little packet I could not but take notice of, which was a complication of all the diseases incident to human nature, and was in the hand of a great many fine people; this was called the spleen. But what most of all surprised me, was a remark I made, that there was not a single vice or folly thrown into the whole heap; at which I was very much astonished, having concluded within myself, that every one would take this opportunity of getting rid of his passions, prejudices, and frailties.

I took notice in particular of a very profligate fellow, who I did not question came loaded with his crimes; but upon searching into his bundle, I found that, instead of throwing his guilt from him, he had only laid down his memory. He was followed by another worthless rogue, who flung away his modesty instead of his ignorance.

When the whole race of mankind had thus cast their burdens, the phantom which had been so busy on this occasion, seeing me an idle spectator of what had passed, approached toward me. I grew uneasy at her presence, when of a sudden she held her magnifying glass full before my eyes. I no sooner saw my face in it, but I was startled by the shortness of it, which now appeared to me in its utmost aggravation. The immoderate breadth of the features made me very much out of humor with my own countenance; upon which I threw it from me like a mask. It happened very luckily, that one who stood by me had just before thrown down his visage, which it seems was too long for him. It was, indeed, extended to a shameful length; I believe the very chin was, modestly speaking, as long as my whole face. We had, both of us, an opportunity of mending ourselves; and all the contributions being now brought in, every man was at liberty to exchange his misfortunes for those of another person. But as there arose many new incidents in the sequel of my vision, I shall reserve them for the subject of my next paper.

In my last paper, I gave my reader a sight of that mountain of miseries, which was made up of those several calamities that afflict the minds of men. I saw, with unspeakable pleasure, the whole species thus delivered from its sorrow; though at the same time, as we stood round the heap, and surveyed the several materials of which it was composed, there was scarcely a mortal, in this vast multitude, who did not discover what he thought pleasures of life; and wondered how the owners of them ever came to look upon them as burdens and grievances.

As we were regarding very attentively this confusion of miseries, this chaos of calamity, Jupiter issued out a second proclamation, that every one was now at liberty to exchange his affliction, and to return to his habitation with any such other bundle as should be delivered to him.

Upon this, Fancy began again to bestir herself, and parceling out the whole heap with incredible activity, recommended to every one his particular packet. The hurry and confusion at this time were not to be expressed. Some observations which I made upon this occasion I shall communicate to the public. A venerable, gray-headed man, who had laid down the colic, and who I found wanted an heir to his estate, snatched up an undutiful son, that had been thrown into the heap by an angry father. The graceless youth, in less than a quarter of an hour, pulled the old gentleman by the beard, and had like to have knocked his brains out; so that meeting the true father, who came toward him with a fit of the gripes, he begged him to take his son again, and give him back his colic; but they were incapable either of them to recede from the choice they had made. A poor galley slave who had thrown down his chains, took up the gout in their stead, but made such wry faces, that one might easily perceive he was no great gainer by the bargain. It was pleasant enough to see the several exchanges that were made, for sickness against poverty, hunger against want of appetite, and care against pain.

The female world were very busy among themselves in bartering for features; one was trucking a lock of gray hairs for a carbuncle; another was making over a short waist for a pair of round shoulders; and a third cheapening a bad face for a lost reputation; but on all these occasions, there was not one of them who did not think the new blemish, as soon as she had got it into her possession, much more disagreeable than the old one. I made the same observation on every other misfortune or calamity, which every one in the assembly brought upon himself, in lieu of what he had parted with; whether it be that all the evils which befall us are in some measure suited and proportioned to our strength, or that every evil becomes more supportable by our being accustomed to it, I shall not determine.

I could not for my heart forbear pitying the poor humpbacked gentleman, mentioned in the former paper, who went off a very well-shaped person with a stone in his bladder; nor the fine gentleman who had struck up his bargain with him, that limped through a whole assembly of ladies who used to admire him, with a pair of shoulders peeping over his head.

I must not omit my own particular adventure. My friend with the long visage had no sooner taken upon him my short face, but he made so grotesque a figure, that as I looked upon him I could not forbear laughing at myself, insomuch that I put my own face out of countenance. The poor gentleman was so sensible of the ridicule, that I found he was ashamed of what he had done; on the other side, I found that I myself had no great reason to triumph, for as I went to touch my forehead I missed the place, and clapped my finger upon my upper lip. Besides, as my nose was exceedingly prominent, I gave it two or three unlucky knocks as I was playing my hand about my face, and aiming at some other part of it. I saw two other gentlemen by me, who were in the same ridiculous circumstances. These had made a foolish exchange between a couple of thick bandy legs, and two long trap sticks that had no calves to them. One of these looked like a man walking upon stilts, and was so lifted up into the air, above his ordinary height, that his head turned round with it; while the other made so awkward circles, as he attempted to walk, that he scarcely knew how to move forward upon his new supporters. Observing him to be a pleasant kind of fellow, I stuck my cane in the ground, and told him I would lay him a bottle of wine, that he did not march up to it, on a line that I drew for him, in a quarter of an hour.

The heap was at last distributed among the two sexes, who made a most piteous sight, as they wandered up and down under the pressure of their several burdens. The whole plain was filled with murmurs and complaints, groans and lamentations. Jupiter, at length, taking compassion on the poor mortals, ordered them a second time to lay down their loads, with a design to give every one his own again. They discharged themselves with a great deal of pleasure; after which, the phantom who had led them into such gross delusions, was commanded to disappear. There was sent in her stead a goddess of a quite different figure; her motions were steady and composed, and her aspect serious but cheerful. She every now and then cast her eyes toward heaven, and fixed them upon Jupiter; her name was *Patience*. She had no sooner placed herself by the Mount of Sorrows, but, what I thought very remarkable, the whole heap sunk to such a degree, that it did not appear a third part so big as it was before. She afterward returned every man his own proper calamity, and, teaching him how to bear it in the most commodious manner, he marched off with it contentedly, being very well pleased that he had not been left to his own choice, as to the kind of evils which fell to his lot.

Besides the several pieces of morality to be drawn out of this vision, I learned from it never to repine at my own misfortunes, or to envy the happiness of another, since it is impossible for any man to form a right judgment of his neighbor's sufferings; for which reason also, I have determined never to think too lightly of another's complaints, but to regard the sorrows of my fellow-creatures with sentiments of humanity and compassion.

In the Garret.

Sarcastic people are wont to say that poets dwell in garrets, and simple people believe it. And others, neither sarcastic nor simple, send them up aloft, among the rubbish, just because they do not know what to do with them downstairs, and "among folks," and so they class them under the head of rubbish, and consign them to the grand receptacle of dilapidated "has been's" and despised "used to be's"—the old garret.

The garret is to the other apartments of the old homestead what the adverb is to the pedagogue in parsing; everything they do not know how to dispose of is consigned to the list of adverbs. And it is for this precise reason that we love garrets; because they do contain the relics of the old and the past—remembrances of other and happier and simpler times. They have come to build houses nowadays without garrets. Impious innovation!

You man of bronze and "bearded like the pard," who would
make people believe, if you could, that you never were a "toddlin'
wee thing;" that you never wore a "ruffle-dress," or jingled a rat-
tle-box with infinite delight; that you never had a mother, and that
she never became an old woman, and wore caps and spectacles,
and, maybe, took snuff; go home once more, after all these years
of absence, all booted and whiskered, and six feet high as you are,
and let us go up the stairs together—in that old-fashioned,
spacious garret, that extends from gable to gable, with its narrow
old windows, with a spider-web of a sash, through which steals
"a dim religious light" upon a museum of things unnamable, that
once figured below stairs, but were long since crowded out by the
Vandal hand of these modern times.

The loose boards of the floor rattle somewhat as they used to
do—don't they?—when beneath your little pattering feet they clat-
tered aforetime, when, of a rainy day, "mother," wearied with
many-tongued importunity, granted the "Let us go up in the garret
and play." And play! Precious little of "play" have you had
since, we'll warrant, with your looks of dignity, and your dream-
ings of ambition.

Here we are now in the midst of the garret. The old barrel
—shall we rummage it? Old files of newspapers—dusty, yellow, a
little tattered! 'Tis the "Columbian Star." How familiar with the
"Letters or papers for father?" And these same Stars, just damp
from the press, were carried one by one from the fireside, and pe-
rused and preserved as they ought to be. Stars? Damp? O many
a star has set since then, and many a new-tufted heap grown dewy
and damp with rain that fell not from the clouds.

Dive deeper into the barrel. There! A bundle, up it comes,
in a cloud of dust. Old almanacs, by all that is memorable! Almanacs! thin-leaved ledgers of time, going back to—let us see how
far; 184-, 183-, 182-,—before our time—180-, when our mothers
were children. And the day-book—how blotted and blurred with
many records and many tears!

There, you have hit your head against that beam. Time was

when you ran to and fro beneath it, but you are nearer to it now, by more than the "altitude of a copine." The beam is strewn with forgotten papers of seeds for the next year's sowing; a distaff, with some few shreds of flax remaining, is thrust in a crevice of the rafters overhead; and tucked away close under the eaves is "the little wheel" that used to stand by the fire in times long gone. Its sweet low song has ceased; and perhaps—perhaps she who drew those flaxen threads—but never mind—you remember the line, don't you?—

"Her wheel at rest, the matron charms no more."

Well, let that pass. Do you see that little craft careened in that dark corner? It was red once; it was the only casket within the house once; and contained a mother's jewels. The old red *cradle*, for all the world! And you occupied it once; ay, great as you are, it was your world once, and over it, the only horizon you beheld, bent the heaven of a mother's eyes, as you rocked in that little bark of love on the hither shore of time—fast by a mother's love to a mother's heart.

And there, attached to two rafters, are the fragments of an untwisted rope. Do you remember it, and what it was for, and who fastened it there? 'Twas "the children's swing." You are here, indeed, but where are NELLY and CHARLEY! There hangs his little cap by the window, and there the little red frock she used to wear. A crown is resting on his cherub brow, and her robes are spotless in the better land.

Anglo-Saxon Influences of Home.

In the sunny climes of Southern Europe, where a sultry and relaxing day is followed by a balmy and refreshing night, and but a brief period intervenes between the fruits of Autumn and the renewed promises of Spring, life, both social and industrial, is chiefly passed beneath the open canopy of heaven. The brightest hours of the livelong day are dragged in drowsy, listless toil, or indolent repose; but the evening breeze invigorates the fainting frame, rouses the flagging spirit, and calls to dance, and revelry, and song, beneath a brilliant moon or a starlit sky. No necessity exists for those household comforts which are indispensable to the inhabitants of colder zones, and the charms of domestic life are scarcely known in their perfect growth. But in the frozen North, for a large portion of the year, the pale and feeble rays of a clouded sun but partially dispel, for a few short hours, the chills and shades of a lingering dawn, and an early and tedious night. Snows impede the closing labors of harvest, and stiffening frosts aggravate the fatigues of the wayfarer, and the toils of the forest. Repose, society, and occupation alike, must, therefore, be sought at the domestic hearth. Secure from the tempest that howls without, the father and the brother here rest from their weary tasks; here the family circle is gathered around the evening meal, and lighter labor, cheered, not interrupted, by social intercourse, is resumed, and often protracted, till, like the student's vigils, it almost "outwatch the Bear." Here the child grows up under the ever watchful eye of the parent, in the first and best of schools, where lisping infancy is taught the rudiments of sacred and profane knowledge, and the older pupil is encouraged to con over by the evening taper, the lessons of the day, and seek from the father or a more advanced brother, a solution of the problems which juvenile industry has found too hard to master.

The members of the domestic circle are thus brought into **closer contact**; parental authority assumes the gentler form of persuasive influences, and filial submission is elevated to affectionate and respectful observance. The necessity of mutual aid and forbearance, and the perpetual interchange of good offices, generate the tenderest kindliness of feeling, and a lasting warmth of attachment to home and its inmates, throughout the patriarchal circle.

Among the most important fruits of this domesticity of life, are the better appreciation of the worth of the female character, woman's higher rank as an object, not of passion, but of reverence, and the reciprocal moral influence which the two sexes exercise over each other.

They are brought into close communion under circumstances most favorable to preserve the purity of woman, and the decorum of man, and the character of each is modified, and its excesses restrained, by the example of the other.

Man's rude energies are softened into something of the ready sympathy and dexterous helpfulness of woman; and woman, as she learns to prize and to reverence the independence, the heroic firmness, the patriotism of man, acquires and appropriates some tinge of his peculiar virtues. Such were the influences which formed the heart of the brave, good daughter of apostolic John Knox, who bearded that truculent pedant, James I, and told him she would rather receive her husband's head in her lap, as it fell from the headsman's axe, than to consent that he should purchase his life by apostasy from the religion he had preached, and the God he had worshiped. To the same noble school belonged that goodly company of the Mothers of New England, who shrank neither from the dangers of the tempestuous sea, nor the hardships and sorrows of that first awful Winter, but were ever at man's side, encouraging, aiding, consoling, in every peril, every trial, every grief.

Had that grand and heroic exodus, like the mere commercial enterprises to which most colonies owe their foundation, been unaccompanied by woman, at its first outgoing, it had, without a visible miracle, assuredly failed, and the world had wanted its fairest example of the Christian virtues, its most unequivocal tokens that the Providence which kindled the pillar of fire to lead the wandering steps of its people, yet has its chosen tribes, to whom it vouchsafes its wisest guidance and its choicest blessings. Other communities, nations, races, may glory in the exploits of their fathers; but it has been reserved to us of New England to know and to boast, that Providence has made the virtues of our mothers a yet more indispensable condition and certain ground, both of our past prosperity and our future hope.

The strength of the domestic feeling engendered by the influences which I have described, and the truer and more intelligent mutual regard between the sexes, which is attributable to the same causes, are the principal reasons why those monastic institutions, which strike at the very root of the social fabric, and are eminently hostile to the practice of the noblest and loveliest public and private virtues, have met with less success, and numbered fewer votaries in Northern than in Southern Christendom. The celibacy of the clergy was last adopted, and first abandoned, in the North; the follies of the Stylites, the lonely hermitages of the Thebaid, the silence of La Trappe, the vows, which, seeming to renounce the pleasures of the world, do but abjure its better sympathies, and, in fine, all the selfish austerities of that corrupted Christianity, which grossly seeks to compound by a mortified body for an unsubdued heart, originated in climates unfavorable to the growth and exercise of the household virtues.

Thoughts on Various Subjects.

It is pleasant to observe how free the present age is in laying taxes on the next: "Future ages shall talk of this; this shall be famous to all posterity;" whereas their time and thoughts will be taken up about present things, as ours are now.

It is in disputes as in armies, where the weaker side setteth up false lights, and maketh a great noise, that the enemy may believe them to be more numerous and strong than they really are.

I have known some men possessed of good qualities, which were very serviceable to others, but useless to themselves; like a sun-dial on the front of a house, to inform the neighbors and passengers, but not the owner within.

If a man would register all his opinions upon love, politics, religion, learning, etc., beginning from his youth, and so go on to old age, what a bundle of inconsistencies and contradictions would appear at last!

The stoical scheme of supplying our wants by lopping off our desires, is like cutting off our feet when we want shoes.

The reason why so few marriages are happy, is because young ladies spend their time in making nets, not in making cages.

Censure is the tax a man payeth to the public for being eminent.

No wise man ever wished to be younger.

An idle reason lessens the weight of the good ones you gave before.

Complaint is the largest tribute Heaven receives, and the sincerest part of our devotion.

The common fluency of speech in many men and most women is owing to a scarcity of matter and scarcity of words; for whoever is a master of language, and hath a mind full of ideas, will be apt, in speaking, to hesitate upon the choice of both; whereas common speakers have only one set of ideas, and one set of words to clothe them in, and these are always ready at the mouth. So people come faster out of a church when it is almost empty, than when a crowd is at the door.

To be vain is rather a mark of humility than pride. Vain men delight in telling what honors have been done them, what great company they have kept, and the like; by which they plainly confess that these honors were more than due, and such as their friends would not believe if they had not been told; whereas a man truly proud thinks the greatest honors below his merit, and consequently scorns to boast. I therefore deliver it as a maxim, that whoever desires the character of a proud man ought to conceal his vanity.

Every man desireth to live long, but no man would be old.

If books and laws continue to increase as they have done for fifty years past, I am in some concern for future ages, how any man will be learned, or any man a lawyer.

If a man maketh me keep my distance, the comfort is, he keepeth his at the same time.

Very few men, properly speaking, *live* at present, but are providing to live another time.

Princes in their infancy, childhood, and youth, are said to discover prodigious parts and wit, to speak things that surprise and astonish; strange, so many hopeful princes, so many shameful kings! If they happened to die young, they would have been prodigies of wisdom and virtue; if they live, they are often prodigies, indeed, but of another sort.

BRET HARTE.

FRANCIS BRET HARTE was born in Albany, New York, August 25, 1837, and is now in the prime of life. His father died while Bret was very young. When but seventeen years of age, young Harte went to California and led a roving life for three years, sometimes digging for gold, sometimes teaching school, and finally acting as an express manager. He was schooled in active life as a miner and teacher, next as a compositor and contributor, subsequently as a member of the editorial staff, and finally as editor of the *Californian*, a literary weekly. From 1864 to 1870, he held the office of secretary of the United States branch mint in San Francisco.

In 1868 the *Overland Monthly* was started, and Bret Harte was selected as editor. In the August number of that year appeared his *Luck of Roaring Camp*, and still later, *The Outcasts of Poker Flat*. From the latter work, we have made our selection. "The Society upon the Stanislan," "John Burns of Gettysburg," "The Pliocene Skull," and "The Heathen Chinee," are his well known productions.

"There is an amusing story to the effect that the proof-reader, a young woman with a superabundance of modesty, reported to the publishers that his *Luck of Roaring Camp* was a most shocking article, unfit for publication, that the publishers took the alarm and besought Harte to withdraw it, and that he made its appearance the condition of his retaining the editorship. This sketch, which met with an enthusiastic reception from the entire reading public, was the

BRET HARTE.

beginning of his most artistic and effective work." Now the best journals and magazines in the country are glad to secure his valuable and interesting contributions. In 1870, Harte held the position as Professor of Recent Literature in the University of California. In 1871, he severed his connection with the literary and school work of the West, and fixed his residence in New York City. His *Condensed Novels*, two volumes of short stories, and volumes of poems, as well as the other works mentioned in this sketch, are deservedly popular.

Mr. Harte is now enjoying the Summer of life as a prominent lyceum lecturer.

The Outcasts of Poker Flat.

The following selections from Bret Harte's pen are beautiful in the extreme. Its length prevents us from giving the entire sketch here:

As the shadows crept slowly up the mountain, a slight breeze rocked the tops of the pine-trees, and moaned through their long and gloomy aisles. The ruined cabin, patched and covered with pine boughs, was set apart for the ladies. As the lovers parted, they unaffectedly exchanged a kiss, so honest and sincere that it might have been heard above the swaying pines. The frail Duchess and the malevolent Mother Shipton were probably too stunned to remark upon this last evidence of simplicity, and so turned without a word to the hut. The fire was replenished, the men lay down before the door, and in a few minutes were asleep.

II

The third day came, and the sun, looking through the white-curtained valley, saw the outcasts divide their slowly decreasing store of provisions for the morning meal. It was one of the peculiarities of that mountain climate that its rays diffused a kindly warmth over the wintry landscape, as if in regretful commiseration of the past. But it revealed drift on drift of snow piled high around the hut—a hopeless, uncharted, trackless sea of white, lying below the rocky shores to which the castaways still clung. Through the marvelously clear air the smoke of the pastoral village of Poker Flat rose miles away. Mother Shipton saw it, and from a remote pinnacle of her rocky fastness hurled in that direction a final malediction. It was her last vituperative attempt, and perhaps for that reason was invested with a certain degree of sublimity. It did her good, she privately informed the Duchess. "Just you go out there and cuss, and see." She then set herself to the task of amusing "the child," as she and the Duchess were pleased to call Piney. Piney was no chicken, but it was a soothing and original theory of the pair thus to account for the fact that she didn't swear and wasn't improper.

When night crept up again through the gorges, the reedy notes of the accordion rose and fell in fitful spasms and long-drawn gasps by the flickering camp-fire. But music failed to fill entirely the aching void left by insufficient food, and a new diversion was proposed by Piney—story-telling.

Neither Mr. Oakhurst nor his female companions caring to relate their personal experiences, this plan would have failed too, but for the Innocent. Some months before he had chanced upon a stray copy of Mr. Pope's ingenious translation of the Iliad. He now proposed to narrate the principal incidents of that poem—having thoroughly mastered the argument and fairly forgotten the words—in the current vernacular of Sandy Bar. And so for the rest of that night the Homeric demigods again walked the earth. Trojan bully and wily Greek wrestled in the winds, and the great pines in the canyon seemed to bow to the wrath of the son of Peleus. Mr. Oakhurst listened with quiet satisfaction. Most especially was he interested in the fate of "Ash-heels," as the Innocent persisted in denominating the "swift-footed Achilles."

So, with small food and much of Homer and the accordion, a week passed over the heads of the outcasts. The sun again forsook them, and again from leaden skies the snow-flakes were sifted over the land. Day by day closer around them drew the snowy circle, until at last they looked from their prison over drifted walls of dazzling white, that towered twenty feet above their heads. It became more and more difficult to replenish their fires, even from the fallen trees beside them, now half hidden in the drifts. And yet no one complained. The lovers turned from the dreary prospect and looked into each other's eyes, and were happy. Mr. Oakhurst settled himself coolly to the losing game before him. The Duchess, more cheerful than she had been, assumed the care of Piney. Only Mother Shipton—once the strongest of the party—seemed to sicken and fade. At midnight on the tenth day she called Oakhurst to her side.

"I'm going," she said in a voice of querulous weakness, "but don't say anything about it. Don't waken the kids. Take the bundle from under my head, and open it." Mr. Oakhurst did so. It contained Mother Shipton's rations for the last week, untouched. "Give 'em to the child," she said, pointing to the sleeping Piney. "You've starved yourself," said the gambler. "That's what they call it," said the woman, querulously, as she lay down again, and, turning her face to the wall, passed quietly away. * * *

III

Night came, but not Mr. Oakhurst. It brought the storm again and the whirling snow. Then the Duchess, feeding the fire, found that some one had quietly piled beside the hut enough fuel to last a few days longer. The tears rose to her eyes, but she hid them from Piney.

The women slept but little. In the morning, looking into each other's faces, they read their fate. Neither spoke; but Piney, accepting the position of the stronger, drew near and placed her arm around the Duchess' waist. They kept this attitude for the rest of the day. That night the storm reached its greatest fury, and rending asunder the protecting pines, invaded the very hut.

Toward morning they found themselves unable to feed the fire, which gradually died away. As the embers slowly blackened, the Duchess crept closer to Piney, and broke the silence of many hours: "Piney, can you pray?"

"No, dear," said Piney, simply. The Duchess, without knowing exactly why, felt relieved, and, putting her head upon Piney's shoulder, spoke no more. And so reclining, the younger and purer pillowing the head of her soiled sister upon her virgin breast, they fell asleep.

The wind lulled as if it feared to waken them. Feathery drifts of snow, shaken from the long pine-boughs, flew like white-winged birds, and settled about them as they slept. The moon, through the rifted clouds, looked down upon what had been the camp. But all human stain, all trace of earthly travail, was hidden beneath the spotless mantle mercifully flung from above.

They slept all that day and the next; nor did they waken when voices and footsteps broke the silence of the camp. And when pitying fingers brushed the snow from their wan faces, you could scarcely have told from the equal peace that dwelt upon them, which was she that had sinned. Even the law of Poker Flat recognized this, and turned away, leaving them still locked in each other's arms.

Gentle Hands.

When and where, it matters not now to relate—but once upon a time, as I was passing through a thinly peopled district of country, night came down upon me, almost unawares. Being on foot, I could not hope to gain the village toward which my steps were directed, until a late hour; and I therefore preferred seeking shelter and a night's lodging at the first humble dwelling that presented itself.

Dusky twilight was giving place to deeper shadows, when I found myself in the vicinity of a dwelling, from the small uncurtained windows of which the light shone with a pleasant promise of good cheer and comfort. The house stood within an enclosure, and a short distance from the road along which I was moving with wearied feet. Turning aside, and passing through the ill-hung gate, I approached the dwelling. Slowly the gate swung on its wooden hinges, and the rattle of its latch, in closing, did not disturb the air until I had nearly reached the little porch in front of the house, in which a slender girl, who had noticed my entrance, stood awaiting my arrival.

A deep, quick bark answered, almost like an echo, the sound of the shutting gate, and, sudden as an apparition, the form of an immense dog loomed in the door-way. At the instant when he was about to spring, a light hand was laid upon his shaggy neck and a low word spoken.

"Go in, Tiger," said the girl, not in a voice of authority, yet in her gentle tones was the consciousness that she would be obeyed; and, as she spoke, she lightly bore upon the animal with her hand, and he turned away, and disappeared within the dwelling. "Who's that?" A rough voice asked the question; and now a heavy-looking man took the dog's place in the door.

"How far is it to G——?" I asked, not deeming it best to say, in the beginning, that I sought a resting-place for the night.

"To G——" growled the man, but not so harshly as at first. "It's good six miles from here."

"A long distance; and I'm a stranger, and on foot," said I. "If you can make room for me until morning, I will be very thankful."

I saw the girl's hand move quickly up his arm, until it rested on his shoulder, and now she leaned to him still closer.

"Come in. We'll try what can be done for you." There was a change in the man's voice that made me wonder.

I entered a large room, in which blazed a brisk fire. Before the fire sat two stout lads, who turned upon me their heavy eyes, with no very welcome greeting. A middle-aged woman was standing at a table and two children were amusing themselves with a kitten on the floor.

"A stranger, mother," said the man who had given me so rude a greeting at the door; "and he wants us to let him stay all night."

The woman looked at me doubtingly for a few moments, and then replied coldly—

"We don't keep a public-house."

"I am aware of that, ma'am," said I; "but night has overtaken me, and it's a long way yet to——."

"Too far for a tired man to go on foot," said the master of the house, kindly, "so it's no use talking about it, mother; we must give him a bed."

So unobtrusively that I scarcely noticed the movement, the

girl had drawn to the woman's side. What she said to her I did not hear, for the brief words were uttered in a low voice; but I noticed, as she spoke, one small, fair hand rested on the woman's hand. Was there magic in that gentle touch? The woman's repulsive aspect changed into one of kindly welcome, and she said:
"Yes, it's a long way to G——. I guess we can find a place for him."

Many times more, during that evening, did I observe the magic power of that hand and voice—the one gentle, yet potent, as the other.

On the next morning, breakfast being over, I was preparing to take my departure, when my host informed me that if I would wait for half an hour he would give me a ride in his wagon to G——, as business required him to go there. I was very well pleased to accept of the invitation. In due time, the farmer's wagon was driven into the road before the house, and I was invited to get in. I noticed the horse as a rough-looking Canadian pony, with a certain air of stubborn endurance. As the farmer took his seat by my side, the family came to the door to see us off.

"Dick!" said the farmer in a peremptory voice, giving the rein a quick jerk as he spoke.

But Dick moved not a step.

"Dick! you vagabond! get up." And the farmer's whip cracked sharply by the pony's ear.

It availed not, however, the second appeal. Dick stood firmly disobedient. Next the whip was brought down upon him with an impatient hand; but the pony only reared up a little. Fast and sharp the strokes were next dealt to the number of half-a-dozen. The man might as well have beaten his wagon, for all his end was gained.

A stout lad now came out into the road, and catching Dick by the bridle, jerked him forward, using, at the same time, the customary language on such occasions, but Dick met this new ally with increased stubbornness, planting his forefeet more firmly, and at a sharper angle with the ground. The impatient boy now struck the pony on the side of his head with his clinched hand, and jerked cruelly at his bridle. It availed nothing, however: Dick was not to be wrought upon by any such arguments.

"Don't do so, John!" I turned my head as the maiden's sweet voice reached my ear. She was passing through the gate into the road, and, in the next moment, had taken hold of the lad and drawn him away from the animal. No strength was exerted in this; she took hold of his arm, and he obeyed her wish as readily as if he had no thought beyond her gratification.

And now that soft hand was laid gently on the pony's neck, and a single low word spoken. How instantly were the tense muscles relaxed—how quickly the stubborn air vanished.

"Poor Dick!" said the maiden, as she stroked his neck lightly, or softly patted it with a child-like hand.

"Now, go along, you provoking fellow!" she added, in a half-chiding, yet affectionate voice, as she drew up the bridle. The pony turned toward her, and rubbed his head against her arm for an instant or two; then, pricking up his ears, he started off at a light, cheerful trot, and went on his way as freely as if no silly crotchet had ever entered his stubborn brain.

"What a wonderful power that hand possesses!" said I, speaking to my companion, as we rode away.

He looked at me for a moment as if my remark had occasioned surprise. Then a light came into his countenance, and he said, briefly,—

"She's good! Everybody and everything loves her."

Was that, indeed, the secret of her power? Was the quality of her soul perceived in the impression of her hand, even by brute beasts! The father's explanation was, doubtless, the true one. Yet, have I, ever since wondered, and still do wonder, at the potency which lay in that maiden's magic touch. I have seen something of the same power, showing itself in the loving and the good, but never to the extent as instanced in her, whom, for want of a better name, I must still call "Gentle hand."

The Ariel among the Shoals.

The extraordinary activity of Griffith, which communicated itself with promptitude to the whole crew, was produced by a sudden alteration in the weather. In place of the well-defined streak along the horizon, that has been already described, an immense body of misty light appeared to be moving in with rapidity from the ocean, while a distinct but distant roaring, announced the sure approach of the tempest that had so long troubled the waters. Even Griffith, while thundering his orders through the trumpet, and urging the men, by his cries, to expedition, would pause for instants to cast anxious glances in the direction of the coming storm, and the faces of the sailors who lay on the yards were turned instinctively toward the same quarter of the heavens, while they knotted the reef-points, or passed the gaskets that were to confine the unruly canvas to the prescribed limits.

The pilot alone, in that confused and busy throng, where voice rose above voice, and cry echoed cry in quick succession, appeared as if he held no interest in the important stake. With his eyes steadily fixed on the approaching mist, and his arms folded together in composure, he stood calmly awaiting the result.

The ship had fallen off with her broadside to the sea, and was become unmanageable, and the sails were already brought into the folds necessary to her security, when the quick and heavy fluttering of canvas was thrown across the water with all the gloomy and chilling sensations that such sounds produce, where darkness and danger unite to appall the seaman.

"The schooner has it!" cried Griffith; "Barnstable has held on, like himself to the last moment—God send that the squall leave him cloth enough to keep him from the shore!"

"His sails are easily handled," the commander observed, "and she must be over the principal danger. We are falling off before it, Mr. Gray; shall we try a cast of the lead?"

The pilot turned from his contemplative posture and moved slowly across the deck before he returned any reply to this question —like a man who not only felt that everything depended on himself, but that he was equal to the emergency.

"'Tis unnecessary," he at length said; "'twould be certain destruction to be taken aback, and it is difficult to say, within several points, how the wind may strike us."

"'Tis difficult no longer," cried Griffith; "for here it comes, and in right earnest!"

The rushing sounds of the wind were now, indeed, heard at hand, and the words were hardly passed the lips of the young lieutenant before the vessel bowed down heavily to one side, and then, as she began to move through the water, rose again majestically to her upright position, as if saluting, like a courteous champion, the powerful antagonist with which she was about to contend. Not another minute elapsed before the ship was throwing the waters aside with a lively progress, and, obedient to her helm, was brought as near to the desired course as the direction of the wind would allow. The hurry and bustle on the yards gradually subsided, and the men slowly descended to the deck, all straining their eyes to pierce the gloom in which they were enveloped, and some shaking their heads in melancholy doubt, afraid to express the apprehensions they really entertained. All on board anxiously waited for the fury of the gale; for there were none so ignorant or inexperienced, in that gallant frigate, as not to know that they as yet only felt the infant efforts of the wind. Each moment, however, it increased in power, though so gradual was the alteration, that the relieved mariners began to believe that all their gloomy forebodings were not to be realized. During this short interval of uncertainty, no other sounds were heard than the whistling of the breeze, as it passed quickly through the mass of rigging that belonged to the vessel, and the dashing of the spray that began to fly from her bows like the foam of a cataract.

"It blows fresh," cried Griffith, who was the first to speak in that moment of doubt and anxiety; "but it is no more than a capful of wind after all. Give us elbow room and the right canvas, Mr. Pilot, and I'll handle the ship like a gentleman's yacht in this breeze."

"Will she stay, think ye, under this sail?" said the low voice of the stranger.

"She will do all that man in reason can ask of wood and iron," returned the lieutenant; "but the vessel don't float the ocean that will tack under double-reefed topsails alone against a heavy sea. Help her with the courses, pilot, and you'll see her come round like a dancing-master."

"Let us feel the strength of the gale first," returned the man who was called Mr. Gray, moving from the side of Griffith to the weather gangway of the vessel, where he stood in silence, looking ahead of the ship with an air of singular coolness and abstraction.

All the lanterns had been extinguished on the deck of the frigate, when her anchor was secured, and as the first mist of the gale had passed over, it was succeeded by a faint light that was a good deal aided by the glittering foam of the waters, which now broke in white curls around the vessel in every direction. The land could be faintly discerned, rising like a heavy bank of black fog above the margin of the waters, and was only distinguishable from the heavens by its deeper gloom and obscurity. The last rope was coiled and deposited in its proper place by the seamen, and for several minutes the stillness of death pervaded the crowded decks. It was evident to every one that their ship was dashing at a prodigious rate through the waves; and, as she was approaching, with such velocity, the quarter of the bay where the shoals and dangers were known to be situated, nothing but the habits of the most exact discipline could suppress the uneasiness of the officers and men within their own bosoms. At length the voice of Captain Munson was heard calling to the pilot.

"Shall I send a hand into the chains, Mr. Gray," he said, "and try our water?—"

"Tack your ship, sir, tack your ship; I would see how she works before we reach the point where she must behave well, or we **perish.**"

Griffith gazed after him in wonder, while the pilot slowly paced the quarter-deck, and then, rousing from his trance, gave forth the cheering order that called each man to his station to perform the desired evolution. The confident assurances which the young officer had given to the pilot respecting the qualities of his vessel, and his own ability to manage her, were fully realized by the result. The helm was no sooner put a-lee, than the huge ship bore up gallantly against the wind, and, dashing directly through the waves, threw the foam high into the air as she looked boldly into the very eye of the wind, and then, yielding gracefully to its power, she fell off on the other tack with her head pointed from those dangerous shoals that she had so recently approached with such terrifying velocity. The heavy yards swung round as if they had been vanes to indicate the currents of the air, and in a few moments the frigate again moved with stately progress through the water, leaving the rocks and shoals behind her on one side of the bay, but advancing toward those that offered equal danger on the other.

During this time, the sea was becoming more agitated, and the violence of the wind was gradually increasing. The latter no longer whistled amid the cordage of the vessel, but it seemed to howl surlily as it passed the complicated machinery that the frigate obtruded on its path. An endless succession of white surges rose above the heavy billows, and the very air was glittering with the light that was disengaged from the ocean. The ship yielded each moment more and more before the storm, and, in less than half an hour from the time that she had lifted her anchor, she was driven along with tremendous fury by the full power of a gale of wind. Still, the hardy and experienced mariners who directed her movements, held her to the course that was necessary to their preservation, and still Griffith gave forth, when directed by their unknown pilot, those orders that turned her in the narrow channel where safety was alone to be found.

So far, the performance of his duty appeared easy to the stranger, and he gave the required directions in those still, calm tones that formed so remarkable a contrast to the responsibility of his situation. But when the land was becoming dim, in distance as well as darkness, and the agitated sea was only to be discovered as it swept by them in foam, he broke in upon the monotonous roaring of the tempest with the sounds of his voice, seeming to shake off his apathy and rouse himself to the occasion.

"Now is the time to watch her closely, Mr. Griffith," he cried; "here we get the true tide and the real danger. Place the best quarter-master of your ship in those chains, and let an officer stand by him and see that he gives us the right water."

"I will take that office on myself," said the captain; "pass a light into the weather main-chains."

"Stand by your braces!" exclaimed the pilot with startling quickness. "Heave away that lead!"

These preparations taught the crew to expect the crisis, and every officer and man stood in fearful silence at his assigned station awaiting the issue of the trial. Even the quarter-master at the gun gave out his orders to the men at the wheel in deeper and hoarser tones than usual, as if anxious not to disturb the quiet and order of the vessel.

While this deep expectation pervaded the frigate, the piercing cry of the leadsman, as he called, "By the mark seven!" rose above the tempest, crossed over the decks, and appeared to pass away to leeward, borne on the blast like the warnings of some water-spirit.

"'Tis well," returned the pilot, calmly; "try it again."

The short pause was succeeded by another cry, "And a half-five!"

"She shoals! she shoals!" exclaimed Griffith; "keep her a good full."

"Ay! you must hold the vessel in command, now," said the pilot, with those cool tones that are most appalling in critical moments, because they seem to denote most preparation and care.

The third call of "By the deep four!" was followed by a prompt direction from the stranger to tack.

Griffith seemed to emulate the coolness of the pilot, in issuing the necessary orders to execute this manœuver.

The vessel rose slowly from the inclined position into which she had been forced by the tempest, and the sails were shaking violently, as if to release themselves from their confinement while the ship stemmed the billows, when the well-known voice of the sailing-master was heard shouting from the forecastle—"Breakers! breakers, dead ahead!"

This appalling sound seemed yet to be lingering about the ship, when a second voice cried—"Breakers on our lee-bow!"

"We are in a bight of the shoals, Mr. Gray," said the commander. "She loses her way; perhaps an anchor might hold her."

"Clear away that best-bower!" shouted Griffith through his trumpet.

"Hold on!" cried the pilot, in a voice that reached the very hearts of all who heard him; "hold on everything."

The young man turned fiercely to the daring stranger who thus defied the discipline of his vessel, and at once demanded—"Who is it that dares to countermand my orders? Is it not enough that you run the ship into danger, but you must interfere to keep her there? If another word—"

"Peace, Mr. Griffith," interrupted the captain, bending from the rigging, his gray locks blowing about in the wind, and adding a look of wildness to the haggard face that he exhibited by the light of his lantern; "yield the trumpet to Mr. Gray; he alone can save us."

Griffith threw his speaking trumpet on the deck, and, as he walked proudly away, muttered in bitterness of feeling—"Then all is lost, indeed, and, among the rest, the foolish hopes with which I visited this coast."

There was, however, no time for reply; the ship had been rapidly running into the wind, and, as the efforts of the crew were paralyzed by the contradictory orders they had heard, she gradually lost her way, and in a few seconds all her sails were taken aback.

Before the crew understood their situation the pilot had applied the trumpet to his mouth, and, in a voice that rose above the tempest, he thundered forth his orders. Each command was given distinctly, and with a precision that showed him to be master of his profession. The helm was kept fast, the head yards swung up heavily against the wind, and the vessel was soon whirling round on her heel with a retrograde movement.

Griffith was too much of a seaman not to perceive that the pilot had seized, with a perception almost intuitive, the only method that promised to extricate the vessel from her situation. He was young, impetuous, and proud; but he was also generous. Forgetting his resentment and his mortification, he rushed forward among the men, and, by his presence and example, added certainty to the experiment. The ship fell off slowly before the gale, and bowed her yards nearly to the water, as she felt the blast pouring its fury on her broadside, while the surly waves beat violently against her stern, as if in reproach at departing from her usual manner of moving.

The voice of the pilot, however, was still heard, steady and calm, and yet so clear and high as to reach every ear; and the obedient seamen whirled the yards at his bidding in despite of the tempest, as if they handled the toys of their childhood. When the ship had fallen off dead before the wind, her head sails were shaken, her after-yards trimmed, and her helm shifted before she had time to run upon the danger that had threatened, as well to leeward as to windward. The beautiful fabric, obedient to her government, threw her bows up gracefully toward the wind again, and, as her sails were trimmed, moved out from amongst the dangerous shoals in which she had been embayed, as steadily and swiftly as she had approached them.

A moment of breathless astonishment succeeded the accomplishment of this nice manœuver, but there was no time for the usual expressions of surprise. The stranger still held the trumpet, and continued to lift his voice amid the howlings of the blast, whenever prudence or skill directed any change in the management of the ship. For an hour longer, there was a fearful struggle for their preservation, the channel becoming at each step more complicated, and the shoals thickening around the mariners on every side. The lead was cast rapidly, and the quick eye of the pilot seemed to pierce the darkness with a keenness of vision that exceeded human power. It was apparent to all in the vessel, that they were under the guidance of one who understood the navigation thoroughly, and their exertions kept pace with their reviving confidence. Again and again the frigate appeared to be rushing blindly on shoals, where the sea was covered with foam, and where destruction would have been as sudden as it was certain, when the clear voice of the stranger was heard warning them of the danger, and inciting them to their duty. The vessel was implicitly yielded to his government, and during those anxious moments, when she was dashing the waters aside, throwing the spray over her enormous yards, each ear would listen eagerly for those sounds that had obtained a command over the crew, that can only be acquired, under such circumstances, by great steadiness and consummate skill. The ship was recovering from the inaction of changing her course in one of those critical tacks that she had made so often, when the pilot for the first time addressed the commander of the frigate, who still continued to superintend the all-important duty of the leadsman.

"Now is the pinch," he said; "and if the ship behaves well, we are safe—but if otherwise, all we have yet done will be useless."

The veteran seaman whom he addressed left the chains at this portentous notice, and, calling to his first lieutenant, required of the stranger an explanation of his warning.

"See you yon light on the southern headland?" returned the pilot; "you may know it from the star near it by its sinking, at times, in the ocean. Now observe the hummock, a little north of it, looking like a shadow in the horizon—'tis a hill far inland. If we keep that light open from the hill, we shall do well—but if not, we surely go to pieces."

"Let us tack again!" exclaimed the lieutenant.

The pilot shook his head, as he replied—"There is no more tacking or box-hauling to be done to-night. We have barely room to pass out of the shoals on this course, and if we can weather the

'Devil's Grip,' we clear their outermost point—but if not, as I said before, there is but an alternative."

"If we had beaten out the way we entered," exclaimed Griffith, "we should have done well."

"Say, also, if the tide would have let us do so," returned the pilot calmly. "Gentlemen, we must be prompt; we have but a mile to go, and the ship appears to fly. That topsail is not enough to keep her up to the wind; we want both jib and mainsail."

" 'Tis a perilous thing to loosen canvas in such a tempest!" observed the doubtful captain.

"It must be done," returned the collected stranger; 'we perish without,—see! the light already touches the edge of the hummock; the sea casts us to leeward!"

"It shall be done!" cried Griffith, seizing the trumpet from the hand of the pilot.

The orders of the lieutenant were executed almost as soon as issued, and, everything being ready, the enormous folds of the mainsail were trusted loose to the blast. There was an instant when the result was doubtful; the tremendous threshing of the heavy sails seeming to bid defiance to all restraint, shaking the ship to her center; but art and strength prevailed, and gradually the canvas was distended, and, bellying as it filled, was drawn down to its usual place by the power of a hundred men. The vessel yielded to this immense addition of force, and bowed before it like a reed bending to a breeze. But the success of the measure was announced by a joyful cry from the stranger, that seemed to burst from his inmost soul.

"She feels it! she springs her luff! observe," he said, "the light opens from the hummock already; if she will only bear her canvas, we shall go clear!"

A report like that of a cannon interrupted his exclamation, and something resembling a white cloud was seen drifting before the wind from the head of the ship, till it was driven into the gloom far to the leeward.

"' Tis the jib blown from the bolt-ropes," said the commander of the frigate. "This is no time to spread light duck,—but the mainsail may stand it yet."

"The sail would laugh at a tornado," returned the lieutenant; "but that mast springs like a piece of steel."

"Silence, all!" cried the pilot. "Now, gentlemen, we shall soon know our fate. Let her luff,—luff you can!"

This warning effectually closed all discourse, and the hardy mariners, knowing that they had already done all in the power of man to insure their safety, stood in breathless anxiety, awaiting the result. At a short distance ahead of them, the whole ocean was white with foam, and the waves, instead of rolling on in regular succession, appeared to be tossing about in mad gambols. A single streak of dark billows, not half a cable's length in width, could be discerned running into this chaos of water; but it was soon lost to the eye amid the confusion of the disturbed element. Along this narrow path the vessel moved more heavily than before, being brought so near the wind as to keep her sails touching. The pilot silently proceeded to the wheel, and with his own hands he undertook the steerage of the ship. No noise proceeded from the frigate to interrupt the horrid tumult of the ocean, and she entered the channel among the breakers with the silence of a desperate calmness. Twenty times, as the foam rolled away to leeward, the crew were on the eve of uttering their joy, as they supposed the vessel past the danger; but breaker after breaker would still rise before them, following each other into the general mass to check their exultation. Occasionally the fluttering of the sails would be heard; and when the looks of the startled seamen were turned to the wheel, they beheld the stranger grasping its spokes, with his quick eye glancing from the water to the canvas. At length the ship reached a point where she appeared to be rushing directly into the jaws of destruction, when suddenly her course was changed, and her head receded rapidly from the wind. At the same instant the voice of the pilot was heard shouting,—

"Square away the yards!—in mainsail!"

A general burst from the crew echoed, "Square away the

yards!" and quick as thought the frigate was seen gliding along the channel before the wind. The eye had hardly time to dwell on the foam, which seemed like clouds driving in the heavens, and directly the gallant vessel issued from her perils, and rose and fell on the heavy waves of the open sea.

The Bald-headed Man.

The other day a lady, accompanied by her son, a very small boy, boarded a train at Little Rock. The woman had a care-worn expression hanging over her face like a tattered veil, and many of the rapid questions asked by the boy were answered by unconscious sighs.

"Ma," said the boy, "that man's like a baby, ain't he?" pointing to a bald-headed man sitting just in front of them.

"Hush!"

"Why must I hush?"

After a few moments' silence: "Ma, what's the matter with that man's head?"

"Hush, I tell you. He's bald."

"What's bald?"

"His head hasn't got any hair on it."

"Did it come off?"

"I guess so."

"Will mine come off?"

"Some time, may be."

"Then I'll be bald, won't I?"

"Yes."

"Will you care?"

"Don't ask so many questions."

After another silence, the boy exclaimed: "Ma, look at that fly on that man's head."

"If you don't hush, I'll whip you when we get home."

"Look! There's another fly. Look at 'em fight; look at 'em!"

"Madam," said the man, putting aside a newspaper and looking around, "what's the matter with that young hyena?"

The woman blushed, stammered out something, and attempted to smooth back the boy's hair.

"One fly, two flies, three flies," said the boy, innocently, following with his eyes a basket of oranges carried by a newsboy.

"Here, you young hedgehog," said the bald-headed man, "if you don't hush, I'll have the conductor put you off the train."

The poor woman, not knowing what else to do, boxed the boy's ears, and then gave him an orange to keep him from crying.

"Ma, have I got red marks on my head?"

"I'll whip you again, if you don't hush."

"Mister," said the boy, after a short silence, "does it hurt to be bald-headed?"

"Youngster," said the man, "if you'll keep quiet, I'll give you a quarter."

The boy promised, and the money was paid over.

The man took up his paper, and resumed his reading.

"This is my bald-headed money," said the boy. "When I get bald-headed, I'm goin' to give boys money. Mister, have all bald-headed men got money?"

The annoyed man threw down his paper, arose, and exclaimed: "Madam, hereafter when you travel, leave that young gorilla at home. Hitherto, I always thought that the old prophet was very cruel for calling the bears to kill the children for making sport of his head, but now I am forced to believe that he did a Christian act. If your boy had been in the crowd, he would have died first. If I can't find another seat on this train, I'll ride on the cow-catcher rather than remain here."

"The bald-headed man is gone," said the boy; and as the woman leaned back a tired sigh escaped from her lips.

An Evening Walk in Virginia.

In truth, the little, solitary nook into which I am just now thrown, bears an aspect so interesting, that it is calculated to call up the most touchingly pleasing exertions in the minds of those who love to indulge in the contemplation of beautiful scenes. We are the sons of earth, and the indissoluble kindred between nature and man is demonstrated by our sense of her beauties. I shall not soon forget last evening, which Oliver and myself spent at this place. It was such as can never be described,—I will therefore not attempt it; but it was still as the sleep of innocence, pure as ether, and bright as immortality. Having traveled only fourteen miles that day, I did not feel as tired as usual, and, after supper, strolled out alone along the windings of a little stream about twenty yards wide, that skirts a narrow strip of green meadows, between the brook and the high mountain at a little distance.

You will confess my landscapes are well watered, for every one has a river. But such is the case in this region, where all the passes of the mountains are made by little rivers, that in process of time have labored through, and left a space for a road on their banks. If nature will do these things, I can't help it,—not I. In the course of the ramble, the moon rose over the mountain to the eastward, which, being just by, seemed to bring the planet equally near; and the bright eyes of the stars began to glisten, as if weeping the dews of evening. I knew not the name of one single star. But what of that? It is not necessary to be an astronomer to contemplate with sublime emotions the glories of the sky at night, and the countless wonders of the universe.

> These earthly godfathers of heaven's lights,
> That give a name to every fixed star,
> Have no more profit of their living nights,
> Than those that walk and wot not what they are.

Men may be too wise to wonder at anything, as they may be too ignorant to see anything without wondering.

There is reason, also, to believe that astronomers may be sometimes so taken up with measuring the distance and magnitude of the stars, as to lose, in the intense minuteness of calculation, that noble expansion of feeling and intellect combined, which lifts from nature up to its great First Cause. As respects myself, I know no more of the planets than the man in the moon. I only contemplate them as unapproachable, unextinguishable fires, glittering afar off, in those azure fields whose beauty and splendor have pointed them out as the abode of the Divinity; as such, they form bright links in the chain of thought that leads directly to a contemplation of the Maker of heaven and earth. Nature is, indeed, the only temple worthy of the Deity. There is a mute eloquence in her smile; a majestic severity in her frown; a divine charm in her harmony; a speechless energy in her silence; a voice in her thunders, that no reflecting being can resist. It is in such scenes and seasons, that the heart is deepest smitten with the power and goodness of Providence, and that the soul demonstrates its capacity for maintaining an existence independent of matter, by abstracting itself from the body, and expatiating alone in the boundless regions of the past and the future.

As I continued strolling forward, there gradually came a perfect calm,—and even the aspen-tree whispered no more. But it was not the death-like calm of a Winter's night, when the northwest wind grows quiet, and the frosts begin in silence to forge fetters for the running brooks, and the gentle current of life that flows through the veins of the forest. The voice of man and beast was indeed unheard; but the river murmured, and the insects chirped in the mild Summer evening. There is something sepulchral in the repose of a Winter night; but in the genial seasons of the year, though the night is the emblem of repose, it is the repose of the couch, not of the tomb; nature still breathes in the buzz of insects, the whisperings of the forests, and the murmur of the running brooks. We know she will awake in the morning, with her smiles, her bloom, her zephyrs, and warbling birds. "In such a night as this," if a man loves any human being in this wide world, he will find it out, for there will his thoughts first center. If he has in store any sweet, or bitter, or bitter-sweet recollections, which are lost in the bustle of the world, they will come without being called. If, in his boyish days he wrestled, and wrangled, and rambled with, yet loved, some chubby boy, he will remember the days of his childhood, its companions, cares, and pleasures. If, in his days of romance, he used to walk of evenings with some blue-eyed, musing, melancholy maid, whom the ever-rolling wave of life dashed away from him forever, he will recall her voice, her eye, and her form. If any heavy and severe disaster has fallen on his riper manhood, and turned the future into a gloomy and unpromising wilderness, he will feel it bitterly at such a time. Or, if it chance that he is grown an old man, and lived to see all that owned his blood, or shared his affections, struck down to the earth like dead leaves in Autumn, in such a night he will call their dear shades around, and wish himself a shadow.

GEORGE BANCROFT.

GEORGE BANCROFT, the eminent American historian, was born at Worcester, Massachusetts, October 3, 1800, and graduated at Harvard College in his seventeenth year. "His college course was but the beginning of his education. He sailed to Europe, and pursued a great variety of studies for five years under the most eminent professors, at Gottingen, Berlin, Heidelberg, Paris, and in several Italian cities, forming acquaintances, also, with many of the most famous scholars and *savants.*" Thus his mind was richly furnished with the treasures of ancient literature, together with the modern metaphysical culture of the German universities. Upon his return to America, Mr. Bancroft was appointed Tutor of Greek at Harvard. He was also connected with the Round Hill Classical School at Northampton, for a short time.

Bancroft's literary record is an important one. It commenced while he was abroad, by the philosophical summaries of Roman history and policy, and of the literature of Germany, which he published in America shortly after his return. "A volume of poems, published at Boston in 1823, witnesses to his poetical enthusiasm for the arts and nature, as he traversed the ruins of Italy and the sublime scenery of Switzerland." Before his twenty-fourth year, he had written a series of poetical translations of some of the chief minor

GEORGE BANCROFT.

poems of Schiller, Goethe, and other German authors. These translations were first published in the "North American Review," and afterward in Bancroft's *Collection of Miscellanies.*

The great work of Bancroft's life is his *History of the United States from the Discovery of the American Continent*, the first volume of which appeared in 1834. His *Colonization of the United States*, published in 1834, and *History of the Revolution*, published in 1852, were included in his *History of the United States.* Up to the present, twelve volumes of his history have been issued, bringing the work down to 1789. In the preparation of his work, he was greatly aided by the free access to the State Paper Office of Great Britain, France and other European states. In 1855 Bancroft published a volume of *Literary and Historical Miscellanies.* While this work is full of merit, his history remains the greatest work of his life, and it proves him to be the greatest of American historians.

Bancroft's political record is also an important part of his life work. In 1838 President Van Buren appointed him to the collectorship of the port of Boston. In 1845 President Polk invited him to a seat in the Cabinet as Secretary of the Navy. His customary energy and efficiency made him a valuable member of the Cabinet. In 1846 Bancroft was appointed Minister Plenipotentiary to Great Britain. This distinguished position he held till 1849, when he returned to the United States and became a resident of the city of New York. In 1867 he was appointed Minister to Berlin, a position he held for several years.

The Aborigines of America.

On the surrender of Acadia to England, the lakes, the rivulets. the granite ledges, of Cape Breton,—of which the irregular outline is guarded by reefs of rocks, and notched and almost rent asunder by the constant action of the sea,—were immediately occupied as a province of France; and, in 1714, fugitives from Newfoundland and Acadia built their huts along its coasts, wherever safe inlets invited fishermen to spread their flakes, and the soil to plant fields and gardens. In a few years, the fortifications of Louisburg began to rise,—the key to the St. Lawrence, the bulwark of the French fisheries, and of French commerce in North America. From Cape Breton, the dominion of Louis XIV extended up the St. Lawrence to Lake Superior, and from that lake, through the whole course of the Mississippi, to the Gulf of Mexico and the Bay of Mobile. Just beyond that bay began the posts of the Spaniards, which continued round the shores of Florida to the fortress of St. Augustine. The English colonies skirted the Atlantic, extending from Florida to the eastern verge of Nova Scotia. Thus, if on the east the Strait of Canso divided France and England, if on the south a narrow range of forests intervened between England and Spain, everywhere else the colonies of the rival nations were separated from each other by tribes of the natives. The Europeans had established a wide circle of plantations, or, at least, of posts; they had encompassed the aborigines that dwelt east of the Mississippi; and, however eager might now be the passion of the intruders for carving their emblems on trees, and designating their lines of anticipated empire on maps, their respective settlements were kept asunder by an unexplored wilderness, of which savages were the occupants.

The great strife of France and England for American territory could not but involve the ancient possessors of the continent in a series of conflicts, which have, at last, banished the Indian tribes from the earlier limits of our republic. The picture of the unequal contest inspires a compassion that is honorable to humanity. The weak demand sympathy. If a melancholy interest attaches to the fall of a hero who is overpowered by superior force, shall we not drop a tear at the fate of nations, whose defeat foreboded the exile, if it did not, indeed, shadow forth the decline and ultimate extinction, of a race?

The earliest books on America contained tales as wild as fancy could invent or credulity repeat. The land was peopled with pygmies and with giants; the tropical forests were said to conceal tribes of negroes; and tenants of the hyperborean regions were white, like the polar bear or the ermine. Jacques Cartier had heard of a nation that did not eat; and the pedant Lafitau believed, if not in a race of headless men, at least, that there was a nation of men with the head not rising above the shoulders.

The first aspect of the original inhabitants of the United States was uniform. Between the Indians of Florida and Canada, the difference was scarcely perceptible. Their manners and institutions, as well as their organization, had a common physiognomy; and, before their languages began to be known, there was no safe method of grouping the nations into families. But when the vast variety of dialects came to be compared, there were found, east of the Mississippi, not more than eight radically distinct languages, of which five still constitute the speech of powerful communities, and three are known only as memorials of tribes that have almost disappeared from the earth.

The study of the structure of the dialects of the red men sheds light on the inquiry into their condition. Language is their oldest monument, and the record and image of their experience. No savage horde has been caught with it in a state of chaos, or as if just emerging from the rudeness of undistinguishable sounds. No American language bears marks of being an arbitrary aggregation of separate parts; but each is possessed of an entire organization, having unity of character, and controlled by exact rules.

Each appears, not as a slow formation by painful processes of invention, but as a perfect whole, springing directly from the powers of man. A savage physiognomy is imprinted on the dialect of the dweller in the wilderness; but each dialect is still not only free from confusion, but is almost absolutely free from irregularities, and is pervaded and governed by undeviating laws. As the bee builds his cells regularly, yet without the recognition of the rules of geometry, so the unreflecting savage, in the use of words, had rule and method and completeness. His speech, like everything else, underwent change; but human pride errs in believing that the art of cultivated man was needed to resolve it into its elements, and give to it new forms, before it could fulfill its office. Each American language was competent of itself, without improvement from scholars, to exemplify every rule of the logician, and give utterance to every passion. Each dialect that has been analyzed has been found to be rich in derivatives and compounds, in combinations and forms. As certainly as every plant which draws juices from the earth has roots and sap vessels, bark and leaves, so certainly each language has its complete organization,—including the same parts of speech, though some of them may lie concealed in mutual coalitions. Human consciousness and human speech exist everywhere, indissolubly united. A tribe has no more been found without an organized language, than without eyesight or memory.

As the languages of the American tribes were limited by the material world, so, in private life, the senses held dominion. The passion of the savage was liberty; he demanded license to gratify his animal instincts. To act for himself, to follow the propensities of his nature, seemed his system of morals. The supremacy of conscience, the rights of reason, were not subjects of reflection to those who had no name for continence. The idea of chastity, as a social duty, was but feebly developed among them, and the observer of their customs would, at first, believe them to have been ignorant of restraint. If "the kindly flames of nature burned in wild humanity," their love never became a frenzy or a devotion; for indulgence destroyed its energy and its purity.

And yet no nation has ever been found without some practical confession of the duty of self-denial. "God hath planted in the hearts of the wildest of the sons of men a high and honorable esteem of the marriage, insomuch that they universally submit unto it, and hold its violation abominable." Neither might marriages be contracted between kindred of near degree; the Iroquois might choose a wife of the same tribe with himself, but not of the same cabin; the Algonquin must look beyond those who used the same *totem*, or family symbol; the Cherokee would marry at once a mother and her daughter, but would never marry his own immediate kindred.

On forming an engagement, the bridegroom, or, if he were poor, his friends and neighbors, made a present to the bride's father, of whom no dowry was expected. The acceptance of the presents perfected the contract; the wife was purchased; and, for a season, at least, the husband, surrendering his gains as a hunter to her family, had a home in her father's lodge.

But, even in marriage, the Indian abhorred constraint; and, from Florida to the St. Lawrence, polygamy was permitted, though at the north it was not common. In a happy union, affection was fostered and preserved; and the wilderness could show wigwams where "couples had lived together thirty, forty years." Yet love did not always light his happiest torch at the nuptials of the children of nature, and marriage among the forests had its sorrows and its crimes. The infidelities of the husband sometimes drove the helpless wife to suicide; the faithless wife had no protector; her husband insulted or disfigured her at will; and death for adultery was unrevenged. Divorce, also, was permitted, even for occasions besides adultery; it took place without formality, by a simple separation or desertion, and, where there was no offspring, was of easy occurrence. Children were the strongest bond; for, if the mother was discarded, it was an unwritten law of the red man that she should herself retain those whom she had borne or nursed.

On quitting the cradle, the children are left nearly naked in the cabin, to grow hardy, and learn the use of their limbs. Juvenile sports are the same everywhere; children invent them for themselves; and the traveler, who finds everywhere in the wide world the same games, may rightly infer, that the Father of the great human family himself instructs the innocence of childhood in its amusements. There is no domestic government; the young do as they will. They are never earnestly reproved, injured or beaten; a dash of cold water in the face is their heaviest punishment. If they assist in the labors of the household, it is as a pastime, not as a charge. Yet they show respect to the chiefs, and defer with docility to those of their cabin. The attachment of savages to their offspring is extreme; and they cannot bear separation from them. Hence every attempt at founding schools for their children was a failure; a missionary would gather a little flock about him, and of a sudden, writes Le Jeune, "my birds flew away." From their insufficient and irregular supplies of clothing and food, they learn to endure hunger and rigorous seasons; of themselves, they become fleet of foot, and skillful in swimming; their courage is nursed by tales respecting their ancestors, till they burn with a love of glory to be acquired by valor and address. So soon as the child can grasp the bow and arrow, they are in his hand; and, as there was joy in the wigwam at his birth, and his first cutting of a tooth, so a festival is kept for his first success in the chase. The Indian young man is educated in the school of nature. The influences by which he is surrounded nurse within him the passion for war; as he grows up, he, in his turn, takes up the war-song, of which the echoes never die away on the boundless plains of the West; he travels the war-path in search of an encounter with an enemy, that he, too, at the great war-dance and feast of his band, may boast of his exploits; may enumerate his gallant deeds by the envied feathers of the war-eagle that decorate his hair; and may keep the record of his wounds by shining marks of vermilion on his skin.

The savages are proud of idleness. At home, they do little but cross their arms and sit listlessly; or engage in games of chance, hazarding all their possessions on the result; or meet in council; or sing, and eat, and play, and sleep. The greatest toils of the men were to perfect the palisades of the forts; to manufacture a boat out of a tree, by means of fire and a stone hatchet; to repair their cabins; to get ready instruments of war or the chase, and to adorn their persons. Woman is the laborer; woman bears the burdens of life. The food that is raised from the earth is the fruit of her industry. With no instrument but a wooden mattock, a shell, or a shoulder-blade of the buffalo, she plants the maize, the beans, and the running vines. She drives the blackbirds from the cornfield, breaks the weeds, and, in due season, gathers the harvest. She pounds the parched corn, dries the buffalo meat, and prepares for Winter the store of wild fruits; she brings home the game which her husband has killed; she bears the wood, and draws the water, and spreads the repast. If the chief constructs the keel of the canoe, it is woman who stitches the bark with split ligaments of the pine root, and sears the seams with resinous gum. If the men prepare the poles for the wigwam, it is woman who builds it, and, in times of journeyings, bears it on her shoulders. The Indian's wife was his slave; and the number of his slaves was a criterion of his wealth.

The Indians of our republic had no calendar of their own; their languages have no word for year, and they reckon time by the return of snow or the springing of the flowers; their months are named from that which the earth produces in them; and their almanac is kept in the sky by the birds, whose flight announces the progress of the seasons. The brute creation gives them warning of the coming storm; the motion of the sun marks the hour of the day; and the distinctions of time are noted, not in numbers, but in words that breathe the grace and poetry of nature.

The aboriginal tribes of the United States depended for food on the chase, the fisheries and agriculture. They kept no herds; they never were shepherds. The bison is difficult to tame, and its female yields little milk, of which the use was unknown to the red man; water was his only drink. The moose, the bear, the deer, and, at the West, the buffalo, besides smaller game and fowl, were pursued with arrows tipped with hart's-horn, or eagle's claws, or pointed stones. With nets and spears, fish were taken, and, for want of salt, were cured by smoke. Wild fruits, and abundant berries, were a resource in their season; and troops of girls, with baskets of bark, would gather the fragrant fruit of the wild strawberry. But all the tribes south of the St. Lawrence, except remote ones on the northeast and the northwest, cultivated the earth. Unlike the people of the Old World, they were at once hunters and tillers of the ground. The contrast was due to the character of their grain. Wheat or rye would have been a useless gift to the Indian, who had neither plough nor sickle. The maize springs luxuriantly from a warm, new field, and in the rich soil, with little aid from culture, outstrips the weeds; bears, not thirty, not fifty, but a thousand-fold; if once dry, is hurt neither by heat nor cold; may be preserved in a pit or a cave for years, aye, and for centuries; is gathered from the field by the hand, without knife or reaping-hook; and becomes nutritious food by a simple roasting before a fire. A little of its parched meal, with water from the brook, was often a dinner and supper; and the warrior, with a small supply of it in a basket at his back, or in a leathern girdle, and with his bow and arrows, is ready for travel at a moment's warning. The tobacco plant was not forgotten; and the cultivation of the vine, which we have learned of them to call the squash, with beans, completed their husbandry.

During the mild season, there may have been little suffering. But thrift was wanting; the stores collected by the industry of the women were squandered in festivities. The hospitality of the Indian has rarely been questioned. The stranger enters his cabin, by day or by night, without asking leave, and is entertained as freely as a thrush or a blackbird that regales himself on the luxuries of the fruitful grove. He will take up his own rest abroad, that he may give his own skin or mat of sedge to his guest. Nor is the traveler questioned as to the purpose of his visit; he chooses his own time freely to deliver his message.

Festivals, too, were common, at some of which it was the rule to eat everything that was offered; and the indulgence of appetite surpassed belief. But what could be more miserable than the tribes of the north and northwest, in the depth of Winter, suffering from an annual famine; driven by the intense cold to sit indolently in the smoke around the fire in the cabin, and to fast for days together; and then, again, compelled, by faintness for want of sustenance, to reel into the woods, and gather moss or bark for a thin decoction, that might, at least, relieve the extremity of hunger?

Famine gives a terrible energy to the brutal part of our nature. A shipwreck will make cannibals of civilized men; a siege changes the refinements of urbanity into excesses at which humanity shudders; a retreating army abandons its wounded. The hunting tribes have the affections of men; but among them, also, extremity of want produces like results. The aged and infirm meet with little tenderness; the hunters, as they roam the wilderness, desert their old men; if provisions fail, the feeble drop down, and are lost, or life is shortened by a blow.

The fate of the desperately ill was equally sad. Diseases were believed to spring, in part, from natural causes, for which natural remedies were prescribed. Of these, the best was the vapor bath, prepared in a tent covered with skins, and warmed by means of hot stones; or decoctions of bark, or roots, or herbs, were used. Graver maladies were inexplicable, and their causes and cures formed a part of their religious superstitions; but those who lingered with them, especially the aged, were sometimes neglected and sometimes put to death.

The clothing of the natives was, in Summer, but a piece of skin, like an apron, round the waist; in Winter, a bear-skin, or, more commonly, robes made of the skins of the fox and the beaver. Their feet were protected by soft moccasins; and to these were bound the broad snow-shoes, on which, though cumbersome to the novice, the Indian hunter could leap like the roe. Of the women, head, arms, and legs, were uncovered; a mat or a skin, neatly prepared, tied over the shoulders, and fastened to the waist by a girdle, extended from the neck to the knees. They glittered with tufts of elk hair, brilliantly dyed in scarlet; and strings of the various kinds of shells were their pearls and diamonds. The Summer garments of moose and deer-skins, were painted of many colors; and the fairest feathers of the turkey, fastened by threads made from wild hemp and nettle, were curiously wrought into mantles. The claws of the grizzly bear formed a proud collar for a war-chief; a piece of an enemy's scalp, with a tuft of long hair, painted red, glittered on the stem of their war-pipes; the wing of a red-bird, or the beak and plumage of a raven, decorated their locks; the skin of a rattlesnake was worn round the arm of their chiefs; the skin of the polecat, bound round the leg, was their order of the Garter—emblem of noble daring. A warrior's dress was often a history of his deeds. His skin was also tattooed with figures of animals, of leaves, of flowers, and painted with lively and shining colors.

Some had the nose tipped with blue, the eyebrows, eyes, and cheeks, tinged with black, and the rest of the face red; others had black, red, and blue stripes drawn from the ears to the mouth; others had a broad, black band, like a ribbon, drawn from ear to ear across the eyes, with smaller bands on the cheeks. When they made visits, and when they assembled in council, they painted themselves gloriously, delighting especially in vermilion.

There can be no society without government; but among the Indian tribes on the soil of our republic, there was not only no written law—there was no traditionary expression of law; government rested on opinion and usage, and the motives to the usage were never embodied in language; they gained utterance only in the fact, and power only from opinion. No ancient legislator believed that human society could be maintained with so little artifice. Unconscious of political principles, they remained under the influence of instincts. Their forms of government grew out of their passions and their wants, and were, therefore, everywhere nearly the same. Without a code of laws, without a distinct recognition of succession in the magistracy, by inheritance or election, government was conducted harmoniously, by the influence of native genius, virtue, and experience.

Prohibitory laws were hardly sanctioned by savage opinion. The wild man hates restraint, and loves to do what is right in his own eyes. As there was no commerce, no coin, no promissory notes, no employment of others for hire, there were no contracts. Exchanges were but a reciprocity of presents, and mutual gifts were the only traffic. Arrests and prisons, lawyers and sheriffs, were unknown. Each man was his own protector, and, as there was no public justice, each man issued to himself his letter of reprisals, and became his own avenger. In case of death by violence, the departed shade could not rest till appeased by a retaliation. His kindred would "go a thousand miles, for the purpose of revenge, over hills and mountains; through large cane swamps, full of grape-vines and briars; over broad lakes, rapid rivers, and deep creeks; and all the way endangered by poisonous snakes, exposed to the extremities of heat and cold, to hunger and thirst." And blood being once shed, the reciprocity of attacks involved family in the mortal strife against family, tribe against tribe, often continuing from generation to generation. Yet mercy could make itself heard, even among barbarians; and peace was restored by atoning presents, if they were enough to cover up the graves of the dead.

The acceptance of the gifts pacified the families of those who were at variance. In savage life, which admits no division of labor, and has but the same pursuit for all, the bonds of relationship are widely extended. Families remain undivided, having a common emblem, which designates all their members as effectually as with us the name. The limit of the family is the limit of the interdicted degrees of consanguinity for marriage. They hold the bonds of brotherhood so dear, that a brother commonly pays the debt of a deceased brother, and assumes his revenge and his perils. There are no beggars among them, no fatherless children unprovided for. The families that dwell together, hunt together, roam together, fight together, constitute a tribe. Danger from neighbors, favoring union, leads to alliances and confederacies, just as pride, which is a pervading element in Indian character, and shelters itself in every lodge, leads to subdivisions.

As the tribe was but a union of families, government was a consequence of family relations, and the head of the family was its chief. The succession depended on birth, and was inherited through the female line. Elsewhere, the hereditary right was modified by opinion. Opinion could crowd a civil chief into retirement, and could dictate his successor. Nor was assassination unknown. The organization of the savage communities was like that which with us takes place at the call of a spontaneous public meeting, where opinion in advance designates the principal actors; or, as with us, at the death of the head of a large family, opinion within the family selects the best fitted of its surviving members to settle its affairs. Doubtless, the succession appeared sometimes to depend on the will of the surviving matron; sometimes to have been consequent on birth; sometimes to have been the result of the free election of the wild democracy, and of silent opinion. There have even been chiefs who could not tell when, where, or how, they obtained power.

In like manner, the different accounts of the power of the chief are contradictory only in appearance. The limit of his authority would be found in his personal character. The humiliating subordination of one will to another was everywhere unknown. The Indian chief has no crown, or scepter, or guards; no outward symbols of supremacy, or means of giving validity to his decrees. The bounds of his authority float with the current of opinion in the tribe; he is not so much obeyed, as followed with the alacrity of free volition; and therefore the extent of his power depends on his personal character. There have been chiefs whose commanding genius could so overawe and sway the common mind, as to gain, for a season, an almost absolute rule—while others had little authority, and, if they used menaces, were abandoned.

Each village governed itself as if independent, and each after the same analogies, without variety. If the observer had regard to the sachems, the government seemed monarchical; but as, of measures that concerned all, "they would not conclude aught unto which the people were averse," and every man of due age was admitted to council, it might also be described as a democracy. In council, the people were guided by the eloquent, were carried away by the brave; and this influence, which was recognized, and regular in its action, appeared to constitute an oligarchy. The affairs relating to the whole nation were transacted in general council, and with such equality, and such zeal for the common good, that, while any one might have dissented with impunity, the voice of the tribe would yet be unanimous in its decisions.

Their delight was in assembling together, and listening to messengers from abroad. Seated in a semicircle on the ground, in double or triple rows, with the knees almost meeting the face— the painted and tattooed chiefs adorned with skins and plumes, with the beaks of the red-bird, or the claws of the bear—each listener perhaps with a pipe in his mouth, and preserving deep silence, they would give solemn attention to the speaker, who, with great action and energy of language, delivered his message; and, if his eloquence pleased, they esteemed him as a god. Decorum was never broken; there were never two speakers struggling to anticipate each other; they did not express their spleen by blows; they restrained passionate invective; the debate was never disturbed by an uproar; questions of order were unknown.

The record of their treaties was kept by strings of wampum; these were their annals. When the envoys of nations met in solemn council, gift replied to gift, and belt to belt; by these, the memory of the speaker was refreshed; or he would hold in his hand a bundle of little sticks, and for each of them deliver a message. To do this well, required capacity and experience. Each tribe had, therefore, its heralds or envoys, selected with reference only to their personal merit, and because they could speak well; and often, an orator, without the aid of rank as a chief, by the brilliancy of his eloquence, swayed the minds of a confederacy. That the words of friendship might be transmitted safely through the wilderness, the red men revered the peace-pipe. The person of him that traveled with it was sacred; he could disarm the young warrior as by a spell, and secure himself a fearless welcome in every cabin. Each village also had its calumet, which was adorned by the chief with eagles' feathers, and consecrated in the general assembly of the nation. The envoys from those desiring peace or an alliance, would come within a short distance of the town, and, uttering a cry, seat themselves on the ground. The great chief, bearing the peace-pipe of his tribe, with its mouth pointing to the skies, goes forth to meet them, accompanied by a long procession of his clansmen, chanting the hymn of peace. The strangers rise to receive them, singing also a song, to put away all wars, and to bury all revenge. As they meet, each party smokes the pipe of the other, and peace is ratified. The strangers are then conducted to the village; the herald goes out into the street that divides the wigwams, and makes repeated proclamation that the guests are friends; and the glory of the tribe is advanced by the profusion of bear's meat, and flesh of dogs, and hominy, which give magnificence to the banquets in honor of the embassy.

But, if councils were their recreation, war alone was the avenue to glory. All other employment seemed unworthy of human dignity; in warfare against the brute creation, but still more against man, they sought liberty, happiness, and renown; thus was gained an honorable appellation, while the mean and the obscure among them had not even a name. Hence, to ask an Indian his name was an offense; a chief would push the question aside with scorn; for it implied that his deeds and the titles conferred by them were unknown.

The code of war of the red men attests the freedom of their life. No war-chief was appointed on account of birth, but was, in every case, elected by opinion; and every war-party was but a band of volunteers, enlisted for one special expedition, and for no more. Any one who, on chanting the war-song, could obtain volunteer followers, became a war-chief.

Solemn feasts and religious rites precede the departure of the warriors; the war-dance must be danced, and the war-song sung. They express in their melodies a contempt of death, a passion for glory; and the chief boasts that "the spirits on high shall repeat his name." A belt painted red or a bundle of bloody sticks, sent to the enemy, is a declaration of defiance. As the war-party leave the village, they address the women in a farewell hymn: "Do not weep for me, loved woman, should I die; weep for yourself alone. I go to revenge our relations fallen and slain; our foes shall lie like them; I go to lay them low." And, with the pride which ever marks the barbarian, each one adds, "If any man thinks himself a great warrior, I think myself the same."

The wars of the red men were terrible; not from their numbers, for, on any one expedition, they rarely exceeded forty men; it was the parties of six or seven which were the most to be dreaded. Skill consisted in surprising the enemy. They follow his trail, to kill him when he sleeps; or they lie in ambush near a village, and watch for an opportunity of suddenly surprising an individual, or, it may be, a woman and her children; and, with three strokes to each, the scalps of the victims being suddenly taken off, the brave flies back with his companions, to hang the trophies in his cabin, to go from village to village in exulting procession, to hear orators recount his deeds to the elders and the chief people, and, by the number of scalps taken with his own hand, to gain the high war-titles of honor. Nay, war-parties of but two or three were not uncommon. Clad in skins, with a supply of red paint, a bow, and quiver full of arrows, they would roam through the wide forest, as a bark would over the ocean; for days and weeks, they would hang on the skirts of their enemy, waiting the moment for striking a blow. It was the danger of such inroads, that, in time of war, made every English family on the frontier insecure.

The Romans, in their triumphal processions, exhibited captives to the gaze of the Roman people; the Indian conqueror compels them to run the gauntlet through the children and women of his tribe. To inflict blows that cannot be returned, is proof of full success, and the entire humiliation of their enemy; it is, moreover, an experiment of courage and patience. Those who show fortitude are applauded; the coward becomes an object of scorn.

Voices of the Dead.

"He being dead yet speaketh." The departed have voices for us. In order to illustrate this, I remark, in the first place, that the dead speak to us, and commune with us, *through the works which they have left behind them.* As the islands of the sea are the built-up casements of myriads of departed lives; as the earth itself is a great catacomb;—so we, who live and move upon its surface, inherit the productions and enjoy the fruits of the dead. They have bequeathed to us by far the larger portion of all that influences our thoughts, or mingles with the circumstances of our daily life. We walk through the streets they laid out. We inhabit the houses they built. We practice the customs they established. We gather wisdom from the books they wrote. We pluck the ripe clusters of their experience. We boast in their achievements. Every device and influence they have left behind tells their story, and is a voice of the dead. We feel this more impressively when we enter the customary place of one recently departed, and look around upon his work. The half-finished labor, the utensils hastily thrown aside, the material that exercised his care and received his last touch, all express him and seem alive with his presence. By them, though dead, he speaketh to us with a freshness and tone like his words of yesterday. How touching are those sketched forms, those unfilled outlines, in that picture which employed so fully the time and genius of the great artist—Belshazzar's Feast! In the incomplete process, the transition state of an idea from its conception to its realization, we are brought closer to the mind of the artist; we detect its springs and hidden workings, and therefore feel its *reality* more than in the finished effort. And this is one reason why we are more impressed at beholding the work just left than in gazing upon one that has been for a long time abandoned. Having had actual communion with the contriving mind, we recognize its presence more readily in its production; or else the recency of the departure heightens the expressiveness with which everything speaks of the departed. The dead child's cast-off garments, the toy just tossed aside, startle us as though with his renewed presence. A year hence they will suggest him to us, but with a different effect.

* * * * * * *

The dead speak to us in *memory* and *association*. If their voices may be constantly heard in their works, we do not always heed them; neither have we that care and attachment for the great congregation of the departed, which will at any time call them up vividly before us. But in that congregation there are those whom we have known intimately and fondly, whom we cherished with our best love, who lay close to our bosoms. And these speak to us in a more private and peculiar manner,—in mementoes that flash upon us the whole person of the departed, every physical and spiritual lineament—in consecrated hours of recollection that open up all the train of the past, and re-twine its broken ties around our hearts, and make its endearments present still. Then, then, though dead, they speak to us. It needs not the vocal utterance nor the living presence, but the mood that transforms the scene and the hour supplies these. That face that has slept so long in the grave, now bending upon us, pale and silent, but affectionate still; that more vivid recollection of every feature, tone, and movement, that brings before us the departed, just as we knew them in the full flush of life and health; that soft and consecrating spell which falls upon us, drawing in our thoughts from the present, arresting, as it were, the current of our being, and turning it back and holding it still as the flood of actual life rushes by us,—while in that trance of soul the beings of the past are shadowed; old friends, old days, old scenes recur; familiar looks beam close upon us; familiar words re-echo in our ears, and we are closed up and absorbed with the by-gone, until tears dissolve the film from our eyes, and some shock of the actual wakes us from our reverie; all these, I say, make the dead to commune with us as really as though in bodily form they should come out from the chambers of their mysterious silence and speak to us. And if life consists in *experiences*, and not mere physical contacts—and if love and communion belong to that experience, though they take place in meditation, or dreams, or by actual contact—then, in that hour of remembrance, have we really lived with the departed, and the departed have come back and lived with us. Though dead, they have spoken to us. And though memory sometimes induces the spirit of heaviness—though it is often the agent of conscience and wakens us to chastise—yet it is wonderful how, from events that were deeply mingled with pain, it will extract an element of sweetness. A writer, in relating one of the experiences of her sick-room, has illustrated this. In an hour of suffering, when no one was near her, she went from her bed and her room to another apartment, and looked upon a glorious landscape of sunrise and Spring-time. "I was suffering too much to enjoy this picture at the moment," she says, "but how was it at the end of the year? The pains of all those hours were annihilated, as completely vanished as if they had never been; while the momentary peep behind the window-curtain made me possessor of this radiant picture forevermore." "Whence this wide difference," she asks, "between the good and the evil? Because the good is indissolubly connected with ideas—with the unseen realities which are indestructible." And though the illustration which she thus gives bears the impression of an individual peculiarity, instead of an universal truth, still, in the instance to which I apply it, I believe it will very generally hold true that memory leaves a pleasant rather than a painful impression. At least, there is so much that is pleasant mingled with it, that we would not willingly lose the faculty of memory—the consciousness that we can thus call back the dead and hear their voices—that we have the power of softening the rugged realities which only suggest our loss and disappointment, by transferring the scene and the hour to the past and the departed. And, as our conceptions become more and more spiritual, we shall find the *real* to be less dependent upon the outward and the visible—we shall learn how much life there is in a thought—how veritable are the communions of spirit with spirit; and the hour in which memory gives us the voices of the dead will be prized by us as an hour of actual experience, and such opportunities will grow more precious to us. No, we would not willingly lose the power of memory.

* * * * * * * * *

Well, then, is it for us at times to listen to the voices of the dead. By so doing we are better fitted for life and for death. From that audience we go purified and strengthened into the varied discipline of our mortal state. We are willing to *stay* knowing that the dead are so near us, and that our communion with them may be so intimate. We are willing to *go* seeing that we shall not be wholly separated from those we leave behind. We will toil in our lot while God pleases, and when He summons us we will calmly depart. When the silver cord becomes untwined, and the golden bowl broken—when the wheel of action stands still in the exhausted cistern of our life, may we lie down in the light of that faith which makes so beautiful the face of the dying Christian, and has converted death's ghastly silence to a peaceful sleep. May we rise to a holier and more visible communing, in the land without a sin and without a tear. Where the dead shall be closer to us than in this life. Where not the partition of a shadow or a doubt shall come between.

The Head-Stone.

The coffin was let down to the bottom of the grave, the planks were removed from the heaped-up brink, the first rattling clods had struck their knell, the quick shoveling was over, and the long, broad, skillfully cut pieces of turf were aptly joined together, and trimly laid by the beating spade, so that the newest mound in the churchyard was scarcely distinguishable from those that were grown over by the undisturbed grass and daisies of a luxuriant Spring. The burial was soon over; and the party, with one consenting motion, having uncovered their heads, in decent reverence of the place and occasion, were beginning to separate, and about to leave the churchyard.

Here, some acquaintances, from distant parts of the parish, who had not had an opportunity of addressing each other in the house that had belonged to the deceased, nor in the course of the few hundred yards that the little procession had to move over from his bed to his grave, were shaking hands quietly, but cheerfully, and inquiring after the welfare of each other's families. There, a small knot of neighbors were speaking, without exaggeration, of the respectable character which the deceased had borne, and mentioning to one another little incidents of his life, some of them so remote as to be known only to the gray-headed persons of the group; while a few yards further removed from the spot, were standing together parties, who discussed ordinary concerns, altogether unconnected with the funeral, such as the state of the markets, the promise of the season, or change of tenants; but still with a sobriety of manner and voice that was insensibly produced by the influence of the simple ceremony now closed, by the quiet graves around, and the shadow of the spire and gray walls of the house of God.

Two men yet stood together at the head of the grave, with

countenances of sincere, but unimpassioned grief. They were brothers, the only sons of him who had been buried. And there was something in their situation that naturally kept the eyes of many directed upon them, for a long time, and more intently than would have been the case, had there been nothing more observable about them than the common symptoms of a common sorrow. But these two brothers, who were now standing at the head of their father's grave, had for some years been totally estranged from each other, and the only words that had passed between them, during all that time, had been uttered within a few days past, during the necessary preparations for the old man's funeral.

No deep and deadly quarrel was between these brothers, and neither of them could distinctly tell the cause of this unnatural estrangement. Perhaps dim jealousies of their father's favor; selfish thoughts that will sometimes force themselves into poor men's hearts respecting temporal expectations; unaccommodating manners on both sides; taunting words, that mean little when uttered, but which rankle and fester in remembrance; imagined opposition of interests, that, duly considered, would have been found one and the same; these, and many other causes, slight when single, but strong when rising up together in one baneful band, had gradually but fatally infected their hearts, till at last they, who in youth had been seldom separate, and truly attached, now met at market and, miserable to say, at church, with dark and averted faces, like different clansmen during a feud.

Surely if anything could have softened their hearts toward each other, it must have been to stand silently, side by side, while the earth, stones, and clods, were falling down upon their father's coffin. And doubtless their hearts were so softened. But pride, though it can not prevent the holy affections of nature from being felt, may prevent them from being shown; and these two brothers stood there together, determined not to let each other know the mutual tenderness that, in spite of them, was gushing up in their hearts, and teaching them the unconfessed folly and wickedness of their causeless quarrel.

A head-stone had been prepared, and a person came forward to plant it. The elder brother directed him how to place it, a plain stone with a sand-glass, skull, and cross-bones, chiseled not rudely, and a few words inscribed. The younger brother regarded the operation with a troubled eye, and said, loudly enough to be heard by several of the bystanders, "William, this was not kind in you; you should have told me of this. I loved my father as well as you could love him. You were the elder, and, it may be, the favorite son; but I had a right in nature to have joined you in ordering this head-stone, had I not?"

During these words, the stone was sinking into the earth, and many persons, who were on their way from the grave, returned. For awhile the elder brother said nothing, for he had a consciousness in his heart that he ought to have consulted his father's son, in designing this last becoming mark of affection and respect to his memory; so the stone was planted in silence, and now stood erect, decently and simply, among the other unostentatious memorials of the humble dead.

The inscription merely gave the name and age of the deceased, and told that the stone had been erected "by his affectionate sons." The sight of these words seemed to soften the displeasure of the angry man, and he said, somewhat more mildly, "Yes, we were his affectionate sons, and since my name is on the stone, I am satisfied, brother. We have not drawn together kindly of late years, and perhaps never may; but I acknowledge and respect your worth; and here, before our own friends, and before the friends of our father, with my foot above his head, I express my willingness to be on other and better terms with you, and if we can not command love in our hearts, let us, at least, brother, bar out all unkindness."

The minister, who had attended the funeral, and had something intrusted to him to say publicly before he left the churchyard, now came forward, and asked the elder brother why he spake not regarding this matter. He saw that there was something of a cold and sullen pride rising up in his heart, for not easily may any man hope to dismiss from the chamber of his heart ever the vilest guest, if once cherished there. With a solemn, and almost severe air, he looked upon the relenting man, and then, changing his countenance into serenity, said gently—

> "Behold how good a thing it is,
> And how becoming well,
> Together such as brethren are,
> In unity to dwell."

The time, the place, and this beautiful expression of a natural sentiment, quite overcame a heart, in which many kind, if not warm affections, dwelt; and the man thus appealed to, bowed down his head and wept. "Give me your hand, brother;" and it was given, while a murmur of satisfaction arose from all present, and all hearts felt kindlier and more humanely toward other.

As the brothers stood fervently, but composedly, grasping each other's hand, in the little hollow that lay between the grave of their mother, long since dead, and of their father, whose shroud was haply not yet still from the fall of dust to dust, the minister stood beside them with a pleasant countenance, and said, "I must fulfill the promise I made to your father on his death-bed. I must read to you a few words which his hand wrote at an hour when his tongue denied its office. I must not say that you did your duty to your old father; for did he not often beseech you, apart from one another, to be reconciled, for your own sakes as Christians, for his sake, and for the sake of the mother who bore you, and, Stephen, who died that you might be born? When the palsy struck him for the last time, you were both absent, nor was it your fault that you were not beside the old man when he died.

"As long as sense continued with him here, did he think of you two, and of you two alone. Tears were in his eyes; I saw them there and on his cheek too, when no breath came from his lips. But of this no more. He died with this in his hand; and he made me know that I was to read it to you over his grave. I now obey him: 'My sons, if you will let my bones lie quiet in the grave, near the dust of your mother, depart not from my burial till, in the name of God and Christ, you promise to love one another as you used to do. Dear boys, receive my blessing.'"

Some turned their heads away to hide the tears that needed not be hidden, and when the brothers had released each other from a long and sobbing embrace, many went up to them, and, in a single word or two, expressed their joy at this perfect reconcilement. The brothers themselves walked away from the church-yard arm in arm with the minister to the manse. On the following Sabbath, they were seen sitting with their families in the same pew, and it was observed that they read together off the same Bible, when the minister gave out the text, and that they sang together, taking hold of the same psalm-book. The same psalm was sung (given out at their own request) of which one verse had been repeated at their father's grave; a larger sum than usual was, on that Sabbath, found in the plate for the poor, for Love and Charity are sisters. And ever after, both during the peace and the troubles of this life, the hearts of the brothers were as one, and in nothing were they divided.

Escape of Harvey Birch and Captain Wharton.

The road which it was necessary for the peddler and the English captain to travel, in order to reach the shelter of the hills, lay, for half a mile, in full view from the door of the building that had so recently been the prison of the latter; running for the whole distance over the rich plain, that spreads to the very foot of the mountains, which here rise in a nearly perpendicular ascent from their bases; it then turned short to the right, and was obliged to follow the windings of nature, as it won its way into the bosom of the Highlands.

To preserve the supposed difference in their stations, Harvey rode a short distance ahead of his companion, and maintained the sober, dignified pace, that was suited to his assumed character. On their right, the regiment of foot, that we have already mentioned, lay in tents; and the sentinels, who guarded their encampment, were to be seen moving, with measured tread, under the skirts of the hills themselves. The first impulse of Henry was, certainly, to urge the beast he rode to his greatest speed at once, and by a *coup-de-main*, not only to accomplish his escape, but relieve himself from the torturing suspense of his situation. But the forward movement that the youth made for this purpose was instantly checked by the peddler.

"Hold up!" he cried, dexterously reining his own horse across the path of the other; "would you ruin us both? Fall into the place of a black following his master. Did you not see their blooded chargers, all saddled and bridled, standing in the sun before the house? How long do you think that miserable Dutch horse you are on would hold his speed, if pursued by the Virginians? Every foot that we can gain without giving the alarm, counts us a day in our lives. Ride steadily after me, and on no account look back. They are as subtle as foxes, ay, and as ravenous for blood as wolves."

Henry reluctantly restrained his impatience, and followed the direction of the peddler. His imagination, however, continually alarmed him with the fancied sounds of pursuit; though Birch, who occasionally looked back under the pretense of addressing his companion, assured him that all continued quiet and peaceful.

"But," said Henry, "it will not be possible for Cæsar to remain long undiscovered; had we not better put our horses to the gallop? and, by the time they can reflect on the cause of our flight, we can reach the corner of the woods."

"Ah! you little know them, Captain Wharton," returned the peddler; "there is a sergeant at this moment looking after us, as if he thought all was not right; the keen-eyed fellow watches me like a tiger laying in wait for his leap; when I stood on the horse block, he half suspected something was wrong. Nay, check your beast; we must let the animals walk a little, for he is laying his hand on the pommel of his saddle; if he mounts now, we are gone. The foot soldiers could reach us with their muskets."

"What does he do?" asked Henry, reining his horse into a walk, but, at the same time, pressing his heels into the animal's sides, to be in readiness for a spring.

"He turns from his charger and looks the other way. Now trot on gently; not so fast, not so fast; observe the sentinel in the field a little ahead of us; he eyes us keenly."

"Never mind the footman," said Henry impatiently, "he can do nothing but shoot us; whereas these dragoons may make me a captive again. Surely, Harvey, there are horsemen moving down the road behind us. Do you see nothing particular?"

"Humph!" ejaculated the peddler; "there is something particular, indeed, to be seen behind the thicket on your left; turn your head a little, and you may see and profit by it too."

Henry eagerly seized his permission to look aside, and his blood curdled to the heart as he observed they were passing a gallows, that had unquestionably been erected for his own execution. He turned his face from the sight in undisguised horror.

"There is a warning to be prudent in that bit of wood," said the peddler, in that sententious manner that he often adopted.

"It is a terrific sight, indeed!" cried Henry, for a moment veiling his face with his hands, as if to drive a vision from before him.

The peddler moved his body partly around, and spoke with energetic but gloomy bitterness—"And yet, Captain Wharton, you see it when the setting sun shines full upon you; the air you breathe is clear, and fresh from the hills before you. Every step that you take leaves that hated gallows behind; and every dark hollow, and every shapeless rock in the mountains, offers you a hiding place from the vengeance of your enemies. But I have seen the gibbet raised when no place of refuge offered. Twice have I been buried in dungeons, where, fettered and in chains, I have passed nights in torture, looking forward to the morning's dawn that was to light me to a death of infamy. The sweat has started from limbs that seemed already drained of their moisture, and if I ventured to the hole that admitted air through grates of iron, to look out upon the smiles of nature, which God has bestowed for the meanest of his creatures, the gibbet has glared before my eyes, like an evil conscience, harrowing the soul of a dying man. Four times have I been in their power, besides this last; but—twice—twice did I think that my hour had come. It is hard to die at the best, Captain Wharton; but to spend your last moments alone and unpitied; to know that none near you so much as think of the fate that is to you the closing of all that is earthly; to think that in a few hours you are to be led from the gloom—which, as you dwell on what follows, becomes dear to you—to the face of day, and there to meet all eyes upon you, as if you were a wild beast; and to lose sight of everything amidst the jeers and scoffs of your fellow creatures; —that, Captain Wharton, is indeed to die."

Henry listened in amazement, as his companion uttered this speech with a vehemence altogether new to him. Both seemed to have forgotten their danger and their disguises, as he cried—

"What! were you ever so near death as that?"

"Have I not been the hunted beast of these hills for three years past?" resumed Harvey, "and once they even led me to the foot of the gallows itself, and I escaped only by an alarm from the royal troops. Had they been a quarter of an hour later, I must have died. There was I placed, in the midst of unfeeling men, and gaping women and children, as a monster to be cursed. When I would pray to God, my ears were insulted with the history of my crimes; and when, in all that multitude, I looked around for a single face that showed me any pity, I could find none—no, not even one—all cursed me as a wretch who would sell his country for gold. The sun was brighter to my eyes than common—but then it was the last time I should see it. The fields were gay and pleasant, and everything seemed as if this world was a kind of heaven. Oh! how sweet life was to me at that moment! 'Twas a dreadful hour, Captain Wharton, and such as you have never known. You have friends to feel for you; but I had none but a father to mourn my loss when he might hear of it; there was no pity, no consolation near to soothe my anguish. Everything seemed to have deserted me—I even thought that He had forgotten that I lived."

"What! did you feel that God had forsaken you, Harvey?" cried the youth, with strong sympathy.

"God never forsakes his servants," returned Birch, with reverence, and exhibiting naturally a devotion that hitherto he had only assumed.

"And who did you mean by He?"

The peddler raised himself in his saddle to the stiff and upright posture that was suited to the outward appearance. The look of fire, that, for a short time, glowed upon his countenance, disappeared in the solemn lines of unbending self-abasement, and, speaking as if addressing a negro, he replied:—

"In heaven, there is no distinction of color, my brother; therefore you have a precious charge within you, that you must hereafter render an account of,"—dropping his voice; "this is the last sentinel near the road; look not back, as you value your life."

Henry remembered his situation, and instantly assumed the humble demeanor of his adopted character. The unaccountable energy of the peddler's manner was soon forgotten in the sense of his own immediate danger; and with the recollection of his critical situation returned all the uneasiness that he had momentarily forgotten.

"What see you, Harvey?" he cried, observing the peddler to gaze toward the building they had left, with ominous interest; "what see you at the house?"

"That which bodes no good to us," returned the pretended priest. "Throw aside the mask and wig—you will need all your senses without much delay—throw them in the road; there are none before us that I dread, but there are those behind us, who will give us a fearful race."

"Nay, then," cried the captain, casting the implements of his disguise into the highway, "let us improve our time to the utmost; we want a full quarter to the turn; why not push for it at once?"

"Be cool—they are in alarm, but they will not mount without an officer, unless they see us fly—now he comes—he moves to the stables—trot briskly—a dozen are in their saddles, but the officer

stops to tighten his girths—they hope to steal a march upon us—
he is mounted—now ride, Captain Wharton, for your life, and keep
at my heels. If you quit me you will be lost."

A second request was unnecessary. The instant that Harvey
put his horse to his speed, Captain Wharton was at his heels, urging the miserable animal that he rode to the utmost. Birch had
selected the beast on which he rode, and, although vastly inferior
to the high-fed and blooded chargers of the dragoons, still it was
much superior to the little pony that had been thought good
enough to carry Cæsar Thompson on an errand. A very few
jumps convinced the captain that his companion was fast leaving
him, and a fearful glance that he threw behind informed the fugi-
tive that his enemies were as speedily approaching. With that
abandonment that makes misery doubly grievous, when it is to be
supported alone, Henry called aloud to the peddler not to desert
him. Harvey instantly drew up, and suffered his companion to
run alongside of his own horse. The cocked hat and wig of the
peddler fell from his head the moment that his steed began to move
briskly, and this development of their disguise, as it might be
termed, was witnessed by the dragoons, who announced their observation by a boisterous shout, that seemed to be uttered in the
very ears of the fugitives—so loud was the cry, and so short the
distance between them.

"Had we not better leave our horses," said Henry, "and make
for the hills across the fields on our left?—the fence will stop our
pursuers."

"That way lies the gallows," returned the peddler; "these fellows go three feet to our two, and would mind those fences no more
than we do these ruts; but it is a short quarter to the turn, and
there are two roads behind the wood. They may stand to choose
until they can take the track, and we shall gain a little upon them
there."

"But this miserable horse is blown already," cried Henry, urging his beast with the end of his bridle, at the same time Harvey
aided his efforts by applying the lash of a heavy riding whip that
he carried; "he will never stand it for half a mile further."

"A quarter will do—a quarter will do," said the pedler, "a single quarter will save us, if you follow my directions."

Somewhat cheered by the cool and confident manner of his companion, Henry continued silently urging his horse forward. A few moments brought them to the desired turn, and, as they doubled round a point of low under-brush, the fugitives caught a glimpse of their pursuers scattered along the highway. Mason and the sergeant, being better mounted than the rest of the party, were much nearer to their heels than even the pedler thought could be possible.

At the foot of the hills, and for some distance up the dark valley that wound among the mountains, a thick underwood of saplings had been suffered to shoot up, when the heavier growth was felled for the sake of fuel. At the sight of this cover, Henry again urged the pedler to dismount, and to plunge into the woods; but his request was promptly refused. The two roads above mentioned met at a very sharp angle, at a short distance from the turn, and both were circuitous, so that but little of either could be seen at a time. The pedler took the one which led to the left, but held it only a moment, for, on reaching a partial opening in the thicket, he darted across the right hand path, and led the way up a steep ascent, which lay directly before them. This manœuver saved them. On reaching the fork, the dragoons followed the track, and passed the spot where the fugitives had crossed to the other road, before they missed the marks of the footsteps. Their loud cries were heard by Henry and the pedler, as their wearied and breathless animals toiled up the hill, ordering their comrades in the rear to ride in the right direction. The captain again proposed to leave their horses, and dash into the thicket.

"Not yet—not yet," said Birch, in a low voice; "the road falls from the top of this hill as steep as it rises—first let us gain the top." While speaking they reached the desired summit, and both threw themselves from their horses. Henry plunged into the thick underwood, which covered the side of the mountain for some distance above them. Harvey stopped to give each of their beasts a few severe blows of his whip, that drove them headlong down the path on the other side of the eminence, and then followed his example.

The peddler entered the thicket with a little caution, and avoided, as much as possible, rustling or breaking the branches in his way. There was but time only to shelter his person from view, when a dragoon led up the ascent, and, on reaching the height, he cried aloud:—

"I saw one of their horses turning the hill this minute."

"Drive on—spur forward, my lads," shouted Mason, "give the Englishman quarter, but cut down the peddler, and make an end of him."

Henry felt his companion gripe his arm hard, as he listened in a great tremor to this cry, which was followed by the passage of a dozen horsemen, with a vigor and speed that showed too plainly how little security their over-tired steeds could have afforded them.

"Now," said the peddler, rising from his cover to reconnoiter, and standing for a moment in suspense, "all that we gain is clear gain; for, as we go up, they go down. Let us be stirring."

"But will they not follow us, and surround this mountain?" said Henry, rising, and imitating the labored but rapid progress of his companion; "remember they have foot as well as horse, and at any rate we shall starve in the hills."

"Fear nothing, Captain Wharton," returned the peddler with confidence; "this is not the mountain that I would be on, but necessity has made me a dexterous pilot among these hills. I will lead you where no man will dare to follow. See, the sun is already setting behind the tops of the western mountains, and it will be two hours to the rising of the moon. Who, think you, will follow us far, on a November night, among these rocks and precipices?"

"But listen!" exclaimed Henry; "the dragoons are shouting to each other—they miss us already."

"Come to the point of this rock, and you may see them," said Harvey, composedly setting himself down to rest. "Nay, they can see us—notice, they are pointing up with their fingers. There! one has fired his pistol, but the distance is too great for even a musket to carry upward."

"They will pursue us," cried the impatient Henry; "let us be moving."

"They will not think of such a thing," returned the peddler, picking the chickerberries that grew on the thin soil where he sat, and very deliberately chewing them, leaves and all, to refresh his mouth. "What progress could they make here, in their boots and spurs, with their long swords, or even pistols? No, no—they may go back and turn out the foot; but the horse pass through these defiles, when they can keep the saddle, with fear and trembling. Come, follow me, Captain Wharton; we have a troublesome march before us, but I will bring you where none will think of venturing this night."

So saying, they both arose, and were soon hid from view amongst the rocks and caverns of the mountain.

Chesterfield's Letters to his Son.

I.

DEAR BOY:—Pleasure is the rock which most young people split upon; they launch out with crowded sails in quest of it, but without a compass to direct their course, or reason sufficient to steer the vessel; for want of which, pain and shame, instead of pleasure, are the returns of their voyage. Do not think that I mean to snarl at pleasure, like a Stoic, or to preach against it, like a parson; no, I mean to point it out and recommend it to you, like an Epicurean; I wish you a great deal, and my only view is to hinder you from mistaking it.

The character which most young men first aim at, is that of a man of pleasure; but they generally take it upon trust; and, instead of consulting their own taste and inclinations, they blindly adopt whatever those, with whom they chiefly converse, are pleased to call by the name of pleasure; and a *man of pleasure*, in the vulgar acceptation of that phrase, means only a beastly drunkard, and a profligate swearer and curser. As it may be of use to you, I am not unwilling, though at the same time ashamed, to own, that the vices of my youth proceeded much more from my silly resolution of being what I heard called a man of pleasure, than from my own inclinations. I always naturally hated drinking; and yet I have often drunk, with disgust at the time, attended by great sickness the next day, only because I then considered drinking as a necessary qualification for a fine gentleman and a man of pleasure.

The same as to gaming. I did not want money, and consequently had no occasion to play for it; but I thought play another necessary ingredient in the composition of a man of pleasure, and accordingly I plunged into it without desire at first, sacrificed a thousand real pleasures to it, and made myself solidly uneasy by it, for thirty of the best years of my life.

I was even absurd enough, for a little while, to swear, by way of adorning and completing the shining character which I affected; but this folly I soon laid aside, upon finding both the guilt and the indecence of it.

Thus seduced by fashion, and blindly adopting nominal pleasures I lost real ones; and my fortune impaired and my constitution shattered are, I must confess, the just punishment of my errors. Take warning by them; choose your pleasures for yourself and do not let them be imposed upon you. Follow nature and not fashion; weigh the present enjoyment of your pleasures against the necessary consequences of them, and then let your own common sense determine your choice.

Were I to begin the world again, with the experience which I now have of it, I would lead a life of real, not of imaginary pleasure. I would enjoy the pleasures of the table and of wine, but stop short of the pains inseparably annexed to an excess in either. I would not, at twenty years, be a preaching missionary of abstemiousness and sobriety; and I should let other people do as they would, without formally and sententiously rebuking them of it; but I would be most firmly resolved not to destroy my own faculties and constitution, in complaisance to those who have no regard to their own. I would play to give me pleasure, but not to give me pain; that is, I would play for trifles, in mixed companies, to amuse myself, and conform to custom; but I would take care not to venture for sums, which, if I won, I should not be the better for, but, if I lost, should be under a difficulty to pay, and, when paid, would oblige me to retrench in several other articles. Not to mention the quarrels which deep play commonly occasions.

I would pass some of my time in reading, and the rest in the company of people of sense and learning, and chiefly those above me; and I would frequent the mixed companies of men and women of fashion, which, though often frivolous, yet unbend and refresh the mind, not uselessly, because they certainly polish and soften the manners.

These would be my pleasures and amusements, if I were to live the last thirty years over again; they are rational ones; and moreover I will tell you, they are really the fashionable ones; for the others are not, in truth, the pleasures of what I call people of fashion, but of those who only call themselves so. Does good company care to have a man reeling drunk among them? or to see another tearing his hair, and blaspheming, for having lost, at play, more than he is able to pay? No; those who practice, and much more, those who brag of them, make no part of good company; and are most unwillingly, if ever, admitted into it. A real man of fashion and pleasure observes decency; at least neither borrows nor affects vices; and if he unfortunately has any, he gratifies them with choice, delicacy and secrecy.

II

DEAR BOY:—People of your age have commonly an unguarded frankness about them, which makes them the easy prey and bubble of the artful and the experienced; they look upon every knave or fool who tells them that he is their friend, to be really so; and pay that profession of simulated friendship with an indiscreet and unbounded confidence, always to their loss, often to their ruin. Beware, therefore, now that you are coming into the world, of these proffered friendships. Receive them with great civility, but with great incredulity, too; and pay them with compliments, but not with confidence. Do not let your vanity and self-love make you suppose that people become your friends at first sight, or even upon a short acquaintance. Real friendship is a slow grower, and never thrives, unless ingrafted upon a stock of known and reciprocal merit. There is another kind of nominal friendship among young people, which is warm for the time, but, by good luck, of short duration. This friendship is hastily produced, by their being accidentally thrown together, and pursuing the same course of riot and debauchery. A fine friendship, truly! and well cemented by drunkenness and lewdness. It should rather be called a conspiracy against good morals and good manners, and be punished as such by the civil magistrate. However, they have the impudence and the folly to call this confederacy a friendship. They lend one another money for bad purposes; they engage in quarrels, offensive and defensive, for their accomplices; they tell one another all they know, and often more too; when, of a sudden, some accident disperses them, and they think no more of each other, unless it be to betray and laugh at their imprudent confidence. Remember to make a great difference between companions and friends; for a very complaisant and agreeable companion may be, and very often proves, a very improper, and a very dangerous, friend. People will, in a great degree, and not without reason, form their opinion of you, upon that which they have of your friends; and there is a Spanish proverb, which says very justly, "Tell me whom you live with, and I will tell you who you are." One may fairly suppose, that a man who makes a knave or a fool his friend, has something very bad to do or to conceal. But, at the same time that you carefully decline the friendship of knaves and fools, if it can be called friendship, there is no occasion to make either of them your enemies, wantonly and unprovoked; for they are numerous bodies;

and I would rather choose a secure neutrality than an alliance or war with either of them. You may be a declared enemy to their vices and follies, without being marked out by them as a personal one. Their enmity is the next dangerous thing to their friendship. Have a real reserve with almost everybody; and have a seeming reserve with almost nobody; for it is very disagreeable to seem reserved, and very dangerous not to be so. Few people find the true medium; many are ridiculously mysterious and reserved upon trifles, and many imprudently communicative of all they know.

The next to the choice of your friends is the choice of your company. Endeavor, as much as you can, to keep company with people above you. There you rise as much as you sink with people below you; for (as I have mentioned before) you are, whatever the company you keep is. Do not mistake, when I say, company above you, and think that I mean with regard to their birth; that is the least consideration; but I mean, with regard to their merit, and the light in which the world considers them.

There are two sorts of good company; one which is called the *beau monde*, and consists of those people who have the lead in courts and in the gay part of life; the other consists of those who are distinguished by some peculiar merit, or who excel in some particular and valuable art or science. For my own part, I used to think myself in company as much above me, when I was with Mr. Addison and Mr. Pope, as if I had been with all the princes in Europe. What I mean by low company, which should by all means be avoided, is the company of those, who, absolutely insignificant and contemptible in themselves, think they are honored by being in your company, and who flatter every vice and every folly you have, in order to engage you to converse with them. The pride of being the first of the company, is but too common; but it is very silly and very prejudicial. Nothing in the world lets down a character more than that wrong turn.

You may possibly ask me whether a man has it always in his power to get into the best company? and how? I say, yes, he has, by deserving it; provided he is but in circumstances which enable him to appear upon the footing of a gentleman. Merit and good breeding will make their way everywhere. Knowledge will introduce him, and good breeding will endear him, to the best companies; for, as I have often told you, politeness and good breeding are absolutely necessary to adorn any or all other good qualities or talents. Without them, no knowledge, no profession whatever, is seen in the best light. The scholar without good breeding is a pedant; the philosopher, a cynic; the soldier, a brute, and every man disagreeable.

Dog-Days.

Doubtless they have their uses, but they are not agreeable. That must be conceded. There is no out-doors. You wake in the morning with a mild sense of strangulation, though all your windows are open at top and bottom. You thrust your head out into the morning air, but there isn't any. It has all run to fog. Fog lies heavy and gray on the grass. Trees and hills and fences are smothered in fog. It creeps into your house, tarnishes all your gilt, swells your drawers and doors so that you can't open them, and when you have opened them you can't shut them. It breathes upon your muslin curtains, and they turn into limpsy strings. It steals into your closet, and little blue specks and white feathery spots appear on your pies. A pungent taste develops itself in your pound cake. The stray cup-custard filched from the general larder for private circulation is a keen and acid disappointment. Milk refuses to curdle into cheese, and cream will tumble about in your churn for hours, and come out mitigated buttermilk at last.

Flies are rampant. If the cover is left off the sugar-bowl, a colony of flies take immediate possession. If your bare arm happens to be carrying a vase of flowers with special care, a fly lights on your elbow, and proceeds by short and easy stages (to him) to your wrist. If you are writing, a horde of flies institute an investigation of your head and hands, with a special commission for your nose. You brush them off, and they only rub their fore-legs together, bob their heads, brush down their wings, and go at it again. Your kitchen ceiling looks like huckleberries and milk. All the while it is very warm, but not so warm as it is sticky, only the stickiness is all on the outside. Within, you feel a constant tendency to fall to pieces, because there isn't *brace* enough in the air to hold you together. If we were English, we should say it was nasty weather. Being Americans, we only sigh, "Dog-days!"

But they must have their uses. Everything is good for something. Let us see. First, they are excellent for the complexion—a matter in which, whatever we say, we are all more or less interested. Bile-y, jaundice-y, sallow faces clear up into healthy tints. Freckles "try out." Pale cheeks tone up into delicate rose, and dry, parched, burning flushes tone down to a cool liquescence. All the pores are opened, and the whole system languishes in a pleasant helplessness—pleasant, if one has been so industrious all the year, that he can afford to be idle during the dog-days.

Dog-days are good as tests. Their effect on curl-paper curls is melancholy, but natural curls laugh them to scorn, and riot in twistings. Just so the temper. Placidity at Christmas often dissolves in an August fog. What you thought was amiability, may have been only oxygen. If you wish to see whether your temper can really bear the strains of wind and weather, just remember how you went to the middle drawer in your bureau for gloves, fearing you should be too late for the cars—how the drawer would only come out by hitches, first one side, then the other, and then not at all,—how you thrust in your hand up to the wrist, and could just not reach the gloves with the end of your longest finger, while your wrist was tortured by the sharp edge of the drawer on one side, and the sharp edge of the bureau on the other. Did you possess your soul in patience? When a shower came suddenly pelting down through the fog, and you tried to close the window, and got yourself wet through for your pains, and couldn't move it an inch for all your shaking and pounding,—when you put your cake into the oven to "scald," and forgot it, till a sense of something burning traveled upstairs to stir your passivity, and you rushed down to snatch too late a burnt and blackened loaf,—did you remember the first three words of Psalm xxxvii, 1?

In the calm complacency of a balmy Spring morning, we look down with a serene smile on the follies of the world. We assume a calm and quiet superiority, give it a pat on the shoulder, and say, condescendingly: "Yes, you will do very well; a little rickety in the joints; a slight softening of the brain; but very passable for your age." Nothing can exceed our amiability when we are pleased and comfortable; but, floundering up to the neck in July; keeping the breath of life in us only by becoming amphibious and web-footed; bound to the earth by no stronger tie than ice-cream and sherbet; wooing to our side every passing breeze, as if it were the king's daughter,—then, a beflowered, bespangled, bedizened abomination, coming betwixt the wind and our nobility, is the spear of Ithuriel to our smiling good nature, and we feel disposed to pluck its eyes out with a demoniac delight.

Dog-days can teach us trust. You have heard of the woman who, when her horse ran away, trusted to Providence till the breeching broke. A good deal of our trust is like this. We call it Providence, but it is really breeching. Not that breeching is not a very good thing to trust to as far as it goes,—only it is not Providence. So, when our doors can be bolted and locked, we lie down in peace and sleep; but when they won't go to, and we have to make a precarious arrangement of sticks and strings, we feel more keenly that we awake because the Lord sustained us.

Dog-days are friendly to greenness. Our lawns smile with velvet verdure. The fog goes into the soil and wraps it around the tender strawberry-vines that we have just transplanted, and in soft swaddling-clothes the young fruit will slumber till next Summer's sun shall bid it leap to luxuriant life, and a creamy and glorious death. Down into the heart of the sweet-pea, deep into the cup of the morning-glory, steals the kindly mist, and a pink and purple splendor crowns the rising day. The cucumber swells its prickly sides and snuffs the coming vinegar. The squash-vine creeps along the ground, sorrowing that it has all turned to pumpkin, but catching from the moist air a deeper shade for the generous gold of its blossom. Ah! in the laboratories of nature the fog has a great work to do.

But the best of dog-days is their departing. Grateful for the returning sun and the sweet west wind, we see a deeper blue in the sky, and a denser green in the fields. The tall corn waves with a statelier grace. The trees are fretted with fresh-springing life. The earth is a billowy and dimpled emerald, tender and smiling; but the sky,—the ever-shifting sky,—is an absorbing and perpetual joy. Sometimes its sweep of stainless blue is glorious afar. Then the dying sun leaves its legacy in the west, of saffron and amber and pale green. Now the clouds sail out white and warm into the central blue, or rush exultant, whirling-up masses of lavender rimmed with gold, or shoot from the glowing west, spires of rosy pink, or mount to the zenith, in delicate shells of pearl, or lie above the horizon, passionate, breathless, and ruddy, floating in seas of fire. Anon they group themselves in all fantastic shapes. A turreted castle sends down shafts of light from its pearly gates. The mailed warrior places his lance in rest, and a couchant lion

> "Scatters across the sunset air
> The golden radiance of his hair."

"Cloud-land! Gorgeous land!" All grace of outline, all wealth of color, are gathered there. Tropical splendor and heavenly purity kiss each other, and the angels of God can almost be seen ascending and descending.

So, gazing with thankful and reverent hearts, we remember that great city, the holy Jerusalem, descending out of heaven from God, whose light is like unto a stone most precious, for the glory of God doth lighten it, and the Lamb is the light thereof.

So, when the west winds come laden with fragrance from the prairies, and the cold winds blow down from the north, bearing us healing and strength, we will gird up our loins anew to the work of the Lord of light, contented to rest and stand in our lot at the end of the days.

www.ingramcontent.com/pod-product-compliance
Lightning Source LLC
Chambersburg PA
CBHW051726300426
44115CB00007B/480